DATE DUE			

THE AUTHENTIC LIFE OF
WILLIAM McKINLEY
Our Third Martyr President

TOGETHER WITH

A LIFE SKETCH OF THEODORE ROOSEVELT
The 26th President of the United States

INTRODUCTION AND BIOGRAPHY	THE LIFE AND PUBLIC CAREER
—BY—	—BY—
ALEXANDER K. McCLURE	**CHARLES MORRIS, LL.D.**
Author of the	Author of the
"Life and Times of Abraham Lincoln."	"Life of Queen Victoria."

Also Memorial Tributes
By STATESMEN, MINISTERS, ORATORS AND
RULERS OF ALL COUNTRIES

Profusely Illustrated with Reproductions from Original Photographs, Original Drawings and Special Pictures of the Family by Express Permission from the Owners

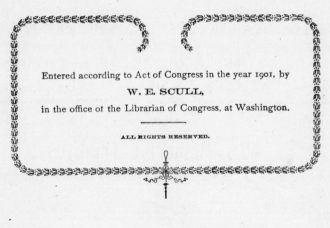

Opening Words
to
The Story of a Martyr

"A GREAT and good man lies dead, and the nation mourns." Such was the sentiment felt in millions of hearts of citizens of the United States of America when, on the morning of Saturday, the 14th of September, 1901, the sad tidings were flashed from end to end of the country that their revered and honored President was no more. During the days of that terrible week which succeeded the treacherous assault upon the life of the National Executive, when trusting himself most fully to the honor and good-will of his people, hope wrestled with dread in the hearts of Americans of every type of political faith, every sentiment of national policy. The opponents as well as the supporters of the President stood in spirit by that bedside where the life of one of their noblest was ebbing away, and if silent prayer could ever change the course of nature, it would have been changed in these fateful days.

Hope for a time triumphed over despair, and the hearts of the people throbbed with gladness when it seemed as if the fell purpose of the assassin was about to be foiled, and our President restored to health and vigor to finish the work which he had been chosen by the voice of the nation to fulfil. Alas! no one knew that dark disease was even then mining deep within, that death had set his lurid seal upon that noble brow, and that minutes, instead of months or years, marked the term of the President's future life.

Hence, when the shock at length came, it was a terrible one. An universal spasm of grief passed from end to end of the land. From far eastern Maine to the western land of gold, from the great lakes of the north to the great gulf of the south, the sentiment of deep regret, the feeling of intense sadness, filled every soul. Never was a man more deeply and widely mourned, not even the sainted Lincoln, nor the warmly esteemed Garfield, America's two former martyrs to integrity and high-mindedness in the Presidential chair. The shock fell with sudden and irresistible force, and for an interval the whole nation swung downward into the vale of grief, only slowly to rise again from under the force of that dread blow.

Never was there a crime more without purpose, more without possible good effect. William McKinley was no oppressor of the people, no irresponsible and cruel autocrat. No act of his had ever, from evil intent, taken the bread from one man's hand, the hope from one man's heart. He was the representative of the people's will, not their master. Chosen by the votes of a majority of the citizens to execute their laws and administer their affairs, he had devoted himself seriously and conscientiously to this purpose, and no one, not even those who most opposed his policy, ever in their hearts accused him of self-seeking, of a disregard for the obligations of his oath of office, of anything other than an earnest desire to do what in his judgment seemed the best thing for the good of the people as a whole.

There was no benefit conceivable to be gained by his cruel taking off; nothing but evil—evil, deep-dyed evil—in the act. Even the opponents of his policy could not hope but that this policy would be pursued by the strong and able man who would succeed him in the Presidential chair. Only the counsels of insensate anarchy, the whisperings of a demon viler than Satan, could have inspired such a deed; and for the man, if it is just to call him man, that struck the blow, only a single excuse exists, that his brain had been turned by the dark conspiracies in which he was involved, and that it was at the instigation of a fanaticism excited to the pitch of insanity that the deed was done.

Anarchy has nothing to gain, it has all to lose, by acts like this. It has been tolerated; it may be, and deserves to be, proscribed. If there is to be no security, for either good man or bad, from its fatalistic hand, the time will surely come when the anarchist will be hunted with the implacable resentment that the man-eating tiger is now followed, the hunt being unremitting until the last assassin of them all is swept from the earth.

The thought of deeds like these inspire us to quote Shakspeare's words:

> "In these cases
> We still have judgment here; and we but teach
> Bloody instructions, which, being taught, return
> To plague the inventor; this even-handed justice
> Commends the ingredients of our poisoned chalice
> To our own lips."

We may quote still further from Macbeth's famous soliloquy, since the qualities ascribed by Shakspeare to the slaughtered Duncan apply with equal or even greater force to a far later victim of the murderer's hand, the martyred McKinley.

> "This Duncan
> Hath borne his faculties so meek, hath been
> So clear in his great office, that his virtues
> Will plead like angels trumpet-tongued against
> The deep damnation of his taking off;
> And pity, like a naked new-born babe,
> Striding the blast, or heaven's cherubim, horsed
> Upon the sightless couriers of the air,
> Shall blow the horrid deed in every eye,
> That tears shall drown the wind."

"The deep damnation of his taking-off," applies with the closest significance to the assassination of William McKinley, for no President before him was more "clear in his great office." It is, indeed, a singular circumstance that the three Presidents marked for death by the assassin were among the noblest and best of the whole Presidential family ; Lincoln, who was loved as no President before his time; Garfield, who was warmly esteemed for his deep probity and earnest desire to administer his high office highly ; and McKinley, whose genial nature, warm heart, and rare devotion to his sense of duty had won him the respect and heartfelt affection of the great mass of his countrymen.

The death of Lincoln, however, came at a time when the passions of men had been intensely roused, and when the waters of strife still rose in billows of wrath. Garfield fell at a time when political passion was similarly aroused by the approaching deposition of the policy "to the victor belongs the spoils" by the civil service or merit system. The murder of McKinley, on the other hand, came like a bolt from a clear sky, when the clouds of war had passed, prosperity reigned, and the country was settling down into security and calm. Its effects, therefore, were the more strongly felt, since it was a blow without a cause, a murder destitute of warrant.

We feel tempted to quote again ; this time not from a master of expression of the past, but from one of the present, William McKinley himself. It is well first to allude to the interesting circumstance that Rutherford B. Hayes, McKinley's old commander and warm friend in the days of war, entered the Presidential office in the same term that McKinley entered the House of Representatives ; their life careers thus seeming strangely united. McKinley, who knew well the virtues and abilities of his lifelong friend, neatly set off his estimate of his character in this telling phrase : " Good in his greatness, and great in his goodness."

We quote it here with a purpose, that of its evident close applicability to the speaker himself. As he said of President Hayes, we may justly say of President McKinley, that he was " Good in his Greatness, and Great in his Goodness," and this motto from his own lips deserves to be carved as an epitaph upon his tomb.

We ask no pardon from the American public for offering this biography of their late martyred ruler for their perusal; feeling that now, while he is warm in their remembrance, the story of his life will be received with gratification and read with enthusiasm. His career has been a varied and deeply interesting one. Born in humble circumstances, in a true sense "One of the People," he engaged, while a mere boy, in the deadly struggle for the permanence of our institutions and the integrity of our territory, the Civil War. In this his story was striking, his services meritorious, his ability conspicuous, and he had the honor, shared by few besides, of rising from the position of a private soldier to the rank of Major in his regiment.

The war ended, he engaged in the practice of the law, but before many years had passed entered the halls of Congress, where his skill as an orator and his earnest and able advocacy of the principles of his party quickly won the admiration of his fellow members. As a Congressman his name became associated with one of the most prominent legislative acts of the closing century, the McKinley Tariff, which first lifted him into high prominence before the eyes of the people.

Serving subsequently as Governor of Ohio, he was in 1896 chosen as President of the United States. He succeeded to this high office at a critical period, that in which the policy of Spain in Cuba was leading inevitably to war between that country and the United States. The results and far-reaching consequences of this war rendered the administration of President McKinley the one most crowded with intricate and momentous questions after that of Lincoln. No matter what course he had chosen to pursue, one of contraction or one of expansion, he would have met with animadversion and called forth hostility. That he chose the course which seemed to him the best adapted to promote the development of his country and the interests of mankind no man can fairly doubt.

That he aroused enmity and opposition during his life must be admitted. But with his sudden death all enmity and recrimination fell to the ground, the nation rose as a man to proclaim his noble character and wealth of good intent, and the world stood, in spirit, beside his bier, to lay upon it the wreath of high respect and heartfelt admiration. Peace be with him in death, as it was not always in life !

The following lines, breathed by the President in his dying moments, are fitting words with which to close this preface :

> Nearer, my God, to Thee,
>   Nearer to Thee,
> E'en though it be a cross
>   That raiseth me,
> Still all my song shall be,
>   Nearer, my God, to Thee,
>   Nearer to Thee !
>
> Or if on joyful wing,
>   Cleaving the sky,
> Sun, moon and stars forgot,
>   Upward I fly,
> Still all my song shall be,
>   Nearer, my God, to Thee,
>   Nearer to Thee !

The Life of William McKinley

A Man of the People

TABLE OF CONTENTS

William McKinley, the Noble American

An Introduction

FOR the third time in a period of little more than a generation, the assassin's bullet has plunged the great republic of the world into the saddest bereavement. Lincoln, Garfield, McKinley; the three Presidents of the United States who would be selected from all the many who have filled that highest civil trust of the world as the most kindly and generous in disposition, and most free from enmity, have fallen by the hand of the assassin. Here in the freest government in the world, with the largest measure of general prosperity enjoyed by any people; under a government so gentle in its operations that it is unfelt in its exactions, and rises to its highest measure of grandeur only when the rights of the citizen or the honor of the nation are imperiled, it is most appalling to record the fall of rulers by unprovoked red-handed murder in a greater degree than has been experienced in any other nation of the world during the last forty years.

It is not surprising that the grinding oppression of despotic governments under which many poverty-stricken subjects are driven to despair, should school the assassin for the terrible work of taking revenge upon rulers who live in boundless luxury; but here, where the President is himself one of the people, lives as they live, mingles with them as one of them, and is accessible to the humblest sovereign of the nation, only some fiend in human form, in

2

whose heart every instinct of manhood was strangled, could plot or execute the murder of the President of the United States.

President McKinley was one of the gentlest and kindest of men. His life was a beautiful poem in many cantos, exhibiting every phase of the best and noblest attributes of human character. Even when racked with pain by the wound of the assassin, he spoke of his murderer only in terms of kindness, asking that he should be treated fairly, and he died as he lived, exhibiting the grandest qualities of Christian manhood. His last words were fitly uttered to the long-suffering, accomplished and devoted wife, at whose home altar there had never been a shadow of discord, and whose life was benignant with that beautiful affection that makes home the sanctuary of its worshippers. With his hand clasped in hers, and just when passing to final unconsciousness, he whispered the sentence that is now immortal: "God's will, not ours, be done."

The life of William McKinley is only one of the many which so impressively illustrate the grandest feature of our great free government that gives opportunity alike to all—the highest and the lowest. He was born at Niles, Trumbull County, Ohio, on the 29th of January, 1843. His early opportunities were limited, but he made the best use of them by attending the public schools until civil war spread its deadly pall over the nation. He was then only eighteen years of age, but he promptly enlisted as a private in the Twenty-third Ohio Volunteers. Other heroes of the war have been honored with the Presidency, but McKinley is the only one who served in the ranks, bearing his musket in the flame of battle. He rose to the rank of captain because of special mention in dispatches for courage and efficiency as a soldier, and at the end of the war he returned to his home, having then just passed his majority, with the rank of brevet major. He promptly resumed his studies, and in due time was admitted to the bar, when he located at Canton, Stark County, Ohio, that has since been his home.

McKinley took an active part in politics in early life, and in 1869 he made his first appearance as a candidate on the Republican ticket for District Attorney, and though the county was strongly Democratic, he was elected by a small majority. He rose rapidly in his profession, but in 1876, at the age of thirty-two, he was elected to Congress, and after that he was continuously in public life. He was chosen to Congress at consecutive elections until 1897. He had become a great political power in his State and also in the councils of the nation, and his political opponents determined to retire him to private life. The Democrats controlled the Legislature in 1890, and enacted a new Congressional apportionment, the chief purpose of which was to connect Stark County, the home of McKinley, with such an overwhelming Democratic majority as to render his re-election impossible. But even with this large adverse majority to overcome, the Democrats feared the popularity of McKinley, and they nominated against him one of the strongest men in the district. The contest became one of national interest, and McKinley made the most aggressive canvass of his life, although to all but himself it seemed to be utterly hopeless. He was defeated by 846 majority where his opponent, by a strict party vote, should have been victor by nearly 4,000. The Republicans of Ohio felt keenly the arbitrary effort made to retire McKinley from public trust by a Congressional gerrymander, and the next year he was unanimously nominated for Governor of the State and elected by an unusually large majority. He filled the executive office with the same conscientious devotion to public duty that had always characterized him, and in 1893 he was unanimously nominated for re-election, and was successful by the largest popular majority ever given in the State, with the single exception of Governor Brough's majority over Valandingham for Governor in 1863.

In both of these State contests his political opponents made desperate efforts to defeat him, or at least to reduce his majority, and thus weaken him as a political factor in State and national affairs, but when he was re-elected Governor by the stupendous majority of 80,995 he was at once recognized by his friends, not only at home but throughout the country, as a promising candidate for the Presidency. Even one year before that election he was made a candidate for the Presidency before the national convention at Minneapolis. He had not been generally discussed as an aspirant at that time, and when the convention met he had no expectation that his name would be presented. He was made President of the convention without a contest, and, to his surprise, a portion of the opposition to Harrison suddenly concentrated upon him, and the vote of his State was cast for himself with the single exception of his own vote, which was given to Harrison. The only ballot for President gave Harrison 535½, Blaine 182½, McKinley 182, Reed 4 and Robert Lincoln 1. McKinley entered the contest of 1892 with great energy and zeal, and was accepted by all as the ablest and most effective of the champions of the Harrison cause. He became recognized in that struggle as the "leader of leaders" in his own party, and it was only logical that after his re-election for Governor of Ohio by an almost unprecedented majority, he should be made the Republican candidate for President in 1896.

The battle for the Presidential succession on the Republican side in 1896 was a very earnest one. That McKinley was the choice of the great mass of the Republican people, excepting when controlled by local preferences, was conceded by all, but he had one of the ablest and most aggressive of the Republican national leaders as his chief competitor in Thomas B. Reed, then Speaker of the House. Senator Hanna cherished a romantic attachment for McKinley, as was shown by his prompt intervention to rescue McKinley from the bankruptcy into which he was suddenly precipitated, when Governor, by the mismanagement of a business enterprise with which he was connected as a partner, but for the direction of which he had neither time nor fitness. Hanna proved himself to be one of the great Warwicks of the Republic, ranking to-day with Thurlow Weed and the elder Francis P. Blair, of olden times. He devoted himself tirelessly for more than a year to

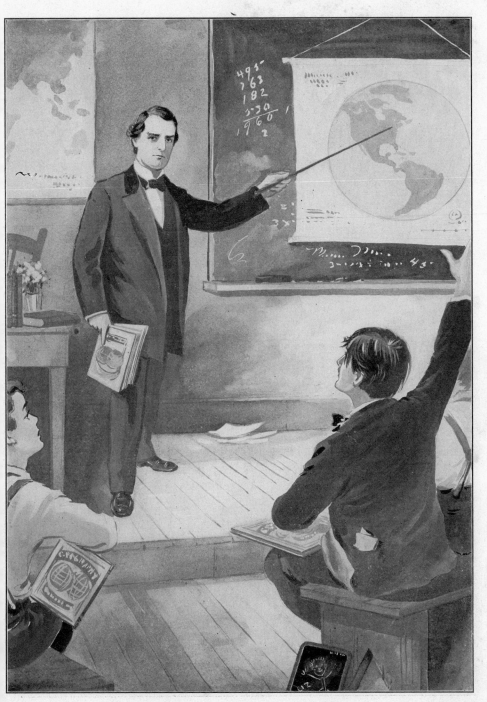

WILLIAM McKINLEY THE YOUNG SCHOOL TEACHER

WILLIAM McKINLEY
The School Teacher—The Soldier—The Lawyer—The Governor

concentrating and organizing the McKinley sentiment throughout the country. With McKinley's great personal strength with the people and Hanna's superb direction, McKinley rapidly took the lead in the race, and finally ended the contest some weeks before the meeting of the Convention, by going into New England and breaking the Reed forces in his own home by carrying Vermont and New Hampshire practically for himself. Reed was thus powerless to make a battle with his New England forces divided, and when the Convention met at St. Louis on the 16th of June, the nomination of McKinley was so generally conceded that the first and only ballot, gave him 661½ votes to 84½ for Reed, 61½ for Quay, 58 for Governor Morton, 35½ for Allison, and 1 for Senator Cameron.

The national battle of 1896 gave a crucial test of the intellectual and personal qualities of the two opposing candidates for President. William Jennings Bryan had by a grand cratorical effort swept away the Democratic Convention in a tempest of applause, and it was a battle royal from start to finish. Bryan's wonderful physical power, his fluency of speech, his great adaptability to all the duties and arts of the platform, and his tireless efforts aroused his supporters to the highest degree of enthusiasm. He spoke not only daily but often many times a day, and in the early part of the contest his election appeared to be more than possible. The vital issue of the conflict was the question of maintaining a sound financial policy, as against the seductive appeals in favor of cheap money at a time when labor was unrequited and industry and trade greatly paralyzed ; but McKinley gave repeated utterances during the struggle which steadily sobered the people, and long before election day the tide was obviously in favor of McKinley's election, notwithstanding the fearful depression which prevailed. In that contest, as uniformly in Congress, he stood resolutely and aggressively for the maintenance of the national credit inviolate, and the great business interests of the country were rallied to his support with such earnestness as to divert from the Democratic party very many of its ablest and most influential leaders to the support of a third ticket or to the direct support of McKinley. The result was McKinley's election by a popular majority of nearly half a million over Bryan, and by a vote of 271 for McKinley in the electoral college to 176 for Bryan.

The election of McKinley to the Presidency in 1896 was a counter revolution of the Democratic revolution that had carried Cleveland into the Presidency in 1892 by large popular and electoral majorities, and it necessarily involved an entire change of the economic policy of the Government. The McKinley administration was supported by a party majority in both branches of Congress, and a new tariff bill, that is yet in existence, was speedily enacted. The severe depression that had continued from 1893 until 1896 was gradually passing away when McKinley was elected, and his success gave new impetus to the great industrial interests of the country. Fortunate conditions gave increased prices for the products of our industry, especially of our farms, and he had every prospect of having a most successful and serene administration until the dark cloud of war that hung over Cuba extended its pall over our Republic. The destruction of the battleship *Maine* quickened the hostility of the American people against the Spanish rule in Cuba to an extent that made war inevitable.

McKinley earnestly strove to avert the calamity of war. Like Lincoln, all his instincts were on the side of humanity, and but for the destruction of the *Maine* that called out a resistless popular sentiment in favor of war, there is little doubt that McKinley, with all his sympathies on the side of peace, would have averted the conflict with Spain. When the grave duty of accepting war was inevitable, he rose to every requirement of the exceptionally grave emergency, and in the short conflict between the armies and navies of the two Governments, the heroism of our army and navy was made to stand out even in grander lustre than ever before. For the first time in the history of naval warfare, two naval battles were fought in which every vessel of the squadrons of the enemy was entirely destroyed, and the Spanish army finally surrendered to a United States army not superior to it in numbers and lacking its advantages of position.

When the first opportunity for securing peace was presented, President McKinley was prompt and tireless in pressing for its attainment. He was compelled to meet the gravest problems ever presented to our statesmanship, with the single exceptions of the problems thrust upon the Government by secession in 1861; but McKinley, always in the forefront to create and maintain the policy he had adopted, speedily accomplished a treaty with Spain that gave to this country all the Spanish possessions in the West Indies with the exception of Cuba, and the entire Philippine archipelago, in the East. He was slow to accept the policy of expansion to the extent to which it was carried, but, like Lincoln, he was ever ready to meet new necessities; and it is well known that while at one time he would have accepted a mere coaling station in the Philippines, and later probably the single province of Luzon, he finally bowed to the resistless logic of events that so clearly demanded the acceptance of all the important Spanish provinces in both the West Indies and in the East. His policy of expansion was fiercely assailed by his political opponents and by some able members of his own party, but the best evidence of the mandatory sentiment of the sovereign people of the nation in requiring the policy of expansion, is given in the fact that when the Paris treaty was before the Senate for confirmation, and was opposed by some of the President's party supporters, Mr. Bryan, his Presidential competitor, went to Washington and publicly and privately urged the confirmation of the treaty. No higher vindication of the policy of the President could have been furnished, and no more conclusive expression could have been given as to the general convictions of the American people.

Beyond the war with Spain and the enactment of a new tariff, the first administration of McKinley was not specially eventful. It was confronted by no great political convulsions, as his party majority was maintained in both branches of Congress during the entire term ; and as the period approached for choosing the candidates for the national battle of 1900, he was in the field practically without a competitor. The Convention was held in Philadelphia on the 19th of June, with Senator Wolcott as temporary chairman and Senator Lodge, of Massachusetts, as permanent chairman. No name was presented or even discussed for the Presidency but that of McKinley. Some of the enthusiastic supporters of Roosevelt meditated an attempt to stampede the Convention to their favorite for President, but the delegates were so solidly devoted to McKinley that the movement was found to be impracticable. McKinley was nominated on the first roll call, receiving 924 votes, being the full membership of the Convention. Theodore Roosevelt was then nominated for Vice-President, receiving 923 votes, being one vote less than the full membership, and that vote his own, as he was at the head of the New York delegation. The Democratic National Convention presented an equally unanimous sentiment in favor of the renomination of William J. Bryan, and thus the two leaders who had locked horns four years before, again took the field in a desperate struggle for political supremacy ; but Bryan was at a great disadvantage because of the general prosperity of the country, the nearly universal employment of labor at fair wages, and the next to universal thrift in all business and industrial channels. Bryan, however, repeated his aggressive campaign of 1896, exhibiting variance only in his somewhat tempered attitude on the financial question. His speeches of this campaign exhibited more of the statesman and not so much of the politician, as did his great speeches in the first struggle, and he commanded very general respect wherever he went, even from those who were politically opposed to him. McKinley was heard only on a few occasions during the conflict, but his utterances were always of the most temperate, forceful and impressive character, and strengthened the already very great confidence that the country reposed in him. The result was his re-election by the largest popular majority ever given to a national candidate. His popular majority over Bryan was 849,455, and his majority over all competitors was 446,719 out of a total vote of 13,969,770. In the electoral college McKinley received 292 votes to 155 for Bryan.

McKinley's friends also carried largely increased majorities in both the Senate and House, and the new Congress chosen to meet on the first Monday in December 1901, that would have been the first under his second administration, was more heartily in accord with the President and the general policy of his administration than any President of the past commanded, with the disappointments of four years to engender opposition. He was re-inaugurated with most imposing ceremonies, and he was thus newly commissioned by the people by a vote of confidence so great and comprehensive that he had every assurance of a most serene and successful administration of his second term in his high office.

The only important event after his second inauguration was his journey to the Pacific, accompanied by his devoted but fragile wife. A tour covering the heart of the different sections of the whole country was planned, and a special train, with every possible comfort and care provided for his invalid wife, started on its journey to the South. The train was stopped at the leading centres of population along the entire route, and the journey was one continued ovation to the honored President of the nation. The fatigue of the journey proved too great for Mrs. McKinley, and in San Francisco it was abruptly ended by her very critical illness, during which her life was despaired of for some days. The authorities and people of San Francisco joined the President and members of the Cabinet in devoting themselves wholly to the care of the beloved woman who so long hovered on the shore of the dark river; but she finally recovered sufficiently to be brought home, and the journey from the Pacific to Washington was made with the utmost speed and popular demonstrations avoided as much as possible.

During McKinley's journey to the Pacific he delivered a succession of speeches largely or wholly extemporized, which proved his wonderful versatility and forcefulness as a disputant and orator. No purer, nobler or better lessons could be given in our schools for the study of our youth than the speeches delivered by McKinley from the time he left Washington until he reached San Francisco. There was not a trace of offensive partisanship in any of them. They were dignified, patriotic, eloquent and chivalrous without exception, and were more carefully studied and approved by the American people than any popular deliverances ever made by a President. When Mrs. McKinley's health improved the President went with her to spend the Summer at their quiet home in Canton, Ohio, where they were universally beloved by their neighbors ; and only the sense of public duty to which President McKinley ever responded, induced him to leave his charming home and home circle to visit the Pan-American Exposition at Buffalo. He was welcomed there as he had been in every part of the country, not only by overwhelming numbers, but by the heartiest applaudits of the people without distinction of party, and his address delivered at the Exposition will stand in literature among the choicest pro- ductions of American statemanship.

The speech in its entirety exhibits the most careful and intelli- gent comprehension of the aims, duties and destiny of our free government, and it will certainly be accepted as a guide, not only by his immediate successor, but for rulers of all parties who may be charged with the destiny of the great republic of the world. His closing paragraph will stand side by side with the immortal deliverance of Abraham Lincoln at Gettysburg. It is as follows :

" Who can tell the new thoughts that have been awakened, the ambitions fired and the high achievements that will be wrought through this Exposition ? Gentlemen, let us ever remember that our interest is in concord, not conflict, and that our real eminence rests in the victories of peace, not those of war. We hope that all who are represented here may be moved to higher and nobler effort for their own and the world's good, and that out of this city may come, not only greater commerce and trade for us all, but, more essential than these, relations of mutual respect, confidence and friendship which will deepen and endure.

"Our earnest prayer is that God will graciously vouchsafe prosperity, happiness and peace to all our neighbors, and like blessings to all the peoples and powers of earth."

On the day following this address, the President yielded to the general desire for a public reception, so that the great mass of people present should have an opportunity to take him by the hand, and while thus receiving the multitude on the afternoon of Friday, September 6th, Leon F. Czolgosz, a young anarchist, approached him with his right hand covered by a handkerchief as if protecting a wound or sore, and extending his left hand to the President, speedily twice fired the pistol concealed in his right hand and two bullets entered the body of the victim. Additional shots would have been fired by the murderer had he not been struck and captured by those immediately about him. The President bore himself most courageously, but finally fell into the arms of his friends, while the murderer was hastened away to prison.

The Emergency Hospital of the Exposition happened to be not only very complete in its equipment, but had connected with it surgeons and physicians of the ripest experience, and the President had the promptest and best treatment known to the profession. After the examinations had been made and an operation performed to aid in healing the breaches in the walls of the stomach, the physicians were hopeful that the distinguished patient might recover. The country was appalled by this third assassin who aimed at the life of the President of the Republic without having suffered any real or imaginary wrong from his victim, and intense anxiety was exhibited every hour of the day and night for the bulletins which came from the bedside of the people's ruler. Day after day the reports were hopeful because no specially unfavorable features were developed, and four days after the wounds had been inflicted, the whole country rejoiced at the official reports from the surgeons in charge that the President was taking food in the natural way and enjoying it and his strength rapidly increasing. Only one day later the shadows again gathered and the hearts of the millions of American people were bowed in woe by the report that most dangerous symptoms had suddenly developed and that the life of the President was trembling in the balance. From that time no hopeful report came from those who watched the tread of death where it would strike a great nation in its dearest hopes and affections, and finally, on Saturday morning, September 14th, at 2.15 A.M., the unconscious effigy of life that dimly flickered in the socket, quietly vanished in the darkness of death, leaving the last sweet utterance of President McKinley imperishably crystallized in the memory of all—"It is God's way. His will be done, not ours."

THE PRESIDENT'S LAST SPEECH AT BUFFALO

Copyrighted by Judge Co.   THE PRESIDENT ADDRESSING THE MULTITUDE AT SAN JOSE, CALIFORNIA

CHAPTER II

The Ancestry of William McKinley

NATIVE AMERICAN STOCK

PRESIDENT McKINLEY came from Crawford County, Ohio, stock, his grandfather and great-grandfather having been leading pioneer citizens. Strange to say, they lived in the banner Democratic township of this rock-ribbed Democratic county, and, what was more, the old gentlemen voted the Democratic ticket. In a little German Lutheran cemetery, a few miles north of Bucyrus, on the State road, can be found a modest gravestone, on which is the following inscription:

DAVID McKINLEY
Revolutionary Soldier
Born 1756. Died 1840

The mound is neatly kept, and from the near-by corners of the old rail fence nod wild roses in fragrant profusion. Just beyond runs the Columbus and Sandusky Short Line Railway, with its stream of commerce; but few of the passengers know that in this little cemetery rests the original stock of Nation's late President.

Beside the grave of McKinley is a companion mound with a similar headstone, on which is inscribed:

HANNAH C. ROSE
Born 1757. Died 1840

These are the graves of the predecessors of the President, and throughout this county there still resides a number of their descendants, while the older pioneers remember well McKinley, the

33

revolutionary soldier.   Among the closest relatives at the present time there are the Waller family, their homestead being a few miles from the lonely graveyard.   Stephen Waller married a sister of the President's father and had many occasions to visit the old home in Canton.   While Mr. Waller and the President differed in politics, the former was always high in his praise of the consistency and character of his famous nephew, and spoke most touchingly of the Christian character of McKinley's mother.

INCIDENTS IN EARLY LIFE

.   After the death of Mrs. Waller the family visits and correspondence were naturally discontinued, but Mr. Waller related many incidents in the early life of the President which illustrate his early Christian training.   On one occasion, during a visit of Mrs. Waller to the home of her brother, William McKinley, Sr., her nephew was a lad of sixteen or seventeen years of age.   He was a student at the time, and was poring over his Latin when his brother David, who was superintendent of a coal mine, came rushing into the room and ordered young William to hitch up his horse and have it ready for him by a certain time, as he was in a hurry, and wanted to drive out to a dance several miles in the country.   After his brother had left the room, young William turned to his aunt, Mrs. Waller, and said, "Aunt Martha, don't you think it rather humiliating for a Methodist and a Latin scholar to be compelled to hitch up a horse for a brother to go to a dance?"

Both the grandfather of the President and his great grandfather were carpenters by trade, and during the early days of the century they were engaged in this work.   The village of Chatfield, which is located on the site of the McKinley farm, was largely built by the McKinleys, and many buildings throughout the county and in Bucyrus are their handiwork.   Of the original buildings on the McKinley farm only one remains, the others having given place to more modern structures.   Upon the site of the old McKinley home has been erected a commodious two-story brick school house, and here the young people of Chatfield are taught in common school branches and imbibe patriotism amidst favorable environments. The only relative bearing the family name who is a resident of this vicinity is William McKinley, of this place, who is in the employ of the Ohio Central. He is an exact counterpart of the President in build and facial mold. Other relatives in Bucyrus are Thomas McCreary and family.

The surviving pioneer citizens who remember the McKinleys when they lived in Crawford County all speak of them in terms of highest praise. Those who knew David McKinley say that he was a highly educated and polished gentleman of the old school. He was a teacher for many years, and was familiar with several languages. In religion he was a strict Presbyterian, and in politics a Democrat of the Jeffersonian school, as were also the other McKinleys of Crawford County in that early day, except James, the President's grandfather, who was a Whig. He also fought in the Revolutionary War, and during the closing years of his life drew a pension for wounds received in the service.

In order to trace the history of the descendants in this county and show their relation to the late President William McKinley, whose career has been so illustrious, it is necessary to follow the history of the family briefly from its first appearance in America to the present time. The first McKinley to arrive in this country was James, who, with his brother William, emigrated from Ireland early in the eighteenth century. His brother William went South and established the Southern branch of the family, but James remained in York County, where he grew to manhood and was married. Among his children was David McKinley, who was born May 16, 1755, and died in this county in 1840. David's second son was James McKinley, who was in turn the father of William McKinley, Sr., father of the President. A brother of James McKinley, Ephraim by name, also located in Crawford County, settling in Bucyrus a year before James located at Chatfield. He married Hannah McCreary, a sister of Thomas McCreary.

well known in Ohio, and they lived in North Bucyrus. Ephraim and family moved from Bucyrus to South Bend, Ind., in 1847, and from there they went to Wisconsin and Dakota, and finally located in Ogden, Ills. When James McKinley located at Chatfield he was accompanied by his children, Hannah, Martha, Ellen and Benjamin, and his son John joined him about two years later, while the other children, including William, father of the President, remained in Columbiana County.

In 1844, James sold his Chatfield farm and bought another, but ultimately moved to South Bend, Ind. About the same time Ephraim moved there from Bucyrus. The country about South Bend was then very swampy, new and full of malaria. The old folks both were stricken with malaria shortly after arriving, and both died on the same day in 1847, on the fortieth anniversary of their marriage, and were buried in the same grave, which is marked by a handsome monument put up by their son, William McKinley, Sr.

THE PRESIDENT'S GRANDFATHER

James McKinley, grandfather of the President, was a remarkable man in many respects, and, like his father, was engaged in fighting England, he having served in the War of 1812. He served under General William Henry Harrison, and was in the battle of Tippecanoe. While in the service Harrison's division passed through this section of the State, and McKinley was so favorably impressed with the country at that time that it led to his locating there. Of their children, Hannah and her husband, Mr. Tilford, continued to live in the vicinity of Lykens for a number of years and also at Sulphur Springs, finally moving to Bloomville. Ellen and her husband, James Winters, lived in the vicinity of Lykens for a number of years after their marriage and then moved to Minnesota, and finally returned to Ohio. Martha and her husband, Mr. Waller, continued to live at Lykens until her death, October 4, 1880. There her husband and some of the children still live.

Let us give, in a little more detail, the story of William McKinley's father and mother. The latter, in her widowhood, found a devoted and loyal supporter in her son, the twenty-fifth President.

It was at New Lisbon that the young iron founder, William McKinley, Sr., wooed, won and married farmer Allison's daughter Nancy, in 1827. This combination of the tillers of the soil and the moulders of the iron was a good one, and no doubt added much to the strength of character in their offspring which manifested itself so decidedly in their daughter Anna, who was a teacher, and found its culminating climax in the Napoleonic face and character of William McKinley, Jr., the late President.

The life of Nancy McKinley was a long one, and its record is a simple narrative of a good wife and devoted mother whose children looked upon her as the embodiment of all that those two sacred names, wife and mother, mean in a Christian American home. Her name will always be recalled with that of her noble son.

The young couple, William and Nancy McKinley, settled, soon after their marriage, at Fairfield, Ohio. There the father established an iron foundry. They were plain and respectable people, without any of the disadvantages and embarrassments of a great name. The father devoted his time to earning a living by honest toil, and the mother to making a happy home for the husband and to the training of the children which came, teaching them the cardinal virtues of truthfulness, honor, and self-dependence.

WILLIAM McKINLEY JR'S BIRTHPLACE

From Fairfield the family removed to Niles, Ohio, a village in an adjoining county, and it was here, about sixteen years after the marriage of his parents, that William McKinley, Jr., was born, January 29, 1843, and named for his father. The little, long, ungainly, two-story, frame house in which the family lived, and in which the embryo President was born, is still standing, as has been said, in Niles. At one end is a portion used for a store. Adjoining this is the

3

vine-covered doorway which constitutes the entrance for the part used as a dwelling. The vine which covers the whole side of the house is very old. It was probably planted by the hand of Nancy Mc-Kinley, and it is undoubtedly associated with the earliest recollections of the President.

Humble as this house appears, it is a palace in comparison with the birthplaces and early homes of Andrew Jackson, Lincoln, and Garfield, and, with them, it goes to show that humble birth is no barrier to greatness, but rather a stimulus to the noble-souled and energetic American youth.

The question of educating the children is always a serious one in a new country. Educational advantages were poor at Niles, and the parents removed to Poland, a small town of some 200 inhabitants not far away, where there was an academy. William was now a young lad, and with his brothers and sisters he entered the school. His sister Anna became a teacher in the academy. William was possessed with a quiet dignity and serious habits, was studious and manly from a child, but he was as vigorous a player at games as he was diligent at his books. The family were held in high esteem at Poland, and the town is yet full of reminiscences concerning the members. Everybody liked William as a boy, and his thoroughness and brightness in his school work caused local prophecies of something great in store for him. He was his mother's chief dependence to run errands and do chores about the house, "because," she said, "he always seemed so pleased to help me."

POLAND, THE HOME OF HIS YOUTH

Poland was a small agricultural and mining town a few miles out from Youngstown, Ohio, and near the Pennsylvania line. It was noted for the integrity, education, and patriotism of its citizens. It is said no soldier was ever drafted there. Every time a call was made, there were more volunteers than the quota of the town required. It was while he was teaching school about two miles from Poland, and studying at the same time, that William

McKinley, then about eighteen years of age, volunteered, and, after receiving his mother's consent and blessing, marched away as a private in the ranks to fight for his country's flag. Before this the boy had advanced so far in his studies that he had already taught one country school in which some of the scholars were older than himself. When fifteen years of age, under his mother's influence, he became an active member in the Methodist Church. He was also a great student of the Bible and a constant attendant of the Sunday Bible class. In fact, he sought every opportunity to increase his knowledge on all profitable subjects.

The career of the boy-soldier is told elsewhere, and we know that at the close of the war he had been many times promoted and commended, and was on the staff of General Hayes.

At the age of twenty-one the boy came home to his mother, and with him he brought a commission of Major. It was dated in 1864, and read : "For gallant and meritorious service at the battles of Opequan, Cedar Creek and Fisher's Hill.

"Signed,   A. LINCOLN."

Perhaps the old mother was not proud to have her boy safe at home? And perhaps she was not prouder still to read that document? The welcome home and the sweet communions of such reunions are too sacred for comment, even if we were possessed of the details. There are thousands of mothers throughout this land, North and South, who know the story, for similar experiences have graven them, in letters that fade not, upon the tablets of their own hearts, where "sacred memories keep them ever fresh" and each advancing year lends them the "sweet mellowing light of age."

Upon the advice of his father, the young soldier decided to study law. The family assisted him by making personal sacrifices, in which Nancy McKinley and her daughter Anna were foremost. After a year and a half reading in the office of Judge Glidden, the unselfishness of mother and sister enabled him to go to the Albany Law School. In 1867, at the suggestion of his sister Anna, he went to Conton, whither she had preceded him as a teacher in the public schools.

It was in this beautiful city—then of 6,000 inhabitants—under the influence and with the help of mother and sister, that the young lawyer of twenty-four opened his office and began the battle of life which afterward crowned him with the laurel wreath of national fame.

HIS HEROIC SISTER ANNA

It would be unjust to President McKinley and his mother, Nancy McKinley, and especially to his heroic sister Anna, should we not add at this point that it was this sister—in her mind and character so like her distinguished brother—who saved her hard earnings, and, aside from assistance given her brother, bought a home and induced her parents to accept it and remove to Canton, that the whole family might live together. It was in this home that the last happy years of these old people, with their children around them, were spent. It was here that their grandchildren came to visit them and the happy family reunions of nearly a quarter of a century were held; and from here both parents were buried—the father in 1892, and the mother in 1897. A special photograph of this plain but comfortable cottage, now made famous by its associations, was taken for this sketch in the month of April, 1898, showing the trees around it, with the buds of Spring putting forth. It is the most unpretentious house in the neighborhood of elegant and palatial homes which surround it; but we doubt if there was a happier home in all Canton than this while Nancy McKinley was its mistress.

Not more than half a mile away, on another street, stands the house which was the home of President McKinley. It, too, is in an elegant community, and its simplicity is in striking contrast with the palaces of the rich by which it is environed.

Every Sunday when he was in Canton the great son of this grand old mother walked over the quiet streets which lay between

WILLIAM McKINLEY
FATHER OF PRESIDENT McKINLEY

MRS. WILLIAM McKINLEY.
MOTHER OF THE PRESIDENT

THE BIRTH PLACE OF WILLIAM McKINLEY

his home and hers and took her to church in the morning, and generally spent a part of the afternoon at her cottage home.

Eight weeks before her death, on his vacation from Washington, her son was with her at the church where they had both been members for many years, and they sat together in the family pew, little dreaming that it was the last time they should accompany each other to the house of worship, and that their next meeting before the altar should be the occasion of her funeral.

The devotion of the President to his mother was always one of the most marked and admirable traits of his character. Even in the most important political events of his life, he seemed never to forget her. On the day of his nomination he was solicitous that she be present at his house when the news of the proceedings came over the wires from the Convention at St. Louis. It was the 18th day of June, 1896, an ideal summer day at Canton, and the air full of golden sunshine. Major McKinley rocked on his porch, enjoying the freshness of the breeze that was balmy, though touched with fire. Telegrams came every few minutes, which he opened, reading to his friends such portions of them as pleased him.

Ladies of the family came up the walk from the street, and as the Major rose to greet them he asked, " Is mother coming up to-day?" and the answer was, "Yes, she will be here." About 1 o'clock the carriage drove up and three ladies descended. The Major hastened forward to greet them. The venerable woman, with Roman features, was the Major's mother, and with her were his sisters.

A TOUCHING INCIDENT

Luncheon was served. Some one mentioned a comforting passage from the Bible as appropriate to the occasion. There was at once a curiosity to read the passage, and Mrs. McKinley's Bible was brought. A gentleman said he presumed the Major was too busy a man to know much of the Bible. " He does, indeed, know the inside of his Bible; no man better, I assure you," said Mrs. McKinley. The passages referred to were found and read by a lady present. They were Jeremiah, xx, 11, beginning, "But the Lord is with me," and Psalm xlvii, 6, beginning "Sing praises to God."

After lunch the company retired to the Major's office, where, with two telegraph lines and one long-distance telephone bringing the news simultaneously, the excitement was too intense for levity. They had not expected the Convention to reach a nomination before night, but it came about 4 o'clock on the first ballot, when Ohio cast her vote, forty-six strong, for her favorite son. Without waiting for further returns a gentleman present arose and exclaimed, "The majority is big enough. Major, I congratulate you. God bless you, and now you have just a quarter of a minute before you are mobbed to greet your wife and mother."

McKinley quickly crossed the hall to the parlor crowded with ladies, and as his wife and mother were seated side by side stooped low to kiss them and clasp their eager hands, the wife responding with a bright smile and sweet exultation in her eyes as he told her the vote of Ohio had given him the nomination. The grand old mother placed her trembling hands on her son's neck, her eyes streaming with tears brighter even than smiles, and whispered to her illustrious boy some holy words for him alone. At this moment the bells rang, the whistles blew, the cannon thundered, and the beautiful little city of Canton went stark, gloriously mad. A vast multitude precipitated themselves in a gigantic, ungovernable procession upon McKinley's unpretentious home, and there, with wife and mother at the windows with him, he acknowledged, in a voice ringing with resolution and sincerity, his gratitude to his neighbors and countrymen.

The world knows the sequel to his nomination. The most bitterly contested campaign followed which ever occurred in the history of America, with the possible exception of that of 1860. when Lincoln was elected and slavery was the issue. McKinley's opponent was William Jennings Bryan, the young and magnetic orator of Nebraska, who was the nominee of the Democratic, the National Republican (Silver Republican), and the People's parties.

The election day came on November 3, 1896. The wires and the telephones brought the news. The Nebraskan had made a gallant fight, but the "favorite son of Ohio" had won. The booming cannon and the blare of trumpets shook the land from Maine to California, and Nancy McKinley, the farmer's daughter, became the mother of the President of the United States.

MOTHER MCKINLEY'S PROUD DAY

On the 4th of March, 1897, at the inauguration—the grandest this country has ever given any man—the proudest witness was Mother McKinley. For a short while she remained at the White House, and saw her son and his wife properly installed. Then she said she was satisfied that they did not need her any longer, and furthermore that she was glad she did not have to stay where there was so much ceremony required. She vastly preferred her own quiet little home and informal friends at Canton.

" Never did the little house seem so dear a home as when I got back to it," she said to a neighbor. "I would not begin to exchange it for the White House."

When the President took a vacation in September he went to Canton to rest, and, as has already been stated, accompanied his mother to church, as he had always done before his exaltation to the highest position in the gift of his countrymen. A few weeks later, news came of the serious illness of the aged woman, and, though in the midst of the most pressing official duties, incident upon the assembling of Congress, the President at the earliest possible moment hastened to her side. After a lingering illness, which followed a stroke of paralysis, the end came at 3 o'clock Sunday morning, December 12, 1897—almost the identical hour at which her husband died on Thanksgiving night five years before.

When the light faded from her eyes and the breathing ceased, the President sat silent and suffused in tears, holding her hand. The wife was by his side, and around the bed stood his brother Abner and his sisters, Mrs. Duncan and Miss Helen McKinley.

Six grandchildren were also there, as was the aged sister of the deceased—Mrs. Abigail Osborne, the only living member of her father's family. For more than an hour after the spirit had flown the President remained sitting at the bedside, gazing silently upon the sacred form which for more than fifty years had been his ideal of noble, exalted womanhood.

At daylight on Sunday morning the bell in the steeple began to toll, and it struck slowly eighty-eight times, once for every year of the long life of the deceased. This was a custom in vogue many years ago, and it was at the suggestion of some of the older members that it was revived for this occasion.

On Sunday afternoon the President and his brother Abner drove to Wood Lawn Cemetery, where they personally made all arrangements to place their mother's remains beside those of their father. While here another touching scene occurred. Under two carefully-kept mounds slept the President's only two children. Before leaving the city he had ordered two beautiful wreaths of flowers, and he laid them gently and reverently on the two little graves while the spot for the mother was being measured off by the workmen.

HIS MOTHER'S FUNERAL

The funeral services were held in the First Methodist Church, already referred to as the sacred spiritual home of mother and son. Here, thirty years before, McKinley had been Superintendent of the Sunday school. Here, for a quarter of a century, mother and son had come together to worship—a fitting spot in which to pay a last public respect to her memory.

Rev. Dr. C. E. Manchester, pastor of the church and a warm personal friend of the President and his mother, who had accompanied them to the inauguration in March, and was a frequent attendant and comforter at the cottage during the illness of Mrs. McKinley, conducted the funeral service, and it is from his address on the occasion and a personal interview which the writer enjoyed with him and his good wife at their home, in Canton, that we are indebted for much of the data contained in this sketch.

All of the thirty pastors in Canton were invited to be present, occupy the pulpit, and participate in the service. The pall-bearers were of the old men who for many years had been neighbors and friends of Mrs. McKinley. Dr. Manchester, in his funeral eulogy, declared, "It was of such as she the wise man spoke when he said, 'The heart of her husband doth safely trust in her. She will do him good, and not evil, all the days of her life. Strength and honor are her clothing, and she shall rejoice in time to come. She openeth her mouth with wisdom, and in her tongue is the law of kindness. She looketh well to the ways of her household, and eateth not the bread of idleness. Her children arise up and call her blessed. Give her of the fruit of her hands, and let her own works praise her in the gates.'"

"It is worth all the cost of trial and sorrow," said Dr. Manchester, "to be worthy of such divine portraiture as this—and she was worthy of it. Her motherhood was the crowning glory of her days. She was by divine right the gentle mistress of her own house. Always tender and true in her loving sympathies, self-poised and sturdy in her personal uprightness, she ruled like a queen over her own home. The law of kindness was the law of her life. Her heart throbbed with tenderest care for those whom God had given her, and her children do rise up and call her blessed.

"Another characteristic of Mother McKinley was her unvarying cheerfulness. It was as if the sunlight from the throne of God played upon her soul and kept it bright. And, after all, that was the sublime secret of her daily existence. She might have said to a sordid, grasping world, 'I have meat to eat that ye know not of.' Her faith that God does all things well, that He makes no mistakes, was the one creed of her Christian life. She grew old beautifully, because she walked with God. She came down to her grave like the well-ripened grain ready for the harvest."

The assemblage was the largest ever gathered at a funeral in Canton, and perhaps the largest ever turned out to honor any mother of the nation's Chief Magistrate. Members of the Cabinet and prominent officials and national celebrities traveled from Washington and all parts of the country to attend. " The church was appropriately draped," said the Canton *Repository*, " and when at 1 o'clock, under the strains of the great organ, the body was carried to the front of the pulpit, it was literally covered with flowers. After the services the undertaker removed the cover, and the vast congregation marched, to a solemn dirge from the organ, past the chancel rail and gazed upon the pale, peaceful face, passing out at one door while crowds passed in at another, until thousands had passed the casket in respectful silence."

After this a brief private service for the immediate family and Washington guests was held at the cottage, and the carriages, headed by the hearse, with its black nodding plumes, moved slowly away to Wood Lawn, where this noble wife, mother, and grandmother was laid to rest. President McKinley was buried from the same church, in the same cemetery, the same minister officiating, September 19, 1901.

MOTHER MCKINLEY'S DEVOTION TO HER CHILDREN

During her life Mrs. McKinley showed a fondness for visiting her children at their homes, as well as having them often at hers. She spent one winter with her son David in California shortly before his death, and frequently went to Somerset, Pennsylvania, the home of her son Abner, as well as to Pittsburg and Cleveland, the home of her daughter, Mrs. Duncan. Some of her grandchildren were nearly always at her cottage with her. Her maiden daughter, Miss Helen, continued to reside at the cottage after her mother's death.

" Did you know Mrs. McKinley ?" the writer asked of Jeremiah Lind, Canton's oldest inhabitant, who claims to have lived in one street seventy-four years.

"Oh, yes," he responded. "She and I were nearly the same age. I often saw her on the street. The old woman was hearty and pleasant all her days. Only a little while before she got sick I saw her with her little market basket on her arm tripping along better than many a woman of fifty years could do."

"Her head was never turned by the glare of society," said another acquaintance. "The common people were always fond of her."

On December 15th Congress adjourned out of respect to her memory ; and coming generations will point to the grave of Nancy McKinley, as they now delight to point to that of Mary Washington, as the resting-place of a model mother.

Pilgrims who, in coming generations, visit Canton will note this one difference between the grave of McKinley and that of any other President, except Garfield — he sleeps close beside his mother. And how fitting it is ! for what man more than the third martyr President avowed his obligation and love to her who gave him birth ?

CHAPTER III

McKinley's Boyhood and Education

THE story of William McKinley as a successful fisherman, a skater, a blackberry picker, as a playmate, and of the boy who "licked" him when he was eight years old, is one which makes every boy's and man's heart warm with memories of similar experiences. Niles, Ohio, was McKinley's birthplace. The house in which he was born has recently been cut in two, and the section which includes the room of his birth has been moved a mile away, to a pretty spot known to the people of Niles as Riverside Park. This half of the house has been newly sided up and is occupied by James Maines and family. The house has been the victim of relic hunters. The room in which Mr. McKinley was born bears the marks of penknives on all sides. A chip from the woodwork, a piece of plaster—anything has served as a memento to the sight-seer, who has been happening this way for the last few years.

Joe Fisher was for a long time the village constable, the truant officer, and an old soldier. "There," said he, as he pointed the small end of his corncob pipe to a red colored building across the street, "is the old school in which 'Bill' and I learned our A. B. C's. 'Bill' is President now, but he hasn't forgotten Joe Fisher. I never asked him for an office, for I don't believe in that sort of thing, but if ever I happen to be where McKinley is he throws his arm around me and gives my hand such a shake as brings back the days when three of us boys were chums, 'Bill' and Mr. Allison and Joe Fisher." Greatness never spoiled the good President, nor kept him aloof from his old friends and neighbors.

The red building, referred to by Mr. Fisher as the schoolhouse, is now occupied by a marble and granite company, and is situated

THE EASTERN PORTICO OF THE CAPITOL
Where the President delivered his Inaugural Address

THEODORE ROOSEVELT AT HIS DESK

on the main street of the town. Just to the rear of its present location once stood the blackberry bushes which McKinley as a boy used to visit with his companions, the blackberry pails suspended in front of them at a convenient height for picking. That section of Niles was then a sort of swamp. To-day it is covered by the nice little homes of the laborers who work in the mills not far distant.

"I declare I never thought 'Bill' would be President," continued Joe Fisher. "Little did I suppose as I sat fishing with him on Mosquito Creek with our legs dangling from the edge of the bridge, or as we caught angle worms to bait our hooks, that I was with a coming President. I well remember his patience with the hook and line. The rest of the boys would get disgusted at not getting a bite and go in bathing, but 'Bill' would keep on fishing. When it came time to go home he would carry a string of fish, while the rest had to be content with their baths. Sometimes we would all have good luck, and the strings of fish we would carry home suspended from a pole across our shoulders would make the eyes of everyone we passed stick 'way out.'"

THE PLACE OF HIS BIRTH

Niles is now a city of 9000 to 10,000 inhabitants. It is a busy centre. Furnaces and steel mills are located in the very boyhood footsteps of President McKinley. Fifty years ago there were a few mills there and a number of blacksmith shops. One of the blacksmith shops made the pair of skates on which McKinley learned to skate. Ice skates could not be purchased in the stores of Niles at that time. They were as much a luxury as diamonds are to-day. Allison, McKinley and Fisher all learned to skate on the same pair of skates. They took turns at using them. After they had learned, the first one to the spot where the skates were kept used them first, in accordance with the maxim, "first come, first served." Mr. McKinley was a good skater, although he is not remembered as having attempted to cut any fancy figures.

The three chums before mentioned lived within a stone's throw of each other, right in what is to-day the centre of the town. They were always together. As a playmate McKinley was very quiet in disposition. The boys bent on mischievousness could never enlist his help or sanction. He would not participate in any "deviltry," as Mr. Fisher puts it.

The Mr. Allison referred to is now in business in Cleveland. "Us three boys used to go down to the saw mill yard and play with the chips of wood," said Joe Fisher, using language which was familiar if it is not entirely grammatical. "'Bill' and Allison sided with each other and picked up all the large chips and left me the small ones. At last I got disgusted and pitched in and licked both of them. 'Bill' was about eight years old then."

The boys' mothers never encouraged the little fellows to tell on each other. In fact, they were punished for tattling every time they were found guilty.

Speaking of a visit to this interesting spot a person says:

"As we passed up Church Street, Mr. Fisher pointed out the high school which McKinley attended after he had completed his studies in the little building now used as a marble shop. As we neared the city hall a Spanish gun was a noticeable acquirement of the grounds. 'That,' said Joe, 'was presented to Niles by the government through the efforts of Mr. McKinley.' As we passed down an alley near the fire engine house, the other part of the McKinley homestead could be seen. It is used for a storehouse now, the principal interest centering around the half in which is the room where McKinley was born."

When about fifteen years of age McKinley moved with his parents to Poland, which is about six miles from Youngstown. There for a long time he helped his father days, and studied nights. Poland once possessed a notable literary society. The Edward Everett Society it was called. President McKinley was a member, and often served as a judge of debates. A picture of Orator Everett was purchased way back in the sixties and placed upon the society walls. It was meant to be an inspiration to the orators which the society was to produce, but when the seventy members were taxed $1 each to pay for the painting, some of them refused to be levied upon, and by action of the society such members were dismissed. Mr. McKinley paid his $1 and took advantage of all the oratorical inspirations which the painting furnished.

President McKinley's youth was passed in comfortable surroundings. His parents were, as we have intimated, in his early years, well-to-do people, though by no means rich. He knew no struggle with grinding poverty in his childhood. Neither was he pampered in the lap of luxury. His childhood was spent, like that of the average healthy, wholesome child of intelligent and thrifty parents, in a simple and unpretentious state of society. No startling tales are told of his precocity. But he was at least rather more than an ordinary boy, in that he was observant in mind and robust in body. He was fond of play and out-of-door sports, and was genial in his companionship with other children. At the same time there was apparent, even in his earliest years, something of that quiet earnestness that was afterwards so marked a characteristic of the man. "A black-haired, grave-faced, but robust and manly little chap," is the memory the older inhabitants of Niles have of their famous townsman's early appearance.

The boy was sent for a few years to the village school at Niles. Then the family removed to Poland, in Mahoning, the county between Trumbull and Columbiana, in order that he and the other children might enjoy the advantages of a high school or academy in that town. In both institutions he showed himself a solid and thorough, rather than a showy student. He already had a leaning towards argument and oratory, and was a prominent figure in all schoolboy debates. At Poland there was a literary society and debating club, and of it he was, for some time president. The story is told that the boys and girls saved up their spending money until they had enough to buy a carpet for the meeting-room of the club. They purchased at a neighboring carpet store what they deemed an exceedingly handsome fabric. Its groundwork was green, and its ornamentation gorgeously golden wreaths. The society unanimously decided that no boots should ever profane that sacred carpet, and the girl members, therefore, volunteered to knit slippers for all the members to wear. Unfortunately, the slippers were not ready for the first meeting, and so all the members who attended, and the visitors, too, were required to put off their shoes from their feet and listen to the debate shod only in stockings. The debaters themselves did likewise, and young McKinley presided over the meeting in his stocking feet.

HIS COLLEGE CAREER

At the Poland Academy McKinley was prepared to enter college, and at the age of sixteen he was matriculated at Allegheny College, Meadville, Pa. Scarcely was he well started in his studies there, however, when he fell ill and was compelled to return home. When his health was restored, he found himself thrown largely on his own resources. William McKinley was a good student. That is shown by the fact that he was able to enter as a junior, coming, as he did, from an academy. He secured a room in a house north of the college campus. The building still stands, and has been enlarged and changed to serve the needs of its present use, that of a home for orphans of Odd Fellows. The hard times of the Buchanan Administration had caused his father some embarrassment in business, and justice to the rest of the family made it necessary for William, at least partially, to support himself. He therefore took to school-teaching in a district school near Poland. He got $25 a month salary and "boarded around." Much of the time, however, he lived at home, walking to and from school every day, a distance of several miles. His intention was to save up a little money and return to college in a year or two. But that was not to be. For the clouds of war were gathering and he was soon to respond to the call of his country. He was among the first to enlist. The story of his war career follows in another chapter.

CHAPTER IV

The Soldier Boy Earns His Spurs

IN April 1861, when Fort Sumter was fired on, the Ohio youth with whose history we are concerned, was still engaged in the creditable profession of teaching. But the call of patriotic citizens to the defence of their country's flag found him quick to drop the tutor's pen and take up the soldier's sword. At Lincoln's summons the whole loyal North sprang to arms ; no part of it with more patriotic ardor than the old Western Reserve, in the borders of which McKinley was living. From every county and town volunteers were soon marching toward the frontier. Every village and hamlet sent its quota. Poland was not behind the rest. In June, 1861, a mass meeting was held, at which some stirring speeches were made, and at its close a company was enlisted.

Among those who composed this company, many of them boys, was our young teacher, then about eighteen years of age, a pale-faced, slender youth of scarcely middle height, but full of boyish energy and vim.

General Fremont inspected and mustered in the recruits. He examined young McKinley, pounded his chest, looked into his eyes and said : "You'll do." That was perhaps the proudest moment the boy had yet known, to be thus treated by the famous " Pathfinder," of whose thrilling adventures he had read with so much zest.

The captain and first lieutenant were selected, the company assembled on the village green, where the last good-byes to parents and sweethearts were said, the final tears of regret and homesickness that sprang to their eyes frowned down, and off they marched for Columbus, the State Capital, where the Governor was then

4

busily mustering the regiments needed for the State quota and despatching them with all speed to the seat of the coming war.

The Poland company was made company E, of the Twenty-third Regiment of Ohio Volunteers, its first colonel being William S. Rosecrans, soon to be raised to the rank of general, and in the end to gain great distinction as commander of the Army of the Cumberland, a military organization, only surpassed in size by the Army of the Potomac. Its major was Rutherford B. Hayes, also destined to rise to the rank of major-general, and to become in after years Governor of Ohio and President of the United States.

HIS REGIMENT MUSTERED IN

The regiment was mustered in by Captain J. C. Robinson, of the Fifth U. S. Infantry, afterwards a major-general of volunteers. It had enlisted for three months' service in response to President Lincoln's call for 75,000 men, but on reaching Columbus it was found that the Ohio quota of twenty-two regiments was already filled. It would have been obliged to disband but for the fact that a second call for volunteers for three years' service had just been made. The regiment, without hesitation, enlisted for this term, and thus took rank as the Twenty-third Regiment, the senior Ohio regiment on the roll of three-year volunteers. Its date of enrollment was June 11, 1861.

For fourteen months McKinley carried a musket in the ranks. He was a good soldier, intelligently obedient to his superior officers and genial and generous to his comrades. There was no more popular man in the regiment, and no harder fighter. Nor was there any lack of fighting to do. Six weeks after it left Columbus the regiment had its baptism of blood and fire at Carnifex Ferry. Then it had to chase the Rebel raiders back and forth across the rugged mountain ranges, was drenched by incessant rains, almost famished at times for lack of food, and exposed to all manner of unpleasant experiences. The young men from Poland thus had their fighting qualities and powers of endurance put to a hard test. But they stood it admirably.

Colonel Rosecrans did not lead the regiment to the field. His abilities as a strategist were recognized and his promotion to a higher command came before the Twenty-third received its orders to march. He was succeeded by Colonel E. S. Scammon, who led his ardent young soldiers to West Virginia, where the country around Clarksburg was being raided by roving bands, threatening to hold that region for the Confederate cause. This state of affairs was doing much to discourage Union sentiment.

Scammon and his men were bidden to drive these wasps from their nests. This was a trying service for raw troops, most of them boys, or just past the period of boyhood, denizens of a level country, heavily laden with arms and accoutrements, and sent into a wild, mountainous region, there to endure the trials and privations of a soldier's life.

HARD MARCHING

The regiment reached Clarksburg on July 27th. It was given but a single day to rest, and on the 28th was ordered to Weston, as a central point from which to deal with the mountain bands. Days and nights of weary and largely profitless labor succeeded, labor from which no fame was to be gained, but which played its part in the effort of the Government to suppress the rebellion and restore peace to the land. Up and down the rugged hills and through the ravines and valleys about Rich Mountain the raw recruits marched and countermarched, exposed to incessant rains and rapidly hardening themselves from untrained countrymen into vigorous and capable soldiers. The enemy being made up of small, scattered bands, it became necessary to divide the regiment into detachments and spread those through the hills. The rovers were hard to find and hard to overtake when found, it being their policy to strike, but to avoid being struck, and for six weary weeks the Twenty-third was employed in chasing elusive foes, who were ever on the alert and were adepts at concealment and ambush.

It may well be believed that the order for the reunion of the detatchments was heard with delight. This took place on September 1, the regiment marching to Bulltown. where it joined the main body of General Rosecrans' command. Thence the army proceeded with rapid marches to Carnifex Ferry, where the Confederate General Floyd, with a strong body of troops, was encamped in a strong position.

The previous service of the regiment had been like fox-hunting. The service before them was more like war. They were now in the face of the foe, as eager, apparently, as themselves for battle, and doubtless many a heart beat high and many a hope of glory and fame was indulged in when the sound of the bugles of the enemy reached their ears. With these feelings, we may be sure, were mingled sentiments of dread and alarm, natural to those who, for the first time, face an enemy on the embattled field. This was a different matter from chasing a flying band or guarding against an ambushed enemy, rarely to be seen until their rifles rang out. Yet the latter service had made men of the untrained boys of the Twenty-third, and we may safely assure ourselves that the youthful McKinley and his brothers-in-arms awaited the battle with more of hope than of dread.

TRYING TO CATCH FLOYD

Whatever their feelings, their fortitude as soldiers was not put to the test, for the expected battle was not fought. There was a sharp skirmish between the advanced lines of the two armies on the evening of the 10th, and the Union troops lay on their arms during the dark hours of the night, fully expecting to be greeted with the rattle of musketry the next day. They were disappointed. General Floyd decided that prudence was the better part of valor, and when day dawned the troops of Rosecrans gazed upon an empty scene. The Confederates had left their camp and slipped away during the night. Pursuit was made, but in vain. A heavy rain made the creeks impassable, and before they could be crossed the enemy was out of reach.

Returning from this fruitless pursuit with nothing to show except a few stragglers taken prisoners, the regiment marched to Camp Ewing, on New River, where it went into winter quarters. The position proved to be an unhealthy one, the air full of the germs of malaria, and the young soldiers, many of them worn out with their unaccustomed hardships and privations, were ill fitted to withstand the insidious assaults of disease. Malarial fever and other diseases attacked them, and the hospital was quickly filled.

We have reason to believe that young McKinley withstood this creeping foe. The winter was well employed in drilling the new troops and recruiting the regiments, the only active service being an occasional foray after some adventurous band of Confederates that came within striking distance of the camp.

When the Spring of 1862 opened, the old work of the regiment was renewed. On May 1st it reached Princeton, in West Virginia, only to find it in flames and the Confederate band which had held it vanished and gone. The tables were turned against the Twenty-third on May 8th, when the regiment was attacked by General Heth, with a strong force of infantry and six pieces of artillery. Much overmatched, it was obliged to retreat, but fell back in good order to East River.

The next camping-place of the Twenty-third Ohio was at Flat Top Mountain, where it remained until July 13th, suffering severely from want of supplies, which were cut off by the activity of the roving foe. Thence they were ordered to Green Meadows, on New River, and on August 8th came a peremptory command for the regiment to march with all speed to Camp Platt, on the Great Kanawha River. In a little more than three days they made the distance of 104 miles on foot—a highly creditable achievement.

This hasty march had its adequate cause. While the minor war we have chronicled was going on in West Virginia, war on a large scale was being waged elsewhere. McClellan's advance against Richmond had been made, the disastrous Seven Days' fight and the Second Bull Run battle had been fought, General

Lee was about to invade Maryland with his victorious army, and the cause of the North was in imminent danger. Every effort was being made to gather forces to meet the threatened peril, and the rapid march of the Twenty-third was a part of this hasty gathering of the hosts.

This midsummer march brought the regiment within the reach of railroad facilities, and the Twenty-third Ohio, then commanded by Lieutenant-Colonel R. B. Hayes, was drawn at the full speed of the iron horse to the national capital, there to join the army which McClellan was rapidly mustering for the defence of Washington and Maryland.

MADE COMMISSARY SERGEANT

Before detailing the stirring events that succeeded, we must return for a moment to the fortunes of William McKinley, the youthful Poland volunteer. He had shown himself from the first an ardent and faithful soldier, and had gone through the trying West Virginia campaign in a manner to attract the favorable attention of his officers. As a result, on April 19, 1862, he was appointed commissary sergeant to the regiment—a responsible and trying position for the ten months' soldier and youth of nineteen. That he was competent to fill the duties of the position with skill and ability the future clearly showed.

From Washington the army, of which the Twenty-third Ohio now formed a part, made a rapid march to South Mountain and Antietam, where the next great struggles of the war were to take place. The story of the great battles that followed does not come within our scope. We are concerned only with the part played by the regiment of which Sergeant McKinley formed a part, and a description of this service we may fitly quote from the work entitled *Ohio in the War*, by the Hon. Whitelaw Reid. This is his account of the doings of the Twenty-third Ohio at South Mountain and Antietam :

"At South Mountain the regiment, under Lieutenant-Colonel Hayes (Gen. J. D. Cox commanding division), was the first infantry engaged, being the advance of the column of that day. It was ordered at an early hour to advance by an unfrequented road leading up the mountain and to attack the enemy. Posted behind stone walls, the enemy, in greatly superior force, poured a destructive fire of musketry, grape, and canister into our ranks at very short range and in a very short space of time. Lieutenant-Colonel Hayes, Captain Skiles, and Lieutenants Hood, Ritter, and Smith were each badly wounded (Colonel Hayes' arm broken; Captain Skiles shot through the elbow, arm amputated; Ritter, leg amputated); and over 100 dead and wounded lay upon the field out of the 350 who went into the action.

BATTLE OF SOUTH MOUNTAIN

"The command now devolved upon Major Comly, and remained with him from that time forward. The enemy suddenly opened fire from the left, and the regiment changed front on first company. Lieutenant-Colonel Hayes soon after again made his appearance on the field, with his wound half-dressed, and fought, against the remonstrances of the whole command, until carried off. Soon after the remainder of the brigade came up, a gallant charge was made up the hill, and the enemy was dislodged and driven into the woods beyond. In this charge a large number of the enemy were killed with the bayonet. During the remainder of the day the regiment fought with its division. Three bayonet-charges were made by the regiment during the day, in each of which the enemy were driven with heavy loss.

"During the day the Twenty-third lost nearly 200, of whom almost one-fourth were killed on the field or afterward died of wounds. Only seven men were unaccounted for at the roll-call after the action. The colors of the regiment were riddled and the blue field almost completely carried away by shells and bullets.

"At Antietam the regiment fought with the Kanawha division. Near the close of the day a disastrous charge was made by the division (the Twenty-third occupying the right of the first brigade), by which the left of the division was exposed to a large force of the enemy, who suddenly emerged from a corn-field in rear of the left.   The colors of the regiment were instantly shot down, at the same time a feint was made in the front.   A battery in the rear opened fire on the advancing column of the enemy, by which also the national forces sustained more loss than the enemy.   After a moment's delay the colors were planted by Major Comly on a new line at right angles with the former front, and without waiting for any further order the regiment, at a run, formed a line in the new direction and opened fire on the enemy, who for some cause retired. Little damage was done by the enemy except a few captures from the left.   The division soon after withdrew, but through some inadvertency no order reached the Twenty-third, and it remained on the field until Colonel Scammon (commanding the division) came back and ordered it to the rear.

"Almost exhausted by several days' hard fighting, the regiment was ordered to support a battery of General Sturgis' division during the night, and was not relieved until the afternoon of the next day."

PRESIDENT HAYES' TRIBUTE

McKinley, made a sergeant in West Virginia, won a commission at Antietam.   This he did by a striking act of coolness and daring and in the practical method which was conspicuous throughout his subsequent career.   There is always a mob of faint hearts in the rear of a line of battle, who seek to shirk their duty.   If these men would not fight they might be otherwise employed.   McKinley knew that the soldiers who had toiled and struggled under a burning sun on that scorching line of battle would be very glad to receive some of the creature comforts of life.   He therefore pressed into service some of these stragglers, whom he set to making coffee.   Then, loading up a couple of wagons, he started with his mule teams for the line of battle.

On July 30, 1891, Ex-President Hayes, while addressing a religious meeting at Lakeside, Ohio, gave the following testimony to this timely act of the young commissary sergeant, with a warm estimate of his general character as man and soldier :

"Rather more than thirty years ago I first made the acquaintance of Major McKinley. He was then a boy—had just passed the age of seventeen. He had before that taught school and was coming from an academy to the camp. He with me entered upon a new, strange life—a soldier's life—in the time of actual war.

"With the Twenty-third Ohio regiment Major McKinley came, the boy I have described, carrying his musket and his knapsack. In every company of that regiment General Rosecrans and Colonel Matthews and myself soon found there were young men of exceptional character and promise. I need not go into any detail of the military history of this young man I have described. At once it was found he had unusual character for the mere business of war. There is a quartermaster's department, which is a very necessary and important department, in every regiment, in every brigade, in every division, in every army.

"Young as he was, we soon found that in business, in executive ability, young McKinley was a man of rare capacity, of unusual and unsurpassed capacity, especially for a boy of his age. When battles were fought, or service was to be performed in warlike things, he always took his place. The night was never too dark ; the weather was never too cold ; there was no sleet, or storm, or hail, or snow or rain that was in the way of his prompt and efficient performance of every duty.

"When I became commander of the regiment he soon came to be upon my staff, and he remained upon my staff for one or two years, so that I did literally and in fact know him like a book and loved him like a brother.

"From that time he naturally progressed, for his talents and capacity could not be unknown to the staff of the commander of the Army of West Virginia, George Crook, a favorite of the army he commanded. He wanted McKinley, and of course it was my duty to tell McKinley he must leave me. The bloodiest day of the war, the day on which more men were killed or wounded than on any other day of the war—observe, I don't say of any other battle, stretching over many days, but any one day—was September 17, 1862, in the battle of Antietam.

SERVING HOT COFFEE ON THE FIGHTING LINE

"That battle began at daylight. Before daylight men were in the ranks and preparing for it. Without breakfast, without coffee, they went into the fight, and it continued until after the sun had set. Early in the afternoon, naturally enough, with the exertion required of the men, they were famished and thirsty and to some extent broken in spirit. The commissary department of that brigade was under Sergeant McKinley's administration and personal supervision. From his hands every man in the regiment was served with hot coffee and warm meats, a thing that had never occurred under similar circumstances in any other army in the world. He passed under fire and delivered, with his own hands, these things, so essential for the men for whom he was laboring.

"Coming to Ohio and recovering from wounds, I called upon Governor Tod and told him this incident. With the emphasis that distinguished that great war governor he said, ' Let McKinley be promoted from sergeant to lieutenant,' and that I might not forget, he requested me to put it upon the roster of the regiment, which I did, and McKinley was promoted. As was the case, perhaps, with very many soldiers, I did not keep a diary regularly from day to day, but I kept notes of what was transpiring. When I knew that I was to come here, it occurred to me to open the old note-book of that period and see what it contained, and I found this entry :

"'Saturday, December 13, 1862.—Our new second lieutenant, McKinley, returned to-day—an exceedingly bright, intelligent, and gentlemanly young officer. He promises to be one of the best.'

"He has kept the promise in every sense of the word."

Twenty years afterward, when the soldier whose story we are telling, himself became Governor of Ohio, one of his first acts was to have an oil portrait of Governor Tod hung in the Executive Chamber. He had not forgotten how his predecessor made him second lieutenant of Company D, in his regiment, the commission dating September 23, 1862.

We have still another account of McKinley's action on that day of stress and strife, written by General J. L. Botsford, quartermaster of his regiment. The General states:

ANOTHER ACCOUNT OF THE SAME INCIDENT

"At the battle of Antietam McKinley was the commissary sergeant of the Twenty-third Regiment, O. V. I., and his duty was, of course, with the commissary supplies, which were at least two miles from the battle-field proper.

"As you no doubt are aware, in all battles, whether large or small, there are numerous stragglers who easily find their way back to where the commissary supplies are. This was the case at Antietam, and McKinley conceived and put into execution the idea of using some of these stragglers to make coffee and carry it to the boys in front. It was nearly dark when we heard tremendous cheering from the left of our regiment. As we had been having heavy fighting right up to this time, our division commander, General Scammon, sent me to find out the cause, which I very soon found to be cheers for McKinley and his hot coffee. You can readily imagine the rousing welcome he received from both officers and men.

"When you consider the fact of his leaving his post of security and driving into the middle of a bloody battle with a team of mules, it needs no words of mine to show the character and determination of McKinley, a boy of, at this time, not twenty years of age. McKinley loaded up two wagons with supplies, but the mules of one wagon were disabled. He was ordered back time and again, but he pushed right on."

After the battle of Antietam the Twenty-third Ohio returned to its former work of Confederate hunting in the mountains of

West Virginia. After many marches they were ordered to Clarksburg in the middle of October. Several changes were here made in the command. Colonel Scammon was appointed brigadier-general; Lieutenant-Colonel Hayes was made colonel, and Comly became lieutenant-colonel. On November 18th the regiment went into winter quarters at the Falls of the Great Kanawha, having during the campaigns of 1862 marched over 600 miles.

The coming winter brought lighter duty, and the regiment did not resume its activity until March 16, 1863, when it was ordered to Charleston. There it lay in camp until July without seeing much field service. Next it was hurried to the Ohio River to help capture Morgan's raiders, whose escapades in the Buckeye State had given rise to much excitement.

Reaching Buffington Bar, on the Ohio River, they succeeded in heading off Morgan's band and picked up a number of his men. They remained in camp at Charleston, W. Va., during the rest of 1863, and up to the preparations made by Grant in the Spring of '64 for the final crushing of the Confederacy.

During this interval McKinley gained a second promotion, being made first lieutenant of Company E, in February, 1863, and serving with that rank during that year. After Hayes was made colonel and placed in command of the first brigade of the Kanawha division, he took the young officer on his staff as brigade quartermaster. He had been very friendly to him from an early period of his service.

CHAPTER V

In the Shenandoah Valley

IN the year 1864, the military affairs of the Union, the conduct of which had been in many respects unsatisfactory, were entrusted to a new hand and took on a new form. General Grant, whose remarkable success in the West had made him famous, was appointed to the command of all the armies of the Union, and laid his plans for a systematic advance from all quarters. The Army of the Potomac, which he joined in person, was to cross the Rapidan River, on the overland route from Washington to Richmond. Sherman received orders to set out simultaneously from Chattanooga, and various contemporary movements were planned. Among the latter was a movement against Lynchburg, Virginia, entrusted to General David Hunter. The Kanawha division, under General Crook, of which the Twenty-third Ohio formed a part, was ordered to join Hunter; but, before doing so, General Crook made a movement of his own against the Virginia & Tennessee Railroad. The column took to the road on April 29, 1864, and, after ten days of hard marching, with an occasional skirmish, Crook's command found itself in front of the enemy at Cloyd's Mountain.

Whitelaw Reid's history of the Ohio volunteers, from which we have already quoted, furnishes the following account of the sharp encounter that took place:

"In this engagement the Twenty-third was on the right of the first brigade. About noon they were ordered to charge the enemy, who occupied the first crest of the mountain with artillery and infantry, behind rudely constructed breastworks. The hill itself was thickly wooded, steep and difficult of ascent, and was skirted by a stream of water from two to three feet deep. The approach was through a beautiful meadow five or six hundred yards in width. At the word of command the regiment advanced at double-quick across the meadow, under a very heavy fire of musketry and artillery, to the foot of the mountain across the stream. The regiment advanced steadily to this point without returning the fire of the enemy, and after a short pause a furious assault was made upon the enemy's works, carrying them and capturing two pieces of artillery, which were brought off the field by Lieutenant Austin. The enemy fell back to the second crest or ridge of the mountain, where a determined attempt was made to form a line, but after a short struggle he was driven from there in full retreat. Reinforcements arriving on the field, a third attempt was made to make a stand, but unsuccessfully. The struggle at the guns was of the fiercest description. The rebel artillerymen attempted to reload ther pieces when our line was not more than ten paces distant. Private Kosht, Company G, a recruit, eighteen years of age, was the first to reach the guns. With a boyish shout he sprang from the ranks and hung his hat over the muzzle of one of the guns."

MCKINLEY IN THE RETREAT AT LYNCHBURG

This affair was followed by several brisk skirmishes and further hard marching, and on June 8th, the column returning, the Twenty-third Ohio joined Hunter at Stanton. On the 11th of that month the three years' service of this regiment expired, but its patriotic members had not yet had enough of war, and most of the men re-enlisted. Hunter's Lynchburg expedition, of which the regiment formed a part, proved a failure. On reaching the vicinity of Lynchburg he found his command heavily outnumbered, and threatened with a serious repulse. The only thing to be done was to retreat with as little loss as possible. The direct route down the valley, however, was not available, and Hunter's only safe way out of his difficulty was to march westward, making his way back to the valley by a long detour along the Kanawha River and up the Ohio. Crook's command took the lead in this difficult movement through a mountainous country. During the long retreat Lieutenant McKinley acted as a staff officer, and took part in all the perilous duties of the march. In truth, Hunter's command had no small difficulty in extricating itself from the situation. This is shown by the diary of an officer which is quoted in Mr. Reed's work.

"June 19.—Marched all day, dragging along very slowly. The men had nothing to eat, the trains being sent in advance. It is almost incredible that men should have been able to endure so much, but they never faltered and not a murmur escaped them. Often men would drop out silently, exhausted, but not a word of complaint was spoken. Shortly after dark, at Liberty, had a brisk little fight with the enemy's advance; reached Buford's Gap about 10 A. M. of the 20th. General Crook remained here with Hayes' brigade, holding the Gap until dark, inviting an attack. The army was, however, too cautious to do much skirmishing. After dark we withdrew and marched all night to overtake the command in advance. Reached Salem about 9 A. M. Hunter had passed through Salem, and a body of the enemy's cavalry fell upon his train and captured the greater part of his artillery.

INTENSE TOIL AND SUFFERING

"About the same time Crook was attacked in front and rear, and after a sharp fight pushed through, losing nothing. Heavy skirmishing all day, and nothing to eat and no sleep. Continued the march until about 10 P. M., when we reached the foot of North Mountain and slept. At 4 A. M. next morning (22d) left in the advance, the first time since the retreat commenced. By a mistake a march of eight miles was made for nothing. Thus we toiled on, suffering intensely with exhaustion, want of food, clothing, etc. Men all crazy. Stopped and ate; marched and ate; camped about dark and ate all night. Marched 180 miles in the last nine days, fighting nearly all the time, and with very little to eat."

Hunter's command ended its long roundabout march at Charleston on July 1st, and remained there to recuperate until the 10th. On that date Crook's command was ordered to Martinsburg to take part in the pursuit of Early, who had invaded Maryland and Pennsylvania. Remaining at Martinsburg until the 18th, it next set out for Cabletown, ten miles from Harper's Ferry, where the enemy's pickets were encountered. Here Hayes' brigade was sent in, without cavalry, and with only two sections of a battery, to attack Early's army, which outnumbered it six to one. It reflects great credit upon General Hunter and his command that, after this futile and perilous attempt, the soldiers engaged, instead of defeating the enemy, escaped a visit to Andersonville Prison. From this point the march was resumed towards Harper's Ferry, and the brigade reached Winchester on July 22d. At Kernstown, near this point, there occurred on the 24th an engagement which proved disastrous to Crook's command. In this affair McKinley again distinguished himself for gallantry. His conduct is described in an account of the events of that date, written by General Russell Hastings.

General Hastings, for many years after the war a prominent resident of Bermuda, but afterwards living at St. Paul, was one of the participants in the following affair described by him:

" The Union forces were commanded by General George Crook; the Confederate forces by General Jubal Early.

" It is not pleasant work for one who participated in a defeat to recount those hours, yet no one can be better informed than he who saw each movement of the command. To lead up to this battle, I feel it necessary to begin at the time General Jubal Early was menacing Washington, twelve days before the battle, when he had his whole army close up to the works north of the city, on July 11th and 12th. For two days he stood before our national capital challenging the Union troops to combat. General Grant soon made such disposition of troops, by sending from the Army of the Potomac, before Richmond, the Sixth and Nineteenth Army

Corps, as caused Early to leisurely retreat toward the Shenandoah Valley, by way of Poolesville, Md., Edward's Ferry, on the Potomac, and Leesburg, Va., reaching Snicker's Gap in the Blue Mountains on the 17th, and crossing the Shenandoah at Snicker's Ford they went into camp on the west bank.

" The Sixth and Nineteenth Corps as leisurely followed, and at or near Snicker's Gap united with one division of General Hunter's infantry (Thoburn's) which had just arrived from the Kanawha Valley over the Baltimore & Ohio Railroad. On the afternoon of the 18th, Thoburn's division was ordered to cross Snicker's Ford and attack Early, but the Sixth Corps, which was to support Thoburn, not coming into action as expected, the latter was driven back through the stream with considerable loss.

MCKINLEY AT WINCHESTER

" On July 19th General Early retreated southward on the road toward Strasburg, safely carrying with him all the plunder he had gathered over Maryland and Pennsylvania, while the whole Union army, consisting of the Sixth and Nineteenth Corps and Hunter's command, which had but lately arrived from the Kanawha Valley, was massed in the vicinity of Berryville and Winchester, quite a formidable army, some 20,000 strong.

" At this time it was supposed by General Grant that General Lee had ordered Early with the main body of his veteran army to Richmond, and Grant, needing the Sixth and Nineteenth Corps with him before Richmond, ordered them to Washington on their way. This left in the valley to confront the Confederates only Hunter's command, consisting of the Eighth Corps, commanded by Gen. George Crook, some 6,000 in number, with a brigade of nondescript troops made up of dismounted cavalrymen and decimated infantry regiments. Such troops were naturally demoralizing to any command. In addition to this infantry was some cavalry under Generals Averill and Duffie, some 2,000 strong.

5

"In the Eighth Corps was a brigade commanded by Gen. Rutherford B. Hayes, and it is of the part taken by this brigade in the battle of Kernstown that I propose to relate. The brigade was formed as follows :

"First Brigade, Second Division, Eighth Corps, Gen. Rutherford B. Hayes commanding ; Twenty-third Ohio Volunteer Infantry, Col. J. M. Comly ; Thirty-sixth Ohio Volunteer Infantry, Col. A. I. Duval ; Fifth West Virginia Infantry, Col. E. H. Enochs ; Thirteenth West Virginia Infantry, Col. William Brown. The brigade staff was as follows : Col. Joseph Webb, surgeon ; Capt. Russell Hastings, adjutant-general ; Lieut. William McKinley, Jr., quartermaster ; Lieut. B. A. Twiner, ordnance ; Lieut. A. W. Delay, commissary ; Lieut. O. J. Wood, aide.

HARD CAMPAIGNING

"General Crook's Eighth Corps, much fatigued and worn, had just returned from a raid to Lynchburg, close to Appomattox, where General Lee surrendered his army in April, 1865. We now felt, with Early and his veterans well off on their way to Richmond, with no enemy of any considerable force in our front, that we should have a few days of much-needed rest. From April 30th up to this date we had made a raid to the New River Bridge, in southwestern Virginia, another to Lynchburg, marching in these raids over 800 miles, often out of food, short of clothing and shoes, were on the skirmish-line daily, either advancing or retreating, and had fought four hard-contested battles. Directly after the close of these raids we had been moved with inconsiderate haste from the Kanawha Valley, near the Kentucky line, to this valley, by forced marches, on steamboats on the Ohio River, and on freight cars on the Baltimore & Ohio Railroad, with no opportunity for sleep or rest. General Crook had now advanced his little army to Winchester, going into camp just south of the town, where there is one of those noted springs of the valley gushing out from a crevice in the limestone rock in sufficient quantities to furnish power for a large flouring mill. Here we rolled ourselves in our blankets upon the luxuriant grass under the shade of large oak trees, and slept away the night and a large part of two delightful days.

"On Sunday morning, July 24th, our 'resting spell' came to a sudden close. While at inspection on this bright, sunny Sunday morning, the sound of cannon, well out on our front toward the south, was heard. Usually such sounds did not worry us, as our cavalry was always 'banging away' with the artillery attached to them. We did not, though, this morning like the sound of it, for to a veteran's ear the frequency of the discharges was such as seemed to mean work before us. Soon cavalry couriers came in from the front, bringing word to General Crook that our cavalry outposts on the valley pike, some ten miles south of Winchester, were being driven in by a seemingly large force. General Crook, still relying on the former information that Early was well off on his way to Richmond, did not feel the necessity of immediately moving out and forming line of battle, but as courier after courier arrived with the additional report of large bodies of the enemy's infantry being seen, he finally ordered all his troops to advance to the front and form line of battle at the little hamlet of Kernstown, some four miles south of Winchester. This ground had already been made historic, as here General Shields met Stonewall Jackson in 1862 and repulsed him.

"At about noon Crook had formed all his available troops in line, with his First Division on the extreme right, extending to the Romney Pike, with his nondescript brigade of mounted cavalry and infantry next and the Second Division on the left, Hayes' brigade occupying the extreme left, extending east of the valley pike out into some open fields, where a view of the country could be had for a mile or more to our left. The Thirteenth West Virginia Infantry, of Hayes' brigade, was posted in an orchard some 500 yards to the rear and left to act as a reserve.

"At this moment Crook discovered he had been deceived about Early's march for Richmond. On July 23d Early had halted at Strasburg, and there learning that the Sixth and Nineteenth Corps had withdrawn toward Washington, and that the forces occupying Winchester were only those of Crook, about one-third his numbers, had determined to return and crush him without delay.

A BATTLE WITH GENERAL EARLY'S FORCES

"Several historians have made an effort to show that General Early was hardly fitted for the position he occupied as commander of the Confederate forces in the valley. The Union army before him, on the contrary, found him always watchful, alert, ready to seize upon such an opportunity as now presented itself; a hard fighter, full of vim and subtle cunning, able to maneuvre his troops in such a way as completely to deceive our commanders. Even after General Sheridan assumed command in the valley, with an army more than three times larger than General Crook had on this day, there was much marching and countermarching, much maneuvering for an advantage, before Sheridan thought it prudent to attack, but when he did attack he gave Early a crushing blow.

"The battle opened with sharp firing all along the line, our artillery on rising ground at our rear firing over our heads, the enemy's artillery replying, with their shells exploding among us. How could we hope to win a battle when so largely outnumbered? On the Union side was only Crook's little corps, some 6,000 strong, combating the whole of Early's army. The Confederate infantry line extended far beyond us on our left, and still beyond that could be seen Confederate cavalry covering the country for a mile or more and rapidly driving back our cavalry in great confusion. Although our infantry could probably manage to keep back the Confederates in our front, this rapidly advancing line on our left, with nothing whatever to oppose them, would soon engulf us. At this moment the nondescript brigade broke in great confusion, leaving a sad gap in our centre. Then, and not till then, and not until the enemy in

THE PRESIDENT CROSSING THE PARADE GROUNDS AT BUFFALO

THE LAST PHOTOGRAPH TAKEN AT REQUEST OF PRESIDENT McKINLEY

our front was severely punished, did Hayes' brigade turn and fall back, with but trifling confusion, in the direction of Winchester, maintaining our organization then and throughout all the afternoon.

"Now came hurrying times for staff officers. Orders had to be carried in all directions. To one would be given orders to gallop rapidly to the rear and try to form a guard line to stop the stragglers; to another to go to the rear and order the wagon train in full retreat toward Martinsburg; to another to go to that battery and order it rapidly to form and unlimber on that adjacent ridge, and play with rapidity upon the advancing enemy with shot and shell; to another to direct the ambulance train down the pike, and so on until this class of officers became scarce. Crook was at one time without a staff officer about him, having already borrowed of Hayes several, and still he had need for more.

MCKINLEY'S PERILOUS RIDE

"Just now it was discovered that one of the regiments was still in the orchard where posted at the beginning of the battle. General Hayes, turning to Lieutenant McKinley, directed him to go for and bring away this regiment if it had not already fallen. McKinley turned his horse and, keenly spurring it, pushed it at a fierce gallop obliquely toward the advancing enemy. A sad look came over Hayes' face as he saw this young, gallant boy pushing rapidly forward to almost certain death. McKinley was much loved in the command—a mere boy at the beginning of the war, who had left his college, his expectation for the future, all, everything, willing to serve his country and his flag in their dire need. With wonderful force of character, then, true, pure, noble and brave, he had, by reason of his ability and wonderful power with men even much older than himself, risen from the ranks to become a noted staff officer; and later was called to the staff of General Crook, and so on up to General Hancock's headquarters; and for his many brave acts and conspicuous gallantry was by President Lincoln brevetted major.

" Hayes loved him as father loves a son, and only imagine what must have been his feelings when the necessities of the moment demanded that he should order this boy to do this dangerous work. None of us expected to see him again as we watched him push his horse through the open fields, over fences, through ditches, while a well-directed fire from the enemy was poured upon him, with shells exploding around, about, and over him. Once he was completely enveloped in the smoke of an exploding shell, and we thought he had gone down; but no, he was saved for better work for his country in his future years. Out of this smoke emerged his wiry little brown horse, with McKinley still firmly seated and as erect as a hussar. Now he had passed under cover from the enemy's fire, and a sense of relief came to us all. Thus far he was all right, but we knew his danger was really but just beginning, for the enemy was still coming on, though not with the fierce energy with which he had attacked the main line a few moments before, no doubt feeling the need of cautious approach, for Crook at this time had planted several batteries on the ridge near by, which then were doing effective work.

MCKINLEY DELIVERS HIS ORDERS

"McKinley gave the colonel the orders from Hayes to fall back, saying, in addition : ' I supposed you would have gone to the rear without orders.' The colonel's reply was : ' I was about concluding I would retire without waiting any longer for orders. I am now ready to go wherever you shall lead, but, lieutenant, I p'intedly believe I ought to give those fellows a volley or two before I go.' McKinley's reply was : ' Then up and at them as quickly as possible,' and as the regiment arose to its feet the enemy came on into full view. Colonel Brown's boys gave the enemy a crushing volley, following it up with a rattling fire, and then slowly retreated towards some woods directly in their rear. At this the enemy halted all along Brown's immediate front and for some distance to his right and left, no doubt feeling he was touching a secondary line, which should be approached with all due caution. During this hesitancy of the enemy McKinley led the regiment through these woods on toward Winchester.

"As Hayes and Crook saw this regiment safely off they turned, and, following the column, with it moved slowly to the rear, down the Winchester pike. At a point near Winchester McKinley brought the regiment to the column and to its place in the brigade. McKinley was greeted by us all with a happy, contented smile—no effusion, no gushing palaver of words, though all of us felt and knew one of the most gallant acts of the war had been performed.

"As McKinley drew up by the side of Hayes to make his verbal report, I heard Hayes say: 'I never expected to see you in life again.' During such scenes as these were our friendly ties knitted, and can you blame us if in our grizzled veteran age the tears will sometimes spring to the eye when we greet each other after a long separation?

"The battle was over, and now began a well-organized retreat, so far as Hayes' brigade was concerned, with the enemy's infantry pushing us from the front and the cavalry harassing us on right and left. Our wagon train was well off toward Martinsburg, and we knew our brigade could take care of itself, no matter how hard Early should push us. We had good, strong legs, plenty of ammunition, and we certainly could march just as rapidly as Early's infantry could follow; and as for the cavalry, no matter where they attacked, right, left, or rear, we could with a few well-directed volleys scatter them.

MCKINLEY'S KINDNESS OF HEART

"All this long, fateful afternoon we marched down the pike, first through Winchester town, where the faces of the inhabitants instantly informed us on which side of the cause were their sympathies. The jubilant faces largely outnumbered the sad ones. One dear old Quaker lady, whom we all knew, stood at her gate as we passed.   Tears were running down her cheeks, and we knew they were caused by sympathy for our misfortunes.   For her own safety, with her Confederate neighbors looking on, we dared not make any effusive display of sorrow at her condition, but McKinley in his great kindness of heart reined his horse to the curbstone and in a low voice said : 'Don't worry, my dear madam. We are not hurt as much as it seems, and we shall be back here again in a few days.'   A smile directly spread over her face, and her heart was made almost happy by these timely spoken words.

"During most of the afternoon we were marching in line of battle on the east side of the pike.   Occasionally, though, after we had given the pushing infantry of the enemy a reminder that there was still some pluck left in us, we would change the column to route march, and on the pike make good time to the rear.   After we were past Winchester the infantry annoyed us very little, but the cavalry harassed us more or less during the afternoon.

AN INTERESTING INCIDENT

"I will relate an incident of the afternoon which occurred some eight miles north of Winchester, to show that valor did not reside alone on either side, that we were brethren of the same Anglo-Saxon lineage, of like characteristics, and the two armies, each in the other, found 'a foe worthy of their steel.'   Some Confederate cavalry had, while we were marching to the rear in line of battle, formed column and charged down upon what had now become our right and front.   On they came with the usual Confederate yell and sabres drawn.   This was a frightful sight to men who a few hours before had become somewhat demoralized by the onset at Kernstown, but not a thought of fear was seen upon the faces of the men.   Cavalry to them was a mere pastime, and, with a few well-directed volleys poured at the charging columns, with many empty saddles this cavalry broke and fled away in great confusion.   Only the officer in command charging at the head of his troops did not flee, but continued right on, veering to his right;

he kept at a respectful distance from us, riding the whole length of our line. We discovered that his horse was running away with him, and the only guiding power he had was exerted to prevent the horse from running into us. Very little firing was directed upon him during these moments, as every one watched with interest his efforts. Finally he stopped his horse and, turning, retraced his steps in the direction where his troops were disappearing over a hill. This again carried him along the front of our line. An occasional shot was fired at him, but now the word passed along our line, 'Don't shoot—he is too brave to kill,' and instead a cheer broke forth, to which he responded by taking off his hat and bowing in the most cavalier style. He soon gained the crest of the hill, seemingly unhurt, halted a moment, and again saluting us, turned away and passed out of sight. After this incident we were not again disturbed by the cavalry. Perhaps a liking for us had sprung up in this officer's breast, and he felt he would no longer, at least for this day, quarrel with us. I have often hoped I might, during the peaceful days after the war, meet that officer and talk things over.

"We now changed our column into route march, and, walking along the pike, settled down to a comparative peace, each man beginning to hunt in his haversack for a stray bit of hard tack which might happen to be there. Up to this time there had been but little opportunity to think of food. It was now nearly dark, and while plodding along, wondering where we would find the balance of the command and the wagon train, so we might go into camp, we discovered that some time during the afternoon there had been a stampede of our wagon train and several wagons had been abandoned and left on the pike. Quick investigation was made for food, but, finding none, a jolly fire was built in each wagon, and they were soon reduced to ashes or so disabled that they would be wholly useless to the enemy. Further along the pike we found a battery of artillery, consisting of four guns with their caissons, which had been abandoned and left for peaceable capture by the enemy.

"Here, again, McKinley showed his force of character and indomitable will-power. He asked the privilege of carrying away these guns, thus saving them from the enemy. It did not, with the exhausted condition of our men, seem practicable, yet he insisted it could be done, and he thought his regiment, the Twenty-third, would gladly aid him. Hayes, with a smile, said: 'Well, McKinley, ask them.' Going first to his old company (E), he called for volunteers; all stepped out to a man, and, the infection spreading, soon the whole regiment took hold of these guns and caissons and hauled them off in triumphal procession. When we went into camp that night long after dark, this artillery captain was found and the guns were turned over to him. He cried like a baby.

"Now this fearful day was over, and in a drizzling rain, dinnerless and supperless, we wound ourselves in our blankets and slept soundly until morning.

"Our losses were very heavy. Hayes' little brigade of 1,700 men alone lost one-fourth of its number in killed and wounded, and most of the wounded were left in the enemy's hands. The balance of the command lost in nearly the same proportion. The cause of the disaster was simply that we were outnumbered three to one, and the surprise is that we were not all captured, as General Early anticipated.

"Considerable effort was made at that time to impugn the bravery of Crook's Eighth Corps in this disaster, but a noted and unbiased historian has said the following, which I quote with much pleasure:

"'Crook's troops had campaigned too well at Floyd's Mountain and during Hunter's march to Lynchburg to be disgraced by this encounter; and while some of them, chiefly the recent additions, had proved of little value, it must be remembered that whatever efforts had been made to challenge Early's retreat from Washington were the work of this command. Their defeat was not strange, for the force soon after assembled in the valley as needful to match Early was thrice Crook's at Kernstown.'"

CHAPTER VI

From Captain to Major

McKINLEY'S gallantry at Kernstown was rewarded by his being raised to the rank of captain, his commission dating from July 25th, the day after the battle. On the succeeding day the command began a series of marches and countermarches in the Shenandoah Valley. These were continued until the middle of August, fighting occurring whenever the enemy could be reached. The campaigns in the valley, which were described in the last chapter, were by no means satisfactory to General Grant. They had so far proved a series of misadventures which were far from acceptable to one accustomed, like himself, to rarely interrupted victory. He was now at the headquarters of the Army of the Potomac, far away to the south, and found communication with Washington far from certain, the lines being often broken. This fact rendered the presence in the valley of some capable leader, who could be trusted to give a good account of himself, indispensable.

The politics of the Administration were then directed by Secretary Stanton, whose judgment was influenced by the effect which military operations were likely to have upon the approaching elections, a line of policy which did not appeal to General Grant. Stanton particularly dreaded a defeat of the Union forces in the valley and the possible capture of Washington by the Confederates. The effect of this mingling of politics with military affairs was to hamper General Hunter to such an extent that he was rendered unable of giving Early a crushing blow should an opportunity arise. General Grant, growing more and more dissatisfied, decided during the first week in August to go to Washington

85

himself and see if the state of affairs in the valley could not be radi-cally changed. He was quite tired of the game of retreat and pursuit which Hunter and Early had been so long playing. Since the war began, this region had been the scene of incessant move-ments by the hostile forces, the Union troops now advancing, now retreating, but the advantage always remaining on the side of the Confederates. No less than four commanders, Banks, Shields, Siegel and Hunter, had succeeded each other in this region, and all had failed in effort to hold the valley and prevent the Confed-erate raids; and what was equally unsatisfactory was the fact that the fertile fields of the Shenandoah were constantly furnishing food for Lee's army.

General Grant saw but one way to put an end to this, which was to put his best fighting general in command of that section. With this view President Lincoln strongly sided. Grant's choice for the position was General Sheridan, who had added greatly to his renown by his performances as chief of cavalry of the Army of the Potomac in the recent campaign. Grant's confidence in Sheridan was not shared by the authorities at Washington, largely on account of his youth, and it may be with some fear that he might be too headstrong for a commander on whom so much depended. His method of driving straight at the enemy was one which would seem to have in it an element of rashness.

MCKINLEY SERVES UNDER GENERAL SHERIDAN

The result of the conference was that the various military departments around Washington were consolidated into what was known as the Middle Military Division, Sheridan being appointed commander. Hunter retired to make way for the new chief. The advent of Sheridan to command in the valley proved especially happy, and rapidly made a change in the state of affairs. With-out hesitation he advanced up the valley, Early at the same time drawing in his scattered commands and concentrating them along Opequan Creek. Here the armies encamped within watching

THE PRESIDENT AT THE CAR WINDOW
Gazing at the busy factories with keen satisfaction

distance of each other. Sheridan had taken the opportunity to reorganize his army, this division now consisting of the Sixth Army Corps under General Wright, the Nineteenth Army Corps under General Emory, and the Army of West Virginia, with General Crook in command. General Torbert commanded the cavalry escort, with Merritt and Averill as division commanders.

Rutherford B. Hayes was at the head of the first brigade of the second division of Crook's army, this being McKinley's regiment. But the young captain was no longer attached to it. On August 9th, Crook had taken him from General Hayes' staff and attached him to his own. From that time until near the end of the year he held the position of acting assistant adjutant general, a capacity in which he served throughout Sheridan's valley campaign. In his new field of duty McKinley seemed to have a knack for getting into danger; in the successive skirmishes that occurred before the battle of Opequan he was frequently under fire. This was the case in a sharp little night engagement with Early's outposts at Berryville on September 3d, when he had his horse killed under him.

The armies lay in front of each other for a month, when as a result of information furnished General Sheridan by Miss Rebecca Wright of Winchester, to the effect that a part of Early's army had been withdrawn by Lee to Richmond, he decided to force a battle. The blow was delivered at dawn on September 19th. Crook's command at this time was in reserve, but, time being lost in getting the troops into position for the main attack, the reserves were soon brought into action, being sent to the right to attack the Confederates in flank.

Here an almost impenetrable growth of cedar and a swampy stream hindered the advance; but finally they emerged from the timber, and, supported by cavalry, advanced rapidly across two or three open fields, which brought them face to face with the enemy's infantry. A galling rifle fire was at once opened upon them, accompanied by artillery, but Crook's men advanced at double quick and swept the enemy before them, charging over his works, and contributing largely to his defeat and demoralization. Sheridan in his Memoirs says :

SHERIDAN'S OWN ACCOUNT OF THE BATTLE

"Crook's success began the moment he started to turn the enemy's left ; and, assured by the fact that Torbert had stampeded the Confederate cavalry and thrown Breckenridge's infantry into such disorder that it could do little to prevent the envelopment of Gordon's left, Crook pressed forward without even a halt. Both Emory and Wright took up the fight as ordered, and as they did so I sent word to Wilson, in the hope that he could partly perform the work originally laid out for Crook, to push along the Senseny and if possible gain the valley pike to the south of Winchester. I then returned toward my right flank, and as I reached the Nineteenth Corps the enemy was contesting the ground in its front with great obstinacy ; but Emory's dogged persistence was at length rewarded with success, just as Crook's command emerged from the morass of Red Bud Run and swept around Gordon toward the right of Breckenridge, who, with two of Horton's brigades, was holding a line at right angles with the valley pike for the protection of the Confederate rear. Early had ordered these two brigades back from Stevenson's Depot in the morning, purposing to protect with them his right flank and line of retreat, but while they were *en route* to this end he was obliged to recall them to his left to meet Crook's attack."

Captain McKinley had been exceedingly active during this fierce struggle, riding rapidly back and forth to the brigade and division commanders, with orders from the commanding general. He acquitted himself so well in this duty that when he received his brevet commission as major, the name of Opequan was mentioned as an occasion when he had distinguished himself by bravery and merit. There is one incident of the day in particular which illustrates his firmness. We describe it as told by an eyewitness :

Crook had sent McKinley with verbal orders to General Duval to move his division into action. Duval on receiving the order, not knowing the country, asked : " By what route shall I move my command ? " Captain McKinley replied : " I would move up this creek." Duval's answer was : " I will not budge without definite orders." McKinley then decisively said : " This is a case of great emergency, general. I order you, by command of General Crook, to move your command up the ravine to a position on the right of the army."

Duval went in as McKinley directed and came out in the right place. It was a great responsibility for so young an officer to take on his hands the fate of a division, but the result demonstrated his good judgment, and he was warmly commended for the service. On reporting to his chief he was told that it was all right, the movement having turned out successfully. If, on the contrary, it had turned out differently, it would certainly have been all wrong.

After winning the battle of Opequan, Sheridan pursued Early up the valley to Fisher's Hill, where he found the Confederate army drawn up in a strong position. Early, in fact, was posted too strong for an assault in front, and Sheridan decided once more to use Crook's forces in a flank movement, and in this way force him to abandon his works. Crook was directed to lead his men into the desired position, under cover of the woods on the eastern slope of the Little North Mountain, the remainder of the army meanwhile engaging the attention of the enemy by a demonstration in front. This completely deceived the Confederate commander as to Sheridan's real intention. Before Early had any conception of what Sheridan was about Crook had completed his movement, and fell upon their rear and left flank, winning the battle almost in a moment. This engagement was conducted with more precision and much less slaughter on both sides than the previous battle. Early again retreated up the valley with Sheridan in hot pursuit.

During this engagement McKinley was still on Crook's staff, and made himself so useful that Fisher's Hill was also mentioned in his commission as brevet major. Sheridan had hoped to capture and destroy Early's army after Fisher's Hill, but the failure of Torbert and Averill to intercept him in his flight gave him an opportunity to escape. The succeeding month was largely taken up by cavalry skirmishes. Early was pursued as far as Harrisonburg, after which Sheridan fell back down the valley, destroying the forage as he went, and finally posting his forces on the north side of Cedar Creek.

ALMOST A DISASTER TO SHERIDAN'S ARMY

Meanwhile the movements of Sheridan's army had become a subject of interest and debate at Washington, and a discussion by telegraph about its future operations went on for some time. In the end he was summoned to Washington by General Halleck for a personal interview. This action well nigh resulted in a very serious disaster to the army, and led to the famous incident known as "Sheridan's Ride."

Crook's command held at this time the left flank of the Union army. On the morning of October 19th, under cover of a dense fog, the Confederates swept down upon his camp with such suddenness and force that the whole Union army was thrown into confusion and driven back in dismay. The story of what followed is told by Sheridan in his Memoirs, in his simple and lucid language. We learn from him how he had reached Winchester on his return from Washington, how he set out from there with the sound of distant artillery ringing in his ears, and how he arrived on the field and turned the tide of battle, changing defeat into victory. The episode is one of the most dramatic in the nation's whole history.

On arriving at Newton, where a portion of the demoralized army was still seeking to hold its own against Early's triumphant forces, Sheridan tells us that he met Major McKinley of Crook's staff, who quickly spread the news of his arrival among the disorganized soldiers, giving them new hope and confidence. McKinley had just been engaged in placing Dupont's battery in a favorable position, by command of General Crook. It was on his return from the performance of this duty that he met Sheridan. This brilliant cavalry leader rode hurriedly from side to side of the field, observing the situation, calling the men to face the enemy, and when, two hours later, at the suggestion of Colonel Forsyth, he decided to ride down the line so that all the troops might see him, McKinley was among the group of officers that accompanied him.

MCKINLEY RECEIVES HIS BREVET OF MAJOR

Sheridan threw off his overcoat and appeared in a new uniform, which he had put on with the purpose of presenting himself at the War Department in Washington. In the hurry of the movement he handed his new epaulets to McKinley, and mounting his black horse, Rienzi, still white with dust and foam from its recent headlong gallop, he rode, hat in hand, and followed by his staff, down the front of the re-formed army, the wildest enthusiasm greeting him as regiment after regiment and brigade after brigade rose with cheers of welcome and waving battle flags. At the sight of their commander the spirit of the army blazed forth again, and at the word of command they sprang to the charge and swept Early's army out of the valley, never to return.

McKinley remained on Crook's staff until after the latter had the misfortune of being captured with General Kelly in West Virginia. Subsequently the young captain was detailed to the staff of General Hancock, then commanding the department. At a later date he was assigned to the staff of General S. S. Carroll at Washington. In this duty he remained until after Lee's surrender at Appomattox. On March 13, 1865, he received his brevet as major, and without seeing any more fighting was mustered out of the United States service on July 26th. Thus closed his military career.

CHAPTER VII

Choosing a Profession

THE close of the Civil War left the young soldier without a profession. He had entered the ranks of the volunteer army as an enthusiastic boy, eager for the active stir of a military life and moved by a warm patriotic impulse. He had risen through sheer force of valor, intelligence, and military ability from the rank of a private soldier to that of a Major, and was still only twenty-two years of age when the close of the conflict left him with the world before him in which to choose a career. It was something for one of his age to be the proud owner of a commission, signed by Abraham Lincoln, appointing him to the rank of Brevet-Major of United States volunteers "for gallant and meritorious services at the battles of Opequan, Cedar Creek, and Fisher's Hill;" but this valued document would not bring him bread, and how to obtain a place in the strife of life was next to be considered.

He was not, indeed, obliged to seek a position in private life. An army career lay before him, if he chose to accept it, and General S. S. Carroll, his personal friend, earnestly advised him to enter the regular army, saying that a young officer with his reputation for gallantry and efficiency could readily secure a commission. He offered, indeed, to use his influence in the young man's behalf, and laid before him the temptation of a life free from business cares and in which his future would be assured.

There can be no doubt that the temptation was a strong one, and that the proffered place was not declined until after long and anxious deliberation. Yet it did not appeal to the young soldier. To remain in the army in times of peace, with none of the excitement

94

of battle, none of the thrill of danger, none of those stirring scenes which set the nerves tingling and the blood bounding through the veins, was by no means to his taste. He had been a soldier. He did not care to become a drill-master. A field of conflict of different character lay before him, that of professional or business life, and the warlike spirit which still inspired his soul counselled him to enter upon a private career, where alone his impulse to fight seemed likely to find a vent.

WITHOUT A TRADE OR PROFESSION

His father and mother, brothers and sisters, still resided in the quiet little village of Poland, whence he had set out as a lad of eighteen to follow his country's flag and give his young life, if need were, to her cause. He had spent in the army the years when most boys are getting their training for business, with the roar of cannon and rattle of rifles in his ears instead of the bustle of trade or the activity of professional life. He had entered the years of manhood without trade or profession, and to begin his 'prentice life at his age was not an attractive prospect. But it must be done; he had chosen the alternative; he must set his shoulder to the wheel.

What career should he choose? No doubt he called the combined experience and judgment of the family to the decision of this important question, and there may have been long and anxious consultations within the precincts of that humble home. However this be, the choice finally fell upon a profession in which many a Western boy has found the route to fame and fortune, that of law. He decided to enter upon a legal career.

Little time was lost after the decision had been made. He obtained admission as a student to the office of Judge Charles E. Glidden, the leading lawyer of the county in which he resided, and then earnestly began his studies, assailing the outworks of the law as vigorously as he had attacked the intrenchments of the Confederate troops in the field.

The young man had days and years to make up. Others of his age were practicing in the courts before he had opened his first legal tome. There was no time to be lost. Only hard and incessant work could regain the vanished time. Night and day found him at his studies, devouring books with an ever unsatisfied appetite. He worked like a Trojan, for he had more than the difficulties of legal lore to overcome. His family were far from wealthy and his father could give him little aid. Wants and demands pressed upon him, and more than once, during his long months of study, he was sorely tempted to abandon his books and enter upon a business career.

We are told that his elder sister was his chief mental support in his persistent study. She assured him that no sacrifice was too great to enable him to accomplish the end which he had deliberately set out to win, and her courageous spirit was, no doubt, of the utmost aid to the struggling and penniless young man. For nearly two years he continued in Judge Glidden's office, and then entered a law school at Albany, New York, where he finished his studies and graduated with success. It was in 1867 that this struggle for a profession ended, and the newly-fledged lawyer gained admission to the bar.

The next question to be decided was that all-important one for a new "limb of the law," of the best place to locate; where, in the growing State of which he was a citizen, a young lawyer might look for a reasonable share of business. Poland, with its 400 people, was no place in which to hope for success. The town finally chosen was Canton, the county-seat of Stark County, and not far away from his boyhood's home. In selecting Canton he was largely influenced by the fact that his elder sister Anna, she whose counsel had done so much towards inducing him to persist in his legal studies, was a teacher in that town, where she had won the good-will and respect of the people by her merit as an instructor and her estimable character as a woman. Her brother had the warmest affection for her, and her residence in Canton was

WILLIAM McKINLEY
A late photograph

MRS. WILLIAM McKINLEY
A late photograph

naturally a strong inducement for him to settle in that town. Thither, then, he made his way, there he hung out his shingle, and there he waited for clients to drift his way. And Canton remained his legal place of residence until the day of his death, his periods of residence in Washington being but passing incidents in his career.

CANTON BECOMES HIS HOME

Canton was not large. It had at that time about 5,000 inhabitants. But to the young man, reared in a village, accustomed for four years to the wild life of a camp, and with little knowledge of large cities, no doubt it seemed a thriving and bustling place, one likely to yield abundant opportunities for legal business. Men will quarrel and do wrong in small places as in large, and in all localities where disputes are settled by the law, instead of by the stick or the sword, a lawyer's services are likely to be called into request.

Stark County, indeed, was well settled, it being a fertile and productive section of land. It lies in the Tuscarawas Valley, covering 500 square miles of productive soil. Originally it was largely settled by Dunkers, a German religious sect, immigrants from Pennsylvania. These sturdy farmers took possession of the fields, leaving to the later-coming Americans the making of the towns. The Germans were Democrats in political faith; the newcomers, English and Scotch-Irish, from the Eastern and Middle States, were stalwart Whigs. Between these two parties the county was divided, with a preponderance in favor of the Democrats.

Stark County, and its county seat, have grown since that day. Its population has more than doubled, while Canton is six times as large as it was when the young lawyer sought it as the seat of his fortunes. Its growth has been due to the founding of numerous manufacturing industries, giving rise to a business activity very likely to make work for the courts. These industries consisted of iron works of various kinds, woolen factories, paper mills, agricultural implement manufactories, etc.

Major McKinley, with his quick intelligence and energetic spirit, took an active interest and soon became a leading man in the affairs of his new place of residence. No one was more alive to the importance of the development of the material welfare of the people, and the older inhabitants of the town soon began to look with attention and respect upon the enterprising young man who had established himself in their midst. His influence was greatly increased by his engaging manners and his readiness and fluency in legal oratory, none the less for the decided opinions and strong common sense which, from the beginning, he displayed. McKinley's first speech had been made just after the close of the war, when he responded for himself and his comrades at a public reception given them on their return from the field. The oratorical power shown at that early date improved steadily as time went on.

HIS PROGRESS IN LAW PRACTICE

But, leaving this phase of our subject for the present, we must return to the story of McKinley's progress in the service of the law. Naturally, as a young and unknown man, litigants were disinclined to trust their interests in his hands. A fortnight passed without a client, and the youthful lawyer was beginning to find the time hang very heavy on his hands. Then, one day, his old preceptor, Judge Glidden, stepped into his little office.

"McKinley," said he, "here are the papers in a case of mine. It comes up to-morrow. I have got to go out of town, and I want you to take charge of it for me."

McKinley was nonplussed. He declared that he could not do justice to the case at so short a notice. "I never have tried a single case yet, Judge," said he.

"Well, begin on this one, then," was the Judge's reply. And it was finally settled that McKinley should do so. He sat up all night working on the case, tried it the next day, and won it. A few days later Judge Glidden entered his office and handed him $25. McKinley demurred at taking it.

" It is too much for one day's work," he said.

" Don't let that worry you," replied Glidden, good-naturedly. " I charged them $100 for the case, and I can well afford a quarter of it to you."

A year or two later McKinley found himself pitted against John McSweeney, then considered one of the most brilliant lawyers of the Ohio bar. The case was a suit for damages for malpractice, the plaintiff charging that a surgeon had set his broken leg in such a way as to make him bow-legged on that side. McKinley defended the surgeon. McSweeney brought his client into court and had the injured limb exposed to the view of the jury. It certainly was very crooked, and the case looked bad for the surgeon. McKinley had both eyes wide open, however, and fixed them to good purpose upon the man's other leg. As soon as the witness was turned over to him, he asked that the other leg should also be bared. The plaintiff and McSweeney vigorously objected, but the Judge ordered it done. Then it appeared that this second leg was still more crooked than that which the surgeon had set.

" My client seems to have done better by this man than nature itself did," said McKinley, "and I move that the suit be dismissed, with a recommendation to the plaintiff that he have the other leg broken and then set by the surgeon who set the first one."

INTEREST IN LOCAL AND STATE POLITICS

Major McKinley no sooner felt himself firmly on his feet as a lawyer than he began to take interest in local and State politics. In political principles he was an ardent Republican. To him Republicanism meant union, freedom and progress—the cause for which he had fought for four years. If political ambition had been uppermost in his mind at that time he would not have selected Stark County for his home, since the Democratic cause was there in the ascendency. Nevertheless, he was drawn into politics almost as soon as he had his first brief. In the Autumn of 1867 there was a hotly contested Gubernatorial campaign in Ohio, and a constitutional amendment giving suffrage to colored men was submitted to the popular vote. The Republicans carried the election, but the amendment was lost. In this canvass McKinley made his first political speech, and it was in favor of the suffrage amendment. This was in New Berlin. The orator, twenty-four years old, spoke from a dry goods box, placed near the steps of the village tavern, to an audience strongly against him.

The story of this, his pioneer political oration, the advance guard of so many more important ones in his later life, is of much interest, and a racy description of it exists, which is well worth repeating.

MCKINLEY'S FIRST SPEECH

On a dry-goods box 4 feet long, 3 feet wide and 3 feet high, President McKinley made his first political speech in the little town of New Berlin. The box stood in front of a house which has since burned down, and just inside the gate of a wooden fence within 100 feet of the four corners of the business centre. The man who introduced him to his first audience afterward lived in a new brick house, built within ten feet of the location of the dry-goods box which supported the President on that memorable night. The benches in front of the post office, next door, furnished a resting-place for the old politicians who here gathered to get their mail daily, and talk over the most notable event in New Berlin's history, made notable by the achievements of the boy orator, McKinley, in succeeding years.

"Can you make a speech?" said Michael Bitzer to William McKinley when the speaker arrived from Canton, ready to follow Judge Underhill upon the improvised stage. Michael Bitzer was the chairman of the meeting. Even at eighty-three years of age, he remembered the night he introduced McKinley as though it were a happening of a yesterday. The somewhat unexpected remark of the chairman of the meeting to the young man who was to make his *début* before a large audience rather took his breath away for a moment, but, on the assurance of Judge Underhill that Mr. Bitzer meant no offense, he regained his pleasant face, showing the kind disposition which was so characteristic of him in later days.

"Could he speak?" said Michael, "Well, I should say he could. Everybody was simply dumfounded. For nearly an hour he talked as never a young man in Stark County had talked before. I told Judge Underhill, who accompanied him, after the meeting, that McKinley did a blamed sight better than he did, and the Judge, too, pronounced him a coming politician."

"I really was surprised when Judge Underhill introduced that young strip of a boy to me, saying that he had come to make a speech in place of another Judge, who was unable to be present. Of course, I only asked McKinley in a joke if he could make a speech. I spoke to him as much as I would to a boy, but I really did have my doubts about such a young man doing justice to the occasion." Mr. Bitzer introduced him as William McKinley, of Canton. He little thought he was introducing the coming President of the United States.

McKinley arose and looked over his audience. There was not a sign of the emotion on his part which usually attends the first speech of a speaker. In stature he was not portly and strong like he was in later days.

"But," said Mr. Bitzer, "as I remember him, the same strong characteristics which were so notable in his public life within the last years stood out forcibly on that night."

He spoke under the glimmer of the street lighted by oil lamps, for that was before the days of electric lights. His strong personality and his kindly manner were noticed by the people of New Berlin. His hearty handshake, his pleasant smile were all there, only waiting for opportunity and strength of purpose to develop them.

As McKinley and Judge Underhill drove into town in the early evening and up to the hotel, many of the admiring audience of an hour and a half later undoubtedly mistook the young man beside the stately Judge for the driver of the carriage.

Mr. McKinley spoke in the open air, but not to the winds. There was a silence which would admit of the audible dropping of a pin. The night was clear. His voice was easily heard by those who sat a hundred feet away on the steps of the store near the corner. He confined himself strictly to the issues of the campaign of 1867, which, however, was not a Presidential one. He did not once refer to notes. His vocabulary and active brain were his only promoters.

"I just wondered," said Mr. Bitzer, "where he got all those words and ideas."

A short time before his death Mr. and Mrs. McKinley took a drive from their home in Canton. Almost before they realized it, they came upon the town of New Berlin. As they passed the place where Mr. McKinley had started his political career upon a dry-goods box, the occupants of the carriage both turned their heads, and a smile spread over the countenance of the President of the United States. They drove past and turned east at the four corners by the post office. After a short drive up that road they returned and again passed the spot where stood the dry-goods box of thirty-five years ago. It was not long after President McKinley had crossed the boundary line of the town from Canton that the people realized that they were very unexpectedly entertaining a notable guest, and one, too, who had more than a passing interest in the little town. They turned out in large numbers. The President bowed to all he met.

WINS HIS FIRST ELECTION

Mr. Bitzer was justly proud of "introducing the President into politics," as he called it. He is an old soldier and a life-long Republican. Once, during McKinley's term as Governor, he called at his office in Columbus. There were not less than a dozen people in the room: "This," said McKinley, "is the man who first introduced me into politics," and Mr. Bitzer's hand was grasped not less than a dozen times. "Yes," said Bitzer, "McKinley and I are fast friends."

The able and ardent young orator was at once welcomed into the Republican party by the leaders, and during the remainder of that campaign, and the campaign for President in 1868, he was frequently called upon to speak in public for the party's principles and candidates. By 1869 he was well known throughout the county as a rising young lawyer, and a speaker of thoughtful force. He was gaining in wisdom and experience.

As a somewhat questionable form of reward for his services, the party put him forward in that year as its candidate for District Attorney. The nomination was looked upon as an empty honor, in view of the fact that Stark was reckoned one of [the banner Democratic counties of the State. An old party leader would have had a very hard battle to win, and for a young and inexperienced man the case seemed hopeless. The nomination appeared a very cheap way of rewarding the rising young orator.

But however the Convention and the people regarded the nomination, McKinley took it in all seriousness, and went into the race determined to win, if youthful energy and hard work could bring success. He made a vigorous canvass of the county, throwing his whole soul into the work, and displaying an enthusiasm which was something new in that district. He assailed the voters as if he was again charging upon the works of the enemy. Day after day he made ardent speeches, inspiring confidence, gaining friends among the people, and making raids upon the ranks of the foe. When the election was over the Democrats were amazed to find that this young man, scarcely known in the county, had defeated their candidate and won the fight by a safe majority. Thus, at the age of twenty-six, Major McKinley won his first political success. The office did not pay a large salary, but it was a stepping-stone alike to legal business and to further political honors.

McKinley gained popular favor in his first office by his honest and able performance of his duties. On the expiration of his two years' term he was again nominated, the party looking upon him as their safest candidate. The Democrats were now thoroughly awakened. This new aspirant for public honors was winning the good-will of his fellow-citizens far too rapidly to please them. They put into the field against him the best man they could find in their ranks, and employed all the devices of political tactics in the campaign. They succeeded, but their majority was so small—only forty-five instead of the usual hundreds—that McKinley rather gained than lost standing by his defeat. His vigorous canvass and growing ability as a speaker brought him into the front rank of his party, and thenceforth he was to be reckoned with as the most powerful political factor in the county. His next step in political life was to be towards a much higher goal, but five years passed before it was taken—years of hard study and diligent practice at the bar.

WINNING A BRIDE

We must now leave politics for the more attractive story of love and matrimony. Six years passed after McKinley left the army, and four years after he engaged in the practice of his profession, before his rising fortunes gave him warrant to seek a wife. It must not be imagined, however, that he had lived in Canton all these years and was not familiar with its attractions in the way of womanly beauty and grace. He was doubtless a favorite in many houses, his genial manners and courtly address being well calculated to win him a host of social friends, and among his fair associates not the least to be considered was she who then reigned as the belle of Canton, the lovely Ida Saxton.

The Saxtons had long been leading people in Canton. John Saxton, the founder of the family in Ohio, was one of the pioneers in that State at the beginning of the last century. There, in 1815, he established the *Ohio Repository*, long the chief journal of the town, and of wide-spread influence in the county; conducting it with success until his death, at an advanced age. For sixty years he was its editor, and had the distinction of printing in it the news of the battle of Waterloo—some five months after it occurred—and the defeat of the Third Napoleon at Sedan, fifty-five years

THE PRESIDENT AND HIS SECOND CABINET

afterward. He was a warm personal friend of Horace Greeley, who was one of the first to put on record the above interesting fact. The paper is still published at Canton, and retains much of its old influence.

One of the veteran editor's sons, James A. Saxton, became a banker in Canton, and a man of much wealth and prominence. Ida Saxton, whom we have above designated as the belle of Canton, was his daughter. She was a girl of many personal charms, a tall blonde, with expressive bright blue eyes, a winning manner, and a lively intelligence.

MRS. MCKINLEY'S GIRLHOOD

As a girl she was busy, whether at work or at play. Her education was begun at the boarding school of Miss Sandford, in Cleveland, and at Miss Eastman's Seminary, Brooke Hall, in Media, Pa. In both of these schools she left the stamp of her personality. She led the other girls in their enterprises, sometimes mischievous ones, and her quickness kept her at the head of her classes, while she spent less time in study than any of the others. One thing is recorded of her by all those who knew her; she never said unkind things of any one. She seems to have been too large in heart to indulge in any petty acts.

Miss Eastman, the principal of the school, lived for long years after that time—long enough to tell many a story of her favorite pupil. She said that Ida Saxton was the one girl in her school who ever caused her to break her rule against favoritism. She believed that this was unfair on a teacher's part, and she fought persistently against it, but Ida Saxton was too much for her. She couldn't help loving her better than she loved any of the others, and in her fear of showing this she was more severe with her than any other.

Ida responded most heartily to her teacher's affection, and afterward, when she became Mrs. McKinley, and with her distinguished husband visited now and then in Philadelphia, she always sent a letter out to Brooke Hall, as the school was called, inviting Miss Eastman to dine with them.

Mr. Saxton was a devoted father, and he lavished upon his daughter every pleasure and accomplishment that was to be had. After her excellent education in this country she went abroad and made a long and extended tour over Europe with her sister. She did not return until 1869.

HER EXPERIENCE AS A CASHIER OF A BANK

Then, after all these years of fashionable education, she did a most unexpected and unconventional thing. She turned bank cashier. Canton found cause for gossip in that fact, but Miss Saxton's serene bearing and her popularity were of a nature to wither gossip. Were the family funds giving out? gossip at first inquired. That was soon found to be not the case. Mr. Saxton himself explained the matter.

"I have seen enough girls left stranded by sudden losses of means," he said, "and I don't intend that this shall ever happen to my daughter. She can be taken care of at home now, but I may be poor some day. Nobody ever knows what is going to happen. I want her to be able to support herself if trouble ever comes her way. Above all, I don't want her to have to marry solely to be supported, as I have seen plenty of girls do. I want her to marry because and whom she wants to."

Through all the flutter that her presence caused in the place of business Miss Saxton preserved a businesslike calm. She was a diligent worker, and became accurate, quick and reliable in her new duties, gaining such a knowledge of the banking business as would have qualified her to hold a position in much larger establishments than that of her father.

It is not to be supposed, however, that a young lady of such attractions would long be left to the dry details of local finance. She was certainly not likely to want devoted friends and suitors, and among these Major McKinley was not the least favored.

He made the acquaintance of his future wife on a visit to his sister Anna, then a teacher at Canton, shortly after his return from the war. In those days the favorite pleasure resort for the young folks of Canton was Meyers' Lake, two miles out of town, and that was where the Major met Miss Ida Saxton.

The acquaintance, there begun, was not suffered to lapse after he became a citizen of Canton, and was renewed with ardor after Miss Saxton's school life and her return from Europe. It was continued with increased warmth during her business life as cashier, friendship now rapidly ripening into love, and social amenities verging into courtship. The young lady saw in Major McKinley not only the most devoted, but the most agreeable of the aspirants to her hand. She returned his affection with a warmth equal to his own. The matter was brought to the usual climax in affairs of this character, and when Mr. Saxton was asked by the young attorney for the hand of his daughter, the latter received the flattering assurance that he was the only man Mr. Saxton knew to whom he would trust the future of his child.

THE WEDDING DAY

The young couple were married on January 25, 1871. The wedding ceremonies took place in the Presbyterian Church of Canton, to the building fund of which the bride's grandfather and father had been the principal contributors. Miss Saxton had been a teacher in the Sunday school, and her marriage was the first in the new church. Major McKinley was a Methodist, Miss Saxton a Presbyterian. She joined her husband's church soon after the marriage. The wedding service was performed by the Rev. E. Buckingham, the bride's pastor, assisted by the Rev. Dr. Endsley, a Methodist clergyman. Abner McKinley was best man and Miss Mary I. Saxton was bridesmaid. The wedding was a great social event in the town, owing alike to the prominence of the bride's family and the popularity of the groom.

They visited several of the Eastern cities on their wedding trip and then went back to Canton to live. Their silver wedding anniversary was celebrated on January 25, 1896, in the same house in which they had begun their home-making. In the meantime Abner McKinley, the Major's brother, had married the daughter of the Rev. Mr. Endsley, and Mr. Barber, one of the ushers at the wedding in 1871, had married the bridesmaid, Miss Mary Saxton. They, and many others who had attended the wedding of Major McKinley and Miss Saxton, were at the celebration of the twenty-fifth anniversary.

The young couple set up their own establishment and began housekeeping in the old-fashioned way. On Christmas Day, 1871, a child was born—a daughter destined to be taken from them when only a little more than three years old. In the meantime, a few months before the birth of a second child, Mrs. McKinley lost her mother, and then her baby died.

The death of her two little girls, together with that of her mother just before Ida was born, was more than Mrs. McKinley's health could stand. She broke down physically because of her grief, and remained an invalid during the rest of her life.

After the death of Mrs. McKinley's mother, she and her husband took up their residence in the Saxton homestead, and there, during his fourteen years' service in Congress, and while he was Governor of Ohio and President of the United States, they passed their time whenever they were at home.

MARRIED LIFE OF THE MCKINLEYS

Of the married life of President and Mrs. McKinley the public needs to be told little, for the devotion of this man and woman was a theme for comment for many years. Their affection appears to have been ideal, almost idealized. On the part of Mrs. McKinley there was a constant, tender, adoring love for the man who won such great success, and at the same time was never too engrossed to pay her delicate attentions. On his part, there was a lifetime of unselfish devotion to a gentle, feeble invalid. The devoted husband saw before him the tragic vision of a childless life and the companionship of an incurable invalid. But he accepted the situation with a cheerfulness which never failed, and which constantly showed the depth of his regard for the woman he loved.

Public affairs never interfered with this, and no biography of William McKinley, as Congressman, Governor or President, is adequate without reference to his unfailing care of his invalid wife. On the other hand, Mrs. McKinley's illness never interfered with her lively interest in public affairs and in the part that her husband took in them.

MRS. MCKINLEY A DEVOTED WIFE

Although she never became very robust in health, she so far recovered as to accompany her husband to Washington, and was his almost constant companion in the long trips he took during his late campaigns. When he went to Washington during the Hayes *régime* his wife, although they lived somewhat quietly at a hotel, became prominent at the White House as the close personal friend of Mrs. Hayes, receiving with her upon public occasions and taking her place in her absence. She was a conspicuous figure at the brilliant wedding at the Executive Mansion when Gen. Russell Hastings, who had been on General Hayes' staff in the army, and Miss Platt, Mrs. Hayes' niece, were married.

After the loss of her own children, whose baby clothes and playthings she always kept near her, Mrs. McKinley's love and care for the children of others became one of her most delightful characteristics. She was "Aunt McKinley" to a host of little folks, and one of her pleasures was in giving entertainments for children at her home.

Because of her illness Mrs. McKinley clung to the pleasures and occupations of the women and wives of a generation past. She could not take an active part in the public charities of the present day, but gave much and did much for the relief and comfort

7

of the unfortunate. Needlework was an occupation at which she became an adept. Another of her little domestic pleasures was afforded by her collection of laces, a rare and valuable one, the nucleus of which was some handkerchiefs which she collected when she was abroad. Besides her laces was a choice assortment of gems, which were given to her by her father and grandfather.

In person Mrs. McKinley was singularly attractive. She had large deep blue eyes, a transparent complexion, and an oval face surmounted by a cluster of brown wavy curls. Although she had none of the reputed characteristics of the so-called "strong-minded woman," she kept her hair cut short, a circumstance which no doubt contributed much to her youthful and girl-like appearance. In spite of the piquancy of the curly head, her bearing was always that of benignant and serene beauty, which captivated all who approached her, causing her to be viewed at once with respect and affectionate interest. Of the many "Ladies of the White House," few equalled Mrs. McKinley in personal attractiveness, though her feeble health prevented her taking the prominent part in public entertainments which fell to the lot of many of her predecessors. To the President's last day he was not alone a careful husband, but a tender and devoted lover, and his deep sympathy and heartfelt grief during her severe illness in California, in the closing year of his life, endeared him more to the people than almost any other act of his life.

The calmness with which the President asked, "Am I shot?" the lack of excitement or of any other expression, the evident absence of any kind of fear of what might be before him in the next hour, was the kind of bravery that sent a feeling of pride in their chief officer through the veins of all Americans. Whatever else Mr. McKinley was, he was a brave man—a man who exhibited in the last critical moment the dignity of a Christian and a soldier.

Very few, if any of us, can begin to appreciate the devotion and affection of Mrs. McKinley for her husband. More than once the President actually saved her life by his influence over her. She believed in him so thoroughly that whatever he told her she knew to be true. Her ill-health, the strain of constantly recurring nervous attacks, would long ago have forced her to give up the struggle, but relying on her husband, filled with absolute confidence and affection for him, she held on to life. And when he lay near death the sick woman bore the news of his danger, and ministered to him with as calm attention as any one of those about him. There is something here that is as old as the hills, but that never fails to seem new and fine, because it shows a little of the beautiful and the true side of humanity.

MRS. MCKINLEY'S FAVORITE POEM

God gives us love. Something to love
　He gives us; but when love is grown
To ripeness, that on which it throve
　Falls off, and love is left alone.

Sleep sweetly, tender heart, in peace !
　Sleep, holy spirit ; blessed soul,
While the stars burn, the moons increase,
　And the great ages onward roll.

Sleep till the end, true soul and sweet !
　Nothing comes to thee new or strange.
Sleep full of rest from head to feet ;
　Lie still, dry dust, secure of change.
　　　　　　　　　　—TENNYSON.

CHAPTER VIII

Member of Congress

IT was in 1876, nine years after Major McKinley engaged in the practice of law, that he entered upon his Congressional career. He had already engaged in politics in his active canvass for the office of prosecuting attorney, of which we have already spoken. Though defeated in his contest for a second term in the latter, his active canvass brought him into very great popularity, and he became an important element in the political conditions of his district. The Congressional District which it was his desire to represent was composed of the counties of Carroll, Columbiana, Mahoning and Stark. It was at that time represented by the Hon. L. D. Woodworth, who was again a candidate for the office. There were a number of other prominent citizens who desired the office, all of them older men than the young Canton lawyer, whose candidacy they looked upon as something of an impertinence. The result was a hot fight for the nomination, which proved a surprise for McKinley's opponents. He very actively canvassed the district, and with such success that he received the nomination on the first ballot.

The district was a very close one, and was rendered the more so in the year 1876 from the fact that the country was suffering from the prostration which succeeded the war; the nation was struggling under an enormous debt, and the Greenback party was vigorously advocating repudiation and fiat money. McKinley ran against a gentleman named Sanborn, one of the strongest the Democrats could have selected. Yet despite these discouraging circumstances, the result of the election was that McKinley received

116

16,489 votes against 13,185 for Sanborn, thus receiving the large majority for the district of 3,304.

The 45th Congress was called in special session in October, 1877, by President Hayes. Ohio had sent a very strong delegation to the House, among the members being James A. Garfield, General Thomas Ewing, and others of prominence, while in the Senate were John Sherman and Allen G. Thurman. Among members from other states who entered Congress at that time was Thomas B. Reed, who was destined to occupy so prominent a position in succeeding Congresses.

Among the more important laws enacted by this Congress was one providing for the coinage of the silver dollar, which had been discontinued in 1873. McKinley was strongly in favor of this measure, which was passed by a large majority, vetoed by the President, and promptly passed again over the veto. The first time that Major McKinley addressed the House was on December 10, 1877, to present a petition from certain iron manufacturers of his district asking Congress to take no action relative to tariff revision until it had thoroughly inquired into the commercial necessities of the country. McKinley, whose name has become so closely associated with tariff legislation, made his first speech on the tariff on April 15, 1878. In this he sustained the doctrine of protection as opposed to tariff for revenue, and was listened to with the greatest attention, from his apparent thorough mastery of the question. In the course of his remarks he said :

" Home competition will always bring prices to a fair and reasonable level and prevent extortion and robbery. Success, or even apparent success, in any business or enterprise, will incite others to engage in like enterprises, and then follows healthful strife, the life of business, which inevitably results in cheapening the article produced.'

He ended with an appeal to the tariff reformers and free traders to let the country have a rest from this agitation until there was time to recover from the effects of the war and the panic of 1873. In this connection he said :

" There never was a time in the history of this country more inauspicious than the present time for the dreamer and the theorist to put into practical operation his impracticable theories of political economy. The country does not want them; the business men of the country do not want them. They want quiet to recuperate their wasted forces; and I am sure I utter no sentiment new or original when I say that if this House will promptly pass the appropriation bills, and other pressing legislation, following this with an immediate adjournment, the people will applaud such a course as the work of statesmen and the wisdom of men of affairs."

HIS DISTRICT GERRYMANDERED

The reputation which McKinley had made in Congress as a protectionist was by no means satisfactory to the Democrats of his district, and when they secured control of the Ohio Legislature, in 1878, they decided to re-district him into private life. To attain this purpose they succeeded in putting Stark County into a group that would certainly return a Democrat to Congress. By this gerrymander Stark County was thrown into the 16th District, along with Ashland, Portage and Wayne counties, it being expected to neutralize the heavy Republican majority in Portage County with the Democratic majorities usually given by the remaining counties. The Democrats nominated Aquila Wiley, of Wooster, a gallant soldier in the Union army, with a splendid military record. The Republicans nominated McKinley, and the two soldiers marshalled their forces for the campaign. Despite this action of the Democratic party, McKinley's popularity and the activity of his canvass were such that he received 15,489 votes to 14,255 for Wiley, and was thus again returned to Congress, where he was given a place on the important Committee of the Judiciary. This Congress, the 46th, was made notable by the return of the Confederate " brigadiers," and was chiefly memorable for its bitter partisan contests. In the heated discussion that followed Major McKinley took a prominent part, occupying an advanced position upon the necessity of fair elections and the protection of the ballot at any cost. The 46th was the first Congress in which Democrats had control of both branches since the Presidency of James Buchanan. The results of this—the ascendency of the Democrats with a Republican President—were constant wrangling and efforts to coerce the President by a practice which led to the now well-established rule in the House of Representatives, forbidding a "rider" on an appropriation bill. As a result of this practice President Hayes was obliged to call two extra sessions of Congress. The Hayes *régime* will go on record as one of the most uncomfortable administrations, in time of peace, in American history.

In the debate on the proposed law to do away with supervisors of national elections, McKinley spoke long and ably. A quotation from his speech will be of interest:

MCKINLEY PUTS A PRACTICAL QUESTION

"If I do not misjudge, the people who fought for free government and maintained it at so great a cost will now be found firm and invincible for a free ballot and fair elections. Let me remind the other side of this chamber that supervisors and marshals will not be needed, and therefore no cost will be incurred, whenever the party which employs tissue ballots and drives colored citizens from the polls shall do so no more forever, and whenever Democratic repeaters shall cease to corrupt the ballot—the great fountain of power in this country; in a single sentence, whenever, throughout this whole country, in every State thereof, citizenship is respected and the rights under it are fully and amply secured; when every citizen who is entitled to vote shall be secure in the free exercise of that right, and the ballot-box shall be protected from illegal voters, from fraud and violence, Federal supervisors of Federal elections will be neither expensive nor oppressive.

"Has any legal voter in the United States been prevented from exercising his right of suffrage by this law or by the officers acting under it? This is the practical question. None that I have ever heard of ; while thousands, yes, tens of thousands, of illegal voters have been deterred from voting by virtue of it. The honest voter has no fear of this law ; it touches him as lightly as the law of larceny touches the honest man, or the law of murder touches him whose hands are stainless of human blood. The thief hates the law of larceny, the murderer the law of homicide. They, too, can truthfully urge the cost of the execution of these laws ; both are expensive and onerous to the taxpayer. But I have never known such arguments seriously entertained as a reason for their repeal. The law is without terror save to wrongdoers. The presence of officers of the law deters only criminals from the commission of crime. They are no restraint upon the honest man. You can form no system of laws which will not be open to some criticism and abuse. These prove nothing against the importance and necessity of their maintenance. If any better method can be offered for preserving the ballot-box in its purity, I will cordially accept it and labor for its passage, but until such better method is proposed we should stand by existing statutes.

MCKINLEY'S POSITION IN 1880

"We cannot afford to break down a single safeguard which has been thrown around the ballot-box. Every guarantee must be kept and maintained. Fair-minded people everywhere are interested in honest elections. It is not a partisan measure ; it falls alike upon all political parties. The law recognizes no political creed, and those who execute it should carefully obey its letter and spirit. It protects Democrats and Republicans and men of all parties alike."

The situation of the Republican party in 1880, when McKinley's name was again presented for nomination, was not in all respects satisfactory. There was dissension among the party leaders in the country at large, and in his own district there was an unwritten law to the effect that two terms in Congress were enough for any one candidate, and that the honor which he had held for the prescribed time should now be transferred to some other candidate. Aspirants for the place presented themselves in every county of the district, all of them anxious for the nomination, largely from the fact that Republican success was now considered assured.

The Republicans having gained control of the Ohio Legislature, had promptly reversed the gerrymandering work of their predecessors, and restored Stark County to its old affiliation with Carroll, Columbiana and Mahoning, thus reconstituting the old Seventeenth District. The district was thus strongly Republican, and a walkover seemed assured for whoever should secure the nomination.

As regards this, McKinley's popularity, and the prestige he had won in his Congressional career, proved sufficient to give him precedence over his untried competitors, and he won the nomination without difficulty. With it came, as a sure result, the election, he receiving 20,221 votes, against 16,660 for Judge Thoman, the Democratic candidate.

As we have said in another chapter, the succeeding election, that of 1882, marked a change in his fortunes. The dissensions between the party managers had gone on to a critical stage, leading to the famous deadlock between President Garfield and the Senate in regard to the appointment of a custom's collector for New York City, and the resignation of Senators Conkling and Platt in consequence, these disputes being followed by the lamentable assassination of the President by a disappointed and evil-minded office-seeker.

The results of these events, and the doubt of President Arthur's fitness for his responsible position, were not favorable to the success of the Republicans in the next campaign, and their opponents did not fail to take the fullest advantage of the situation.

In fact, the party was in such a demoralized state that its Democratic opponents were enabled to make a successful assault upon its lines. The support by the Administration of the nomination of Secretary Folger for Governor of New York proved seriously adverse to his success, and he was beaten by a tremendous majority by Grover Cleveland, the Mayor of Buffalo. The gallant General Beaver was defeated in the Keystone State, and Pennsylvania, for the first time since the war, had a Democratic Governor. A raid was made in all parts of the country upon the members of Congress who had voted for a river and harbor improvement bill vetoed by the President, despite the fact that its proportions were insignificant compared with several which have passed since without comment.

MCKINLEY UNSEATED IN CONGRESS

As one result of this rise of the Democrats to power, McKinley, for the first time in his Congressional career, came perilously near defeat. The election resulted in giving him 16,906 votes to 16,898 for Wallace, the Democratic candidate. This slight majority of eight gave him the election, the State Canvassing Board presenting him the necessary certificate. There were but seven Republicans besides himself who were sent to represent Ohio in that Congress. As it happened, he was returned to a Congress with a strong Democratic majority in the House, and his bare eight votes exposed him to a contest for his seat. In this his opponents prevailed, McKinley was unseated, and his competitor took his place.

In 1884 the Ohio Legislature was again Democratic, and the old policy of redistricting was again brought into play. A special effort was made to defeat McKinley, whose growing prominence as a high-tariff advocate was by no means agreeable to his political opponents. With this in view, Stark County was once more made a political football, being now driven to a new goal in the Twentieth District and united with Medina, Summit and Wayne Counties. This time they felt secure, since political arithmetic gave the new district a Democratic majority of from 1,200 to 1,500 votes. But there are influences stronger than figures, and here personal popularity and known ability as a statesman prevailed over the "tricks that are vain" of State politics. McKinley had for adversary

David R. Paige, then a member of the House. He received 22,672 votes, against 20,643 for Paige, being elected with a majority of 2,029.

Before the next election the Republicans returned to power in Ohio, Stark County was again footballed back into its old family of counties, and Major McKinley was once more elected, this time with 2,557 majority. The election of 1888 yielded a similar result, though with a larger majority, McKinley now winning by 4,090 votes.

MCKINLEY'S WATERLOO

In 1890, in his eighth Congressional campaign, came McKinley's Waterloo. He had now succeeded Kelley as the leading advocate of high protection, and was becoming so sharp a thorn in the side of Democracy that his political foes resorted to desperate measures to shelve him. Once more they controlled the Ohio Legislature, and, knowing that a campaign against McKinley in his old district was hopeless, they determined upon a still more indefensible act of gerrymandering than in previous instances. A more outrageous partitioning of a State for partisan ends was never before performed, McKinley being railroaded into a district which had the year before given a Democratic plurality of 2,900. He accepted the challenge, made a gallant fight, and was defeated by only 302 votes.

It is interesting to recall, in view of this one defeat, that McKinley had been some years before twitted in Congress, by Mr. Springer, on having been returned at the previous election by a somewhat diminished majority. Mr. Springer said: "Your constituents do not seem to support you." McKinley's reply is worthy of all remembrance: "My fidelity to my constituents," he said, "is not measured by the support they give me. I have convictions which I would not surrender if 10,000 majority had been entered against me."

The opinion of the people of his State upon this operation was definitely shown in the succeeding year, by his election as

Governor by a large majority. This matter, which we mention here in passing, will be dealt with in a later chapter.

HIS RELATION TO CONGRESSIONAL COMMITTEES

As regards Representative McKinley's relation to Congressional committees, a few words must suffice. On his first entry to the House, Speaker Randall placed him, as a new and untried member, in a position of minor importance, that of the Committee for the Revision of the Laws of the United States. In his second term he was given a much more important place, being appointed to the Committee on the Judiciary. In December, 1880, he succeeded James A. Garfield in one of the leading posts of Congress, as a member of the Committee on Ways and Means, on which he continued until the close of his Congressional career. In the preceding Congress he had also been appointed on the Committee of Visitors to the United States Military Academy, and in 1881 was made chairman of the committee to conduct the Garfield memorial exercises in the House.

In 1889, on the organization of the Fifty-first Congress, he became a candidate for Speaker, but was defeated on the third ballot by Thomas B. Reed, who, as already stated, had entered Congress in the same year with him.

In April, 1890, as Judge Kelley's successor in the chairmanship of the Ways and Means Committee, he had the honor of introducing the famous tariff measure afterwards known by his name.

During the period of his Congressional career, in addition to his speeches on the silver question, dealt with in this chapter, and those on the tariff, his great subject, to be hereafter treated, McKinley had taken an active part in the discussion of other questions. Among these we may name one on the subject of arbitration as a remedy for labor troubles; his speech of December 17, 1889, introducing the Customs Administration Bill to simplify the laws relating to the collection of revenue; and his forceful address of April 24, 1890, sustaining the Civil Service Law.

Coming now to the consideration of Major McKinley's attitude on the silver question, which has given rise to some controversy, and was made use of by his political opponents during the canvass preliminary to the St. Louis nomination to discredit him, it can readily be shown that he was consistent throughout. His position on this question was always strictly that of his party, and when the Republicans found it expedient to modify their views in regard to silver coinage, McKinley kept strictly in line with them, finding their reasons for this change of policy expedient and judicious. His views on finance during his career were always in unison with those of John Sherman, whom no one would think of charging with unwise radicalism or lack of sound views on finance.

ATTITUDE ON THE SILVER QUESTION

The change of views was not due simply to conditions existing in this country, but to the changing attitude of the world in regard to silver coinage and its effect on the market value of silver bullion. A brief review of the situation will demonstrate this.

In the period with which we are now concerned there had been constant changes in the condition of the currency, this being due largely to two causes, the action of Germany, and the great increase in the production of silver in the United States. Before the establishment of the German Empire in 1871, all the states of Germany were on the silver basis except Bremen, where the gold standard prevailed. After the war with France and the establishment of the Empire it became necessary to adopt a system for the whole country. The subject was widely discussed, and as a result the German Empire adopted the gold standard, in July, 1873. Germany at that time had $300,000,000 worth of silver. This it was decided to melt up and sell abroad in exchange for gold. The government entered cautiously upon this process, selling the silver gradually.

At the same time the act of the United States Congress, made in 1873, establishing the gold standard in this country, and similar legislation in the Netherlands and Scandinavia, all tended to decrease the market value of silver. Silver coinage was also discontinued by the Latin Union, and the demand for silver from India decreased every year, thus cutting off Germany's chief market for her bullion.

AGITATION FOR BI-METALLISM

In the meantime, a vigorous agitation for bi-metallism arose in Europe, and active efforts were made to reinstate silver. The Hon. William G. Kelley, of Pennsylvania, at that time traveling in Germany, took part in this agitation in favor of bi-metallism, and he was aided in his efforts by several prominent German and French statesmen. The movement was encouraged by the fact that Germany had ceased melting and selling her silver, about $100,000,000 of the old silver coin remaining in 1879 in circulation.

An active agitation had arisen in the United States in favor of the free coinage of silver, which was largely supported by eminent leaders of the Republican party, Major McKinley among them. It was believed that, by an international arrangement, silver might regain its old status and a bi-metallic standard be established. As is well known, these efforts proved futile, and the market value of silver continued to decrease.

In order that a silver dollar shall equal a gold dollar in value, silver bullion must be worth $1.2939 per ounce of fine metal. Before 1873 the value of silver was considerably above this figure, the bullion in the silver dollar at that time being worth from two to five cents more than the standard gold dollar. It was, therefore, more valuable in trade than gold, and could not be kept in circulation. As an inevitable result there was little demand for it, and between 1834 and 1873 the total coinage of silver dollars was only about 8,000,000. In fact, the so-called dollar of our "daddies" was rarely to be seen, and was still more rarely used. Only after silver bullion decreased in price was there any special demand noticed for silver as money. In 1876 the value of silver had fallen to $1.15 per ounce, and the belief arose that if at least $2,000,000 per month were coined the price of the white metal would be increased.

HE SUPPORTED THE BLAND-ALLISON LAW

For this purpose the Bland-Allison law was passed, among its supporters being Major McKinley. The result, however, did not accord with the theory. The value of silver continued to decline. In 1879 the silver dollar was worth about eighty-seven cents, in 1885 it had fallen to eighty-four cents, in 1887 to seventy-five cents, and in 1889 it fell to seventy-two cents. These facts rendered it apparent that, in view of the practical mono-metallism of other nations, the United States could not bear the silver burden alone. In consequence the Republican leaders took a stand against the free and unlimited coinage of the standard silver dollar, Major McKinley taking the same ground and voting to that effect on every occasion on which the question was brought up in Congress during the remainder of his Congressional career.

He never hesitated to give his reasons for what some were pleased to call his change of front, and his utterances on the subject certainly had the ring of solid metal. Before quoting from his speeches we may give Senator John Sherman's opinion concerning McKinley's position on the question of coinage. It occurs in a letter written to the Young Men's Republican Club, of Brooklyn, N. Y. The veteran financier says :

JOHN SHERMAN ON MCKINLEY'S POSITION

" There can be no doubt as to the opinions of Major McKinley on the money question. He is committed in every form, by speech and otherwise, to the Republican policy of maintaining the present gold coin of the United States as the standard of value. He, in common with myself and others, believes that silver should be employed as money, always, however, to be maintained at par with gold. The convenience of silver coin for the minor transactions of life is so manifest that no sound-money man would desire its discontinuance, but upon the primary condition that its coinage should be limited and its purchasing power maintained by the fiat of the Government at par with gold."

A second testimony to the same effect from Hon. Charles Emory Smith, then editor of the Philadelphia *Press*, afterward Postmaster-General of the United States, may be fitly given. Referring to McKinley's position on the money question, he says:

" He has been the earnest, intelligent, and unvarying advocate of honest money measured by the world's best standard. Some of his antagonists have misrepresented him by garbling and distorting his utterances. No fair and honest citation of his expressions can be made which will not satisfy the most exacting friend of a sound currency. As to Governor McKinley's critics, we challenge any of them to copy these declarations and impeach them if they can.

" One cardinal and central thought runs through all of these utterances—that the standard of value must be preserved sacred and inviolate, and that it must be the one recognized, established standard of the commercial world. If there is to be paper or representative money, it must be redeemable in real money of that standard, so that for purposes of currency it will be as good. If there is to be silver, it must be so limited and so constantly exchangeable for gold that the parity of the metals will be maintained. In the later years there is a recognition that the limit has been reached. Governor McKinley gives constant warning against any debasement of the standard."

MCKINLEY'S OWN EXPLANATION

We shall now let Major McKinley speak for himself. In a speech delivered at Niles, Ohio, in 1891, during the contest for the governorship of that State, he spoke as follows:

" The Democratic platform declares for the free and unlimited coinage of the silver of the world, to be coined, as freely as gold is now, upon the same terms and under the existing ratio. The platform of the Republican party stands in opposition to anything short of a full and complete dollar. The legislation of the last Congress is the strongest evidence which can be furnished of the purpose of the Republican party to maintain silver as money, and of its resolution to keep it in use as part of our circulating medium equal with gold. The law which the Republican party put upon the statute-books declared the settled policy of the Government to be 'to maintain the two metals upon a parity with each other upon the present legal ratio or such ratio as may be provided by law.'

"The free and unlimited coinage of silver demanded by the Democratic Convention recently held in Cleveland amount to this : That all the silver of the world, and from every quarter of the world, can be brought to the mints of the United States and coined at the expense of the Government ; that is, that the mints of the United States must receive 412½ grains of silver, which is now worth but 80 cents the world over, and coin therefor a silver dollar, which by the fiat of the Government is to be received by the people of the United States and to circulate among them as worth a full dollar of 100 cents.

"The silver producer, whose 412½ grains of silver are worth only 80 cents or less in the markets of this country and the world, is thus enabled to demand that the Government shall take it at 100 cents. Will the Government be as kind to the producer of wheat and pay him 20 cents more per bushel than the market price ? The silver dollar now issued under a limited coinage has 80 cents of intrinsic value in it, so accredited the world over, and the other 20 cents is legislative will—the mere breath of Congress. That is, what the coin lacks of value to make it a perfect dollar Congress supplies by public declaration, and holds the extra 20 cents in the Treasury for its protection. The Government, buying the silver at its market value, takes to itself the profit between the market value of 412½ grains of silver and the face value of the silver dollar. Now it is proposed to remove the limit and to make the Government coin, not for account of the Treasury, but for the benefit of the silver-mine owner.

"It does not take a wise man to see that if a dollar worth only 80 cents intrinsically, coined without limit, is made a legal tender to the amount of its face value for the payment of all debts, public and private, a legal tender in all business transactions among the people, it will become in time the exclusive circulating medium of the country. Gold, which is 20 per cent. more valuable on every dollar, will not be paid out in any transactions in this country when an 80-cent silver dollar will answer the purpose. Nor will the greenback be long in returning to the Treasury for redemption in gold. We shall do our business, therefore, with short dollars, rather than with full dollars as we are now doing. The gold dollar will be taken from the circulating medium of the country and hoarded, and the effect will be that the circulating medium will not be increased, but reduced to the extent of the gold circulating, and we will be compelled to do the business of the country with a silver dollar exclusively, which under present conditions is confessedly the poorest, instead of doing our business with gold and silver and paper money, all equal and all alike good."

MCKINLEY ANSWERS OBJECTIONS

After quoting from President Cleveland and the Hon. M. D. Harter, a Democratic Representative in Congress, he proceeded:

"My competitor [Governor Campbell] has said in his reported interviews that in sentiment upon this subject the Democrats of Ohio are very much divided; that the vote in the convention was a very close one. This close vote not only emphasizes the danger of the free-coinage declaration in the minds of a large number of the Democrats in the State, but enjoins the importance and necessity of the friends of honest money standing together, and in all the contests of the past they have been forced to stand together for an honest currency. Governor Campbell declared in one of his interviews that while he had his doubts about it, he was willing 'to chance free and unlimited coinage of silver.' I am not willing to 'chance' it. Under present conditions the country cannot afford to chance it. We cannot gamble with anything so sacred as money, which is the standard and measure of all values. I can imagine nothing which would be more disturbing to our credit and more deranging in our commercial and financial affairs than to make this the dumping-ground of the world's silver. The silver producer might be benefited, but the silver user never. If there is to be any profit in the coinage of silver, it should go to the Government. It has gone to the Government ever since the Bland-Allison law went into effect. The new declaration would take it from the Government and give it to the silver producer,"

FURTHER DEFENCE OF HIS VIEWS

In a later speech during the same campaign, alluding to his own record upon the money question in Congress, he said:

"In 1877 I voted to reinstate the ancient silver dollar as a part of the coinage of the United States. Silver had been stricken from our coinage in 1873—stricken by both political parties, the one just as responsible as the other—and in 1878, being in favor of both gold and silver as money, to be kept at parity, one with the other, I voted for the restoration of the silver dollar. When I did it we had but 8,000,000 silver dollars in circulation. When I did it silver was more valuable than it is to-day. We have 405,000,000 silver dollars to-day, and that is as much as we can maintain at par with gold with the price of silver that prevails throughout the world. I took every occasion to re-instate silver to its ancient place in our monetary system, because I wanted both metals. I am opposed to free and unlimited coinage, because it means that we will be put upon a silver basis and do business with silver alone instead of with gold, silver, and paper money, with which we do the business of the country to-day—every one of them as good as gold.

"I want to tell the workingmen here, and the farmers, that it takes just as many blows of the hammer, it takes just as many strokes of the pick, it takes just as much digging, just as much sowing, and just as much reaping to get a short dollar as it does to get a full dollar."

Upon another occasion he declared himself concerning a debased dollar and its effect upon the business interests of the people as follows :

"A one hundred-cent dollar will go out of circulation along-side an eighty-cent dollar, which is a legal tender by the fiat of the Government. And no class of people will suffer so much as the wage-earner and the agriculturist. If it is the farmer you would benefit, there is one way to do it. Make the bushel measure with which he measures his wheat for the buyer three pecks instead of four, and require the buyer to pay as much for three pecks as he now pays for four. No man knows what the future may be, but in our present condition and with our present light every consideration of safety requires us to hold our present status until the other great nations shall agree to an international ratio."

He had remarked in Congress on May 25, 1890 :

"I do not propose by any vote of mine to force the people of the United States, the farmers and laborers, to the cheapest money of the world or to any policy which might tend in that direction. Whatever dollars we have in this country must be good dollars, as good in the hands of the poor as the rich ; equal dollars, equal in inherent merit, equal in purchasing power, whether they be paper dollars, gold dollars, or silver dollars, or treasury notes—each convertible into the other and each exchangeable for the other, because each is based upon an equal value and has behind it equal security ; good not by the fiat of law alone, but good because the whole commercial world recognizes its inherent and inextinguishable value. There should be no speculative features in our money, no opportunity for speculation in the exchanges of the people. They must be safe and stable."

In the course of his address at the Academy of Music in Philadelphia on September 23, 1892, he used these words :

JAMES A. GARFIELD
Assassinated July 2, 1881 by Charles J. Guiteau

ABRAHAM LINCOLN
Assassinated April 14, 1865 By John Wilkes Booth

WILLIAM McKINLEY
A late photograph

" My fellow-citizens, there is one thing which this country cannot afford to trifle with, and that is its currency, its measure of
value, the money which passes among the people in return for their
labor and the products of their toil or of their land.   There is no
contrivance so successful in cheating labor and the poor people of
the country as unstable, worthless, and easily counterfeited currency. . . .   The money of this country should be as national
as its flag, as sacred as the national honor, and as sound as the
Government itself.   That is the character of the money we have
to-day.   That is the kind of money which it is the paramount
interest of every citizen of this country, no matter to what political
party he may belong, to want to maintain and continue."

Drawn by Hamilton

WILLIAM McKINLEY, Jr.

Just before making his Great Tariff Speech, 1890

CHAPTER IX

McKinley and the Protective Tariff

TO tell the story of McKinley's seven terms would be to tell the history of Congress and the nation for fourteen years. From the beginning he was an active and conspicuous member of the House. He lost his seat, indeed, in the election of 1882, in which he received a majority of eight votes over Wallace, his Democratic competitor. As the House of Representatives was then strongly Democratic it was not difficult to count out this small majority, and McKinley was unseated. Speaking to Secretary Folger of his small majority, the shrewd old man replied: "Young man, eight votes is a very large majority this fall." In the succeeding election of 1884, McKinley was returned with a majority of over 2000. William McKinley was an American, and he reckoned nothing that concerned Americans to be unworthy of his notice. He recognized, however, that in view of the vast development, extension and multiplication of human interests, there was little hope for success as a universal genius. A man must be a specialist if he would attain the greatest eminence and the greatest usefulness. Already, indeed, he had devoted his attention especially to the subject of the tariff and its bearings upon American industry.

The story is told that soon after he opened his law office at Canton, while he was as yet an untrained youth, he was drawn into a debate upon that subject. Pitted against him was a trained, shrewd and experienced lawyer, who had at his tongue's end all the specious sophistries of free trade. The older and more expert debater won a seeming victory, but McKinley, though silenced for a

136

time, was not convinced. "No one will ever overcome me again in that way," he said to a companion. "I know I am right, and I know I can prove it." Thenceforth the study of books and men and conditions of industry to attain that end was the chief labor of his life.

Mr. Blaine, in his "Twenty Years in Congress," made fitting mention of this feature of his younger colleague's work. "The interests of his constituency," he wrote, "and his own bent of mind led him to the study of industrial questions, and he was soon recognized in the House as one of the most thorough statisticians and one of the ablest defenders of the doctrine of protection." For "one of the ablest" it was soon necessary to substitute "the foremost." It was reserved, indeed, for Major McKinley to bring the American protective system to its highest degree of perfection, to proclaim it a permanent and abiding principle, and to vindicate it as such before the world.

AN INCIDENT IN CONGRESS

Almost his first speech in Congress, as we have already said, was on the subject of the tariff, and it was one that made a marked impression upon the House. Thenceforth its author was looked to in every tariff debate to be one of the chief upholders of protection. An incident related by Judge Kelley, in his eulogy upon Dudley C. Haskell, shows how effectively McKinley answered this expectation. It was when the famous Mills bill was before the House. Kelley was to open the debate on the Republican side and McKinley was to close it. Haskell, who was a member of the Ways and Means Committee, and a particularly strong debater, desired the honor of closing the debate, and asked Judge Kelley to persuade McKinley to give way to him. The Judge went to McKinley and repeated Haskell's request. McKinley readily consented, saying that he did not care in what order he spoke. So it happened that McKinley was the fourth or fifth speaker, and Haskell was to talk last. At the conclusion of McKinley's speech a number of the members crowded around to congratulate him. Foremost among them was Haskell, who seized McKinley's hand enthusiastically, exclaiming: 'Major, I shall speak last; but you, sir, have closed the debate.'"

With such years of preparation Major McKinley was universally recognized as the one man of all best qualified to frame a new tariff law, which it seemed desirable to enact when the Republicans resumed full control of the Government in 1889. He was appointed Chairman of the Ways and Means Committee, and presently gave to the nation the great measure which bears his name. Of his work in connection with it he spoke modestly. "I was Chairman of the Committee," he said, "and I performed my duties as best I could. That is all. Some of the strongest men in Congress were on the Committee, and the eight of us heard everybody, considered everything, and made up the best tariff law we knew how to frame."

It was, indeed, as a high tariff advocate that McKinley made his reputation, alike as a Congressional debater and an earnest and indefatigable worker for what appeared to him the best interests of the country. It was his record in this field of public labor that carried him to the governorship of Ohio and to the Presidency. The tariff question, in brief, was the main-spring of his career, and as such some more detailed account of his work in this direction, with illustrative extracts from his speeches on the subject, is an essential feature of any record of his life.

PROMINENT IN TARIFF DISCUSSION

He began his work in the tariff, as we have said, almost upon his first entrance to the halls of Congress. In 1880, while speaking at Cooper Institute, New York, he definitely stated his position upon the subject; saying that, while the Democratic party professed to favor a tariff for revenue with incidental protection, he preferred a tariff for protection with incidental revenue. This happy way of putting the subject was caught up by Republican speakers and newspapers throughout the country and set the people to thinking seriously upon it. No bolder proposition in favor of the doctrine of protection had been made for many years.

McKinley took a prominent part in the discussion of the tariff bill of 1882, speaking very effectively upon the subject. As a member of the Ways and Means Committee he was actively concerned in the preparation of the bill. This bill, however, was greatly modified by the action of the Senate, and as finally offered proved far from satisfactory to the Republicans. It was especially unsatisfactory to the wool interest. As a result, on its final passage McKinley voted against it, with most of the Ohio delegation.

During the debate he expressed himself very decisively on the subject of protection, and claimed that it was steadily growing in popular favor and appreciation. He said:

" The sentiment is surely growing. It has friends to-day that it never had in the past. Its adherents are no longer confined to the Nort'i and the East, but are found in the South and in the West. The idea travels with industry and is the associate of enterprise and thrift. It encourages the development of skill, labor, and inventive genius as part of the great productive forces. Its advocacy is no longer limited to the manufacturer, but it has friends the most devoted among the farmers, the wool-growers, the laborers, and the producers of the land. It is as strong in the country as in the manufacturing towns or the cities ; and while it is not taught generally in our colleges, and our young men fresh from universities join with the free-trade thought of the country, practical business and every-day experience later teach them that there are other sources of knowledge besides books, that demonstration is better than theory, and that actual results outweigh an idle philosophy. But while it is not favored in the colleges, it is taught in the schools of experience, in the workshop, where honest men perform an honest day's labor, and where capital seeks the development of national wealth. It is, in my judgment, fixed in our national policy, and no party is strong enough to overthrow it.

"When the South depended upon the labor of the slaves and employed little or no free labor it was as earnest an advocate of free trade as is England to-day. Now that it must resort to free labor, it is placed upon the same footing as Northern producers; it is compelled to pay a like rate of wages for a day's work, and therefore demands protection against the foreign producer, whose product is made or grown by a cheaper labor. And we find, all through the South, a demand for protection to American industry against a foreign competition, bent upon their destruction and determined to possess the American market.

"Free trade may be suitable to Great Britain and its peculiar social and political structure, but it has no place in this Republic, where classes are unknown and where caste has long since been banished; where equality is the rule; where labor is dignified and honorable; where education and improvement are the individual striving of every citizen, no matter what may be the accident of his birth or the poverty of his early surroundings. Here the mechanic of to-day is the manufacturer of a few years hence. Under such conditions, free trade can have no abiding-place here. We are doing very well; no other nation has done better or makes a better showing in the world's balance-sheet. We ought to be satisfied with the outlook for the future. We know what we have done and what we can do under the policy of protection. We have had some experience with a revenue tariff, which inspires neither hope, nor courage, nor confidence. Our own history condemns the policy we oppose and is the best vindication of the policy which we advocate. It needs no other."

MCKINLEY'S ADDRESS AT PETERSBURG

In 1885, while on a visit to Petersburg, Va., he made an address to the people on the tariff, delivered in a familiar but effective way which must have set the people to thinking. It attracted widespread attention alike in the South and the North. He put his view of the business aspect of a protective tariff in a homely and practical way calculated to make it clear to school-boy, farmer, and business man alike. We append the following extract:

"Now, my fellow-citizens, what is this tariff? It is very largely misunderstood, and if I can to-night make this audience, the humblest and the youngest in it, understand what the tariff means, I will feel that I have been well paid for my trip to Virginia. What, then, is the tariff? The tariff, my fellow-citizens, is a tax put upon goods made outside of the United States and brought into the United States for sale and consumption. That is, we say to England, we say to Germany, we say to France: 'If you want to sell your goods to the people of the United States, you must pay so much for the privilege of doing it; you must pay so much per ton, so much per yard, so much per foot, as the case may be, for the privilege of selling to the American people, and what you pay in that form goes into the public treasury to help discharge the public burdens.' It is just like the little city of Petersburg, for example. I do not know what your customs may be, but in many cities of the North, if a man comes to our cities and wants to sell goods to our people on the streets, not to occupy any of our business houses, not being a permanent resident or trader, not living there, but traveling and selling from town to town—if he comes to one of our little cities in Ohio we say to him: 'Sir, you must pay so much into the city treasury for the privilege of selling goods to our people here.' Now, why do we do that? We do it to protect our own merchants.

"Just so our Government says to the countries of the Old World—it says to England and the rest: 'If you want to come in and sell to our people you must pay something for the privilege of doing it, and pay it at the Treasury at the custom-houses,' and that goes into the Treasury of the United States to help discharge the public debt and pay the current expenses of the Government. Now, that is the tariff, and if any man at this point wants to ask me any questions about it I want him to do it now, for I don't want, when I am gone, to have some Democrat say: 'If I could only have had an opportunity to ask him a question I would like to have done it, because I could have exposed the fallacy of his argument.' So I want him to do it now.

"Do you think there would be an idle man in America if we manufactured everything that Americans use? Do you think if we didn't buy anything from abroad at all, but made everything we needed, that every man would not be employed in the United States, and employed at a profitable remuneration? Why, everybody is benefited by protection, even the people who do not believe in it—for they get great benefit out of it, but will not confess it; and that is what is the matter with Virginia. Heretofore she has not believed in it. You have not had a public man that I know of in Washington for twenty-five years, save one, except the Republicans, who did not vote against the great doctrine of American protection, American industries, and American labor; and do you imagine that anybody is coming to Virginia with his money to build a mill, or a factory, or a furnace, and develop your coal and your ore—bring his money down here when you vote every time against his interests and don't let those who favor them vote at all? No! If you think so you might just as well be undeceived now, for they will not come.

"Why, old John Randolph, I don't know how many years ago, said on the floor of the American Congress, in opposing a protective tariff, he did not believe in manufactories. 'Why,' said he, 'if you have manufactories in Philadelphia you will have cholera six months in the year.' That was what the 'Sage of Roanoke' said, and Virginia seems to be still following the sentiments he uttered years and years ago.

"I tell you, manufactories do not bring cholera—they bring coin, coin; coin for the poor man, coin for the rich, coin for everybody who will work; comfort and contentment for all deserving people. And if you vote for increasing manufactories, my fellow-citizens, you will vote for the best interests of your own State, and you will be making iron, and steel, and pottery, and all the great

WILLIAM McKINLEY, THE PRESIDENT

AT HIS DESK IN THE WHITE HOUSE

This picture is the best profile likeness of the late President. It was obtained for exclusive use in this work by the publishers and is protected by copyright.

Copyright, 1900, by James Henry Harper

THE UNITED STATES PEACE COMMISSIONERS OF THE SPANISH WAR.

Appointed September 9, 1898. Met Spanish Commissioners at Paris, October 1st. Treaty of Peace signed by the Commissioners at Paris, December 10th. Ratified by the United States Senate at Washington, February 6, 1899.

leading products just as Ohio and Pennsylvania are making them to-day.

"Be assured that the Republicans of the North harbor no resentments—only ask for the results of the war. They wish you the highest prosperity and greatest development. They bid you, in the language of Whittier :

> " 'A school-house plant on every hill,
> Stretching in radiate nerve-lines thence
> The quick wires of intelligence ;
> Till North and South, together brought,
> Shall own the same electric thought ;
> In peace a common flag salute;
> And, side by side, in labor's free
> And unresentful rivalry,
> Harvest the fields wherein they fought.' "

MCKINLEY AND THE MILLS BILL

In the Congress of 1887, which had a Democratic majority, Roger Q. Mills, of Texas, was chairman of the Committee on Ways and Means. This committee prepared a tariff bill, popularly known as the Mills' Bill, the debate upon which was one of the longest and most spirited that had occurred in Congress during many years. McKinley took a very active part in the opposition, his private office in the hotel being a meeting place for manufacturers from all parts of the country. Major McKinley heard them all with great patience. In addition, he was surrounded by a small library of printed volumes and a mass of reports and statistics bearing upon the conditions of industry alike in the United States and foreign countries.

Great as was the labor involved, he never seemed to weary of it, and was constantly accessible to visitors on business pertaining to the proposed bill. All who came in contact with him greatly admired his mastery of the subject in its highly varied details. The report which gave the views of the Republican minority was drawn by him, and in it he cited the various objections to the measure, and made manifest the fallacy of the theory upon which it was based. In the discussion of the bill which followed occurred the incident related by Judge Kelley which we have quoted above.

The debate on the Mills' Bill was very spirited, and the part taken in it by McKinley was active and effective. An amusing *recontre* took place between him and Leopold Morse, a Democratic member from Massachusetts. Much has been said about how free wool would cheapen the workingman's clothing. Morse was a member of a firm of dealers in clothing, and McKinley, with the purpose of giving an effective object lesson on this point, had procured a suit of cheap clothes from this firm. We quote from his speech as given in the *Congressional Record*:

AN AMUSING ENCOUNTER

"The expectation of cheaper clothes is not sufficient to justify the action of the majority. This is too narrow for a national issue. Nobody, so far as I have learned, has expressed dissatisfaction with the present price of clothing. It is a political objection; it is a party slogan. Certainly nobody is unhappy over the cost of clothing except those who are amply able to pay even a higher price than is now exacted. And besides, if this bill should pass, and the effect would be (as it inevitably must be) to destroy our domestic manufactures, the era of low prices would vanish, and the foreign manufacturer would compel the American consumer to pay higher prices than he had been accustomed to pay under the 'robber tariff,' so called.

"Mr. Chairman, I represent a district comprising some 200,000 people, a large majority of the voters in the district being workingmen. I have represented them for a good many years, and I have never had a complaint from one of them that their clothes were too high. Have you? [Applause on the Republican side.] Has any gentleman on this floor met with such complaint in his district?

"Mr. Morse: They did not buy them of me.

"Mr. McKinley: No! Let us see. If they had bought of the gentleman from Massachusetts it would have made no difference, and there could have been no complaint. Let us examine the matter.

"[Mr. McKinley here produced a bundle containing a suit of clothes, which he opened and displayed, amid great laughter and applause.]

MR. MCKINLEY AND THE TEN-DOLLAR SUIT

"Come, now, will the gentleman from Massachusetts know his own goods? [Renewed laughter.] We recall, Mr. Chairman, that the Committee on Ways and Means talked about the laboring man who worked ten days at a dollar a day, and then went with his $10 wages to buy a suit of clothes. It is the old story. It is found in the works of Adam Smith. [Laughter and applause on the Republican side.] I have heard it in this House for ten years past. It has served many a free trader. It is the old story, I repeat, of the man who gets a dollar a day for his wages, and having worked for the ten days goes to buy his suit of clothes. He believes he can buy it for just $10, but the 'robber manufacturers' have been to Congress and have got 100 per cent. put upon the goods in the shape of a tariff, and the suit of clothes he finds cannot be bought for $10, but he is asked $20 for it, and so he has to go back to ten days more of sweat, ten days more of toil, ten days more of wear and tear of muscle and brain to earn the $10 to purchase the suit of clothes. Then the chairman gravely asks, is not ten days entirely annihilated?

"Now, a gentleman who read that speech, or heard it, was so touched by the pathetic story that he looked into it and sent me a suit of clothes identical with that described by the gentleman from Texas, and he sent me also a bill for it, and here is the entire suit; 'robber tariffs and taxes and all' have been added, and the retail cost is what? Just $10. [Laughter and applause on the Republican side.] So the poor fellow does not have to go back to work ten days more to get that suit of clothes.   He takes the suit with him and pays for it just $10. [Applause.] But in order that there might be no mistake about it, knowing the honor and honesty of the gentleman from Massachusetts [Mr. Morse], he went to his store and bought the suit. [Laughter and cheers on the Republican side.]   I hold in my hand the bill.

"Mr. Struble :   Read it.

"Mr. McKinley (reading) :

'Boston, May 4, 1888.

J. D. Williams, bought of Leopold Morse & Co., men's, youths' and boys' clothing, 131 to 137 Washington Street, corner of Brattle'—I believe it is.

"Mr. Morse : Yes, Brattle.

"Mr. McKinley (reading): 'To one suit of woolen clothes, $10. Paid.' [Renewed laughter and applause.] And now, Mr. Chairman, I never knew of a gentleman engaged in this business who sold his clothes without profit. [Laughter.] And there is the same $10 suit described by the gentleman from Texas that can be bought in the city of Boston, can be bought in Philadelphia, in New York, in Chicago, in Pittsburg, anywhere throughout the country, at $10 retail the whole suit—coat, trousers, and vest—and 40 per cent. less than it could have been bought for in 1860 under your low tariff and low wages of that period. [Great applause.] It is a pity to destroy the sad picture of the gentleman from Texas which was to be used in the campaign, but the truth must be told. But do you know that if it were not for protection you would pay a great deal more for these clothes? I do not intend to go into that branch of the question, but I want to give one brief illustration of how the absence of American competition immediately sends up the foreign prices, and it is an illustration that every man will remember. My friend from Missouri [Mr. Clardy], who sits in front of me, will remember it. The Missouri Glass Company, was organized several years ago for the manufacture of coarse fluted glass and cathedral glass. Last November the factory was

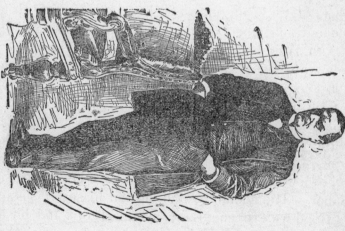

"Nobody can well dispute this proposition."

"What boots it whether our commerce is on the seas to foreign ports or on inland seas to domestic ports?"

Drawn by Hamilton

THE TARIFF DEBATE IN CONGRESS, 1890

Hon. William McKinley, Jr. Making his Great Argument for Protection

9

149

destroyed by fire. Cathedral glass was their specialty. Within ten days from the time that splendid property was reduced to ashes the foreign price of cathedral glass advanced 28 per cent. to the American consumer. [Applause on the Republican side.] Showing that whether you destroy the American production by free trade or by fire, it is the same thing ; the prices go up to the American consumer, and all you can do is to pay the price the foreigner chooses to ask." [Renewed applause.]

When the bill came to a vote, only one Republican member of the House voted in the affirmative. With this exception, the Republicans of the House were a unit against the Mills' Bill, which, as is well known, failed to become a law.

MCKINLEY AND HIS TARIFF BILL, 1890

The Congress of 1889–90 was largely concerned in the preparation and passage of the bill which became famous as the McKinley Tariff Bill. As has been stated, he was chairman of the Ways and Means Committee of that Congress. Among the other members of the Congress were J. C. Burrows and John H. Gear, subsequently members of the United States Senate, John G. Carlisle, who later became Secretary of the Treasury, Roswell P. Flower, who had been Governor of the State of New York, and Nelson Dingley, whose name became associated with a later Republican tariff bill.

Chairman McKinley at once set out to prepare a bill fitted to voice the verdict of the people, who had declared for the American doctrine of protection and the preservation of our home markets for our own workmen. No man could have been better qualified for this labor. The committee did not sit in secret sessions, but the doors stood wide open to the manufacturers and business men of the country. It mattered not what were the political views of the visitor, if he had anything of a practical nature to propose he was sure of a respectful audience. The end desired by the chairman

"We do not depreciate the value of our foreign trade; we are proud of it."

THE TARIFF DEBATE IN CONGRESS

Hon. William McKinley, Jr. Making his Great Argument for Protection

"What advantage can come from passing by the best market that we may reach the poorest by distant seas?"

Drawn by Hamilton

151

was the greatest good of the people of the United States, not the advancement of party interests.

No measure was ever so perfectly prepared for the consideration of the House as the McKinley Bill on the day on which it was reported. The committee had been engaged upon it from the meeting of the House in December, 1889, until April 16, 1890, on which day the bill was reported. It was not called up for consideration until May 7th, the general debate upon it lasting until the 10th, after which it was passed by a strict party vote, 164 Republicans voting for it and 141 Democrats and one Populist voting against it. It was reported to the Senate on June 18th, the amended bill was sent to the Conference Committee September 15th, and the measure was finally passed on September 30th.

Of the changes made in the tariff by the Act of 1890 more than two-thirds were in the original bill as proposed by McKinley, and 492 out of 641 were placed in the bill before it left his committee. Great credit is due to all the able statesmen in both Houses of Congress who aided in passing the measure, but it deserves to be put upon record that William McKinley did the greater part of the work. The bill was vigorously attacked by such able opponents as Carlisle, Breckenridge, Mills, and others, the best debaters that the ranks of the Southern Congressmen could furnish. McKinley led his party safely through these assaults, and was master of the field throughout the whole battle.

MCKINLEY'S SPEECHES IN CONGRESS ON THE TARIFF

His opening address called attention to the fact that the country, in the election of 1888 had declared itself in favor of the policy of protection, and that the long discussion of the Mills' Bill, and subsequent debates during the Presidential campaign, had familiarized the people with the principles underlying the tariff ; he therefore deemed it unnecessary to expound these abstract doctrines.

With reference to the tariff itself, he stated that the entire system was to be remodeled. Among the several changes, the United

"But, Mr. Chairman, in the presence of our magnificent domestic commerce, why need we vex
ourselves about foreign commerce?"

"With me this position is a deep conviction,
not a theory."

Drawn by Hamilton

THE TARIFF DEBATE IN CONGRESS, 1890

Hon. William McKinley, Jr. Making his Great Argument for Protection

153

States Government was to be deprived of the privilege it had long enjoyed of importing foreign articles for its own use free of duty. Under this provision of the old law great abuses had grown up, for not only did the Government pass its goods free through the custom houses, but its officers, agents and contractors did the same thing, much to the disadvantage of our manufacturers.

It placed a limit upon the merchandise that tourists could bring into the country under the guise of personal effects ; thus escaping their share of taxation while, through their purchases abroad, the country was drained of its money for the benefit of foreign tradesmen. It further required that all imported merchandise should be plainly stamped with the name of the country where it was produced. This was to stop the fraudulent use of American brands and trade-marks by foreign manufacturers.

The Democratic minority had argued in its report that the proposed bill would not diminish the revenues because it increased various duties. Major McKinley, replying to this, stated that all experience taught that whenever the duty was raised to the protective point, or above the highest revenue point, on goods or articles produced at home, the amount of importations always decreased and the resulting revenue diminished. When the duty was raised to a point where the foreign manufacturer could not compete in our market with our own products the revenue was abolished altogether. The bill would therefore not increase revenue because it increased duties.

As regards the relation of agriculture to the tariff, Major McKinley showed that the depression of farming, which had become during late years serious in this country, was much greater in England, so that free trade was no remedy for this evil. He showed that we imported eggs by the million, cattle, horses and sheep, barley, hay, and other agricultural products that we ought to produce, to the extent of nearly $300,000,000 a year. Canada agriculturists alone took $25,000,000 a year out of the pockets of our farmers. The bill proposed to correct all this and give the American farmer his full share of the advantages of a protective tariff. It showed how this vast amount of money spent every year for foreign farm products, if kept at home, would relieve the distress of our own landholders and stimulate all branches of trade and manufactures dependent upon the farming classes.

Many articles were taken off the dutiable list and put on the free list, far the most important of these being sugar and kindred products. Steps were taken to encourage the cultivation of the sugar beet, it being proposed to pay a bounty upon all sugar made in this country. The speaker called attention to the fact that eighteen articles had been taken from the free list and put upon the dutiable list, ten of these being farm products. Among these were eggs, broom corn, plants, trees and shrubs, straw, apples, teazels, flax and hemp.

HE REVIEWED THE GAIN OF PROTECTION

Major McKinley briefly reviewed the service which this country had gained from protection. We had lived, he stated, under a protective tariff for twenty-nine years, the longest consecutive period since the Government was founded. As a result, we found ourselves in a condition of prosperity and independence which had never before been witnessed in our country, and had no parallel in the recorded history of the world. We had made remarkable progress in all that goes to make a nation great and strong. In the arts, in science, literature, manufactures, and inventions, in the application of science to manufacturing and agriculture, in wealth and credit, and in national honor, we were abreast of the best of foreign nations and behind none. In 1860 at the close of fourteen years in which the country had been under a revenue tariff,—just the kind the Democratic party wished to put in force again,—the business of the country was prostrated, agriculture was depressed, manufactures were in a decline, and the nation was destitute of credit in the financial centres of the world.

Under protection we had gained a surplus revenue and a spotless credit. The Morrill protective tariff of 1861, had enabled us to equip vast armies and carry the war to a successful termination. At the same time flourishing industries sprang up under it in all parts of the country. Thus, after the war closed, with our burden of over $2,000,000,000 of debt, this tariff had enabled us to pay it off at the rate of $174,000 every twenty-four hours for twenty years. Under this tariff we had led all nations in the savings-bank deposits of our laboring classes. We led them all in mining, in agriculture and in manufacturing. Such were the results of twenty-nine years of protection.

Major McKinley next depicted the disastrous results which would follow a departure from the safe paths by which we had been led into the green pastures of national prosperity through the action of the American protective system. One of the most popular features of the bill presented by him was the clause providing for reciprocity in trade. The credit of securing the enactment of this part of the law has generally been given to James G. Blaine, who at that time was Secretary of State. There is no doubt, it may be admitted, that Mr. Blaine did play an important part in securing the adoption of this clause, but it is not true, as has been reported, that Major McKinley was opposed to the idea. In almost his final words, those spoken in his remarks at Buffalo the day before he received his fatal wound, the extension of the reciprocity policy was earnestly advocated by him. In this same speech he eulogized Blaine as the one to whom the chief credit should be given for this important policy.

Mr. William E. Cartes, formerly chief of the Bureau of American Republics, clearly states the relations of Mr. Blaine and Mr. McKinley to this measure. He says:

"When Mr. Blaine found that it was proposed to remove the duty on sugar, he sent me to Mr. McKinley with a proposition which he wanted added to the bill as an amendment. It afterward became known as the Hale Amendment. It provided that the

President should be authorized to take off the duty on sugar whenever the sugar-producing nations removed their duties on our farm products and certain other articles. Mr. McKinley presented this amendment to the Committee on Ways and Means. It was not adopted. Mr. McKinley voted for it the first time it was presented. Then a second proposition containing some modifications was presented, and Mr. McKinley voted for that, as he voted for the Blaine reciprocity amendment every time it was submitted.

"It has been currently reported that Mr. Blaine denounced the McKinley Bill with such vigor that he smashed his hat. Mr. Blaine's opposition to the bill was because of the free-sugar clause. He criticized the refusal of Congress to take advantage of conditions which he thought were favorable to our trade. They proposed to throw away the duty on sugar when he wanted them to trade with it.

"When what was known as the Aldrich Amendment was adopted, Mr. Blaine was perfectly satisfied, and there was nothing in the current tales that he was unfriendly to Major McKinley. On the contrary, he was one of his warmest friends. Had it not been for Mr. McKinley and Senator Aldrich, of Rhode Island, the reciprocity clause in the tariff act would never have been adopted."

In conclusion of our consideration of this famous commercial and fiscal measure, it must be said that no opportunity arose to test its effect upon the national revenues. The vast quantity of goods, of the classes upon which the rates of duty were increased, that were rushed into our ports before the law became operative, and a concurrent holding back of those that were to be placed upon the free list, prevented the new tariff from pursuing its normal course. It was little more than a month in existence before the Fall elections gave it its death-blow. The advent of a Democratic Congress alarmed those whose business the tariff would have benefited, and the deadlock in trade which was soon to show itself early began to manifest itself in the commerce of the country. The McKinley tariff fell before it could be fairly tried.

CHAPTER X

Governor of Ohio

AT the election of 1890, as we have said, the Democrats so manipulated the districts as to defeat Mr. McKinley by 300 votes in a district normally Democratic by 2,900, and thus prevent his return to Congress. Great was their rejoicing at this. They thought they had crushed their arch-enemy at last. But they reckoned without the chief factor in the problem. The answer to their exultation came unhesitatingly. Mr. McKinley in the following year was nominated by the Republicans by acclamation for Governor of the State.

The platform of the Convention re-affirmed the devotion of the party to the patriotic doctrine of protection, and recognized the McKinley bill as the ablest expression of a principle enacted in fulfillment of Republican promises. It made declarations in favor of such legislation by Congress as would in every practical mode encourage, protect, and promote agriculture. It demanded protection of the wool industry. It declared that gold and silver should form the basis of all circulating mediums, and expressed the desire to add the entire production of the silver mines of the United States to the currency of the people.

A MEMORABLE CAMPAIGN

Then followed one of the most memorable campaigns ever waged in the Buckeye State. Mr. McKinley began his campaign on August 1, and for three months he traveled night and day, making from two to a dozen speeches a day, until he had visited eighty-four out of the eighty-eight counties of the State, and made in all 130 speeches. His campaign was on national issues, on the tariff, on protection; and so eloquently and passionately did he defend his principles that great crowds turned out to hear him. The attention of the whole country was drawn to the State of Ohio and the campaign. Newspaper correspondents followed the champion of protection in his tour of the State, and filled the press of the country with descriptions of scenes novel in political campaigns.

The Democrats contested every inch of the ground stubbornly, but the people turned to McKinley as the apostle of the true dispensation, and women and children said he had made protection and tariff plain to them. In that campaign, the first general campaign Mr. McKinley had ever made, he was pronounced the best vote-getter ever seen on the stump in Ohio. He won the admiration of Democrats, as he won the devotion of Republicans, and his election by a majority of over 21,000 votes was gratifying to one party, without being a source of bitterness to the rank and file of the other party.

MCKINLEY RENOMINATED FOR GOVERNOR

The opening of the second Cleveland Administration in 1893, was followed by a business distrust that in a brief time developed into a widespread panic. Even the greatest financial combination in the land, the Associated Banks of New York, practically suspended payment, issuing clearing-house certificates in place of money. Dismay took the place of hope; ruin succeeded prosperity.

In the height of the panic Governor McKinley was renominated by the Republicans of Ohio by acclamation. A spirited contest followed. His opponent was the Hon. L. T. Teal. Nothing was to be said of the personal fitness of the candidates, and the campaign was conducted on the basis of party issues. The revulsion against the protective policy was reaching its end, the people were repenting of their temporary change of sentiment, and the issue brought before them was that of protection or free trade.

The discussion extended throughout the Fall; when at length the people came to indicate their opinion at the ballot-box, their verdict showed the change in public opinion. McKinley was re-elected Governor with a plurality of 80,955 ; up to that time the largest but one in the history of the State.

Mr. McKinley's record as Governor was an admirable one. He never forgot that he was not alone the representative of the party which had elected him, but the Chief Magistrate of the whole State, and he was untiring in his efforts to secure for the State a wise, economical, and honorable administration. He took great interest in the management of the public institutions, making a special study of means for their betterment, and securing many important and much-needed reforms. He urged the preserving and improving of the canal system, and was an earnest promoter of the movement for good roads. To the question of tax reform he paid much attention and repeatedly urged its importance upon the Legislature. Many questions relating to the welfare of workingmen became acute during his administration, and were dealt with by him in a spirit of intelligent sympathy.

MCKINLEY A WISE AND FIRM GOVERNOR

He had already long been known as an advocate of an eight-hour system, and of arbitration as a means of settling disputes between employers and employees. It was due to his initiative that the State Board of Arbitration was established in Ohio, and to its successful operation he gave for nearly four years his close personal attention. He made various wise recommendations for legislation for the better protection of life and limb in industrial pursuits, and as a result several salutary laws to such effect were put upon the statute books. When destitution and distress prevailed among the miners of the Hocking Valley, he acted with characteristic promptness and decision. News that many families were in danger of starving reached him at midnight. Before sunrise he had a carload of provisions on the way to their relief.

Many times during his administration the peace of the State was disturbed by unseemly outbreaks requiring the application of the restraining power of the Government. This power McKinley exercised with great firmness and discretion. Fifteen times it was necessary to call out the State troops for the maintenance or restoration of order, but on no occasion was the use of them in any respect oppressive. During the summer of 1894 strikes and other disturbances prevailed, especially on the chief railroad lines, and for three weeks the regiments were on duty, acquitting themselves most creditably for the protection of property and enforcement of the law, without any unnecessary harshness towards either party to the disputes. On two noteworthy occasions desperate efforts were made by ill-advised mobs to commit the crime of lynching. Governor McKinley promptly used the military forces of the State to prevent such violence of law and dishonor of the Commonwealth, and showed himself a thorough master of the trying situation.

A distinctive feature of the McKinley administration was the absence of red tape and needless formality. In his method of transacting business the Governor was concise and direct, and in his intercourse with the people, though dignified, he was always approachable and genial. Access was readily had to him at all reasonable times, and no matter of actual interest ever failed to receive his courteous, prompt, and painstaking attention.

HIS FINANCIAL MISFORTUNE

During the period of Mr. McKinley's governorship occurred a most serious misfortune, due to his misplaced confidence in an old friend, and unhesitating readiness in coming to the rescue of one in financial straits. The result of his overconfidence and unquestioning kindness of heart was the sweeping away of the small fortune which he had spent his life in accumulating. Some attempt was made to attach discredit to his name on account of his failure, there being a few who suggested that there was some wrong-doing connected with it. But when the facts became known, they were found to redound to his generosity and goodness of heart, and served to add to his already great popularity.

The misfortune was due to the business failure of his friend, Robert L. Walker, of Youngstown, Ohio, which swept away not only all his own wealth, but that of Governor McKinley as well. The facts of the case are briefly as follows:

The two men had known each other from boyhood, and had always been close friends. As a young law student, a struggling lawyer, and a Congressman, Major McKinley had several times been aided with loans of money by Mr. Walker. These loans were chiefly needed to enable Major McKinley to meet his campaign assessment. As his reputation grew, the assessments ceased, he paid back the loans, and in the last ten years of his Congressional career, he succeeded in accumulating about $20,000, which he invested in real estate and securities. His wife had inherited a fortune of about $75,000 from her father. Early in 1893, Mr. Walker went to the Governor and asked him for assistance. The banker said that he was hard pressed for ready money, and he wished the Governor to indorse his notes, which he then intended to have discounted. Without hesitation, the Governor cheerfully consented to give this aid to the old friend who had helped him in his early years, and indorsed about $15,000 worth of paper, payable in thirty, sixty and ninety days. This paper, he was assured, would be discounted in three well-known banks. Later on he indorsed a number of notes which, he understood, were made for the purpose of taking up the notes which he had first indorsed, and which had become due. Mr. Walker was at this time the president of a national bank, a savings bank, a stamping mill company and a stove and range company, and was interested in several coal mines in Ohio and Pennsylvania. He was credited with possessing a fortune of more than $250,000, and his personal and business standing was so high that a prominent Ohio business man said that he would have indorsed Mr. Walker's paper for half a million dollars the day before his failure.

When, in addition to these facts, it is remembered that he had been a boyhood companion and generous friend of Governor

McKinley, it is not to be wondered at that the latter trusted him implicitly. On the day that the Walker failure was announced, Governor McKinley was about to start for New York to attend the annual dinner of the Ohio Society in that city. He at once cancelled the engagement, and went to Youngstown. There he found that banks all over the State held Walker paper indorsed by him, and that, instead of being liable for $15,000 worth, he was liable for nearly $100,000 worth. Five days afterward he and his wife made an assignment of all their property to three trustees, to be used, without preference, for the equal benefit of the Walker creditors. Mrs. McKinley was urged to keep her interest in her property, but she declined to do so. The news of the misfortune and of the position taken by Mr. McKinley and his wife aroused a wide-spread feeling of sympathy and a desire to help them in their trouble. A popular fund was started, but the Governor returned the contributions that were forwarded to him, thanking those who sent them for the good will shown, but positively refusing to accept the profferred aid. Then a number of personal friends decided to raise a private fund. Again the Governor, as soon as he heard of it, interposed, and declined absolutely to receive any assistance ; but his friends persisted in the plan, pointing out to him that many of the subscriptions were anonymous, and, therefore, could not be returned. To his last day, with the possible exception of four or five subscribers, he did not know who contributed to the fund. As fast as the Walker notes were presented the treasurer of the fund took them up, and when the last one had been paid Mrs. McKinley's property was restored to her, and the Governor's original modest fortune of $20,000, with a little more added, was returned to him.

At the close of his second term as Governor there was no question of his renomination. He had grown above the level of serving as the chief magistrate of a State and was about to be called to a much more exalted position, that of the executive head of the nation.

CHAPTER XI

The St. Louis Convention and Nomination

AS an essential preliminary to the story of McKinley's nomination for the Presidency in 1896, his standing and honorable attitude before the two preceding Conventions must be given. In 1884 Mr. McKinley was a Delegate-at-Large from Ohio to the Republican Nominating Convention, and helped to place James G. Blaine on the ticket. At the National Convention of 1888 he represented Ohio in the same capacity and was an earnest and loyal supporter of John Sherman. At that Convention, after the first day's balloting, the indications were that Mr. McKinley himself might be made the candidate. Then his strength of purpose and his high ideas of loyalty and honor showed themselves, for in an earnest and stirring speech he demanded that no vote be cast for him. From the first, two delegates had been voting persistently for him, although he had not, of course, been formally placed in nomination. Now the number of his supporters rose to fourteen. All the Republican Congressmen at Washington telegraphed to the Convention urging his nomination. The air became electrified with premonitions of a stampede.

Mr. McKinley had listened to the announcement of the two votes for him on each ballot with mingled annoyance and amusement. But now the case was growing serious. The next ballot might give him a majority of the whole Convention. He had only to sit still and the ripe fruit would drop into his hands. He had only to utter an equivocal protest and the result would be the same. But there was nothing equivocal about William McKinley. On one side was his personal honor; on the other side the Presidency of the United States. In choosing between the two, hesitation was impossible. He sprang to his feet with an expression upon his face and an accent in his voice that thrilled the vast assembly, but hushed it mute and silent as the grave while he spoke :—

"I am here as one of the chosen representatives of my State. I am here by resolution of the Republican State Convention, passed without a single dissenting vote, commanding me to cast my vote for John Sherman for President and to use every worthy endeavor for his nomination. I accepted the trust because my heart and my judgment were in accord with the letter and spirit and purpose of that resolution. It has pleased certain delegates to cast their votes for me for President. I am not insensible to the honor they would do me, but in the presence of the duty resting upon me, I cannot remain silent with honor.

"I cannot, consistently with the wish of the State whose credentials I bear and which has trusted me ; I cannot with honorable fidelity to John Sherman ; I cannot, consistently with my own views of personal integrity, consent, or seem to consent, to permit my name to be used as a candidate before this Convention. I would not respect myself if I should find it in my heart to do so, or permit to be done that which would ever be ground for any one to suspect that I wavered in my loyalty to Ohio or my devotion to the chief of her choice and the chief of mine. I do not request, I demand, that no delegate who would not cast reflection upon me shall cast a ballot for me."

That ended it, and the threatened stampede was averted. But, although the nomination was not forced upon Mr. McKinley, neither could he secure it for Mr. Sherman, although he loyally strove to do so till the end.

Mr. McKinley again occupied a seat as a Delegate-at-Large from Ohio in the National Convention of 1892, and was made the Permanent Chairman of the Convention. On this occasion an incident similar to that of 1888 occurred. Mr. McKinley was pledged in honor to the support of President Harrison for renomination, and he, as earnestly and as loyally as he had supported Mr. Sherman

10

four years before, labored for Mr. Harrison's success. The Republican leaders who were opposed to Harrison's renomination sought to accomplish their purpose by stampeding the Convention for McKinley himself.

When the roll was being called and Ohio was reached, Governor Foraker, one of the delegates from that State, rose and said that Ohio wanted time to consult. After a pause Mr. Nash, a district delegate, announced the vote as 2 for Harrison and 44 for McKinley. Chairman McKinley sprang from his seat and shouted back that he challenged the vote. Mr. Foraker responded that the chairman was not a member of the delegation.

" I am a member of the delegation," retorted Chairman McKinley.

" The gentleman's alternate has taken his place in the delegation, and the gentleman is not recognized as a member of the delegation now, and we make that point of order," came back from Foraker.

"The Chair overrules the point of order and asks the secretary to call the roll of Ohio," said Mr. McKinley.

The reading clerk called the roll, and the result was McKinley 44, Harrison 2. A delegate changed his vote, and then it stood McKinley 45, Harrison 1.

The contest between the chairman and the Ohio delegation and the calling of the roll had consumed some time, and the stampede was checked.

The roll-call proceeded, Harrison receiving 535 votes, McKinley 182, Thomas B. Reed 4, Robert T. Lincoln 1.

So General Harrison was renominated, and he owed the honor largely to McKinley. The latter was chairman of the committee that went to Washington to notify President Harrison officially of his renomination. In the address made by him on that occasion there was no tone of disappointment, but the speech rang with words of hope and cheer for the party.

At the opening of the national election campaign of 1894 it was evident to all that McKinley was the leader whom people in all parts of the country most desired to see and hear. From every State in the Union calls poured in for him, and he finally consented to enter the campaign outside of Ohio, agreeing to make forty-six speeches. The result was a tour which has never been equaled in the political history of the country. The people refused to be so easily satisfied as the orator hoped. State after State called for him with a persistence that would not be denied, and, instead of forty-six speeches, he actually made 371. His route extended through the States of Indiana, Illinois, Missouri, Nebraska, Iowa, Wisconsin, Michigan, Kentucky, Tennessee, Alabama, Mississippi, Louisiana, West Virginia, New York, New Jersey, Pennsylvania and Ohio, through which he journeyed in all over 10,000 miles.

MCKINLEY A POPULAR FAVORITE

During eight weeks' time he averaged seven speeches a day, extending from ten minutes to an hour in length. In all he addressed over two million people. Wherever he went he was received with an ovation, people gathering in thousands and clamoring to hear him at all the railroad stations on his line of travel. Everywhere his fame spread in advance, and the people flocked in numbers, coming hundreds of miles to see him at the larger cities where he was engaged to speak.

On September 26th, he faced at Indianapolis the largest audience ever gathered in the Hoosier State. At Chicago over 9,000 gathered to hear him, and over 7,000 in St. Louis. In the State of Kansas he addressed at Hutchison a meeting of over 40,000 people, the largest ever held in that State, many of them coming from adjoining States and Territories. At Topeka it was estimated that 24,000 people were present. Altogether he spoke to over 150,000 people at various points in Kansas. At Omaha, Nebraska, an audience of 12,000 listened to his explanation of the protection policy. In Iowa the multitudes in all aggregated 50,000. The same popular enthusiasm was manifested in Minnesota, he speaking to 10,000 in St. Paul and 15,000 in Duluth. At Springfield, Illinois, more than 20,000 people came to hear him.

MCKINLEY SPEAKS TO THE SOUTH

Subsequently, turning south towards New Orleans, he met with the same gratifying experience; 3,000 people gathered to hear him as he passed through Lexington, Kentucky. There was a tremendous gathering at Chattanooga, and at New Orleans he was received with an ovation, addressing over 8,000 people. He subsequently journeyed north through Alabama and other States, reaching the North at Pittsburg, where he addressed a large audience. At Philadelphia he spoke three times in one evening to enormous gatherings of people. In New York his campaign began at Buffalo, where it was necessary to call three meetings to accommodate the number who wished to see him. Passing eastward through the State, he was greeted by 10,000 people at Albany, whence he made his way down the Hudson valley, speaking at various points, and finally addressing a great multitude at Weehawken, New Jersey. On his way home to Ohio he stopped at Erie, Pennsylvania, speaking there to a gathering of 10,000 people.

Daily hundreds of columns of the newspapers were devoted to his remarks during this extended tour. His first formal nomination for President of the United States was made at the Ohio State Convention at Zanesville, May 29, 1895. This convention had met to nominate his successor as Governor. During the gubernatorial campaign McKinley entered the field as a speaker in favor of his successor, who was elected by a very large majority.

With the opening of the year 1896 the question of the Presidential election became prominent in all men's minds, and the Republican conventions in the several States began to select their delegates and declare their choice. The first State convention to endorse the Ohio candidate was Oregon, and other States followed

PRESIDENT McKINLEY'S LOVE FOR CHILDREN
Giving his buttonhole carnation to a little girl at one of his receptions

ELECTION NIGHT IN NEW YORK CITY

in rapid succession. Important opposition was made in only a few States, those in New England being Massachusetts and Rhode Island, whose favorite was Thomas B. Reed. New Hampshire, while declaring for Reed, named McKinley as second choice. Vermont selected him as first choice, and Connecticut evaded the issue. Maine, as was to be expected, spoke for its favorite son.

NUMEROUS PRESIDENTIAL CANDIDATES

The candidate of New York was Governor Levi P. Morton, whose political record had won for him the affection of the people. The Commonwealth of Pennsylvania named Matthew Stanley Quay, then the most prominent name in the ranks of the Republican party of that State. Iowa chose for its candidate the veteran Senator Allison. The remaining States of the Union unanimously declared for McKinley. Such were the encouraging preliminaries to the opening of the St. Louis Convention.

The result of the coming nomination seemed so evident in advance that the opposition press made a vigorous assault upon McKinley, attacking his financial record, and endeavoring to divert attention from the industrial issue to that of the currency. Such was the state of affairs in the country at large when the time for the assembling of the convention arrived.

The remarkable popularity of William McKinley, in view of the fact that he was but one of numerous prominent Congressmen, deserving for their services and available as candidates, seems to demand some explanation. He was not in the position of several of his predecessors, whose fame as military leaders had carried them to a position for which they were poorly fitted by nature or experience. He was not a "new man," borne suddenly upward on a billow of public favor like his coming competitor. He was in no sense a "dark horse," to be sprung suddenly upon a convention weary of a long and hopeless contest. He had made his way slowly and surely into public favor by the force of his character and the merit of his services, by his long and able record as a Congressman, and especially by his persistent labors in advocacy of the doctrine of protection. Of this, the sheet-anchor of the Republican party, McKinley had grown to be the leading exponent, and his recent service as the chief author of the 1890 tariff had lifted him into the highest rank among the leaders of his party.

OPPORTUNITIES FOR MCKINLEY

As we have already seen, the nomination of 1892 might have been his for the asking. It was fortunate for him that he positively declined it. The year 1892 was an off-year for the Republicans. Various causes of public dissatisfaction existed, and in the Autumn elections of that year Democracy swept the field. A different story had 1894 to tell. A Democratic administration had been two years in power, the McKinley "tariff for protection" had been replaced by a Democratic "tariff for revenue," business had utterly gone to pieces, and ruin loomed over the whole land.

The workmen of the country became convinced that their distress was due to the radical change in policy, and to this must largely be ascribed the extraordinary ovation which he received in his speech-making tour of that year. It was as if the people with one voice had exclaimed : "Give us back the McKinley tariff !"

Election day came, and with it a political revolution greater than that of 1892. In the latter the Democrats had been widely victorious. In the former an equal victory rested upon the Republican banners, the Democrats in much the larger number of States meeting with an overwhelming defeat. The House elected in 1892 contained 219 Democrats and 127 Republicans ; that elected in 1894 contained 245 Republicans and 100 Democrats.

When 1896 rolled around the same state of affairs prevailed. The depression in business had not ended and was still widely attributed to the substitution of the Wilson for the McKinley tariff. The election of a Republican President seemed assured, and the people had given their verdict with no uncertain voice for William McKinley as the standard-bearer of his party.

It must not be supposed, however, that the tariff problem was the only one to be considered. That was the question on which the party had always rested, and on which there was likely to be only one opinion. A second great question had grown strongly prominent, that of gold and silver coinage, and on this, if on anything, dissension would arise. The Democrats, largely setting aside the tariff issue, were prepared to make the fight with "free silver" engraved on their banners. Gold as the single standard of money was the Republican slogan, but on this question the party was far from unanimous, its members in the silver-mining States of the West being strongly in favor of unlimited silver coinage. This was the rock on which the counsels of the party threatened to split. McKinley's views on the question were well known. He had stated them often on the floors of Congress and the public rostrum. Now he kept silent. He was in the hands of his friends and his record lay open before the country. His had become a case in which "silence is golden."

FIRST DAY OF THE ST. LOUIS CONVENTION

It was about half an hour past noon, on Tuesday, June 16, 1896, that the eleventh national convention of the Republican party was called to order by the Hon. Thomas Henry Carter, chairman of the Republican National Committee. The large structure, known as the Auditorium or Convention Hall, was capable of accommodating an immense assemblage, and it is estimated that more than 40,000 visitors had flocked to St. Louis. Forty years had passed since the origin of the Republican party, and once more its representatives had come together to chose a national leader.

For the first time in the history of national conventions, the opening prayer was made by an Israelite, in the person of Rabbi Samuel Sale, pastor of the Shaare Emeth congregation. His invocation was devout, and at its close the secretary read the call issued by the National Committee for the convention. He was

not heard fifty feet away, not so much because of his weakness of
voice, as on account of the wretched acoustic qualities of the building. Chairman Carter then presented the name of Hon. Charles
W. Fairbanks, of Indiana, as temporary chairman. No voice was
raised in opposition, and the tall, slender man, with close-cropped
beard and mustache, came forward and delivered an address that
was frequently interrupted by applause. At its conclusion, the
necessary officials of the convention were appointed, the members
of the various committees announced, and, after a session of less
than two hours, an adjournment was had until ten o'clock
Wednesday.

WEDNESDAY'S PROCEEDINGS—ADOPTION OF THE GOLD PLANK

Between the adjournment and the coming together on the
morrow, much effective work was done. While the sentiment of
the delegates was overwhelmingly in favor of "sound currency,"
or the single gold standard, there was a diversity of opinion in
many quarters as to whether the word "gold" should be used in
the platform. A considerable number thought the latter was sufficiently explicit without the word, but the insistence of others
compelled a yielding of the point; it was decided that the all-
potent word should appear.

The convention reassembled at a quarter to eleven on Wednesday, and was opened with prayer by Rev. Dr. W. G. Williams, after
which the report of the Committee on Permanent Organization
presented the name of Senator J. N. Thurston, of Nebraska, as
chairman, made the secretaries, sergeant-at-arms and other temporary officers permanent officers of the convention, and gave a list
of vice-presidents, consisting of one from each State. It was
accepted, and Senator Thurston was loudly applauded as he took
his seat.

The address of Mr. Thurston pleased all by its terseness and
brevity. Great as is his ability, the sultry atmosphere and the
general impatience to get to work led the majority to look with

some dread upon a long and labored speech. Great, therefore, was the gratification of the delegates when the honorable gentleman said:

"Gentlemen of the convention: The happy memory of your kindness and confidence will abide in my grateful heart forever. My sole ambition is to meet your expectations, and I pledge myself to exercise the important powers of this high office with absolute justice and impartiality. I bespeak your cordial co-operation and support, to the end that our proceedings may be orderly and dignified, as befits the deliberations of the supreme council of the Republican party.

"Eight years ago I had the distinguished honor to preside over the convention which nominated the last Republican President of the United States. To-day I have the further distinguished honor to preside over the convention which is to nominate the next President of the United States. This generation has had its object-lesson, and the doom of the Democratic party is already pronounced. The American people will return the Republican party to power because they know that its administration will mean:

"The supremacy of the Constitution of the United States.

"The maintenance of law and order.

"The protection of every American citizen in his right to live, to labor and to vote.

"A vigorous foreign policy.

"The enforcement of the Monroe Doctrine.

"The restoration of our merchant marine.

"Safety under the Stars and Stripes on every sea, in every port.

"A revenue adequate for all governmental expenditures and the gradual extinguishment of the national debt.

"A currency 'as sound as the government and as untarnished as its honor,' whose dollars, whether of gold, silver or paper, shall have equal purchasing and debt paying power with the best dollars of the civilized world.

" A protective tariff which protects, coupled with a reciprocity which reciprocates, securing American markets for American products and opening American factories to the free coinage of American muscle.

" A pension policy just and generous to our living heroes and to the widows and orphans of their dead comrades.

" The governmental supervision and control of transportation lines and rates.

" The protection of the people from all unlawful combinations and unjust exactions of aggregated capital and corporate power.

" An American welcome to every God-fearing, liberty-loving, Constitution-respecting, law-abiding, labor-seeking, decent man.

" The exclusion of all whose birth, whose blood, whose conditions, whose teachings, whose practices, would menace the permanency of free institutions, endanger the safety of American society, or lessen the opportunities of American labor.

" The abolition of sectionalism—every star in the flag shining for the honor and welfare and happiness of every Commonwealth and of all the people.

" A deathless loyalty to all that is truly American and a patriotism eternal as the stars."

It was quietly growing evident, however, that the convention was far from a unit, the financial plank of the platform being that in which it was destined to split.

THURSDAY'S PROCEEDINGS

The first order of business on the assembling of the convention on Thursday, was the reading, by Senator Foraker, of Ohio, of the report of the Committee on Resolutions, the proposed platform of the party. The reading of this was greeted with great applause, in particular the currency plank, which stated : " We are opposed to the free coinage of silver, except by international agreement."

He was followed by Senator Teller, of Colorado, who read a minority report which demanded a declaration in favor of the free and unlimited coinage of silver at the ratio of 16 to 1, and made a strong and telling appeal in its favor. His motion was not without considerable support, there being 105 votes cast for it. It was overthrown, however, by the decisive vote of 818 for the majority report. We may briefly conclude this part of our subject by stating that, in consequence of this divergence of opinion, Teller and twenty other delegates withdrew from the convention. The remaining free-silver men did not feel called upon to take this extreme step.

The platform being adopted, the business next before the convention was the call of the States for nominations of candidates for the Presidency. The first response came from Iowa, R. M. Baldwin, of Council Bluffs, nominating Senator W. B. Allison, and offering a glowing tribute in his favor.

The voice of Massachusetts was next heard; Senator Lodge, of that State, eloquently presenting the claims of the Hon. Thomas B. Reed. The great popularity of the "man from Maine" was indicated by the uproar of enthusiasm with which his name was received. New York came next in order, Chauncey M. Depew placing in nomination the name of Governor Levi P. Morton, of whose services to the country he spoke in his usual felicitous style.

When Ohio was called, Joseph B. Foraker, of that State, arose, and, after giving his opinion of the record of the recent Democratic Administration and its results, and depicting the kind of man that he thought the country needed, said : " I stand here to present to this convention such a man. His name is William McKinley."

At this point pandemonium was let loose, and the convention gave up to unrestrained yelling, cheering, horn-blowing, whistling, cat-calling and all the other devices common to such occasions. A number of red, white and blue plumes, which (carefully wrapped up) had been brought into the convention earlier in the proceedings, were uncovered and waved, while almost every delegate seemed to be wildly gesticulating with either a fan or a flag in the air. The band tried in vain to compete with the ear-splitting clamor, but at last the strains of "Marching Through Georgia" caught the ears of the crowd, and they joined in the chorus and gradually quieted down.

Then a portrait of McKinley was hoisted on a line with the United States flag on the gallery facing the platform, and the cheering began over again, to which the band responded by playing "Rally Round the Flag," the convention joining in the chorus. Nearly a half hour passed before order was fully restored, and Senator Foraker able to proceed with his speech. After eulogizing the great leaders of the party, with special reference to Mr. Blaine, he continued :

GOVERNOR FORAKER'S EULOGY OF MCKINLEY

"But, greatest of all, measured by present requirements, is the leader of the House of Representatives, the author of the McKinley Bill, which gave to labor its richest awards. No other name so completely meets the requirements of the occasion, and no other name so absolutely commands all hearts. The shafts of envy and malice and slander and libel and detraction that have been aimed at him lie broken and harmless at his feet. The quiver is empty, and he is untouched. That is because the people know him, trust him, believe in him, love him, and will not permit any human power to disparage him unjustly in their estimation.

"They know that he is an American of Americans. They know that he is just and able and brave, and they want him for President of the United States. [Applause.] They have already shown it—not in this or that State, nor in this or that section, but in the States and in all the sections from ocean to ocean, and from the Gulf to the Lakes. They expect of you to give them a chance to vote for him. It is our duty to do it. If we discharge that duty we will give joy to their hearts, enthusiasm to their souls and triumphant victory to our cause. [Applause.] And he, in turn,

PRESIDENT McKINLEY CROSSING THE MOUNTAINS TO CONGRESS GOLD MINES.

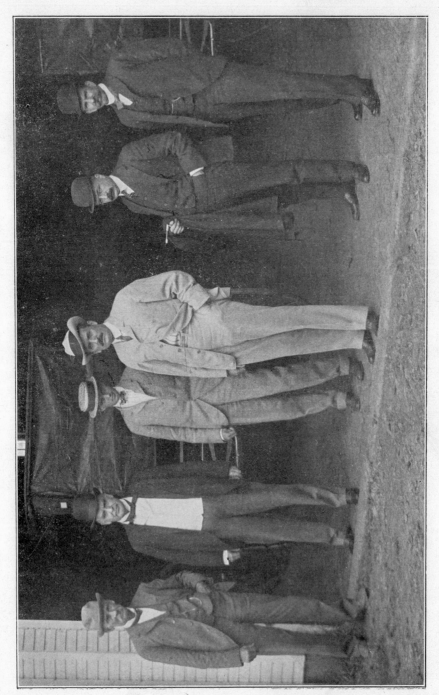

PRESIDENT McKINLEY ON HIS FARM

Shows also his manager, Jack Adams

will give us an administration under which the country will enter on a new era of prosperity at home and of glory and honor abroad, by all these tokens of the present and all these promises of the future. In the name of the forty-six delegates of Ohio, I submit his claim to your consideration." [More applause.]

Senator Thurston seconded the nomination, in an address of considerable length and great eloquence, in which he stated succintly what McKinley stood for, eulogizing his position on finance and protection, and concluding :

" On behalf of those stalwart workmen, and all the vast army of American toilers ; that their employment may be certain, their wages just, their dollars the best in the civilized world ; on behalf of that dismantled chimney, and the deserted factory at its base ; that the furnaces may once more flame, the mighty wheels revolve, the whistles scream, the anvils ring, the spindles hum ; on behalf of the thousand cottages round about, and all the humble homes of this broad land ; that comfort and contentment may again abide, the firesides glow, the women sing, the children laugh ; yes, and on behalf of that American flag, and all it stands for and represents ; for the honor of every stripe, for the glory of every star ; that its power may fill the earth and its splendor span the sky, I ask the nomination of that loyal American, that Christian gentleman, soldier, statesman, patriot, William McKinley."

THE BALLOTING

In the midst of cries of "vote," Governor Hastings, of Pennsylvania, placed in nomination Matthew Stanley Quay, at the conclusion of which, amid a profound hush, the convention began balloting for a nominee for President of the United States.

Alabama led off with 1 for Morton and 19 for McKinley, Arkansas and California following with a solid vote for McKinley. Connecticut gave 5 for Reed and 7 for McKinley ; Delaware, its full vote for McKinley ; Florida, 8 for McKinley ; Georgia, 2 for Quay, and 22 for McKinley.

At this point one of the colored delegates from Florida challenged the vote of his State, and, on a recount, 2 of the votes went to Morton and 6 to McKinley. The vote of Georgia was also challenged, but the vote as announced was confirmed. Then a colored delegate from Alabama demanded a recount of his State, with the result that Morton received 1 vote, Reed 2, and McKinley 19.

Illinois gave 46 for McKinley, and 2 to Reed; Indiana all of its 30 votes for McKinley, while Iowa cast her 26 for Allison; Kansas, 20 for McKinley; Kentucky, 26 for McKinley. The vote of Louisiana was curious—11 for McKinley, 4 for Reed, half a vote for Allison and half a vote for Quay.

So the vote progressed, with the McKinley column steadily growing, Massachusetts casting 1 of her votes for him. New York cast 54 for Morton and 17 for McKinley. It was a curious fact that when Ohio was reached, her vote gave her candidate the requisite number to secure his nomination, recognizing which, the convention broke into cheers.

MCKINLEY NOMINATED

When all of the States had been called, the chairman stated, before the announcement of the result, that application had been made to him for recognition by delegates of the defeated candidates to make a certain motion. He thought it the fairest way to recognize them in the order in which the nominations had been made. He then announced that William McKinley had received 661½ votes.

Before the chairman could get any further, the enthusiasm of the convention broke all bounds. Every man was on his feet, shouting, hurrahing, cheering, swinging hats and canes in the air, waving flags and banners and the pampas plumes of California, while through the Niagara-like rush and roar were caught the notes of "My Country, 'tis of Thee," as the band played with might and main in its attempt to gain the mastery of the cyclone. The women were, if possible, more frantic than the men. Parasols, fans, opera-glasses, gloves—anything, everything—were compelled to help in the magnificent burst of enthusiasm which swept over and submerged all alike, until it looked as if order could never again be evolved from the swirling pandemonium.

One fancy caught on with wonderful effect. A young man on the platform waved on the point of the national banner a laced cocked hat, such as appears in most of popular representations of the mighty Napoleon. This symbol of enthusiasm was greeted with rapturous applause, to which the booming of artillery on the outside contributed.

Finally, after a long, long time, the Chairman gained a chance to complete the announcement of the vote. It was : Thomas B. Reed, 84½ ; Senator Quay, 61½ ; Levi P. Morton, 58 ; Senator Allison, 35½, and Don Cameron 1.

Senator Lodge, rising in his delegation, in a forceful speech moved to make the nomination of Mr. McKinley unanimous. Mr. Hastings of Pennsylvania who had nominated Quay, seconded the motion, as did Thomas C. Platt on behalf of New York, Mr. Henderson, of Iowa, and J. Modison Vance, of Louisiana. In answer to loud calls Mr. Depew mounted his chair in the back of the room, where the rays of the sun beamed on his countenance, which itself was beaming with good humor and said :

MR. DEPEW SPEAKS OF MCKINLEY

"I am in the happy position now of making a speech for the man who is going to be elected. [Laughter and applause.] It is a great thing for an amateur, when his first nomination has failed, to come in and second the man who succeeded. New York is here, without bitter feeling and no disappointment. We recognize that the waves have submerged us, but we have bobbed up serenely. [Loud laughter.] It was a cannon from New York that sounded first the news of McKinley's nomination. They said of Governor Morton's father that he was a New England clergyman who brought up a family of ten children on $300 a year, and was, notwithstanding, gifted in prayer. [Laughter.] It does not make any difference how poor he may be, how out of work, how ragged, how next door to a tramp anybody may be in the United States to-night, he will be 'gifted in prayer' at the result of this convention. [Cheers and laughter.] There is a principle dear to the American heart. It is the principle which moves American spindles, starts its industries, and makes the wage-earners sought for instead of seeking employment. That principle is embodied in McKinley. His personality explains the nomination to-day. And his personality will carry into the Presidential Chair the aspirations of the voters of America, of the families of America, of the homes of America, protection to American industry, and America for Americans." [Cheers.]

The Chair then put the question: "Shall the nomination be made unanimous?" and by a rising vote it was so ordered, and the Chair announced that Mr. William McKinley, of Ohio, was the candidate of the Republican party for President of the United States.

The convention ended its work with the nomination of a candidate for Vice-President. A considerable number of names having been voted for, Garret A. Hobart, of New Jersey, received the nomination by a large majority of the whole.

During the sessions of the convention McKinley remained quietly at home in the pleasant little city of Canton, 600 miles away. Yet such had been the advance of science within the closing years of the century, that he was enabled to hear what was going on in the convention almost as well as if he had occupied one of its seats. The telephone faithfully reported to him all the essential facts that took place, and the whirlwind of shouts and cheers with which his name was greeted came to his ears over that interval of more than half-a-thousand miles.

On that eventful Thursday, in which the work was completed, Mrs. McKinley was in the parlor, surrounded by relatives and near friends, including the Major's mother, when the husband in his office caught the words as they were uttered in the Auditorium at St. Louis, "Ohio, McKinley." Without speaking he arose from his chair, hurried across the hall to his wife and bending over, kissed her with the words: "Ida, Ohio's vote has just nominated me."

THE DEMOCRATIC CONVENTION

The Democratic Party held its Seventeenth Convention in Chicago, commencing July 17th. The delegates were from the start, like the Republicans, divided into two factions; but with them the free coinage element predominated. The Committee on Platform reported in favor of independent bi-metallism. Senator Hill, of New York, backed by sixteen other members of the committee, presented a minority report practically recommending the Republican position on the coinage question, and suggesting the endorsement of President Cleveland's administration. The most stormy and exciting debate, perhaps, ever witnessed in a national party convention ensued. Governor Russell, of Massachusetts, Senator Vilas and others supported Mr. Hill. Senator Tillman introduced a denunciatory resolution condemning the administration, and made a fiery speech, causing intense commotion. Senator Jones, of Arkansas, attempted to palliate Mr. Tillman's radical utterances, but the temper of the convention was at the boiling point, and excited men moved about among the delegations.

At this juncture the man for the hour appeared. William Jennings Bryan, of Nebraska, a young man of thirty-six years, who had won distinction as an orator, ascended the platform. The conditions which Webster declared necessary for a great oration— "the man, the audience, the occasion"—were present. The speech he delivered has been regarded as a masterpiece. The burning eloquence, earnestness, zeal and magnetic presence of the man were irresistible. When he closed he was borne from the stage amid the wildest enthusiasm. The report of the minority was laid on the table. Senator Tillman's resolution was also defeated.

11

The platform as reported by the majority was adopted. The financial clause read : " We demand the free and unlimited coinage of both silver and gold at the present legal ratio of 16 to 1, without waiting for the aid or consent of any other nation." They also declared against injunction proceedings on the part of the Government in settling labor troubles, as interfering with State sovereignty. This clause was no doubt instigated by a disapproval of President Cleveland's course in quelling the Chicago riot in 1894. Other radical departures from previous Democratic platforms were also introduced.

Prior to this speech Mr. Bryan had not been considered as a presidential possibility; but from that moment he became the most popular candidate. Five ballots were cast duly complimenting such "silver" leaders as Hon. Richard P. Bland, of Missouri, Horace Boies, of Iowa, and others, but resulting in the nomination of Mr. Bryan by a vote of 528 out of 930. Arthur Sewall, of Maine, was nominated for Vice-President.

Such were the results of the national conventions of the two leading parties. But the 1896 campaign was remarkable in the fact of the large number of parties in the field, seven in all.

In the lively contest that followed Mr. Bryan threw all his energy into the canvass and displayed wonderful industry and vigor. He made whirlwind tours through the country, speaking several times a day and in the evening, and won many converts. Mr. McKinley made no speech-making tours, being quite willing to let his record speak for him. But he was obliged to speak many times to the crowds who called upon him at his home in Canton, Ohio. The official vote in November was as follows :

McKinley and Hobart, Republican, 7,101,401 popular votes; 271 electoral votes.

Bryan and Sewall, Democrat and Populist, 6,470,656 popular votes ; 176 electoral votes.

Thus William McKinley was elected President of the United States by the decisive majority of ninety-five electoral votes.

CHAPTER XII

Estimate of McKinley's First Term

ON the 4th of March, 1897, William McKinley assumed the duties of the exalted office of President of the United States. It was a time of marked industrial depression. Business and commerce were lagging, and large numbers of people throughout the country were seeking employment. The platform upon which he had been elected declared for a change in our tariff laws which would recognize more fully the protective principle, and for the enactment of a law which would firmly establish gold as the monetary standard of the nation. The new president, without hesitation, assembled Congress in extraordinary session, and addressed to it a message urging a revision of the existing tariff laws, under which business was suffering, while a deficiency in revenue was endangering the nation's credit and the stability of its currency. This prompt action in convening Congress, and the resultant passage of the Dingley law, unquestionably hastened the return of national prosperity.

Under that law revenues revived, and with stable tariff conditions assured, the industries of the country slowly recovered from their depression. The intimate relations existing under the old financial laws between adequate revenues and the credit of governmental currency soon led to a restoration of public confidence; and even before the passage of the gold-standard law, gold was freely offered at the Treasury in exchange for greenbacks.

CURRENCY REFORM

The deficiency in revenues under the Wilson law, and the commercial panic of 1893, with the ensuing business depression, had exposed the inherent weakness of our currency system. This weakness resulted from a disproportion between the demand currency liabilities of the Government and the gold in the Treasury to redeem them; while the awkward fact existed that after these currency liabilities had been redeemed in gold they could again be paid out for expenses, thus enabling the public to present them again for redemption, causing what was commonly known as the "endless chain."

After the success of the Republican party upon its platform of sound money, in a campaign in which this weakness formed one of the chief subjects of discussion, several plans of currency and banking reform were presented to the public and discussed generally in the press. It is highly creditable to the President's discernment and breadth of view that he avoided complicated recommendations, confining himself to urging the enactment of a provision which would remedy the weakness of our financial system without involving the business of the country in the dangers incident to radical legislative experiments with currency laws.

His recommendation, made in his first annual message and repeated in his second, went to the very gist of the trouble; and it is the corner-stone of the financial law which Congress passed at its session in March, 1900.

In his first annual message to Congress, the President said:

" I earnestly recommend, as soon as the receipts of the Government are quite sufficient to pay all the expenses of the Government, that when any of the United States notes are presented for redemption in gold and are redeemed in gold, such notes shall be kept and set apart and only paid out in exchange for gold."

In his second annual message to Congress, after renewing his recommendation of the year before, he said:

" In my judgment the condition of the Treasury amply justifies the immediate enactment of the legislation recommended one year ago, under which a portion of the gold holdings shall be placed in a trust fund from which greenbacks should be redeemed

HOME OF PRESIDENT McKINLEY AT CANTON

REPORTER'S AT THE LINE WAITING NEWS

GEN. FITZHUGH LEE

U.S. BATTLESHIP MAINE.

FROM ALBERTYPE CO.
PROVIDENCE, R.I.

OFFICERS OF THE MAINE.

CAPT. SIGSBEE

This magnificent second-class battleship was blown up in Havana Harbor, February 15, 1898 and 266 American sailors lost their lives through the explosion. The vessel believed that the ship was destroyed through Spanish treachery; and this sentiment did much to upon presentation, but when once redeemed should not thereafter be paid out except for gold."

To the President's plain and simple presentation of a fundamental remedy, and his avoidance of the recommendation of extensive and experimental plans, the people of the country largely owe the present stable and safe condition of our entire financial system.

THE ANNEXATION OF HAWAII

Almost as if foreseeing by intuition the necessity for the annexation of Hawaii, as later revealed by the tremendous events of the following years, the President early in his administration recommended to Congress the annexation of those islands, the movement towards which had been decisively checked by the preceding President. The importance of this step, both from the standpoint of the best interests of the islanders and of our own people, now seen so clearly by all, was not then so apparent; and, but for the earnest and aggressive attitude of the President, annexation would have failed. During the pendency of the Hawaiian question, speaking of the islands, he said to a visitor: "We need Hawaii just as much as, and a good deal more than, we did California." The annexation of these beautiful islands was the first step in the new and broader life upon which this republic has entered, and from which neither duty nor self-interest will allow it to turn back.

THE MERIT SYSTEM

The delicate problem of such a revision of the merit system of civil service as would remove therefrom the dangers to its permanence, arising from too rigid application of theory, was for many months a subject of the most serious consideration by the President and the members of his cabinet, and the operation of the amendments finally adopted is daily proving their wisdom.

The country sees the rise and disposition of questions of great moment to its welfare, but, from want of knowledge of details, gives little heed to the daily round of a President's labors, including the constant direction of affairs of state, the consideration of appointments, the handling of such matters as the Pacific Railroad's indebtedness, domestic difficulties requiring federal intervention, the approval of the countless minor acts of Congress, and a multitude of other duties. As evidence of President McKinley's tact may be cited his policy in regard to the vetoing of bills which came before him for action. The statement has frequently been made that he never vetoed bills, implying either that he gave them but slight examination or left it for others to do for him. Probably no incumbent of the executive office gave more thorough examination and careful thought to every document to which he appended his signature. But the object of the veto was compassed in many instances by sending for the authors of the objectionable bills and pointing out to them their evident inaccuracies or inconsistencies. The result was usually a request from Congress for the return of the bill. Where the case was meritorious, a new bill, without the objections of the old one, was passed and approved by the President. This in no way abridged the prerogative of the executive ; but it expedited legislation, and tended to maintain cordial relations.

THE DISAPPEARANCE OF SECTIONALISM

For the complete obliteration of sectional lines, of the spirit of exultation and intolerance on the one side, defiance and intolerance on the other, the United States is deeply indebted to President McKinley. The influence of his example, the power of his position, and all the force of his ability were constantly given to this end ; and his gratification at the fulfillment of so noble an inspiration found voice at Atlanta in words deserving of perpetuation—"Reunited—one country again and one country forever! Proclaim it from the press and pulpit ; teach it in the schools ; write it across the skies ! The world sees and feels it ; it cheers every heart North and South, and brightens the life of every American home ! Let nothing ever strain it again ! At peace with all the world and with each other, what can stand in the pathway of our progress and prosperity?"

Upon the field of Antietam the President later spoke upon this subject, and said: " Standing here to-day, one reflection only has crowded my mind—the difference between this scene and that of thirty-eight years ago. Then the men who wore the blue and the men who wore the gray greeted each other with shot and shell, and visited death upon their respective ranks. We meet, after all these intervening years, with but one sentiment—that of loyalty to the Government of the United States, love of our flag and our free institutions, and determined, men of the North and men of the South, to make any sacrifice for the honor and perpetuity of the American nation."

THE SPANISH-AMERICAN WAR

Mr. Cleveland had realized, during his second administration, the gravity of the Cuban problem, but had been obliged to hand it over unsolved to his successor; and on March 4, 1897, William McKinley assumed it, with results now known to the world.

The successive steps in the war that followed have been told in many forms, and from various points of view. But there is one story of this war that has not yet been written, and can even now be but imperfectly outlined—that of the sagacious, far-seeing man who, though kindly and sympathetic in all the relations of life, was ever inflexible of purpose for the recognition of the righteous principles which should control our conduct throughout the struggle, and masterful in the vigor and celerity with which he organized and directed the land and naval forces of the United States. And when the defeated and humiliated kingdom, recognizing the hopelessness of the strife, sought peace, he was magnanimous and merciful.

In the dark days preceding the opening of hostilities, amid increasing excitement, the importunities of well-wishing friends and advisers, and the abuse of the sensational press, the President of the United States never swerved from the line of duty he had marked out for himself and the Republiche had sworn faithfully to serve. His long legislative experience, his knowledge of men and events, had taught him that often many of the people form hasty opinions, at variance with the greater knowledge and wider sources of information available to those in high executive authority. But the provocation was great. The feelings of our people were outraged by scenes enacted in the island near our shores, and by the continuance of the unhappy conditions which from time to time appeared there, culminating in merciless proclamations and degrading requirements that shocked the moral sense of this nation. From all sections came the imperious demand that a stop must be put to these things, and that no longer should there be tolerated upon the American Continent a condition so menacing to our tranquility and security.

THE PRESIDENT AS HARMONIZER

The President knew that to interfere meant war. He had faith in the people, and believed that with a fuller knowledge of the facts on their part, and with still greater endeavor upon the part of the United States, the authorities in Madrid would yet find a way to meet the requirements of civilization and evade the horrible alternative of hositilities.

The war with Spain he sought by every honorable means to avert, steadfastly adhering to his conception of the American ideal— peace with honor, war rather than dishonor; justice to other nations, loyalty to his own. Foreseeing the conflict, he foresaw its certain and many of its possible evils. The one class could not be escaped; to the avoidance of the other he gave his full energy and intelligence. That we entered upon the war so well prepared, so little hampered by mortgages on the future, and so generally united in purpose, was the result of long weeks of self-sacrificing, patriotic, devoted labor on the part of the dominant men among those entrusted at the time with our national fortunes—a labor in which the President led, and gave the best that was in him.

During those trying days, when the war fever was constantly and rapidly increasing, there were frequent illustrations of the truth of a statement made by one of his associates in public life that " McKinley was one of the greatest harmonizers America had ever known." Daily and nightly consultations were had at the White House between the President and little groups of Senators and Representatives whom he invited to be present ; these meetings were utterly non-partisan in character, composed of Republican rivals and Republican followers, and of "Silver" as well as "Gold" Democrats. The requests to attend the conferences were invariably acceded to with respect and cordiality ; and the results which followed so broad-minded a course were of incalculable value in the preparation for and conduct of the war.

Does anyone believe that with a less conciliatory policy, with less of the courteous considerateness that characterized the intercourse of the President with the Congress and prominent officials throughout the country, the marvelous results would have been achieved as quickly and as completely as they were ?

RESPONSIBILITY OF THE EXECUTIVE

In this time of great national excitement, a responsibility was suddenly imposed upon the President of an intensity unknown since the days of Lincoln. That he then realized that war was inevitable cannot be doubted, and under his direction the War and Navy Departments were straining every resource in preparation for the coming conflict.

The general feeling of indignation ran high, and the halls of Congress rang with the demands and denunciations of the impatient ones who ascribed to the man upon whose shoulders the terrible burden of decision rested unworthy and unpatriotic motives for his refusal to take thoughtless, hasty, and half-considered steps. It was at this time that the President, from a sense of duty, took his position against the recognition on the part of this Government of the so-called Cuban republic. He had superior sources of knowledge

of the actual conditions existing in the island, and fully comprehending the fact that this recognition would have placed the
officers of our army who might enter Cuba under the command of
Cuban generals, and that there existed no form of government
among the insurgents such as could be properly recognized under
international law, knew that such recognition would be fraught with
the gravest consequences.   Under the conditions which existed in
the island, a recognition of the so-called republic meant helpless
confusion and conflict, and humiliation in event of war.   A false
step then would have been irremediable.

During the time the President was preparing his message to
Congress he was called upon personally by the great majority of
members of both houses, and the executive mansion was thronged
each day with excited men protesting against anything short of
complete recognition of the Cuban republic.   He stated his reasons
calmly and firmly to the people who called by hundreds to demand
that his position be altered, decisively declining to recognize
the so-called republic, and by so doing involve the United States in
all the political and diplomatic difficulties to which such a recognition would have led.

A PATRIOT IN THE WHITE HOUSE

His political leadership hung in the balance, and every argument of expediency which political ingenuity could devise was
urged upon him.   But he was adamant; and to the aid of that
position which he knew to be right he called every legitimate
resource of his great power as chief executive, and every proper
resource of his power as an individual.

Our present calm retrospect makes the course of William
McKinley at this juncture seem one of courageous patriotism.
We recall the violent denunciation, the scathing contumely, heaped
upon him for his refusal to take the precipitate action which was
widely demanded; the deliberate manner in which he directed an
investigation of the *Maine* explosion, awaited the report and

communicated its substance to the Spanish Government. With wisdom gained by the lapse of time, we review the turbulent scenes in Congress, and remember the outcry then so much in accord with our own feelings. We see the President stubbornly battling against the hasty indignation of the moment, because he felt that the time was not ripe for war, yet quietly and skillfully preparing to meet the crisis when it should come ; and we see him not long after the recipient of a verdict of popular approval nearly as enthusiastic and quite as general as the denunciation of a few months before.

When in his message to Congress of April 11, 1898, he uttered the words, "In the name of humanity, in the name of civilization, in behalf of endangered American interest, which gives us the right and the duty to speak and to act, the war in Cuba must stop," he realized the expectations of those who had followed his career through all its activities, and those who had prophesied for him a weak and un-American administration saw how erroneous had been their estimate of the man.

Every effort put forth by the President and his Cabinet having failed, and the gage of battle having been accepted in obedience to the dictates of humanity and civilization, and in accordance with the authority given the Executive by Congress, the people learned that they had placed in the White House one who was Commander-in-Chief in fact as well as in name—a man of iron will in the prosecution of his country's battles and in the exaction of honor and respect for its flag.

THE TRYING POSITION OF THE PRESIDENT

The burdens of the executive office during those weeks, and at the time when by message the Congress was made to share them, were more severe than have been placed upon any President since the Civil War. Out of the rancor and excitement the nation emerged prepared for conflict ; partisan feeling was hushed in the presence of a great emergency, a vast sum was appropriated for national defense, and, with a unanimity not paralleled in our history, its expenditure was entrusted to the President of the United States. The discordant notes of sensationalism died away; the tread of volunteers responding to the call to arms drowned the ill-natured comments of fault-finders, and carried messages of cheer and encouragement to the White House.

President McKinley rarely left his office until 1 or 2 o'clock at night; frequently he was there until a much later hour. He personally supervised the details of preparation. He gathered from his Cabinet advisers the latest information upon vital points of equipment. His orders for instant and thorough preparation and ceaseless vigilance reached the utmost limits of our national authority. The suggestions and criticisms that came to him from all parts of the country would fill volumes. The incessant stream of callers, always great, became larger, and every hour was filled with vast responsibilities.

IN THE WAR ROOM

The war came on; the President led in its prosecution. He was constantly in direct telegraphic communication with the front, and the "war room" adjoining his office in the executive mansion, was his first resort in the morning and his last at night. Maps, elaborate in detail, covered the walls of the room; and by means of tiny flags, with pins for sticks, the positions and changes of position of the ships and land forces of both sides were always before his eyes.

Frequent Cabinet meetings and less formal conferences with his immediate advisers, the formulation and consideration of plans, the organization and movement of the army, the extension of the navy and its manipulation—these and many kindred duties engaged his time.

And when the struggle was over, how prompt was his recognition of the loyalty, bravery, and self-sacrifice of our soldiers, our sailors, and our marines! And how ready he was to accord all

CHARLES EMORY SMITH.
POSTMASTER-GENERAL.

HENRY CABOT LODGE.
SENATOR FROM MASSACHUSETTS.

LYMAN J. GAGE,
Sec'y of the Treasury

JAS. WILSON,
Sec'y of Agriculture.

C. N. BLISS,
Sec'y of the Interior.

Copyrighted
by
C. M. Bell
1898.

PRESIDENT McKINLEY AND THE WAR CABINET

PRESIDENT McKINLEY

JOHN W. GRIGGS,

JOHN D. LONG,

WM. R. DAY,
Sec'y of State

RUSSELL A. ALGER,
Sec'y of War

CHAS. EMORY SMITH,
Postmaster-General

praise to the defenders of the national honor in the Philippines, whose duty was nobly done, and who came to feel that their Commander-in-Chief at Washington was never so busy as to overlook merit or so exacting as to ignore their personality.

With the cessation of hostilities came the problems of peace. The Peace Conference at Paris felt the guiding hand and far-seeing Americanism of the President at every stage of its proceedings. With no uncharitableness, he yet insisted upon those things which were the nation's right, and which the verdict of the future will establish as incalculable blessings, not only to our own people, but to the distant peoples who have come under our authority and within the beneficent influence of our free institutions.

MCKINLEY AND THE PHILIPPINES

Among the opponents of the President's course in the Philippines, none has yet expressed a wish that the battle of Manila Bay had not been fought. In the President's view, the acquisition of the Philippines was the only result of that battle consistent with the American ideal of duty, and with characteristic strength he did his share in its accomplishment. Some of those who thought the battle could be fought without consequences, while applauding the victory, decried the outcome; but he steadfastly pursued the purpose he believed to be right.

No Administration of recent years has dealt with such grave questions as confronted that of McKinley. The problems which were crowded into any one of its years would have made or unmade the fortunes of any Administration. But during these busy years the country took note of things done, of promises fulfilled, of good faith and fair-dealing. In the excitement of debate, in the fancied necessities of political strategy, it is easy to state fallacies and natural to exaggerate evils. To the opponents of the President and his Administration, the conduct of the War with Spain appeared open to severe criticism; to the impartial student of history, it was a record of marvelous preparation and execution. To those opposed to the results secured by the Administration in the fields of finance, they presaged an unstable currency and disaster to both capital and labor.   To the practical, hard-headed, far-sighted business man, who knows confidence to be the bulwark of the financial world, the strengthening of the gold standard, and the enactment into law of the platform promises of the Republican party meant the permanence of public credit, the assurance of increased employ-ment for labor, and the advancement of the country in its material interests. To many of the opponents of the Administration, new possessions meant a weakening of tradition and a departure from right principle.   To its adherents, who believed they read aright the nation's destiny in the light of what had come from former expansion, they meant the quickening of national spirit, the exten-sion of free institutions among peoples who have hitherto striven in darkness and doubt, the steady advancement of the Republic in its mission of liberty and enlightenment.

MCKINLEY A TYPICAL AMERICAN

A great political leader is almost necessarily a type of the nation he leads—the embodiment of the characteristics of his time—the manifest product of the circumstances and conditions of the people he governs and directs.   This is more especially true in the critical period of a nation's history.   When a people are pro-foundly absorbed in events—when it is necessary for them to come to conclusions upon vital matters—the man who most nearly repre-sents them in character, rearing, and environment, as well as in thought, is most likely to reach a position of commanding power.

Washington embodied, as did no other of the Revolutionary heroes, the virtues and the limitations of the colonial community to whom fell the task of maintaining for Americans their rights and of constructing a new nation.   Lincoln was the type of the fron-tiersman—the American engaged in conquering the wilderness— of the democracy which spread over the continent from east to west, carrying the idea of God and an eternal Justice, and which struggled too hard for its own life and happiness to be willing that any others should be denied them.

William McKinley was just as much the inevitable product of his time as these two great predecessors in the Presidency. His origin, his profession, his career, his manners, his methods, his own personality, and all his achievements, evidenced this.

The end of the Civil War marked a sharp change in American life. New national activities, new currents of public thought, new conditions, tended to create a new type of political leader. President McKinley's unquestioned leadership in economic and financial policies was followed by as complete and successful leadership in international and diplomatic questions. Many of those who differed from him most widely did not question that he dealt with the gravest international matters—those involving the very future of the nation—masterfully, courageously, and consistently. Through the confused conflicts of our political life, the jealousies of eager competition in Congress, the hurly-burly of conventions, along a rough path full of pitfalls, over the obstacles of temporary failure, of inevitable misunderstandings of his purposes and underratings of his abilities, in spite of the alternations of party success, a fit man survived, and was the President of this nation at a time fraught with grave consequences for the future.

MCKINLEY'S PERSONAL CHARACTERISTICS

The impression of William McKinley which a casual caller at the White House received was that of a sincere, patient, and kindly man of great natural dignity and tact. In his personal contact with others, he was generous of his time in the extreme, and listened to the stories of the unfortunate and complaining with a patience which surprised his associates, when he himself was bearing well-nigh crushing burdens of administrative responsibility. He was naturally sympathetic, obliging, and self-sacrificing. Yet all this reflects but one side of his character, although it was the side which most impressed those who met him but casually.

His most predominant characteristics, which bound great bodies of men to him with rivets of steel, which lifted him from the position of a private soldier to that of Chief Magistrate of the nation, which sustained him and carried him through the many great crises confronting him, and gave him the trust and confidence of the American people—were his moral strength and his unflinching courage to do the right as he saw it, irrespective of temporary consequences. His natural gentleness and his tendency to ignore small and non-essential differences, his willingness to oblige even his enemies, and his utter lack of vindictiveness,—all these, when the times of crisis came and the eyes of the people were turned to him alone, gave him added strength to achieve great results in public affairs. At such times he found that behind him was a multitude of men who believed in the sincerity of his purpose and his unselfishness, and were willing to trust his judgment. These characteristics of moral strength and courage were constantly apparent to those whose connection with the administration of national affairs gives them intimate knowledge of the true relation of the President to public questions. They were manifest to the people of the United States whenever great issues placed responsibility upon him.

THE FAME OF PRESIDENTS

In a country whose social and political systems offer a wide range of opportunity to the individual, some of the greatest possibilities for development and for fame are open to him who has seemingly reached the end of American ambition by attaining to the Chief Magistracy of the nation. The fame of Presidents has been perpetuated or lost according as they have grasped or failed to grasp the American ideal of nationality. It seems hardly necessary now after the many evidences of this embodied in our history, to assert that this ideal is not always contained in the popular agitation of the day—so often a delusion that by the morrow has vanished from the public mind.

The clear vision to see through an effervescence of feeling to the enduring principle beneath it, and the strength and integrity to act in accordance with such a perception of the real aspirations of the people, make public men great. The absence of these traits accounts for the oblivion into which our prominent statesmen so often pass. Whether the fame of William McKinley shall remain a part of our national glory depends not altogether on the present popular estimate of his deeds, which even his contemporaries accord high rank. Another epoch, another generation, will pronounce the final verdict. A few years ago he was one of a number of popular leaders—an untried President. To-day his place is fixed by that severest of all tests, the faithful performance of high public duties in a series of great crises.

TWO EXTREME TYPES

In personal traits and disposition, Mr. McKinley and his predecessor represented absolute extremes. Mr. Cleveland grew more and more conservative, unapproachable, sensitive and self-conscious as time went on. In his every message, document and public utterance, there was always revealed that somewhat painful sense of his own personal responsibility. The Executive became constantly more hedged in and mysterious. The old public path across the White House grounds was barred up. Extra policemen, unwonted sentries, and undreamed-of contingents of secret service men and detectives were requisitioned to keep the person of the President the better guarded against the intrusion of his fellow-citizens. Mr. Thurber, as private secretary, seemed for four years to be chiefly occupied in mystifying reporters and correspondents as to Mr. Cleveland's comings, and goings, and in excluding callers from his presence—Senators and Representatives being excluded along with the unofficial herd. The process was successful ; for at length the public ceased to intrude, and the callers—including the Senators and Congressmen—kept scrupulously away from the White House.

12

Every President must work out his own method for himself; and all reasonable people are ready to believe that Mr. Cleveland's method, was, in his judgment, the one which enabled him best to do his duty and serve the country. But Mr. McKinley's method was radically different, though fully as natural to the man. An assumed affability for the sake of popularity will not in the end strengthen the hand or hold of any President. But Mr. McKinley's affability seemed a part of his nature; and its indulgence did not apparently exhaust his vitality. Instead of interposing all sorts of obstacles between the public and himself as Mr. Cleveland did, he adopted precisely the opposite plan. Perhaps he reasoned that the great human tide flowing toward the White House must have some eventual metes and bounds, and that the most logical plan would be to remove every barrier in order that the flow might the sooner spend itself. Furthermore, the President gave himself the pleasure and benefit of a long walk through the public streets every afternoon. His face thus became familiar, and the public the sooner learned to understand that in those hours when he was not visible he had a right to deal uninterruptedly with the affairs of state. He had shown that he could systematize his work, keep certain hours for certain duties, assign tasks to his advisers, and make good use of the services of other men.

The general statements given in this chapter regarding President McKinley's personal relations to the Spanish-American War are preliminary to a description of that war itself. This, as the great event of his administration, cannot be omitted from a story of his career, and we shall devote a subsequent chapter to a concise account of this momentous conflict, so far reaching in its results.

CHAPTER XIII

First Year as President

THE inauguration of William McKinley as President of the United States, on March 3, 1897, was the opening of a new and vital era in the political and military history of this country. Important events loomed up which no man even then could foresee, and the seeming calm which lay upon the surface of social and political affairs concealed the germs of a series of storms which were destined, before the close of the term, to change the whole policy and international position of the great republic of the West.

While these great events were hidden in the mists of the future, there were questions of high importance that called for immediate solution. There had been not alone a change of administration, but also a change of party control. A Republican had succeeded a Democratic President, a fact which in itself called for radical changes in the management of affairs. But, added to this, the outgoing administration had left to the incoming one an industrial and financial problem strongly calling for solution. The effects of the panic of 1892 had not yet fully passed away. For more than four years the shadow of ruin had lain upon the land, poverty and misery had visited a myriad households, and when McKinley was elected to the Presidency a widespread commercial and industrial depression still prevailed. For years the wheels of a thousand factories practically ceased to revolve, artisans in great numbers found employment impossible to obtain, commerce was in a state of collapse, the public and national finances were seriously depressed, and in many hearts hope had given place to despair.

This gloomy state of affairs, which had existed in its intensity during the opening years of President Cleveland's second administration, had not fully passed away when the election of McKinley took place, and an unsatisfactory condition of business depression continued when the new President took his seat. The lack of business activity was reflected in the state of the national finances, the receipts of the Treasury having fallen off so greatly that there was not money enough to meet the current expenses of the Government, and the expenditures were growing alarmingly in excess of the receipts.

Naturally various explanations were given of this unfortunate state of affairs. The party in power, in accordance with its basic fiscal policy, attributed the depression to the change in the tariff made by the late administration, and President McKinley was in full sympathy with this view. His name had been long associated with the policy of high tariff, and his natural view of the remedy for the public evil was the restoration, in some degree, of the tariff measures which the Democratic Congress had changed.

CALLS CONGRESS IN SPECIAL SESSION

The necessity of some immediate action to relieve the prevailing distress seemed to the President so great, that he felt it incumbent upon him to call Congress together in extra session at once, that it might deliberate upon this pressing problem and take such action as seemed in its wisdom most advisable and best adapted to relieve the financial stringency. He accordingly called the Houses of Congress into extra session on March 15, 1897, and, on their convening, had read before them the following message:

" *To the Congress of the United States:*
" Regretting the necessity which has required me to call you together, I feel that your assembling in extraordinary session is indispensable because of the condition in which we find the revenues of the Government.

"It is conceded that its current expenditures are greater than its receipts and that such a condition has existed for now more than three years. With unlimited means at our command, we are presenting the remarkable spectacle of increasing our public debt by borrowing money to meet the ordinary outlays incident upon even an economical and prudent administration of the Government. An examination of the subject discloses this fact in every detail, and leads inevitably to the conclusion that the condition of the revenue which allows it is unjustifiable and should be corrected.

"We find by the reports of the Secretary of the Treasury that the revenues for the fiscal year ending June 30, 1892, from all sources were $425,868,260.22, and the expenditures for all purposes were $415,953,806.56, leaving an excess of receipts over expenditures of $9,914,453.66. During that fiscal year $40,570,467.98 were paid upon the public debt, which had been reduced since March 1, 1889, $259,076,890, and the annual interest charge decreased $11,684,576.60. The receipts of the Government from all sources during the fiscal year ending June 30, 1893, amounted to $461,716,661.94, and its expenditures to $459,374,887.65, showing an excess of receipts over expenditures of $2,341,674.29.

"Since that time the receipts of no fiscal year, and with but few exceptions, of no month of any fiscal year have exceeded the expenditures. The receipts of the Government from all sources during the fiscal year ending June 30, 1894, were $372,802,498.89, and its expenditures $442,605,758.87, leaving a deficit, the first since the resumption of specie payments, of $69,803,260.58. Notwithstanding there was a decrease of $16,769,128.78 in the ordinary expenses of the Government, as compared with the previous year, its income was still not sufficient to provide for its daily necessities, and the gold reserve in the Treasury for the redemption of greenbacks was drawn upon to meet them. But this did not suffice, and the Government then resorted to loans to replenish the reserve.

"In February, 1894, $50,000,000 in bonds were issued, and in November following a second issue of $50,000,000 was deemed necessary. The sum of $117,171,795 was realized by the sale of these bonds, but the reserve was steadily decreased until, on February 8, 1895, a third sale of $62,315,400 in bonds for $65,116,244 was announced to Congress.

"The receipts of the Government for the fiscal year ending June 30, 1895, were $390,373,203.30, and the expenditures $433,178,426.45, showing a deficit of $42,805,223.19. A further loan of 100,000,000 was negotiated by the Government in February, 1896, the sale netting $111,166,246, and swelling the aggregate of bonds issued within three years to $262,315,400. For the fiscal year ending June 30, 1896, the revenues of the Government from all sources amounted to $409,475,408.78, while its expenditures were $434,678,654.48, or an excess of expenditures over receipts of $25,203,245.70. In other words, the total receipts for the three fiscal years ending June 30, 1896, were insufficient by $137,811,729.46 to meet the total expenditures.

"Nor has this condition since improved. For the first half of the present fiscal year the receipts of the Government, exclusive of postal revenue, were $157,507,603.76, and its expenditures, exclusive of postal service, $195,410,000.22, or an excess of expenditures over receipts of $37,902,396.46. In January of this year the receipts, exclusive of postal revenues, were $24,316,994.05, and the expenditures, exclusive of postal service, $30,269,389.29, a deficit of $5,952,395.24 for the month. In February of this year the receipts, exclusive of postal revenues, were $24,400,997.38, and expenditures, exclusive of postal service, $28,796,056.68, a deficit of $4,395,059.28, or a total deficiency of $186,061,580.44 for the three years and eight months ending March 1, 1897. Not only are we without a surplus in the Treasury, but with an increase in public debt there has been a corresponding increase in the annual interest charge from $22,893,883.20 in 1892, the lowest of any year since 1862, to $34,387,297.60 in 1896, or an increase of $11,493,414.40.

"It may be urged that, even if the revenues of the Government had been sufficient to meet all its ordinary expenses during the past three years, the gold reserve would still have been insufficient to meet the demands upon it, and that bonds would necessarily have been issued for its repletion. Be this as it may, it is clearly manifest, without denying or affirming the correctness of such a conclusion, that the debt would have been decreased in at least the amount of the deficiency, and business confidence immeasurably strengthened throughout the country.

"Congress should promptly correct the existing condition. Ample revenues must be supplied, not only for the ordinary expenses of the Government, but for the prompt payment of liberal pensions and the liquidation of the principal and interest of the public debt. In raising revenue, duties should be so levied upon foreign products as to preserve the home market, so far as possible, to our own producers; to revive and increase manufactures; to relieve and encourage agriculture; to increase our domestic and foreign commerce; to aid and develop mining and building, and to render to labor in every field of useful occupation the liberal wages and adequate rewards to which skill and industry are justly entitled. The necessity of the passage of a tariff law which shall provide ample revenue need not be further urged. The imperative demand of the hour is the prompt enactment of such a measure, and to this object I earnestly recommend that Congress shall make every endeavor. Before other business is transacted let us first provide sufficient revenue to faithfully administer the Government without the contracting of further debt or the continued disturbance of our finances.

"WILLIAM McKINLEY.

"EXECUTIVE MANSION, March 15, 1897."

In anticipation of the extra session of the Fifty-fifth Congress, thus called for, the Committee of Ways and Means, or at least Nelson Dingley, its chairman, and his Republican colleagues in that committee, had been steadily working upon a new tariff measure.

They had allowed various interests to appear before the committee at public hearings, and had worked industriously in private sessions. The new bill was ready for presentation to the House as soon as it was convened.

This method, evidently, had saved a great deal of time. Four months had elapsed since Mr. McKinley's election, and there had been abundant opportunity for consultation with him upon the main features of the new tariff bill. It was obviously desirable that the new measure should provide fifty or sixty million dollars a year more than the Wilson-Gorman tariff then in force. It was also deemed desirable that the reciprocity features of the McKinley tariff of 1890—which had begun to operate so advantageously, and which were so ruthlessly abandoned by the Wilson Bill,—should, so far as possible, be revived.

DISPLAY OF PARTY ANTAGONISM

The abrogation of those features was not merely a matter of domestic policy. It seemed, indeed, a rather ill-mannered and wholly unnecessary breach of essential good faith toward the countries which had entered into treaty relations with us in pursuance of the reciprocity plan. Those nations had to a greater or less extent re-adjusted their domestic revenue laws and arrangements to meet the results of the reciprocity treaties; and the manner in which the policy was abandoned by this country seemed a cheap display of mere party antagonism.

The revenue measure here adverted to, which subsequently became known as the Dingley Tariff, in many respects reversed the so-called "reform tariff" of the Cleveland Administration, and restored the McKinley Tariff, in spirit, if not in fact. Of course, the lapse of years, and the growing expansion of American commercial interests, rendered necessary provisions adapted to the new conditions, among them being a considerable extension of the free list. But the features of this tariff bill, which became law on July 24, 1897, were in close accordance with Mr. McKinley's views on the subject, as calculated to advance the purpose he had in view in calling Congress in extra session, "to provide revenue for the Government and encourage the industries of the United States. The Reciprocity measure, a feature of the tariff of 1890, which had been abrogated in the Wilson Tariff, was restored. In view of the fact that President McKinley, in his last speech, advocated the "encouragement and extension of this feature of our commercial policy," we append the legislation concerning it in the Dingley tariff:

RECIPROCITY SECTION OF THE TARIFF ACT OF 1897

"That whenever the President of the United States, by and with the advice and consent of the Senate, with a view to secure reciprocal trade with foreign countries, shall, within the period of two years from and after the passage of this act, enter into commercial treaty or treaties with any other country or countries concerning the admission into any such country or countries of the goods, wares and merchandise of the United States and their use and disposition therein, deemed to be for the interests of the United States, and in such treaty or treaties, in consideration of the advantages accruing to the United States therefrom, shall provide for the reduction during a specified period, not exceeding five years, of the duties imposed by this act, to the extent of not more than twenty per centum thereof, upon such goods, wares, or merchandise as may be designated therein of the country or countries with which such treaty or treaties shall be made, as in this section provided for; or shall provide for the transfer during such period from the dutiable list of this act to the free list thereof of such goods, wares, and merchandise, being the natural products of such foreign country or countries, and not of the United States; or shall provide for the retention upon the free list of this act during a specified period, not exceeding five years, of such goods, wares, and merchandise now included in said free list, as may be designated therein; and when any such treaty shall have been ratified by the Senate and approved by Congress, and public proclamation made

accordingly, then and thereafter the duties which shall be collected
by the United States upon any of the designated goods, wares, and
merchandise from the foreign country with which such treaty has
been made, shall, during the period provided for, be the duties
specified and provided for in such treaty, and none other.

" That whenever any country, dependency, or colony shall pay or
bestow, directly or indirectly, any bounty or grant upon the expor-
tation of any article or merchandise from such country, dependency,
or colony, and such article or merchandise is dutiable under the
provisions of this act, then upon the importation of any such article
or merchandise into the United States, whether the same shall be
imported directly from the country of production or otherwise, and
whether such article or merchandise is imported in the same condition as when exported from the country of production or has been
changed in condition by manufacture or otherwise, there shall be
levied and paid, in all such cases, in addition to the duties otherwise
imposed by this act, an additional duty equal to the net amount of
such bounty or grant, however the same be paid or bestowed. The
net amount of all such bounties or grants shall be from time to
time, ascertained, determined, and declared by the Secretary of the
Treasury, who shall make all needful regulations for the identification of such articles and merchandise and for the assessment and
collection of such additional duties.

" That there shall be levied, collected, and paid on the importation of all raw or unmanufactured articles, not enumerated or
provided for in this act, a duty of ten per cent. ad valorem, and on
all articles manufactured, in whole or in part, not provided for in
this act, a duty of twenty per cent. ad valorem."

It is here in place to take a brief glance into the future of the
fiscal measure whose legislative history we have just briefly given.
President McKinley had two objects in view in suggesting it and
convening Congress in extra session for its consideration. One of
these was the endeavor to place the national finances in a more
healthy condition than they had been in during the past four years,

and especially to bring the receipts info excess of the expenditures. The other was to overcome the business depression which had so long prevailed, to restore commercial and industrial confidence, to furnish orders for the manufacturers of the land and work at living wages for the widely idle mechanics.

BUSINESS DEPRESSION OVERCOME

It need scarcely be said that both these ends were fully, indeed, magnificently gained. This is a matter of history with which all our people are familiar and which very many of them have providently felt. The wearisome, truly hopeless depression which had so long prevailed, showed evident signs of quick amelioration as soon as the tidings of McKinley's triumphant election were received. By the day he took his seat the hopeful signs in the air had grown stronger and brighter. The new tariff proved the Rubicon of the advancing good times. That passed, the indications of a coming industrial "boom" were everywhere to be seen. They grew and expanded, they rose and swelled, until such a wave of prosperity swept over the land as this western world had rarely seen. Never in the history of the world had there been a more marked contrast of bad and good times than between the second Cleveland and the first McKinley administrations. And let what may be said, the fact stands largely self-evident that this wondrous change in conditions was due to the opposed fiscal measures of the two administrations, the Wilson tariff for revenue and the Dingley tariff for protection.

The improvement in conditions was as remarkably manifested in still another way, that of the extraordinary increase in the commerce of the United States, a ratio of growth in commercial prosperity never equalled or approached, in so brief a time, in the commercial history of any other country in the world.

As our export trade augmented with extraordinary rapidity, our import trade correspondingly fell off, the balance of trade in our favor becoming much greater, by the opening year of the new century, than any other nation had ever known during the thousands of years of the world's history. And this striking phenomenon belonged almost solely to the McKinley administration and was mainly, perhaps wholly, due to its commercial and fiscal policy.

The exports of merchandise of the United States for the year ending June 30, 1897, amounted in value to $1,032,007,603. The imports for the same fiscal year to $764,730,412. This left a balance of trade in our favor of $257,877,189. This was a far better showing than in preceding years, and not many years before the balance tended to the other side. If now we consider the returns for the fiscal year ending June 30, 1901, we find the figures to sum up as follows: Exports, $1,487,656,544; imports, $822,756,533; making the balance of trade in our favor, $664,900,011; being more than $400,000,000 over that of 1896-97, and immensely greater than in the history of earlier administrations. Here is an object lesson for the people that needs no words of arguments. It speaks for itself for the results of the policy of the McKinley administration.

HOW PRESIDENT MCKINLEY SELECTED HIS CABINET

An essential duty in the beginning of every new administration is the selection of a Cabinet, the official family of Presidential advisers. President McKinley's long Congressional service and familiar acquaintance with the leading Statesmen and business men of the day fitted him admirably for the duty of selection, and he was ready to announce, in the first days of his administration, an exceptionally strong list of Departmental Secretaries. Names were offered by hundreds, by politicians and party newspapers, for his consideration. Not fewer than two hundred of these were presented to him by men of influence, and probably as many as fifty were carefully weighed in his mind before his final selection was made.

Among the prominent leaders who preferred to retain their seats in Congress to accepting Cabinet positions, were Senator

Allison, Speaker Reed, and Representative Dingley. The last named, then Chairman of the Ways and Means Committee, was offered the position of Secretary of the Treasury, but declined it on the plea that his feeble health would not enable him to stand the strain. Marcus A. Hanna, the President's close friend and political adviser, was also seriously considered. But he did not desire a Cabinet position, preferring a seat in the Senate to the labor of Departmental duties.

HIS SECRETARY OF STATE

For the responsible position of Secretary of State, one name presented itself above all others, that of the veteran and able statesman, Hon. John Sherman, then one of the leading figures in Congress and the country. Mr. Sherman seemed, above all others, to possess the requisite prestige, and he was at length persuaded to accept the Secretaryship of State, it being tacitly understood that Governor Bushnell of Ohio, would appoint Mr. Hanna to Mr. Sherman's vacant place in the Senate.

While more familiar with public finance than with diplomacy and international law, John Sherman had for more than forty years been in the centre of our political life, and in constant touch with our national policy in its every aspect, domestic and foreign alike. The principal doubt raised in the public mind as regarded the wisdom of his appointment to the post, had reference to his great age. It was objected that the duties of the "foreign office" impose an exceptionally heavy burden upon the Secretary personally, and require, therefore, exceptional vigor and physical strength.

But, despite this, it was felt that Mr. Sherman would know how to husband his strength, while the respect with which he was regarded abroad, and his known conservative views and lack of aggressive sentiments in international affairs, were sure to make him a safe and suitable incumbent of the office. His selection met with the cordial approbation of the country, and was very favorably commented on in Europe.

Not less important in the administrative duties of the Government stands the Secretary of the Treasury, the man to whom the vast and complicated financial interests of our country are intrusted, the official who, by an unwise move, may succeed in sending a wave of dismay and distress through the delicately poised financial institutions of our States, and on the other hand, by a judicious and well-considered act, may save the land from panic ; coming to the aid of the community in those critical moments when disaster impends and ruin seems inevitable.

HIS SECRETARY OF THE TREASURY

Before selecting this highly important official, Mr. McKinley long and anxiously surveyed the field, studying the records of the foremost financiers of the country. He finally called from private life a man whose appointment was hailed not merely with approval but with enthusiasm. There was no longer any doubt about the wise control of the finances. The President-elect had not been looking for a popular man, but for one who had the requisite qualifications. And it is not likely that Mr. McKinley suspected how much he was enhancing his own popularity when he offered the Treasury portfolio to Mr. Lyman J. Gage, the Chicago banker.

Mr. Gage had won a national reputation as a banker of exceptionally quick conception and original genius in finance. It was feared, indeed, that his appointment might prove unsatisfactory to the wage-earners and farmers of the country, who distrusted and were prejudiced against bankers and capitalists. But, as it quickly proved, these classes were the ones best pleased.

They knew Mr. Gage as a man of high character, of broad views, of a sincere desire for the welfare of all his fellow-citizens, absolutely devoid of the arts and wiles of the professional politician, and fitted by virtue of great financial knowledge and experience for the work of conducting the national finances.

For Secretary of War was chosen General Russell A. Alger, in every respect a self-made man. He had been, somewhat like

McKinley himself, successively a farmer's son in Ohio, a farm laborer, a school-teacher, a lawyer, and a soldier, in the latter capacity rising from captain to major-general, and having a record of wounds, capture, imprisonment and escape. Subsequently he became an active business man in Michigan, and rose to the possession of great wealth, and to the position of Governor of that State. His record as an active and successful man of affairs, and his long and varied experience as a soldier, seemed to fit him well as a controller of the military affairs of the United States.

HIS OTHER SECRETARIES

The remaining members of the Cabinet were John D. Long, of Massachusetts, Secretary of the Navy; Cornelius N. Bliss, of New York, Secretary of the Interior; James Wilson, of Iowa, Secretary of Agriculture; James A. Gary, of Maryland, Postmaster-General, and Joseph McKenna, of California, Attorney-General. Of these it must serve to speak in general. Mr. Wilson, Mr. Long and Mr. McKenna had been long in State Legislature service and in Congress, while Mr. Long had been one of the most brilliant Governors of his State. Mr. Bliss might more than once have been Governor of New York, had he so desired, and Mr. Gary would have held the same office in Maryland but for its large Democratic majority. We may say further that the Cabinet was one of self-made men, nearly every member of it having been the architect of his own fortune.

As time went on, various changes were made in the *personnel* of the Cabinet, there being one resignation before the end of the year, that of Attorney-General McKenna, who gave up his post on December 17th, to become Associate Justice of the Supreme Court of the United States. He was succeeded by John W. Griggs, of New Jersey, appointed January 21, 1898.

Secretary of State Sherman resigned April 27, 1898, when war with Spain had become certain, being unable to bear the additional burdens of labor which warlike conditions would bring. He was succeeded by W. R. Day, then Assistant Secretary. Secretary Day resigned on September 16th, on account of the responsible duties before him as a member of the commission to arrange terms of peace with Spain, and was succeeded by John Hay, who had been Ambassador to England during the earlier period of the administration. Secretary Day's resignation was made with the understanding that he would be subsequently appointed to a seat on the bench of the United States Court. This has been done, he being appointed Justice of the Northern District of Ohio.

OTHER CHANGES IN THE CABINET

On April 21, 1898, Postmaster-General Gary resigned, and was succeeded by Charles Emory Smith, proprietor and editor of the *Press*, the leading Republican newspaper of Philadelphia. On December 22, 1898, Secretary Bliss retired, and was succeeded by Ethan A. Hitchcock, until then Ambassador to Russia. On August 1, 1899, Russell A. Alger retired from the War Department, as a consequence of the severe assault made upon him for alleged incompetence and mismanagement in connection with the commissary supplies of the army in Cuba. He was succeeded by Elihu Root, of New York. It is of interest to remark, in this connection, that Theodore Roosevelt, now President of the United States, served for a short time as Assistant Secretary of the Navy, resigning when war became inevitable to take part with the " Rough Riders " in the field. We may say further that Vice-President Hobart did not survive his term of office, dying in 1899.

The Administration was represented at foreign courts as follows : Ambassador to Great Britain, John Hay, of Ohio—succeeded in 1899 by Joseph H. Choate, of New York ; to France, Horace Porter of New York ; to Austria and Austria-Hungary, Charlemagne Tower, of Pennsylvania—succeeded in 1899 by Addison C. Harris, of Indiana ; United States Minister to Russia, Ethan A. Hitchcock, of Missouri, raised to Ambassador in 1898, and succeeded in 1899 by Charlemagne Tower ; Ambassador to Germany,

Andrew D. White, of New York; Ambassador to Italy, William F. Draper, of Massachussets—succeeded in 1901 by George von L. Meyer, of Massachusetts; Ambassador to Spain, Stewart L. Woodford, of New York, who served until official relations were broken off in April, 1898, and in April, 1899, was succeeded by Bellamy Storer, of Ohio.

Among the events of importance during McKinley's first year in office, not adverted to above, may be named the discovery of gold in Alaska and the intense excitement to which it gave rise. A rush of miners to that Territory began in the latter half of 1897 and continued during the following years, the result being a great increase in the white population of Alaska and a considerable addition to the gold supply of the world.

In the same year a highly important municipal event was consummated, namely, the consolidation of the cities of New York and Brooklyn and the adjoining populous districts into one enormous city, which was popularly named Greater New York. As thus constituted, the city of New York covered an area of 317.77 square miles, and had a population of over 3,000,000, becoming the second city in the world. McKinley's administration was signalized by no more momentous event than this remarkable example of our civic growth in a little over a century of national existence.

The most exciting events of the year were those in connection with the savage acts of the Spanish generals and forces in their endeavor to suppress the rebellion in Cuba. The indignation to which these gave rise in the United States, and the slow but steady drift of this country into warlike relations with Spain, must be left for treatment in the next chapter.

We may here fitly close with reference to an impressive event, in which President McKinley took part, the removal of the remains of General Grant to their final resting place in the magnificent tomb erected on Morningside Heights, overlooking the Hudson, in the city of New York.

The ceremonies attending the removal of the remains on April 27, 1897, included three impressive displays, the ceremony at the tomb, the parade of the troops, National Guard and civic bodies, and the review of the navy and merchant marine on the Hudson. Those who gathered to take part in the final tribute to the great soldier included the President and Vice-President of the United States, the Cabinet, many State governors, prominent American citizens, and representatives of foreign nations. From 129th Street to the Battery, and from Whitehall up East River to the Bridge, thousands of American and foreign flags were displayed, while the parade of men on foot included 60,000 persons.

MCKINLEY AT DEDICATION OF GRANT'S TOMB

Bishop Newman opened the exercises with prayer, and President McKinley made one of the finest speeches of his life, the opening words of which were :

"A great life, dedicated to the welfare of the nation, here finds its earthly coronation. Even if this day lacked the impressiveness of ceremony and was devoid of pageantry, it would still be memorable, because it is the anniversary of the birth of the most famous and best beloved of American soldiers."

The President concluded with the words :

"With Washington and Lincoln, Grant had an exalted place in the history and the affections of the people. To-day his memory is held in equal esteem by those whom he led to victory, and by those who accepted his generous terms of peace. The veteran leaders of the Blue and Gray here meet not only to honor the name of Grant, but to testify to the living reality of a fraternal national spirit which has triumphed over the differences of the past and transcends the limitations of sectional lines. Its completion— which we pray God to speed—will be the nation's greatest glory.

"It is right that General Grant should have a memorial commensurate with his greatness, and that his last resting-place should be in the city of his choice, to which he was so attached, and of whose ties he was not forgetful even in death. Fitting, too, is it that the great soldier should sleep beside the noble river on whose banks he first learned the art of war, of which he became master and leader without a rival.

" But let us not forget the glorious distinction with which the metropolis among the fair sisterhood of American cities has honored his life and memory. With all that riches and sculpture can do to render the edifice worthy of the man, upon a site unsurpassed for magnificence, has this monument been reared by New York as a perpetual record of his illustrious deeds, in the certainty that, as time passes, around it will assemble, with gratitude and veneration, men of all climes, races, and nationalities.

" New York holds in its keeping the precious dust of the silent soldier, but his achievements—what he and his brave comrades wrought for mankind—are in the keeping of seventy millions of American citizens, who will guard the sacred heritage forever and forevermore."

While the events of which we have spoken were taking place various important questions and new political issues had arisen for the government to deal with. Throughout President McKinley's administration the prosperity of the country had immensely increased. We have elsewhere given the figures for the extraordinarily great commercial development, while home industries had shown a corresponding progress. Among the much debated questions that came to the front may be mentioned that of popular control of municipal affairs, such as street railways, water, gas, and other civic requisites, and also the parallel demand for public control of the railroads and telegraphs of the country, and other so-called public utilities. These questions, while still exciting much discussion, remain for future settlement.

Among the leading measures considered in Congress, that of governmental support of the mercantile navy, by national subsidies, excited an animated discussion, but led to no final decision. In March, 1900, a new financial law was enacted, its purpose being the fixing of the monetary standard of value. It re-established the gold standard and made important provisions for the facile control of the finances, containing a provision for breaking the "endless chain," by prohibiting the re-issue of notes that had been redeemed to meet deficiencies in the current revenues. This, it will be remembered, had more than once been earnestly advocated by the President. One clause of the bill provided for the coining of the silver bullion on hand into subsidiary silver coins up to the limit of $100,000,000. Various changes were made in the National Banking Act, mainly for the purpose of permitting banks to be organized with small capital in places of 3,000 inhabitants or less.

"THE PRESIDENT AT THE HELM"

Showing McKinley in the War Room dictating his famous message to Admiral Sampson not to cripple his fleet against ortifications but to bottle up the enemy at Santiago

THE CHILDREN OF PRESIDENT ROOSEVELT

CHAPTER XIV

Revolution in Cuba and War with Spain

THE most momentous and striking event of McKinley's first administration was the war of 1898, between the United States and Spain. This highly important conflict was due to a concurrence of circumstances, by which this country was irresistibly forced into drawing the sword in defence of its national honor and in retribution for the horrors of Spanish rule in Cuba, an island in the closest contiguity to our own territory, and whose long record of wrongs had for years appealed to the sympathy and aroused the indignation of the people of the United States. That the origin of this conflict may be the better understood, it becomes necessary to review in brief the relations between Spain and her island colony.

The history of Spain may best illustrate the decline of the Latin race, and the rise of the Anglo-Saxon. When America was discovered, that country was the leading maritime power of the world, but it was corrupt, rapacious, ferocious, and totally devoid of what is best expressed by the term "common sense." So lacking indeed was it in this prime requisite that it alienated, when it was just as easy to attract, the weaker nations and colonies which came under its influence and control. This was especially the case with Cuba, the only important colony which remained to Spain after her colonial territories on the American continent had been driven into revolt and won their independence.

The steadiness with which Cuba clung to the mother country won for her the title of the "Ever Faithful Isle." Had she received any consideration at all, she would still have held fast. She poured princely revenues into the lap of Spain, and when

227

other colonies revolted, she refused to be moved. It required long years of outrage, robbery and injustice to turn her affection into hate, but Spain persisted until the time came when human nature could stand no more.

The truth gradually worked its way into the Cuban mind that the only thing a Spaniard could be depended upon to do is to violate his most solemn promise. Secret societies began forming in the island, whose plottings and aims were to wrest their country from the cruel domination of Spain. We shall not dwell on the several unsuccessful attempts at revolt made by these organizations during the first half of the nineteenth century.

The first important revolutionary movement took place in 1868, the Cuban patriots availing themselves of an uprising in Spain against the hated Queen Isabella. The war that followed lasted ten years, with varying fortunes, but all that Cuba won were promises of reform, definitely stated in the treaty of El Zanjon, February 10, 1878, but deliberately broken before many years had passed. The Cubans had again trusted to Spanish honor, and had again been deceived. They quietly prepared for another rising, and in February, 1895, the fires of revolt were again kindled.

We are not concerned with this war, our interest as Americans being solely in the way in which it was conducted and the consequences to which it led. The methods adopted by General Weyler made it a tale of horror. He spread ruin and desolation over the land, and, collecting the non-combatants into camps, under the guns of his troops, left them to slowly starve. More than a hundred thousand are said to have died from sheer starvation.

This inhumanity called forth the strongest sympathy in the United States for the sufferers, and aroused an indignation which threatened to carry the country into war. Congressmen visited the island, and their hearts wept at sight of the cruelties they beheld. So indignant was the protest of this country that Weyler was recalled and General Blanco took his place. But the change in captains-general caused little alleviation of the situation.

Matters were in this state of extreme tension when the blowing up of the *Maine* occurred. While riding quietly at anchor in the harbor of Havana, on the night of February 15, 1898, this American battleship was utterly destroyed by a terrific explosion, which killed 266 officers and men. The news thrilled the land with horror and rage, for it was taken at once for granted that the appalling crime had been committed by Spaniards, and this feeling was deepened by the report of the investigating committee, to the effect that, beyond question, the *Maine* was destroyed by an outside explosion, or submarine mine. It was everywhere felt that this could only have been purposely planted, by Spanish hands.

The war between the United States and Spain was, in brief, a war for humanity, for America could no longer close her ears to the wails of the starving people who lay perishing, as may be said, on her very doorsteps. It was not a war for conquest or gain, nor was it in revenge for the awful destruction of the *Maine*, though few nations would have restrained their wrath with such sublime patience as did our countrymen while the investigation was in progress. Yet it cannot be denied that this unparalleled outrage intensified the war fever in the United States, and thousands were eager for the opportunity to punish Spanish cruelty and treachery. Congress reflected this spirit when by a unanimous vote it appropriated $50,000,000 "for the national defense." The War and Navy Departments hummed with the activity of recruiting, the preparations of vessels and coast defenses, the purchase of war material and vessels at home, while agents were sent to Europe to procure all the war-ships in the market. Unlimited capital was at their command, and the question of price was never an obstacle. When hostilities impended the United States was unprepared for war, but by amazing activity, energy, and skill the preparations were pushed and completed with a rapidity that approached the marvelous.

War being inevitable, President McKinley sought to gain time for our consular representatives to leave Cuba, where the situation daily and hourly grew more dangerous. On April 18th the two houses of Congress adopted the following

RESOLUTIONS

WHEREAS, The abhorrent conditions which have existed for more than three years in the island of Cuba, so near to our own borders, have shocked the moral sense of the people of the United States, have been a disgrace to Christian civilization, culminating as they have, in the destruction of a United States battle-ship with 266 of its officers and crew, while on a friendly visit in the harbor of Havana, and cannot longer be endured, as has been set forth by the President of the United States in his message to Congress of April 11, 1898, upon which the action of Congress was invited; therefore,

Resolved, By the Senate and House of Representatives of the United States of America, in Congress assembled—

First—That the people of the island of Cuba are, and of right ought to be, free and independent.

Second—That it is the duty of the United States to demand, and the government of the United States does hereby demand, that the government of Spain at once relinquish its authority and government in the island of Cuba, and withdraw its land and naval forces from Cuba and Cuban waters.

Third—That the President of the United States be, and he hereby is, directed and empowered to use the entire land and naval forces of the United States, and to call into the actual service of the United States the militia of the several states, to such an extent as may be necessary to carry these resolutions into effect.

Fourth—That the United States hereby disclaims any disposition or intention to exercise sovereignty, jurisdiction, or control over said island, except for the pacification thereof, and asserts its determination when that is completed to leave the government and control of the island to its people.

This resolution was signed by the President April 20th, and a copy served on the Spanish minister, who demanded his passports, and immediately left Washington. The contents were telegraphed to United States Minister Woodford at Madrid, with instructions to officially communicate them to the Spanish government, giving it until the 23d to answer. The Spanish authorities, however, anticipated this action by sending the American minister his passports on the morning of the 21st. This act was of itself equivalent to a declaration of war.

15

The making of history now went forward with impressive swiftness.

War Preparations

On April 22d the United States fleet was ordered to blockade Havana. On the 24th Spain declared war, and the United States Congress followed with a similar declaration on the 25th. The call for 75,000 volunteer troops was increased to 125,000 and subsequently to 200,000. The massing of men and stores was rapidly begun throughout the country. Within a month expeditions were organized for various points of attack, war-vessels were bought, and ocean passenger steamers were converted into auxiliary cruisers and transports. By the first of July 40,000 soldiers had been sent to Cuba and the Philippine Islands. The rapidity with which preparations were made and the victories gained and the progress shown by the Americans at once astonished and challenged the admiration of foreign nations who had regarded America as a country unprepared for war by land or sea. On April 27th, following the declaration of war on the 25th, Admiral Sampson, having previously blockaded the harbor of Havana, was reconnoitering with three vessels in the vicinity of Matanzas, Cuba, when he discovered the Spanish forces building earthworks, and ventured so close in his efforts to investigate the same that a challenge shot was fired from the fortification, Rubal Cava. Admiral Sampson quickly formed the *New York, Cincinnati* and *Puritan* into a triangle and opened fire with their eight-inch guns. The action was very spirited on both sides for the space of eighteen minutes, at the expiration of which time the Spanish batteries were silenced and the earthworks destroyed, without casualty on the American side, though two shells burst dangerously near the *New York*. The last shot fired by the Americans was from one of the *Puritan's* thirteen-inch guns, which landed with deadly accuracy in the very centre of Rubal Cava, and, exploding, completely destroyed the earthworks. This was the first action of the war, thoug it could hardly be dignified by the name of a battle.

It was expected that the next engagement would be the bombardment of Morro Castle, at Havana. But it is the unexpected that often happens in war. In the Philippine Islands, on the other side of the world, the first real battle—one of the most remarkable in history—was next to occur.

The Battle of Manila

On April 25th the following dispatch of eight potent words was cabled to Commodore Dewey on the Coast of China: "Capture or destroy the Spanish squadron at Manila." "Never," says James Gordon Bennett, "were instructions more effectively carried out. Within seven hours after arriving on the scene of action nothing remained to be done." It was on the 27th that Dewey sailed from Mirs Bay, China, and on the night of the 30th he lay before the entrance of the harbor of, Manila, 700 miles away. Under the cover of darkness, with all lights extinguished on his ships, he daringly steamed into this unknown harbor, which he believed to be strewn with mines, and at daybreak engaged the Spanish fleet. Commodore Dewey knew it meant everything for him and his fleet to win or lose this battle. He was in the enemy's country, 7,000 miles from home. The issue of this battle must mean victory, Spanish dungeons, or the bottom of the ocean. "*Keep cool and obey orders*" was the signal he gave to his fleet, and then came the order to fire. The Americans had seven ships, the *Olympia*, *Baltimore*, *Raleigh*, *Petrel*, *Concord*, *Boston*, and the dispatch boat *McCullough*. The Spaniards had eleven, the *Reina Christina*, *Castilla*, *Don Antonio de Ulloa*, *Isla de Luzon*, *Isla de Cuba*, *General Lezo*, *Marquis de Duero*, *Cano*, *Velasco*, *Isla de Mindanao*, and a transport.

From the beginning Commodore Dewey fought on the offensive, and, after the manner of Nelson and Farragut, concentrated his fire upon the strongest ships one after another with terrible execution. The Spanish ships were inferior to his, but there were more of them, and they were under the protection of the land batteries. The fire of the Americans was especially noted for its terrific rapidity and the wonderful accuracy of its aim. The battle lasted for about five hours, and resulted in the destruction of all the Spanish ships and the silencing of the land batteries. The Spanish loss in killed and wounded was estimated to be fully 1,000 men, while on the American side not a ship was even seriously damaged, and not a single man was killed outright, and only six were wounded.

THANKED AND PROMOTED BY HIS COUNTRY

More than a month after the battle, Captain Charles B. Gridley, commander of the *Olympia*, died, though his death was the result of an accident received in the discharge of his duty during the battle, and not from a wound. On May 2d Commodore Dewey cut the cable connecting Manila with Hong Kong, and destroyed the fortifications at the entrance of Manila Bay, and took possession of the naval station at Cavite. This was to prevent communication between the Philippine Islands and the government at Madrid, and necessitated the sending of Commodore Dewey's official account of the battle by the dispatch boat *McCullough* to Hong Kong, whence it was cabled to the United States. After its receipt, May 9th, both Houses abopted resolutions of congratulation to Commodore Dewey and his officers and men for their gallantry at Manila, voted an appropriation for medals for the crew and a fine sword for the gallant Commander, and also passed a bill authorizing the President to appoint another rear-admiral, which honor was promptly conferred upon Commodore Dewey, accompanied by the thanks of the President and of the nation for the admirable and heroic services rendered his country.

The Battle of Manila must ever remain a monument to the daring and courage of Admiral Dewey. However unevenly matched the two fleets may have been, the world agrees with the eminent naval critic who declared: "This complete victory was the product of forethought, cool, well-balanced judgment, discipline, and bravery. It was a magnificent achievement, and Dewey will go down in history ranking with John Paul Jones and Lord Nelson as a naval hero."

Admiral Dewey might have taken possession of the city of Manila immediately. He cabled the United States that he could do so, but the fact remained that he had not sufficient men to care for his ships and at the same time effect a successful landing in the town of Manila. Therefore he chose to remain on his ships, and though the city was at his mercy, he refrained from a bombardment because he believed it would lead to a massacre of the Spaniards on the part of the insurgents surrounding the city, which it would be beyond his power to stop. This humane manifestation toward the conquered foe adds to the lustre of the hero's crown, and at the same time places the seal of greatness upon the brow of the victor. He not only refrained from bombarding the city, but received and cared for the wounded Spaniards upon his own vessels. Thus, while he did all that was required of him without costing his country the life of a single citizen, he manifested a spirit of humanity and generosity toward the vanquished foe fully in keeping with the sympathetic spirit which involved this nation in the war for humanity's sake.

DIFFICULTIES FOR THE GOVERNMENT

The Battle of Manila further demonstrated that a fleet with heavier guns is virtually invulnerable in a campaign with a squadron bearing lighter metal, however gallantly the crew of the latter may fight.

Before the Battle of Manila it was recognized that the government had serious trouble on its hands. On May 4th President McKinley nominated ten new Major-Generals, including James H. Wilson, Fitzhugh Lee, William J. Sewell (who was not commissioned), and Joseph Wheeler, from private life, and promoted Brigadier-Generals Breckinridge, Otis, Coppinger, Shafter, Graham, Wade, and Merriam, from the regular army. The organization and mobilization of troops was promptly begun and rapidly pushed. Meantime our naval vessels were actively cruising around the Island of Cuba, expecting the appearance of the Spanish fleet.

On May 11th the gunboat *Wilmington*, revenue-cutter *Hudson*, and the torpedo-boat *Winslow* entered Cardenas Bay, Cuba, to

CHAIRMAN OF THE REPUBLICAN NATIONAL COMMITTEE.

MARCUS A. HANNA.
SENATOR FROM OHIO.

JOSEPH B. FORAKER.
SENATOR FROM OHIO.

attack the defences and three small Spanish gunboats that had taken refuge in the harbor. The *Winslow*, being of light draft, took the lead, and when within eight hundred yards of the fort was fired upon with disastrous effect, being struck eighteen times and rendered helpless. Ensign Worth Bagley, of the *Winslow*, who had recently entered active service, was one of the killed. He was the first officer who lost his life in the war.

On the same date Admiral Sampson's squadron arrived at San Juan, Porto Rico, whither it had gone in the expectation of meeting with Admiral Cervera's fleet, which had sailed westward from the Cape Verde Islands on April 29th, after Portugal's declaration of neutrality. The Spanish fleet, however, did not materialize.

Deeming it unnecessary to wait for the Spanish war-ships in the vicinity of San Juan, Sampson withdrew his squadron and sailed westward in the hope of finding Cervera's fleet, which was dodging about the Caribbean Sea. For many days the hunt of the war-ships went on like a fox-chase. On May 21st Commodore Schley blockaded Cienfuegos, supposing that Cervera was inside the harbor, but on the 24th he discovered his mistake and sailed to Santiago, where he lay before the entrance to the harbor for three days, not knowing whether or not the Spaniard was inside. On May 30th it was positively discovered that he had Cervera bottled up in the narrow harbor of Santiago. He had been there since the 19th, and had landed 800 men, 20,000 Mauser rifles, a great supply of ammunition, and four great guns for the defense of the city.

Operations Against Santiago

On May 31st Commodore Schley opened fire on the fortifications at the mouth of the harbor, which lasted for about half an hour. This was for the purpose of discovering the location and strength of the batteries, some of which were concealed, and in this he was completely successful. Two of the batteries were silenced, and the flagship of the Spaniards, which took part in the engagement, was damaged. The Americans received no injury to vessels and no loss of men. On June 1st Admiral Sampson arrived before

Santiago, and relieved Commodore Schley of the chief command of the forces, then consisting of sixteen war-ships.

Admiral Sampson, naturally a cautious commander, suffered great apprehension lest Cervera might slip out of the harbor and escape during the darkness of the night or the progress of a storm, which would compel the blockading fleet to stand far off shore. There was a point in the channel wide enough for only one war-ship to pass at a time, and if this could be rendered impassable Cervera's doom would be sealed. How to reach and close this passage was the difficult problem to be solved. On either shore of the narrow channel stood frowning forts with cannon, and there were other fortifications to be passed before it could be reached.

Lieutenant Hobson's Heroism

Lieutenant Richmond Pearson Hobson, a naval engineer, at 3 o'clock A. M., June 3d, in company with seven volunteers from the *New York* and other ships, took the United States collier *Merrimac*, a large vessel with 600 tons of coal on board, and started with the purpose of sinking it in the channel. The ship had not gone far when the forts opened fire, and amid the thunder of artillery and a rain of steel and bursting shells the boat with its eight brave heroes held on its way, as steadily as if they knew not their danger. The channel was reached, and the boat turned across the channel. The sea-doors were opened and torpedoes exploded by the intrepid crew, sinking the vessel almost instantly, but not in the position desired. As the ship went down the men, with side-arms buckled on, took to a small boat, and, escape being impossible, they surrendered to the enemy. The Spaniards were so impressed with this act of bravery and heroism that they treated the prisoners with the greatest courtesy, confined them in Morro Castle, and Admiral Cervera promptly sent a special officer, under a flag of truce, to inform Admiral Sampson of their safety. The prisoners were kept confined in Morro Castle for some days, when they were removed to a place of greater safety, where they were held until exchanged on July 7th.

The danger of entering the narrow harbor in the face of Cevera's fleet rendered it necessary to take the city by land, and the government began preparations to send General Shafter with a large force from Tampa to aid the fleet in reducing the city. Some 15,000 men, including the now famous Rough Riders, cowboy cavalry, were hurried upon transports, and under the greatest convoy of gunboats, cruisers, and battle-ships which ever escorted an army started for the western end of the island of Cuba.

The Landing of Shafter's Army

On June 13th troops began to leave Tampa and Key West for operations against Santiago, and on June 20th the transports bearing them arrived off that city. Two days later General Shafter landed his army of 16,000 soldiers at Daiquiri, a short distance east of the entrance to the harbor, with the loss of only two men, and these by accident.

The Victory of the Rough Riders

On June 24th the force under General Shafter reached Juragua, and the battle by land was now really to begin. It was about ten miles out from Santiago, at a point known as La Guasima. The country was covered with high grass and chaparral, and in this and on the wooded hills a strong force of Spaniards was hidden. Lieutenant-Colonel Roosevelt's Rough Riders, technically known as the First Volunteer Cavalry, under command of Colonel Wood, were in the fight, and it is to their bravery and dash that the glory of the day chiefly belongs. Troops under command of General Young had been sent out in advance, with the Rough Riders on his flank. There were about 1,200 of the cavalry in all, including the Rough Riders and the First and Tenth Regulars. They encountered a body of two thousand Spaniards in a thicket, whom they fought dismounted.

For an hour they held their position in the midst of an unseen force, which poured a perfect hail of bullets upon them from in front and on both sides. At length, seeing that their only way of escape was by dashing boldly at the hidden foe, Colonel Wood took command on the right of his column of Rough Riders, placing Lieutenant Colonel Roosevelt at the left, and thus, with a rousing yell, they led their soldiers in a rushing charge before which the Spaniards fled from the hills and the victorious assailants took the blockhouses. The Americans had sixteen killed and fifty-two wounded, forty-two of the casualties occurring to the Rough Riders and twenty-six among the Regulars. It is estimated that the Spanish-killed were nearly or quite one hundred. Thirty-seven were found by the Americans dead on the ground. They had carried off their wounded, and doubtless thought they had taken most of the killed away also.

General Garcia with 5,000 Cuban insurgents had placed himself some time before at the command of the American leader. On the 28th of June another large expedition of troops was landed, so that the entire force under General Shafter, including the Cuban allies, numbered over 22,000 fighting men.

The Battle of El Caney

The attack began July 1st, involving the whole line, but the main struggle occurred opposite the left centre of the column, on the heights of San Juan, and the next greatest engagement was on the right of the American line, at the little town of El Caney. These two points are several miles apart, the City of Santiago occupying very nearly the apex of a triangle of which a line connecting these two positions would form the base. John R. Church thus described the battles of July 1st and 2d:

"El Caney was taken by General Lawton's men after a sharp contest and severe loss on both sides. Here as everywhere there were blockhouses and trenches to be carried in the face of a hot fire from Mauser rifles, and the rifles were well served. The jungle must disturb the aim seriously, for our men did not suffer severely while under its cover, but in crossing clearings the rapid fire of the repeating rifles told with deadly effect. The object of the attack on El Caney was to crush the Spanish lines at a point near the city and allow us to gain a high hill from which the place could be bombarded if necessary. In all of this we were entirely successful. The engagement began at 6.40 A. M., and at 4 o'clock the Spaniards were forced to abandon the place and retreat toward their lines nearer the city. The fight was opened by Capron's battery, at a range of 2,400 yards, and the troops engaged were Chaffee's brigade, the Seventh, Twelfth, and Seventeenth Infantry, who moved on Caney from the east; Colonel Miles' brigade of the First, Fourth, and Twenty-fifth Infantry, operating from the south; while Ludlow's brigade, containing the Eighth and Twenty-second Infantry and Second Massachusetts, made a detour to attack from the southwest. The Spanish force is thought to have been 1,500 to 2,000 strong. It certainly fought our men for nine hours, but, of course, had the advantage of a fort and strong intrenchments.

The operations of our centre were calculated to cut the communications of Santiago with El Morro, and permit our forces to advance to the bay, and the principal effort of General Linares, the Spanish commander in the field, seems to have been to defeat this movement. He had fortified San Juan strongly, throwing up on it intrenchments that, in the hands of a more determined force, would have been impregnable.

THE BATTLE OF SAN JUAN

The battle of San Juan was opened by Grimes' battery, to which the enemy replied with shrapnell. The cavalry, dismounted, supported by Hawkins' brigade, advanced up the valley from the hill of El Pozo, forded several streams, where they lost heavily, and deployed at the foot of the series of hills known as San Juan, under a sharp fire from all sides, which was exceedingly annoying because the enemy could not be discerned, owing to the long range and smokeless powder. They were under fire for two hours before the charge could be made and a position reached under the brow of the hill. It was not until nearly 4 o'clock that the neighboring hills were occupied by our troops and the final successful effort to crown the ridge could be made. The obstacles interposed by the Spaniards

14

made these charges anything but the 'rushes' which war histories mention so often. They were slow and painful advances through difficult obstacles and a withering fire The last 'charge' continued an hour, but at 4.45 the firing ceased, with San Juan in our possession.

The object of our attack was a blockhouse on the top of the hill of San Juan, guarded by trenches and the defenses spoken of, a mile and a half long. Our troops advanced steadily against a hot fire maintained by the enemy, who used their rifles with accuracy, but did not cling to their works stubbornly when we reached them. San Juan was carried in the afternoon. The attack on Aguadores was also successful, though it was not intended to be more than a feint to draw off men who might otherwise have increased our difficulties at San Juan. By nightfall General Shafter was able to telegraph that he had carried all outworks and was within three-quarters of a mile of the city.

THE MOST IMPORTANT BATTLE OF THE WAR

It was on Sunday morning July 3d. Admiral Cervera, in obedience to commands from his home government, endeavored to run his fleet past the blockading squadron of the Americans, with the result that all of his ships were destroyed, nearly 500 of his men killed and wounded, and himself and about 1,300 others were made prisoners. This naval engagement was one of the most dramatic and terrible in all the history of conflict upon the seas, and, as it was really the beginning of the end of what promised to be a long and terrible struggle, it was undoubtedly the most important battle of the war.

For nearly one month and a half the fleets of Schley and Sampson had lain, like watch-dogs before the mouth of the harbor, without for one moment relaxing their vigilance. The quiet of Sunday morning brooded over the scene. For two days before, July 1st and 2d, the fleets had bombarded the forts of Santiago for the fourth time, and all the ships, except the *Oregon*, had steam down so low as to allow them a speed of only five knots an hour.

At half-past nine o'clock the bugler sounded the call to quarters, and the Jackies appeared on deck rigged in their cleanest clothes for their regular Sunday inspection. On board the *Texas* the devout Captain Philip had sounded the trumpet-call to religious services. In an instant a line of smoke was seen coming out of the harbor by the watch on the *Iowa*, and from that vessel's yard a signal was run up—"The enemy is escaping to the westward." Simultaneously, from her bridge a six-pounder boomed on the still air to draw the attention of the other ships to her fluttering signal. On every vessel white masses were seen scrambling forward. Jackies and firemen tumbled over one another rushing to their stations. Officers jumped into the turrets through manholes, dressed in their best uniforms, and captains rushed to their conning towers. There was no time to waste—scarcely enough to get the battle-hatches screwed on tight.

THE BATTLE ON

One minute after the *Iowa* fired her signal-gun she was moving toward the harbor. From under the Castle of Morro came Admiral Cervera's flagship, the *Infanta Maria Teresa*, followed by her sister armored cruisers, *Almirante Oquendo and Vizcaya*—so much alike that they could not be distinguished at any distance. There was also the splendid *Cristobal Colon*, and after them all the two fine torpedo-boat destroyers, *Pluton* and *Furor*. The *Teresa* opened fire as she sighted the American vessels, as did all of her companions, and the forts from the heights belched forth at the same time. Countless geysers around our slowly approaching battle-ships showed where the Spanish shells exploded in the water. The Americans replied. The battle was on, but at a long range of two or three miles, so that the secondary batteries could not be called into use; but 13-inch shells from the *Oregon* and *Indiana* and the 12-inch shells from the *Texas* and *Iowa* were churning up the water around the enemy. At this juncture it seemed impossible for the Americans to head off the Spanish cruisers from passing the western point, for they had come out of the harbor at a speed of thirteen and one-half knots an hour, for which the blockading fleet was not prepared. But Admiral Sampson's instructions were simple and well understood—"Should the enemy come out, close in and head him off"—and every ship was now endeavoring to obey that standing command while they piled on coal and steamed up. As it happened, the command in the coming contest fell to Admiral Schley, Admiral Sampson, with the flag-ship *New York*, having gone up the coast that morning for a consultation with General Shafter. A vessel was sent with all speed to bring him back, but the battle was at an end before he reached the scene.

How the Fight was Won

It was not until the leading Spanish cruiser had almost reached the western point of the bay, and when it was evident that Cervera was leading his entire fleet in one direction, that the battle commenced in its fury. The *Iowa* and the *Oregon* headed straight for the shore, intending to ram if possible one or more of the Spaniards. The *Indiana* and the *Texas* were following, and the *Brooklyn*, in the endeavor to cut off the advance ship, was headed straight for the western point. The little unprotected *Gloucester* steamed right across the harbor mouth and engaged the *Oquendo* at closer range than any of the other ships, at the same time firing on the *Furor* and *Pluton*, which were rapidly approaching.

It then became apparent that the *Oregon* and *Iowa* could not ram, and that the *Brooklyn* could not head them off, as she had hoped, and, turning in a parallel course with them, a running fight ensued. Broadside after broadside came fast with terrific slaughter. The rapid-fire guns of the *Iowa* nearest the *Teresa* enveloped the former vessel in a mantle of smoke and flame. She was followed by the *Oregon*, *Indiana*, *Texas*, and *Brooklyn*, all pouring a rain of red-hot steel and exploding shell into the fleeing cruisers as they passed along in their desperate effort to escape. The *Furor* and *Pluton* dashed like mad colts for the *Brooklyn*, and Commodore Schley signaled—"Repel torpedo-destroyers." Some of the heavy ships turned their guns upon the little monsters. It was short work.   Clouds of black smoke rising ftom their thin sides showed how seriously they suffered as they floundered in the sea.

The *Brooklyn* and *Oregon* dashed on after the cruisers, followed by the other big ships, leaving the *Furor* and *Pluton* to the *Gloucester*, hoping the *New York*, which was coming in the distance, would arrive in time to help her out if she needed it.   The firing from the main and second batteries of all the battle-ships—*Oregon, Iowa, Texas*—and the cruiser *Brooklyn* was turned upon the *Vizcaya, Teresa*, and *Oquendo* with such terrific broadsides and accuracy of aim that the Spaniards were driven from their guns repeatedly; but the officers gave the men liquor and drove them back, beating and sometimes shooting down those who weakened, without mercy; but under the terrific fire of the Americans, the poor wretches were again driven away or fell mangled by their guns or stunned from the concussions of the missiles on the sides of their ships.

They are on Fire ! We've Finished Them

Presently flames and smoke burst out from the *Teresa* and the *Oquendo.* The fire leaped from the port-holes; and amid the din of battle and above it all, rose the wild cheers of the Americans, as both these splendid ships slowly reeled like drunken men and headed for the shore. "They are on fire ! We've finished them," shouted the gunners. Down came the Spanish flags. The news went all over the ships—it being commanded by Commodore Schley to keep everyone informed, even those far below in the fire-rooms—and from engineers and firemen in the hot bowels of the great leviathans to the men in the fighting-tops the welkin rang until the ships reverberated with exuberant cheers.

In twenty-four minutes after the sinking of the *Teresa* and *Oquendo*, the *Vizcaya*, riddled by the *Oregon's* great shells and burning fiercely, hauled down her flag and headed for the shore, where she hung upon the rocks. In a dying effort, she had tried to ram the *Brooklyn*, but the fire of the big cruiser was too hot for her. The *Texas* and the little *Vixen* were seen to be about a mile to the rear, and the *Vizcaya* was left to them and the *Iowa*, the latter staying by her finally, while the *Texas* and *Vixen* followed on.

It looked like a forlorn hope to catch the *Colon*. She was four and one-half miles away. But the *Brooklyn* and the *Oregon* were running like express trains, and the *Texas* sped after the fugitives with all her might. The chase lasted two hours. Firing ceased, and every power of the ship and the nerve of commodore, captains, and officers were devoted to increasing the speed. Men from the guns, naked to the waist and perspiring in streams, were called on deck for rest and an airing. It was a grimy and dirty but jolly set of Jackies, and jokes were merrily cracked as they sped on and waited. Only the men in the fire-rooms were working as never before. It was their battle now, a battle of speed. At 12.30 it was seen the Americans were gaining, and the *Brooklyn*, a few minutes later, with 8-inch guns, began to pelt her sides. Everyone expected a game fight from the proud and splendid *Colon*, with her smokeless powder and rapid-fire guns; but all were surprised when, after a feeble resistance, at 1.15 o'clock, her captain struck his colors and ran his ship ashore sixty miles from Santiago, opening her sea-valves to sink her after she had surrendered.

Victory Complete

Victory was at last complete. As the *Brooklyn* and *Oregon* moved upon the prey word of the surrender was sent below, and naked men poured out of the fire-rooms, black with smoke and dirt and glistening with perspiration, but wild with joy. Commodore Schley gazed down at the grimy, gruesome, joyous firemen with glistening eyes suspicious of tears, and said, in a husky voice, eloquent with emotion, " *Those are the fellows who made this day.*" Then he signaled—" The enemy has surrendered." The *Texas*, five miles to the east, repeated the signal to Admiral Sampson some miles further away, coming at top speed of the *New York*. Next the commodore signaled the admiral—" *A glorious victory has been achieved. Details communicated later.*" And then to all the ships, " *This is a great day for our country,*" all of which were repeated by the *Texas* to the ships further east. The cheering was wild. Such a scene was never, perhaps, witnessed upon the ocean. Admiral Sampson arrived before the *Colon* sank, and placing the great nose of the *New York* against that vessel pushed her into shallow water, where she sank, but was not entirely submerged. Thus perished from the earth the bulk of the sea power of Spain.

The Spanish losses were 1,800 men killed, wounded, and made prisoners, and six ships destroyed or sunk, the property loss being about $12,000,000. The American loss was one man killed and three wounded, all from the *Brooklyn*, a result little short of a miracle from the fact that the *Brooklyn* was hit thirty-six times, and nearly all the ships were struck more than once.

The Last Battle and the Surrender of Santiago

On July 8th and 10th the two expeditions of General Miles arrived, reinforcing General Shafter's army with over 6,000 men. General Toral was acquainted with the fact of their presence, and General Miles urgently impressed upon him that further resistance could but result in a useless loss of life. The Spanish commander replied that he and his men would die fighting. Accordingly a joint bombardment by the army and navy was begun. The artillery reply of the Spaniards was feeble and spiritless, though our attack on the city was chiefly with artillery. They seemed to depend most upon their small arms, and returned the volleys fired from the trenches vigorously. Our lines were elaborately protected with over 22,000 sand-bags, while the Spaniards were protected with bamboo poles filled with earth. In this engagement the dynamite gun of the Rough Riders did excellent service, striking the enemy's trenches and blowing field-pieces into the air. The bombardment continued until the afternoon of the second day, when a flag of truce was displayed over the city. It was thought that General Toral was about to surrender, but instead he only asked more time.

On the advice of General Miles, General Shafter consented to another truce, and, at last, on July 14th, after an interview with

General Miles and Shafter, in which he agreed to give up the city on condition that the army would be returned to Spain at the expense of America, General Toral surrendered. On July 16th the agreement, with the formal approval of the Madrid and Washington governments, was signed in duplicate by the commissioners, each side retaining a copy. This event was accepted throughout the world as marking the end of the Spanish-American War.

THE CONQUEST OF THE PHILIPPINES

After Dewey's victory at Manila, already referred to, it became evident that he must have the co-operation of an army in capturing and controlling the city. The insurgents under General Aguinaldo appeared anxious to assist Admiral Dewey, but it was feared that he could not control them. Accordingly, the big monitor *Monterey* was started for Manila and orders were given for the immediate outfitting of expeditions from San Francisco under command of Major-General Wesley Merritt. The first expedition consisted of between 2,500 and 3,000 troops, commanded by Brigadier-General Anderson, carried on three ships, the *Charleston*, the *City of Pekin*, and the *City of Sydney*. This was the longest expedition (about 6,000 miles) on which American troops were ever sent, and the men carried supplies to last a year. The *Charleston* got away on the 22d, and the other two vessels followed three days later. The expedition went through safely, arriving at Manila July 1st. The *Charleston* had stopped on June 21st at the Ladrone Islands and captured the island of Guam without resistance. The soldiers of the garrison were taken on as prisoners to Manila and a garrison of American soldiers left in charge, with the stars and stripes waving over the fortifications.

The second expedition of 3,500 men sailed June 15th under General Greene, who used the steamer *China* as his flagship. This expedition landed July 16th at Cavite in the midst of considerable excitement on account of the aggressive movements of the insurgents and the daily encounters and skirmishes between them and the Spanish forces.

On June 23d the monitor *Monadnoc* sailed to further reinforce Admiral Dewey, and four days later the third expedition of 4,000 troops under General McArthur passed out of the Golden Gate amid the cheers of the multitude, as the others had done ; and on the 29th General Merritt followed on the *Newport.* Nearly one month later, July 23d, General H. G. Otis, with 900 men, sailed on the *City of Rio de Janeiro* from San Francisco, thus making a total of nearly 12,000 men, all told, sent to the Philippine Islands.

General Merritt arrived at Cavite July 25th, and on July 29th the American forces advanced from Cavite toward Manila. On the 31st, while enroute, they were attacked at Malate by 3,000 Spaniards, whom they repulsed, but sustained a loss of nine men killed and forty-seven wounded, nine of them seriously. This was the first loss of life on the part of the Americans in action in the Philippines. The Spanish casualties were much heavier. On the same day General McArthur's re-inforcements arrived at Cavite, and several days were devoted to preparations for a combined land and naval attack.

THE SURRENDER OF THE CITY DEMANDED

On August 7th Admiral Dewey and General Merritt demanded the surrender of the city within forty-eight hours, and foreign war-ships took their respective subjects on board for protection. On August 9th the Spaniards asked more time to hear from Madrid, but this was refused, and on the 13th a final demand was made for immediate surrender, which Governor-General Augusti refused and embarked with his family on board a German man-of-war, which sailed with him for Hong Kong. At 9.30 o'clock the bombardment began with fury, all the vessels sending hot shot at the doomed city.

In the midst of the bombardment by the fleet American soldiers under Generals McArthur and Greene were ordered to storm the Spanish trenches which extended ten miles around the city. The soldiers rose cheering and dashed for the Spanish earthworks. A deadly fire met them, but the men rushed on and **swept the enemy** from their outer defenses, forcing them to their inner trenches. A second charge was made upon these, and the Spaniards retreated into the walled city, where they promptly sent up a white flag. The ships at once ceased firing, and the victorious Americans entered the city after six hours' fighting. General Merritt took command as military governor. The Spanish forces numbered 7,000 and the Americans 10,000 men. The loss to the Americans was about fifty killed, wounded, and missing, which was very small under the circumstances.

In the meantime the insurgents had formed a government with Aguinaldo as president. They declared themselves most friendly to American occupation of the islands, with a view to aiding them to establish an independent government, which they hoped would be granted to them. On September 15th they opened their republican congress at Malolos, and President Aguinaldo made the opening address, expressing warm appreciation of Americans and indulging the hope that they meant to establish the independence of the islands. On September 16th, however, in obedience to the command of General Otis, they withdrew their forces from the vicinity of Manila.

Peace Negotiations and the Protocol

Precisely how to open the negotiations for peace was a delicate and difficult question. Its solution, however, proved easy enough when the attempt was made. During the latter part of July the Spanish government, through M. Jules Cambon, the French ambassador at Washington, submitted a note, asking the United States government for a statement of the ground on which it would be willing to cease hostilities and arrange for a peaceable settlement. Accordingly, on July 30th, a statement, embodying President McKinley's views, was transmitted to Spain, and on August 2d Spain virtually accepted the terms by cable. On August 9th Spain's formal reply was presented by M. Cambon, and on the next day he and Secretary Day agreed upon terms of a protocol, to be sent to Spain for her approval. Two days later, the 12th inst., the French ambassador was authorized to sign the protocol for Spain, and the signatures were affixed the same afternoon at the White House (M. Cambon signing for Spain and Secretary Day for the United States), in the presence of President McKinley and the chief assistants of the Department of State. The six main points covered by the protocol were as follows:

THE MAIN POINTS OF THE PROTOCOL

1. That Spain will relinquish all claim of sovereignty over and title to Cuba.

2. That Porto Rico and other Spanish islands in the West Indies, and an island in the Ladrones, to be selected by the United States, shall be ceded to the latter.

3. That the United States will occupy and hold the city, bay, and harbor of Manila, pending the conclusion of a treaty of peace which shall determine the control, disposition, and government of the Philippines.

4. That Cuba, Porto Rico, and other Spanish islands in the West Indies shall be immediately evacuated, and that commissioners, to be appointed within ten days, shall, within thirty days from the signing of the protocol, meet at Havana and San Juan, respectively, to arrange and execute the details of the evacuation.

5. That the United States and Spain will each appoint not more than five commissioners to negotiate and conclude a treaty of peace. The commissioners are to meet at Paris not later than October 1st.

6. On the signing of the protocol, hostilities will be suspended and notice to that effect be given as soon as possible by each government to the commanders of its military and naval forces.

On the very same afternoon President McKinley issued a proclamation announcing on the part of the United States a suspension of hostilities, and over the wires the word went ringing throughout the length and breadth of the land and under the ocean that peace was restored. The cable from Hong Kong to Manila, however, had not been repaired for use since Dewey had cut it in May; consequently it was several days before tidings could reach General Merritt and Admiral Dewey; and meantime the battle of Manila, which occured on the 13th, was fought.

President McKinley appointed as the National Peace Commission, Secretary of State Wm. R. Day, Senator Cushman K. Davis of Minnesota, Senator Wm. P. Frye of Maine, Senator George Gray of Delaware, and Mr. Whitelaw Reid of New York. Secretray Day resigned his State portfolio September 16th, in which he was succeeded by Colonel John Hay, former Ambassador to England. With ex-Secretary Day at their head the Americans sailed from New York, September 17th, met the Spanish Commissioners at Paris, France, as agreed, and arranged the details of the final peace between the two nations. Thus ended the Spanish-American War.

THE TREATY OF PEACE

December 10, 1898, was one of the most eventful days in the past decade—one fraught with great interest to the world, and involving the destiny of more than 10,000,000 of people. At 9 o'clock on the evening of that day the Commissioners of the United States and those of Spain met for the last time, after about eleven weeks of deliberation, in the magnificent apartments of the foreign ministry at the French capital, and signed the Treaty of Peace, which finally marked the end of the Spanish-American War.

This treaty transformed the political geography of the world by establishing the United States' authority in both hemispheres, and also in the tropics, where it had never before extended. It, furthermore, brought under our dominion and obligated us for the government of strange and widely isolated peoples, who have little or no knowledge of liberty and government as measured by the American standards.

On January 3, 1899, the Hon. John Hay, Secretary of State, delivered the Treaty of Peace to President McKinley, who, on January 4th, forwarded the same to the Senate of the United States and after careful consideration was ratified.

PRESIDENT McKINLEY IN PHILADELPHIA
Delivering an address at the unveiling of the Washington Monument, 1899.

PRESIDENT McKINLEY INSPECTING A GOVERNMENT TRANSPORT

SIGNING THE PEACE PROTOCOL

Secretary of the State Day signing the historic document which marked the cessation of hostilities, in the presence of President McKinley, the French Ambassador, and other distinguished persons.—*Copyrighted, 1898, by Francis B. Johnston.*

CHAPTER XV

McKinley and the Closing Century

TWO years after the signing of the treaty of peace with Spain the nineteenth century—an era of great achievements and remarkable progress—came to an end. Many of its years had become famous for striking events and significant steps of political development, and not the least among these was the period here in question, the closing years of the century. These years were marked by events of vast significance in the history of several countries of the world, notably Great Britain, China, and the United States.

The outcome of the war with Spain gave an extraordinary impetus to the great republic of the West, which thenceforth assumed a new and momentous position, that of a world power, a leading factor in the concert of nations, a ruling element in the "parliament of the world."

NOTABLE CAUSES AND EFFECTS

There were various causes leading to this result, notable among them being the addition to our territory of the Philippine Islands, a populous archipelago near the coast of Asia. The new position thus taken by the United States as an Asiatic power remarkably modified its relation to the other great nations. The possession of these islands by Spain, a minor European power, had long been viewed with complacency by the courts of Europe, as of no political importance. Their possession by the United States was a very different affair, and stirred the councils of the Old World as if an earthquake had suddenly rolled beneath their national foundations.

They had in earlier years looked upon this country with almost as much complacency as upon Spain. Regarding it simply as an American power, interested only in the affairs of the Western continent, and with no concern in what was taking place abroad, they had troubled themselves little about it as a political factor. In commerce, indeed, they were beginning sorely to feel its competition, but in politics the two continents seemed as widely apart as the poles.

But the results of the war and the sudden expansion of American territory put a new aspect on the case, and Europe began to look askance on the young world-power rising in the West. The war in the Philippines, the intervention of the United States in the Chinese outbreak, and the general attitude taken by the American Government added to their uneasiness, and the position of President McKinley as chief magistrate of a nation that must be considered in all future national movements, assumed a new importance in their eyes.

The same was the case at home. The new problem became equally prominent on our own soil. Two parties arose, their war-cries being expansion and non-expansion, imperialism and republicanism, and a war of words went briskly on, promising to become a political conflict when the time for the next Presidential election should arise.

MCKINLEY AND THE GREAT PROBLEMS OF HIS TIME

In the settlement of this problem William McKinley, as the Executive of the nation, occupied the most prominent position. Question after question arose which he had to settle at once, having no opportunity to submit them to Congress. He was constantly forced to take a definite side, to adopt some fixed policy, and in doing so was at every turn exposed to hostile criticism. Opinion on the problem of expansion or non-expansion grew hot, party divisions and animosities arose; whatever side the President might take, he was sure to be bitterly assailed by the adherents of the opposite view. He was like an officer between two armies, exposed to the full fire of the one and not safe from the glancing shots of the other. The battle of words raged hotly, and President McKinley stood as a shining mark in the midst of it all. Yet he stood there serenely, doing with firm hand what he conceived to be his duty, and calmly sustaining the weight of recrimination which he was obliged to bear.

Before considering further the aspects of this political warfare, it seems advisable to give in outline the story of what took place in the Philippines and elsewhere, by way of completing the history of the first McKinley administration.

THE UNITED STATES BECOMES A WORLD POWER

On the last day of 1898 the Spanish troops were withdrawn from Havana, and on the first day of 1899 the stars and stripes proudly floated over that queen city of the American tropics. But this was only for a time. The United States was pledged to give freedom to Cuba, and no man in authority thought of breaking this pledge, for the honor of the country was involved.

In the Summer of 1900, the Cuban people were asked to hold a convention and form a Constitution, with the single proviso that it should contain no clauses favoring European aggression or inimical to American interests. This done, American troops and officials would be withdrawn and Cuba be given over to the Cubans.

The occupation of Porto Rico, on the contrary, was permanent. It had been fully ceded to the United States, and steps were taken to make it a constituent part of that country. But the period of transition from Spanish to American rule was not favorable to the interests of the people, who suffered severely, their business being wrecked by tariff discrimination. Action by Congress was demanded, and a bill was passed greatly reducing the tariff in Porto Rico, but not giving free trade with the United States, though many held that this was the Constitutional right of the islanders. Under this new tariff business was resumed, and the lost prosperity of the island was gradually restored.

The occupation of our new possessions in the Pacific presented serious difficulties. This was not the case with Hawaii, which fell peacefully under its new rule, and in 1900 was made a Territory of the United States. With the Philippine Islands the case was different. There hostility to American rule soon showed itself, and eventually an insurrection began, leading to a war, which proved far more protracted and sanguinary than that with Spain.

THE PHILIPPINE INSURRECTION

On the 30th of December, 1898, President McKinley had issued a proclamation offering the natives, under American supremacy, a considerable measure of home rule, including a voice in local government, the right to hold office, a fair judiciary, and freedom of speech and of the press. These concessions were not satisfactory to Emilio Aguinaldo, the leader in the late insurrection against Spain, who demanded independence for the islands. He claimed that Dewey had promised it to him in return for his aid in the capture of Manila—a claim which Dewey positively denied.

General Elwell S. Otis, who had succeeded General Merritt as military governor of the islands, found himself plunged into the midst of an active war. Admiral Dewey's aid was not needed in this conflict, and soon after it began he returned to the United States. On the 3d of March, 1899, he had been promoted to the exalted naval rank of full admiral, which only Farragut and Porter had previously held, and which was looked upon as the sole fitting reward for his services. During his journey home he received the highest honors at every halting-place on the route, and in the United States he was greeted as the chief hero of the Spanish war. His reception in New York was one of the events of the century, and his admiring countrymen showed their appreciation by purchasing him a beautiful home in the city of Washington.

Before his return he had served on a commission, appointed by the President, with the hope of reaching a peaceful end of the difficulties. The other members of the commission were General Otis, Jacob G. Shurman, President of Cornell University, Professor Dean Worcester, and Charles Denby, late Minister to China. The commission began its work on April 4, 1899, by issuing a proclamation to the Philippine people, offering them, under the supremacy of the United States, an abundant measure of civil rights, honest administration, reform of abuses, and development of the resources of the country. This proclamation fell stillborn, so far as the insurgent forces were concerned, Aguinaldo issuing counter proclamations and calling on the people to fight for complete independence. It was evident that the settlement of the affair would depend on the rifle and the sword rather than on paper proclamations and promises.

THE INSURRECTION IN LUZON

In January, 1899, a conference was held between General Otis and Aguinaldo and other leading Filipinos, in which the latter demanded a greater degree of self-government than Otis had authority to grant. The conference, therefore, led to no satisfactory result, and the situation arising from the irritation of the natives grew daily more critical.

As the debate in the Senate upon the treaty of peace with Spain approached its termination, and promised to end in the ratification of the treaty and the cession of the islands to the United States, the restlessness and hostility of the natives increased, and on the night of February 4th the threatened outbreak came, in a fierce attack on the American outposts at Manila. A severe battle ensued, continuing for two days, and ending in the defeat of the natives, who had suffered severely and were driven back for miles beyond the city limits.

Meanwhile a republic had been proclaimed by the Philippine leaders, Aguinaldo being chosen president and commander-in-chief of the native armies.   He immediately issued a declaration of war, and both sides prepared for active hostilities.   The next step taken by the Filipinos was a desperate one—an attempt at wholesale arson.   On the night of February 22d the city of Manila was set on fire at several points, and the soldiers and firemen who sought to extinguish the flames were fired upon from many of the houses. The result was not serious except to the natives themselves, since the conflagration was in great part confined to their quarter of the city. General Otis took vigilant precautions to prevent the recurrence of such an attempt, and from that time forward Manila, though full of secret hostiles, was safe from the peril of incendiarism.

THE CAMPAIGN OF 1899

The American forces, being strengthened with reinforcements, began their advance on March 25th.   They met with sharp resistance, the Filipinos having thrown up earthworks at every defensible point, and being well armed with Mauser rifles.   But they nowhere seemed able to sustain the vigorous onsets of the Americans, who did not hesitate to charge their works and swim wide rivers in face of their fire, and they were driven back from a long succession of fortified places.   On March 31st, Malolos, the capital of Aguinaldo, was occupied.   Calumpit, another Philippine stronghold, was taken near the end of April.   General Lawton, an old Indian fighter, who had recently reached the islands, led an expedition northward through the foothills and captured San Isidro, the second insurgent capital.   Various other places were taken, and at the beginning of July, when the coming on of the rainy season put an end to active operations, a large and populous district to the north and west of Manila was in American hands.

By this time it had become evident that a larger army was needed to complete the task, and reinforcements were now hurried across the ocean.   With them was sent a considerable body of cavalry, the lack of which had seriously handicapped the troops in the spring campaign.   Fighting was resumed in mid-autumn, and

Aguinaldo's new capital of Tarlac fell. The insurgents seemed to have lost heart from their reverses in the spring, and defended themselves with less courage and persistence, the result being that by the 1st of December the Americans were masters of the whole line of the Manila-Dagupan Railway and the broad plain through which it ran, and the Filipinos were in full flight for the mountains, pursued by Lawton and Young, with their cavalry and scouts.

From that time forward there was no Filipino army, properly so-called, Aguinaldo's forces being broken up into fugitive bands, capable only of guerilla warfare. The American troops traversed the island from end to end, having frequent collisions with small parties of the enemy, in one of which, unfortunately, the gallant Lawton was shot dead. Many of the insurgent leaders were captured or surrendered, but Aguinaldo continued at large, and the hope of a final end of the war came to depend largely upon the event of his capture.

In November the Philippine Commission made its report to the Government, and a system which was thought to be well adapted to the situation was formulated at Washington. This declared that the people of the Philippines, while many of them were intelligent and capable, had no experience in self-government, and that it was necessary for the United States to retain a firm political control, while giving them such share in the government as they were fitted to exercise, increasing this as they gained political training. In accordance with this policy, local governments were established in those localities which had become pacified, and with very promising effect. By the Summer of 1900 the resistance to American domination had so much decreased that President McKinley issued a proclamation of amnesty, with the hope that the natives still in arms would take advantage of the opportunity to cease their desultory resistance.

In March, 1901, an event of leading importance took place in the Philippine Islands, in the capture of Emilio Aguinaldo, President of the Philippine government and commander-in-chief of its forces. On February 28th, General Funston had captured a messenger bearing letters from the insurgent leader, which revealed the fact that he was then at the town of Palanan, in northwest Luzon. Funston at once devised a plan and organized a force for his capture.

The expedition consisted of seventy-eight Macabebe scouts, dressed as insurgents and laborers, and four ex-insurgent officers. The only Americans were General Fred. Funston and four other officers, who had disguised themselves as privates. Funston had prepared two decoy letters, apparently signed by the insurgent general Lacuna, whose seal and correspondence he had captured some time before. These stated that Lacuna was sending his superior the best company under his command.

THE CAPTURE OF AGUINALDO

Landing from the gunboat *Vicksburg*, the party made a toilsome march over a very rugged country. They reached Palanan on March 23d. Aguinaldo was completely deceived by the letters, and by the story told him that the Americans were part of a surveying party which had been surprised on the march, part being killed and part taken. His household guards were drawn up to receive the visitors and their captives. Suddenly the mask was thrown off, firing began, and one of the ex-insurgent officers seized and held him firmly. His attendants and body-guard at once took to flight, and in a few minutes the affair was at an end, and the Filipino leader was a captive to the Americans. The expedition had proved a complete success. The important prisoner was brought to Manila, and confined there in the Malacanan Palace. Here he soon regained his calmness, talked freely, and was visited by a number of prominent Filipinos, who sought to convince him that the struggle was hopeless, and advised him to use his influence with the people to establish peace. Their arguments were effective, Aguinaldo expressed his satisfaction with the form of government, and on April 2d he took the oath of allegiance to the United States.

PRESIDENTIAL PARTY LEAVING CANTON FOR THE INAUGURATION

The President-elect escorting his mother

WILLIAM McKINLEY READING THE NEWS OF THE ELECTION TO HIS MOTHER

The effect of his capture proved highly favorable. Several prominent insurgent leaders at once surrendered themselves and their bands, and it seemed as if a new era of peace was about to dawn. Aguinaldo, who had apparently experienced a change of opinion, did his share towards hastening it by sending peace emissaries to the chiefs still in arms and signing a peace manifesto for distribution among his people. General Funston's brilliant exploit was not left unrewarded. Its value was heightened by the great risk he had run in his daring deed, and on March 30th President McKinley promoted him to the rank of Brigadier-General in the United States army. His comrades were also suitably rewarded for their participation in the exploit, which was looked upon as the most signal instance of courage and daring during the entire war.

THE SITUATION IN CHINA

While this was going on in the Philippines a disturbed condition of affairs suddenly developed in a new quarter, the ancient and populous empire of China. It is necessary to go a step backward to trace the course of events leading to this unlooked-for situation. The whole intercourse of European nations with China had been of a character to create indignation and hatred of foreigners in the populace of that country. The Japano-Chinese war increased this feeling, while demonstrating the incapacity of the Chinese to cope in war with modern nations. In the years that followed, the best statesmen of China vividly realized the defects of their system, and recognized that a radical reform was necessary to save the nation from a total collapse. The nations of Europe were seizing the best ports of the empire and threatening to divide the whole country between them, a peril which it needed vigorous measures to avert.

The result was an effort to modernize the administration. Railroads had long been practically forbidden, but now concessions for the building of hundreds of miles of road were granted. Modern implements of war were purchased in great quantities, and the European drill and discipline were introduced into the imperial army. The young emperor became strongly imbued with the spirit of reform, and ordered radical changes in the administration of affairs. In short, a promising beginning was made in the modernization of the ancient empire.

A movement of this kind in a country so rigidly conservative as China could scarcely fail to produce a revulsion. The party of ancient prejudice and conservative sentiment—a party comprising the bulk of the nation—took the alarm. The empress-dowager, who had recently laid down the reins of government as regent, took them up again, under the support of the conservative leaders, seized and held in palace seclusion the emperor, put to death his advisers, and restored the old methods of administration.

THE BOXER OUTBREAK 1900.

This revolution in the palace soon made itself felt in the hovel. A secret society of the common people, known as "The Boxers," rose in arms, made an onslaught upon the missionaries, who were widely domiciled within the realm, and soon appeared in the capital. Here, aided by many of the soldiers, and led by men high in rank in the anti-foreign party, they made a virulent assault upon the legation buildings, and put the ministers of the nations in imminent peril of their lives. These exalted officials were cut off from all communication with their governments, stories of their massacre alone filtering through, and the powers, roused to desperation by the danger of their envoys, sent ships and troops in all haste to the nearest point to Peking. In this movement the United States actively joined, its minister, Edwin H. Conger, and the members of the embassy sharing the common peril.

What followed must be briefly told. A small force, made up of soldiers and marines of various nations, including the United States, under Admiral Seymour, of the British navy, set out on June 11th for Peking. This movement failed. The railroad was found to be torn up, a strong force of Chinese blocked the way, and Seymour and his men were forced to turn back and barely escaped with their lives.

At the same time a naval attack was made on the forts at Taku ; Admiral Remey, of the United States navy, refusing to take part in this ill-advised action. Its immediate result was an assault in force by Boxers and troops on the foreign quarter of the city of Tien Tsin, in which the Chinese fought with an unexpected skill and persistence. They were repulsed, but only after the hardest fight which foreigners had ever experienced on Chinese soil.

THE RESCUE OF THE MINISTERS

As the month of July went on the mystery at Peking deepened. It became known that the German minister had been murdered, and doubtful reports of the slaughter of all the foreigners in the capital were cabled. As it seemed impossible to obtain authentic news, the greatest possible haste was made to collect an army strong enough to march to Peking, and early in August this force, consisting of some 16,000 Japanese, Russians, Americans and British, set out. A severe struggle was looked for, and their ability to reach Peking seemed very doubtful. At Peitsang, some twelve miles on the route, the Chinese made a desperate resistance, which augured ill for the enterprise ; but their defeat there seemed to rob them of spirit, and the gates of Peking were reached with little more fighting. On the 14th the gates were assailed, the feeble opposition from within was overcome, and the troops marched in triumph to the British legation, the stout walls of which had offered a haven of refuge to the imperilled legationers.

Glad, indeed, were the souls of the beleaguered men and women within, so long in peril of death from torture or starvation, to see the stars and stripes and the union jack waving over the coming troops. Only then was the mystery surrounding their fate made clear and the safety of all the ministers, except the representative of Germany, assured. So far as the United States was concerned, the work was at an end. That country wanted no share in the partition of China. All it demanded was an "open door" to commerce, an equal share in the important Chinese trade. No sooner was its minister rescued than it was announced that the American troops would be withdrawn as soon as proper relations with the Chinese government had been consummated, and that in no case would the United States support any land-seizing projects of the nations of Europe.

A few words will suffice to tell the final outcome of this notable work. For a year following, the foreign troops held possession of the capital of China, while negotiations went on with the Chinese government, then in a location remote from Peking. During this occupation the troops of several foreign powers committed great ravages, looting freely in the Chinese city and palace, and treating the people with violence and indignity. In these outrages the American troops took no part, being held under the strictest discipline, and so greatly winning the respect and confidence of the Chinese that they were appealed to for protection where the troops of other powers were regarded with hatred and fear. The occupation ended in the Summer of 1901, China engaging to pay a large indemnity to the powers, and consenting to other severe measures of retribution. The foreign troops were thereupon withdrawn and the Chinese regained possession of their capital.

RECENT MEASURES CONSIDERED BY CONGRESS

Throughout the administration the question of an interoceanic canal continued prominent, the problem being whether this canal should be built across Nicaragua or the Isthmus of Panama. A commission was appointed by President McKinley early in the administration for the purpose of making surveys and reporting upon the most feasible route. The provisions of the Bulwer-Clayton treaty with Great Britain seriously interfered with the construction and placing under American control of a Nicaragua canal, and an international question arose with England in regard to the modification of this treaty, but no final action resulted.

Meanwhile a French company was engaged in endeavoring to complete the Panama canal. Large sums of money had been spent on this enterprise, and near the close of the administration this company offered to make a sale of its work, so far as completed, to the United States. At the end of the century this important question remained to be acted upon by Congress, it being then impossible to foresee which route would be chosen.

The discovery of gold in Alaska had given rise to a question of some importance between Great Britain and the United States. The Klondike gold diggings proved to be in British territory, and it became important to fix definitely the boundary line between Alaska and British America. This matter has been temporarily adjusted, but the permanent settlement of the boundary still remains to be effected.

Another question which had remained unsettled for a considerable period was that concerning the Samoan Islands. In the year 1900 this was definitely adjusted by the partition of these islands between England, Germany and the United States. By this agreement the United States obtained the island of Tutuila. This gives us the magnificent harbor of Panga Panga, where for more than twenty years we have had a coaling station. The treaty was negotiated by Secretary Hay, and approved by the Senate on January 16, 1900.

THE OPEN DOOR IN CHINA

Every American voter will be interested in the results secured and the benefits arising from Secretary Hay's negotiation with foreign powers, by which was acquired an equal footing for our commerce in China. There had been an attempt on the part of several European powers to secure a permanent influence over portions of China, to control all grants for the purpose of constructing railroads and developing mines. In acquiring these rights there was danger that the United States would be excluded from its commercial rights with the Chinese. By treaty China had already granted to the United States the privileges allowed to the most favored nations, and under this treaty our commerce had thrived. Beginning with September 6, 1899, Secretary Hay held correspondence with the governments of other nations respecting the maintaining of an " open door " in China. He secured the assent of Great Britain, Germany, France, Italy, Russia and Japan to an international declaration, by which each government agreed substantially as follows :

First. That it would in no wise interfere with any treaty port or any vested interest within any so-called "sphere of interest " or leased territory it might in the future control in China.

Second. That the Chinese treaty tariff of the time being should apply to all merchandise landed or shipped to all such ports as were within such "spheres of interest" (unless they should be "free ports "), no matter to what nationality it might belong, and that duties so leviable should be collected by the Chinese Government.

Third. That it would levy no higher harbor dues on vessels of another nationality frequenting any port in such "sphere" than should be levied on vessels of its own nationality ; and no higher railroad charges over lines built, controlled or operated within its "sphere," on merchandise belonging to citizens or subjects of other nationalities transported through such "sphere," than should be levied on similar merchandise belonging to its own nationality transported over equal distances.

The special point in this triumph of American diplomacy is that the United States surrendered nothing in acquiring these valuable concessions from the powers named. The United States will have an equal footing with all other nations in the Orient, and American merchandise can be shipped to and landed in all Chinese ports where the nations named have their spheres of influence. There will be no discriminating harbor dues or railroad charges. Consequently, the western shore of the Pacific will become the most inviting field for American enterprise, since the Chinese Empire, with its great requirements, has been opened to commerce and trade.

As regards our new acquisition of Porto Rico, the President in his message of 1900 used this much quoted language : " Our plain duty is to abolish the customs tariffs between the United States and Porto Rico, and give her products free access to our markets." The people of Porto Rico at that time had been brought into a state of poverty and despair as the result of a severe tropical hurricane, which had devastated the coffee plantations and done great damage to all kinds of property. It occurred to the President that the most effective measure of relief would be to give the islanders free access to our markets. Congress, however, dissented from this view, but reduced temporarily the tariff duties with Porto Rico. It may be said in this connection that in the second McKinley administration this duty was removed and commerce between the United States and Porto Rico was made free.

OUR NEW POSSESSIONS

The most important question that had arisen, however, was that indicated by the much used words " Imperialism" and "Expansion." The position taken by the Government in regard to the Philippine Islands had created a vigorous opposition. A party not large in numbers, but strongly outspoken, denounced the movement towards retaining possession of the Philippine Islands. Among other arguments was the great cost of the war in the Philippines, which amounted to nearly $500,000,000, the drain upon the youths of this country and the barbarities of the warfare. Serious objection was also made to the large increase in the army rendered necessary, leading to expected burdens of militarism and increased taxation. The issue of this controversy will be considered in the next chapter.

CHAPTER XVI

The Campaign of 1900

ON the 19th of June, 1900, for the third time in its 'history, the National Republican Convention assembled in Philadelphia. Like its predecessors, it was an historic event of unusual importance. Philadelphia responded fittingly to the honor of its choice by the Republican party, and to the enthusiasm of the hour, bedecked itself with bunting and national emblems, and opened its doors in generous hospitality to the thousands who poured in from every State and Territory of the Union. Long before the Convention met, it was evident that President McKinley would receive a unanimous re-nomination for the first place on the ticket, and that the policy of his administration would be heartily indorsed. The name and portrait of the President headed every combination for the Republican ticket, and no doubt of his enthusiastic selection existed.

But who would get the nomination for the second place was a question of keen interest to politicians and friends of rival candidates. Among the illustrious names mentioned, Governor Roosevelt, of New York State, headed the list, closely followed by Secretary John D. Long of Massachusetts, William B. Allison and William Dolliver, favorite sons of Iowa, Timothy L. Woodruff, New York's Lieutenant-Governor, and ex-Secretary Cornelius N. Bliss, of New York.

Republican National assemblies have always boasted a distinguished membership. But in this respect the roll of the Convention which met in Philadelphia in 1900 probably surpassed any of its eleven predecessors. The roll of the Convention which assembled forty-four years ago contained the names of men who have

ROTUNDA OF THE CAPITOL

Where the leaders sat to th' Hall

THEIR PARTING VIEW OF NIAGARA FALLS

since passed into history. But most of them were almost unknown in 1856. It will probably be so with the membership of the National Republican Convention of 1900. When the history of the next forty-four years shall have been written, many of its prominent actors will doubtless be found to have sat in the Convention which re-nominated William McKinley.

A HARMONIOUS CONVENTION

The Convention met without contest or difference, collision or controversy over the platform, and the leaders claimed that it had done its work, accomplished its declared purpose, and presented to the voters of the country a record of good deeds done and intended when it outlined its past achievements and proposed its future policy.

When it had met four years before in St. Louis the gold standard needed to be asserted, and was disputed even within the party, the national credit was lower than for twenty years before, the tariff demanded revision to save the industries of the country, whose foreign trade had declined, while its protests against misgovernment in Cuba had been contemned by Spain. The party at the Convention of 1900 claimed that these issues had all been met; that they had all been solved; that the arduous labor they demanded had been done. No differences were left to be adjusted, and the country stood ready to approve the success of the past by giving the party another term of office.

This, the twelfth Convention, showed no less enthusiasm and buoyant party spirit than was shown at the meeting of previous Conventions. There were in attendance the distinguished leaders of the party, and men of thought and action in State and national counsels. The speeches delivered reached the "highwater mark" of earnestness and eloquence, all of which presaged one of the most important and interesting campaigns in the nation's history.

The hall selected for the meeting of the Convention, probably the largest and finest in the United States for this purpose, seated fully 25,000 people, and was arranged with all the conveniences and equipments for handling and moving large assemblies. It had been erected for the Philadelphia Commercial Museum, one of the most important institutions in the land, and used for the National Export Exposition of 1899.

FIRST DAY OF THE CONVENTION

Men who have attended previous Conventions recall that Harrison was nominated in the Minneapolis Exposition building, in which the lack of acoustic properties defied all the forensic forces of the speakers, and McKinley was nominated at St. Louis in a wigwam which was a terror to every man who tried to impress his colleagues with his eloquence.

All these Convention halls failed immeasurably in comparison with the splendid auditorium in which the twelfth Convention of the Republican party was assembled. The expressions of delight at its majestic proportions were followed by others of surprise and profound satisfaction that the voice from the platform carried to the remotest door, and brought the personality, the logic, and the oratory of the speakers to every one of the thousands of eager listeners who filled the structure. It was a testimony, moreover, of the metropolitan way in which Philadelphia does things, and the word was certain to be carried to the remotest corners of the land, that no quadrennial assemblage of either of the great parties had been so comfortably and delightfully lodged as this one.

Chairman Hanna called the Convention to order at 12.35 P.M., and introduced the Rev. Gray J. Bolton, who delivered the invocation. Senator Dick, of the National Committee, read the call for the Convention, and the entire audience rose to its feet when the band began to play " The Star-Spangled Banner." Senator Hanna, in his opening remarks, eulogized Philadelphia as the " Cradle of Liberty," and said that this " beehive of industry " is all the evidence necessary to demonstrate the great principles of the Republican party. He thanked the people for their hospitality. When he referred to President McKinley the Convention went into an uproar.

. . . .

He closed by introducing Senator E. O. Wolcott, of Colorado, as temporary chairman of the Convention. Senator Wolcott, in a few graceful words, accepted the appointment, and spoke in a most eloquent manner, in which he eulogized President McKinley as a patriotic, wise and courageous leader, and an example of the highest type of American manhood. After speaking of the President as one of the greatest leaders the party has ever had, he paid a glowing tribute to the memory of the late Vice-President Hobart, and spoke of him as always a trusted friend and adviser of the President, "Sage in counsel, and wise in judgment."

SENATOR WOLCOTT THE TEMPORARY CHAIRMAN

As to the excessive war tax, Senator Wolcott predicted that before President McKinley's term would expire many of the duties would be lightened; that new legislation would be passed, which would rebuild our merchant marine, and provide for building, owning and operating, under exclusive American control, a ship canal connecting the Atlantic and Pacific. He referred in eloquent language to the war with Spain, and the noble sacrifices the North and the South had made in behalf of home and country, to alleviate the sufferings of the neighboring people, and secure for them the same liberties which we ourselves enjoy. He discussed our relations with Porto Rico and our power to deal with foreign possessions, claiming that the action taken by the administration was a wise one. He also asserted that the Republican party would adhere literally to its declaration in regard to the freedom of Cuba. In scathing terms he spoke of the American citizens who had gone to Cuba for the purpose of perpetrating frauds which had brought a blush of shame to every American. He declared that the Republican party would be the first to right any wrongs that had been done, and to bring to justice those who had done wrong; and in regard to the Philippines that it was our duty to keep them, and that their abandonment would be a confession that we were not able to protect them, and that we would be doing what no other civilized nation of the world would do, turning them back to Spain or else consigning them to anarchy and confusion.

In conclusion he said:

"The American people are neither poltroons nor pessimists, and they will not signalize the dawn of the new century by the surrender of either convictions or territory. Every soldier back from the islands—and they are in almost every hamlet in the land—returns an advocate of their retention. Our dead are buried along the sands of Luzon, and on its soil no foreign flag shall ever salute the dawn.

"Whatever may be in store for us in the new and unbeaten track upon which we are entering, we shall not be found 'with the unlit lamp and the ungirt loin.' Our way is new, but it is dark. In the re-adjustment of world-conditions, where we must take our place with the other great nations of the earth, we shall move with caution, but not with fear. We seek only to lift up men to better things, to bless and not to destroy. The fathers of the republic accepted with courage such responsibilities as devolved upon them. The same heavens bend over us, and the same power that shielded them will guard and protect us, for what we seek is to build still more firmly, always upon foundations of probity and of virtue, the glorious edifice of the republic."

SECOND DAY OF THE CONVENTION

The second day's session of the Republican National Convention was called to order at 12.30 o'clock, by Senator Wolcott. He introduced the Rev. Charles E. Boswell, who opened the proceedings with prayer. A very significant scene followed when the presiding officer rose to introduce the fifteen survivors of the first Republican Convention, called at Pittsburg forty-four years before, who had with them the same old flag used at that convention. The audience arose as the line of white-haired patriarchs appeared on the platform carrying the faded American flag, tattered and barely holding together. A deafening salute went up for the faded standard and its venerable bearers. The fifteen white-haired men arranged themselves side by side and looked out upon the sea of faces.

When the storm of applause had ceased, the leader of the delegation read the resolutions which declared the unswerving allegiance to the party they had helped to bring forth. The resolutions regretted the inability of many of the members of the National Fremont Association to be present because of their advanced age. The resolutions were concluded with the declaration that "We heartily endorse the administration of William McKinley, which gives such unbounded prosperity."

After this interesting incident the regular order of the day was commenced, and the report of the Committee on Credentials was read by Honorable Sereno E. Payne, its chairman. General Grosvenor, of Ohio, Chairman of the Committee on Permanent Organization, announced the selection of Henry Cabot Lodge as permanent chairman. Governor Roosevelt, of New York, and Governor Shaw, of Iowa, were appointed to escort the permanent chairman to the platform.

In the able and well-considered address delivered by Senator Lodge, all the national questions involved in the coming contest were reviewed. Here we shall content ourselves with a single extract, that in which he referred to the question of expansion and strongly approved President McKinley's policy in regard to our newly-gained island possessions.

SENATOR LODGE PRAISES MCKINLEY'S POLICY

"War is ever like the sword of Alexander. It cuts the knots. It is a great solvent and brings many results not to be foreseen. The world forces unchained in war perform in hours the work of years of quiet. Spain sued for peace. How was that peace to be made? The answer to this great question had to be given by the President of the United States. We were victorious in Cuba, Porto Rico, and the Philippines. Should we give those islands back

16

to Spain? Never! was the President's reply. Would any American wish that he had answered otherwise? Should we hand them over to some other power? Never! was again the answer. Would our pride and self-respect as a nation have submitted to any other reply? Should we turn the islands, where we had destroyed all existing sovereignty, loose upon the world to be a prey to domestic anarchy and the helpless spoil of some other nation? Again the inevitable negative. Again the President answered as the nation he represented would have him answer. He boldly took the islands, took them, knowing well the burden and the responsibility; took them from a deep sense of duty to ourselves and others, guided by a just foresight as to our future in the East, and with entire faith in the ability of the American people to grapple with the new task. When future conventions point to the deeds by which the Republican party has made history, they will proclaim with especial pride that under a Republican administration the war of 1898 was fought, and that the peace with Spain was the work of William McKinley."

The remaining interesting feature of the day's session was the report of the Committee on Resolutions, read by its chairman, Senator Fairbanks, of Indiana. The platform was accepted without hesitation, and the announcement of its approval by the committee was received with enthusiastic applause.

The following is a brief synopsis of the Republican platform:

The party endorsed President McKinley's administration; asserted its allegiance to the gold standard and its steadfast opposition to the free coinage of silver; condemned conspiracies and combinations to restrict business; re-affirmed its policy of protection and reciprocity; declared for more effective restriction of immigration of cheap labor; and upheld Civil Service reform.

It declared that there would be no discrimination on account of race or color; stood for good roads, rural free delivery, free homes, and reclamation of arid lands; favored statehood for New Mexico, Arizona and Oklahoma; promised reduction of war taxes;

declared for an Isthmian Canal and an open door in China ; congratulated women on their work in camp and hospital ; re-affirmed the Monroe Doctrine ; approved the tender of good offices to end the war in South Africa ; and promised restoration of order and establishment of self-government in the Philippines and independence to Cuba.

THE CLOSING DAY'S SESSION

On June 21st came the great day of the convention. People who had thronged the building on the previous days, expecting to hear the nominating speeches for President McKinley, went away disappointed; but they returned at an early hour of the last day's convention, fully confident that their expectations would be realized. The indecision of the previous days as to the probable candidate for second place on the ticket had given away to practical certainty that New York's popular Governor, Theodore Roosevelt, would be unanimously nominated. So enterprising and generous had the daily papers been in securing and publishing the news, that practically the plans of the day were known. All that remained for the last day's session was the enthusiasm which attended the nomination of two men whose popularity has seldom been exceeded in American history, and equaled only by the popularity which surrounded the name of James G. Blaine, the " Plumed Knight " of more than one campaign.

The Convention Hall was gay with colors of bunting, with badges of delegates and spectators, with the bright-colored dresses and hats of the ladies, and the beautiful flowers which were banked upon the platform. As the crowds assembled, the bands discoursed popular airs. A band from Canton, Ohio, known as McKinley's Band, was again in attendance and very popular with the convention. Everyone felt, when Chairman Henry Cabot Lodge rapped with his gavel upon the table, that this was to be the day for the Republican party. More than 20,000 people were present to witness it. Before this audience were the grandeur of peaceful symbolism, the splendors of ecclesiastical vestment, and the exciting influence of dramatic climaxes, set as it were upon a stage, all to yield to the enthralment of fervent oratory, and the delirium of unrestrained enthusiasm.

The chairman introduced Archbishop Ryan, who came forward in the purple vestments of his office to offer prayer. The vast audience arose, as the venerable prelate stepped forward, and stood with bowed heads, hearing in the silence which ensued the strong voice and the fervent and solemn invocation. After a few moments for announcements and preliminary business, the chairman declared that it was now in order to proceed with the nominations, and ordered the States to be called in alphabetical order.

ROLL-CALL OF THE STATES

Alabama, being the first called upon, responded that it would yield its place to Ohio, and immediately a gray-haired man with whitening moustache came down the aisle, and was recognized in an instant as Senator Foraker, of Ohio. Everyone seemed to be aware of the task which had been set for the venerable Senator, and knew well who was the incomparable statesman that the speaker so eloquently portrayed without naming him, yet from ancient custom his hearers pretended to be ignorant. When Mr. Foraker, in closing, thundered, "William McKinley," the assembly arose to its feet as one man, and gave forth a shout of approval which seemed to have been stored up for three days. A thousand hands among the delegates were uplifted and ten thousand handkerchiefs among the spectators fluttered, and here and there tricolored bunches of pampas plumes waved back and forth ; then another and another, like magic, sprang into view, and the pit occupied by the delegates seemed one mass of waving color. The band in the gallery began playing, but nobody could recognize the air. The cornet and bass-drum only were recognizable. Even the dignified officials and guests on the platform seemed to forget themselves and join in the pandemonium. Mark Hanna could restrain himself no longer, but jumped to his feet and, seizing a

THE PRESIDENT'S TRAIN ON HIS CALIFORNIA TRIP

bunch of brilliant plumes, dropped his handkerchief and fan and led the audience, waving his plumes like a baton. Every banner of every State which had been fastened in its socket to mark the position of the delegates was torn from its moorings, and soon there was a procession of banners moving through the aisles. Even the banner of little Hawaii was held aloft by the dark-skinned native delegate. This sight swept the audience beyond control.

GOVERNOR ROOSEVELT SPEAKS

For nearly twenty minutes this popular outburst was maintained, until from pure weariness the audience finally subsided and the sound of the chairman's gavel was heard. On the whole the great demonstration was a success. It was loud, it was long, it satisfied the convention and the spectators. When the chairman could be heard he recognized a delegate from New York, who desired to second the nomination of William McKinley. Of course, it was Governor Theodore Roosevelt, the rough rider, statesman and popular hero, who spoke. For nearly five minutes he was compelled to face this vast audience, again on its feet, thundering forth applauses with cheers and waving of banners. In vain he raised his hand and motioned for silence. Finally the strenuous Governor made himself heard. He spoke as though he would drive every sentence home, and expected to carry conviction with it. His clenched fist, heavy-set jaw, and poise of body bespoke a kind of angry conviction. He praised the administration, and with sharp and emphatic sentences brought down the house with his description of the Ice Trust as "one that is thoroughly infamous in character and may be criminal."

He was followed by John W. Yerkes, of Kentucky, and by Senator Thurston, of Nebraska, who without much effort filled the hall with the volume of his voice, and affirmed that "the steamships which plowed the main took up the glad refrain, William McKinley! William McKinley! William McKinley!" He was followed by George A. Knight, of California, who paid a tribute to his own State and its enthusiastic opinion of President McKinley's policy. Soon there began to be heard the call, "Vote! Vote!" and the calling of the roll of the States began in the usual impressive manner. As the name of each State was called, a delegate arose and answered, with the number of votes from each State, "For William McKinley." Little Hawaii again became the centre of attraction when she cast her two votes for the President. In this way there were 930 votes, and they were unanimously for William McKinley; and upon the announcement of the result by the chairman there was another grand demonstration.

NOMINATION OF VICE-PRESIDENT

When the convention could be brought to order, the nomination for Vice-President became the order of the day. In accordance with a prearranged program, Colonel Lafe Young, of Iowa, in a graceful speech, announced that his State, whose first choice had been one of her own sons, William Dolliver, now recognized that there was one man more than all others demanded by the people of this broad country for second place. He gracefully joined in the popular demand, and proposed the name of Governor Roosevelt, of New York, as the people's choice for Vice-President. Upon this announcement, the audience again rose to their feet, and shouted and cheered and marched with an enthusiasm almost equal to that displayed upon the nomination of the President. The roll of the States being called, the choice was unanimous, the total number of votes cast for the nominees being 930 for President and 929 for Vice-President, Theodore Roosevelt not voting with his delegation for himself.

The interesting fact, that the candidates for both President and Vice-President were unanimously nominated on the first ballot, is, we believe, the first instance of the kind in American history.

The Democratic National Convention, held in Kansas City, July 4, 1900, unanimously chose as its candidate William Jennings Bryan, the standard-bearer of the party four years before. For

Vice-President, Adlai E. Stevenson, who had already served one term in the office during Cleveland's second administration, triumphed over all competitors. Bryan was also chosen, as previously, by the People's Party, Charles A. Towne, of Minnesota, being named for Vice-President. Nominations were also made by the Prohibition and several other organizations, among them being a Silver Republican faction, by which the Democratic nominees were endorsed.

The platforms of the parties were significant in that the old party war-cries sank into the background and new principles rose into prominence. The tariff, so long the leading issue, practically vanished from sight. The question of free silver coinage, so prominent in 1896, became a minor issue. The new points in debate were the trusts and the policy of so-called Imperialism. It was not easy, however, to make the trusts a leading question. Both parties condemned them in their platforms, though the Democrats maintained that they were supported by the existing administration, and that the Republican party was the sustainer of monopoly. This left as the most prominent issue the question of Imperialism *versus* Anti-Imperialism, a controversy based on the effort of the administration to subdue and control the people of the Philippines. The persons opposed to this policy, at first comparatively few, had grown in numbers until Anti-Imperialism was taken up as a basic principle of the Democratic platform. The country became divided upon this great question, and the campaign orators fulminated *pro* and *con*, with all their eloquence, upon the grand problem of the conquest or the independence of the Filipinos.

SENATOR HANNA'S IDEA OF CAMPAIGNING

Senator Hanna, Chairman of the Republican National Committee, and President McKinley's closest friend and most ardent supporter, was opposed to a campaign on the rostrum of the usual rhetorical kind. Oratorical fireworks were not to his taste. He was content to let the other party deal in them, and proposed that the Republican orators and pamphleteers should confine themselves to argument instead of indulging in invective and recrimination. He said:

"Let the other fellows have the fiddles and the barbecues! Our argument exists *per se* at the bench, in the workshop, at the desk, in the counting-room, at the chair by the fireside. Let them do the shouting; we will do the showing. They may have the hysterics; we have the conditions. 'Let well enough alone' is a mighty good saying, if it *is* well enough, as it is now for a good many more than a majority of the voters of these United States. We need not wave the flag. If they force it—the people of our country are patriotic. We need not win any gory victories on the stump, nor storm any Spanish armies from wagon-ends. The war is over, and over with the utmost credit to the Republican administration. The people know that, and we need not weary them by dwelling upon it. Our appeal, and it need not be an appeal—still less a defense—is to sober common-sense as against visions; to what is, and is satisfactory, as against what may be, and may be disastrous; to present prosperity, as against probable panic; to what has been tried and found true, as against what is untried and likely to be found wanting,—in short, to the sanity of the nation."

Mr. Bryan did not look upon it in this way. He was, above all else, an orator, with a remarkable power of influencing audiences and with extraordinary energy and endurance. While the President remained quietly at home in Canton, giving his views only to such as called on him there, Bryan traversed the country from end to end, speaking to large audiences, and vigorously promulgating the Democratic political doctrines.

AN ACTIVE CAMPAIGN

As the campaign progressed, the Democrats avoided the silver question even more than at the beginning; and, generally speaking, they seemed to find the Philippine issue less profitable than they had hoped to make it. Toward the middle of October they began to concentrate their oratory, to a marked extent, upon phases of the Trust question and kindred matters, in a way designed to stir up the prejudices of labor against capital. They sought to identify the Republican party with all that is objectionable in the rapid tendency toward the amalgamation of industries, and claimed for Mr. Bryan the position of the highest special authority on the whole subject of trusts—their causes, their development, and especially the means by which they are to be destroyed or rendered harmless. This was the favorite theme of Mr. Bryan's many speeches in the State of New York.

Mr. Bryan, indeed, was embarrassed by the multiplicity of his issues. He found himself the foremost champion on too many different fields. He could not abdicate his place as head and forefront of the great free silver movement. Nor could he repudiate a position in which the Olneys, Schurzes, and Atkinsons of the anti-Imperialist movement, as well as the Kansas City Convention, had recognized him as the leader in a crusade that proposed to preserve the republic and avert the "empire." But, for political purposes, an even greater question, if possible, than either of the others became, as above said, that involved in the hue and cry against trusts and plutocratic tendencies in government.

Here, again, he found practically the whole work of saving the country thrown upon his one pair of sturdy shoulders. Single-handed, he fought for an income tax. It was he, moreover, who was selected to champion the cause of the Boers ; to denounce the alleged secret alliance of Mr. McKinley and Secretary Hay with Lord Salisbury ; and to proclaim the grievances, if they could be found, of the Porto Ricans and the Cubans against this country. The load was too heavy for any candidate that ever lived. The only wonder is that Mr. Bryan carried it so well. He made perhaps more out of the situation than any one else could have done. Now, as four years before, the Democratic and Populist standard-bearer made a wonderful speaking campaign.

But he was seeking in vain to talk down a firmly fixed public opinion. Despite the active controversy of the Anti-imperialists, their lurid pamphlets and overwrought discourses, the great majority of the people favored the retention of the islands. Bishop Potter, of New York, after a visit to Manila, expressed what was undoubtedly a widely held public opinion :

"Whatever we might have done a year or more back, there is but one thing for us to do now, and that is to hold on to the islands and assume the responsibility for their future. One thing is evident, and that is that the Filipinos are in no condition for self-government. If a civil government were imposed it would need a large military force to maintain it.

"Several friends of Aguinaldo called upon me in Hong Kong, and they told me that they were satisfied that there could be no success for his undertaking. The better class of Filipinos are satisfied that American occupation means increased prosperity, and are not raising any objections."

The Trust issue proved of little more cogency. The great combinations of capital, which were increasing with alarming rapidity, no doubt excited widespread dread and distrust. But the attempt to convert the Trust question into a political one could not be sustained. It was a business issue, pure and simple, for which neither party could justly be held responsible. The effort to saddle it on the back of Republicanism necessarily failed. The people were fully conversant with the subject, and were unwilling to have it injected into their politics. Both parties had declared against trusts in their platforms. Such legislation as favored them was of old date, and had been framed to meet other conditions. There had been recent legislation against trusts, and on this question the record of Republicanism was as clear as that of Democracy.

When the November election came on, the result decisively showed that a large majority of the people were in favor of William McKinley and his party principles. He was re-elected to the office by a popular vote of 7,206,777 against a vote for Bryan of 6,374,397. The electoral vote for McKinley and Roosevelt was 292; that for Bryan and Stevenson, 155, yielding the very large Republican majority of 137 electoral votes. McKinley's popular majority was 230,000, his electoral majority 42, greater than the large majorities of 1896.

MCKINLEY RE-ELECTED

Thus William McKinley was once more chosen President of the United States, and went on without a break in the duties of his great office, no dream of fate coming to warn him how soon and fatally this was to end. Theodore Roosevelt, who had very reluctantly accepted the nomination for Vice-President, was fully prepared to spend four years as presiding officer of the Senate, similarly without a dream of the great future fate was preparing for him. Thus events move on in the progress of human life. The past lies behind us like an open scroll; the face of the future is deeply veiled. None can say whether sunshine or cloud, sorrow or joy, life or death, awaits any man in the coming days or years.

CHAPTER XVII

Nearing the End

ON the 1st of January, 1901, the United States entered a new century admirably equipped for the journey that lay before it. In wealth and promise of prosperity it had become the foremost nation of the world. In commercial development it stood supreme; not in the sum of its exports and imports, in which it was surpassed by Great Britain, but in the enormous balance of trade in its favor, in which it far exceeded all the other nations of the world. In manufacturing activity and the value of its annual products, and in the superabundant yield of its farms and pastures, it similarly had attained a foremost place, while its working classes enjoyed a degree of comfort and prosperity nowhere else approached. It was capable not only of feeding its own people, but had become the granary of Europe, which trusted to the United States to save it from possible starvation. And its surplus of manufactured goods was sent abroad in similar profusion. In a word, the great republic had become the grand almoner of mankind, the "Lady Bountiful" whose generous hand gave freely from its abundance to the crowding millions of the outer world.

Its progress was not alone in material things. The mental wealth of its people was expanding equally with their physical conditions. Within its broad domain there was no privileged class, no pampered and idle aristocracy, no political magnates with hereditary power and authority; all were equal, all sovereign citizens, the poorest in the land being equal before the laws and in political opportunities with the richest and highest. Education was the privilege of all, rich and poor alike. In art, in music, in literature, in science, in invention, the West had attained the level of the

THE PRESIDENT IN FRONT OF THE ALAMO, SAN ANTONIO, TEXAS

East, and spiritually as well as materially the United States recognized no superior upon the earth.

In respect to power and influence, its development had been
equally great. It began the new century with a population of
76,304,799, the greatest of any justly entitled civilized nation of the
world—for though Russia surpassed it in mere numbers, it did so by
including a vast host of people to whom the term civilized could not
properly be applied. In wealth and financial resources it stood
supreme, while its debt was the smallest among those of the leading
nations. Removed by two great oceans from warlike peoples, it
was free from the incubus of a great standing army, trusting to its
patriotic people and to its naval resources for ample protection
should hostile relations arise.

Such was the great and commanding nation of which William
McKinley had a second time been elected President, and into whose
highest official position he was re-inaugurated on the 4th of March,
1901. We speak of this growing supremacy of the United States
not without purpose, since much of it had been gained after
McKinley was first inaugurated President, four years before.

FROM PANIC TO PROSPERITY

He first became chief ruler of the country when at a low level
in its financial and business conditions. For years the shadow of
ruin had lain upon the land. Its business was depressed, its people
were despairing, its finances were disorganized, its debt was increasing, its expenses surpassed its income, in every respect its condition
was discouraging, its outlook the reverse of hopeful.

Four years of a McKinley administration had passed, and an
extraordinary change had come upon the land. The clouds of dis-
couragement had broken and rolled like a scroll away, and the full
sunshine of prosperity poured down upon our cities, homes, and
fields. Business depression was replaced by a magnificent activity,
despair had been swept away by hopefulness, money poured into
our treasury far more rapidly than it flowed out, the country had,

metaphorically, thrown off its coat and grasped its tools, and in city and country alike an extraordinary energy manifested itself, while on every sea a great fleet of merchantmen bore the products of our factories and fields to all quarters of the earth.

In political importance the progress had been no less stupendous. Not many years had passed since Europe looked upon our country with disdain, as a nation of shopkeepers, without ambition for aught but coin, and unworthy of being considered in the great national movements of mankind. Even in 1896, when McKinley was first elected, this sentiment had by no means passed away. Europe had begun to look with distrust upon the growing giant of the West, but viewed it still as limited to the interests of its own continent and not worthy of consideration in world affairs.

DAWN OF A NEW ERA

A new era had dawned and how great the change! The giant had broken its bonds and for the first time stood before mankind in its true proportions. In a single leap it had sprung into the position of a world power, one of the great national magnates of the earth, and the nations gazed askance upon this mighty form in their midst, destined, hereafter, to have a voice in the councils of the world, to aid in moving the pieces which settled the destinies of mankind.

In this grand form it was that the United States entered the twentieth century. We cannot give William McKinley the credit of setting in train this mighty and rapid change. Most of it was inevitable, the result of causes which had been developing for many years. But in the final days of the voyage he stood at the helm and aided the great craft to weather the dangerous storms through which it passed, to avoid the rocks which threatened it with wreck, and to bring it safely at last into the port for which its course was laid.

On the 4th of March, 1901, our well proved and tried President entered upon a new four-year term in our national career, with every promise before him of guiding the ship of state safely onward in the great voyage upon which it had once more set sail. Sadly enough, it was for the pilot now that the rocks of peril arose, not for the mighty ship. In the most hopeful days of the voyage his hand was snatched from the helm, death fell upon him at his post, and nothing was left of him to his people but the beloved memory of one of their noblest and greatest men. Fortunately there was a new and strong hand ready to seize the helm, and still the Ship of State sailed grandly on.

Like Lincoln and Garfield before him, he was stricken down in the year of his inauguration. Lincoln had fallen in the month after he again took the chair of office. The hand of the assassin struck Garfield in the fourth month of his term. Six months of his new administration passed ere McKinley fell. The events of these few months it is our purpose here to briefly relate. They were of no great political importance. The country was for the time at rest after the years of struggle and excitement it had just passed through. It was a brief breathing time before new questions of moment should arise, and its few events may quickly be told.

THE PHILIPPINE WAR

After two years of more or less active warfare the struggle in the Philippines was practically at an end. There were still some bands of brigands in the mountains, as there had been for centuries, and a rapidly expiring guerrilla contest, but the leading revolutionists had ceased their opposition, and the Taft Commission, appointed by President McKinley to establish a liberal form of government in the islands, met with the greatest success in its work. At the same time a large number of teachers were sent out from the United States to establish schools in the islands, and thus confer upon their people the highest boon which this country was able to bestow—that of education on liberal principles.

Among the events of the opening year of the twentieth century one of the most interesting was the Pan-American Exposition, held in the city of Buffalo, N. Y., from May 1st to November 1st. This project was first planned in 1897, the exposition to be held on a small scale, in 1899, on Cayuga Island, near Niagara Falls. The Spanish-American War, however, checked the project, and when it was revived it was on a more ambitious scale. Buffalo was chosen as the site, and the original fifty acres were expanded into 330 acres, the ground chosen including the most beautiful portions of Delaware Park. A fund of $5,000,000 was provided by the city and citizens of Buffalo, appropriations were made by the State of New York and the Federal Government, and the work was begun on an estimate of $10,000,000 of expenditures.

PAN-AMERICAN EXPOSITION

The purpose of this Exposition is clearly indicated in its name. It concerned itself solely with the countries of the two Americas and the new possessions of the United States, of which it was proposed to show the progress during the nineteenth century, a leading object of the enterprise being to bring into closer relations, commercially and socially, the republics and colonies of the Western Hemisphere and promote intercourse between their peoples. The Department of State, in June, 1899, invited the various governments of the American Continents to take part in the enterprise, and acceptances were very generally received.

The preparations made for the Exposition were of the most admirable character, and, when completed, the grounds and buildings presented a magnificent scene. While on a smaller scale than the Philadelphia and Chicago World's Fairs, the Buffalo Fair surpassed all previous ones in architectural beauty. Instead of presenting the pure white of the Columbian Exposition, there was a generous use of brilliant colors and rich tints, which gave a glowing rainbow effect to the artistically grouped buildings; the general style of architecture being a free treatment of the Spanish Renaissance, in compliment to the Latin American countries taking part. The elaborate hydraulic and fountain arrangements, the horticultural and floral settings, and the sculptural ornamentation, added greatly to the general effect.

Of the varied elements of the display, that of electricity stood first, the enormous electrical plant at Niagara and its connection by wire with Buffalo affording unequalled facilities in this direction. The Electric Tower, 375 feet high, was the centre-piece of the Exposition, the edifice itself being stately and beautiful and its electric display on the grandest scale. The vari-colored electrical fountain was strikingly beautiful. There were winding canals, caverns, and grottoes, water cascades, towers, domes and pinnacles, and other objects of attraction, not the least of them the Midway, with its diversified display, a feature which has become indispensable to all recent enterprises of this character. We have spoken especially of this superb Fair from the sad relations which President McKinley was to hold to it—a subject of national grief which we reserve for later treatment.

TRANS-CONTINENTAL TOUR OF THE PRESIDENT

Another event of much public interest which marked the year 1901 was a grand tour of the entire country projected by President McKinley, on a scale far surpassing those undertaken by preceding Presidents, its limits being the Atlantic and Pacific in the East and West, and the Gulf and Lake States in the North and South. Leaving Washington on April 29th, in a special train, whose cars were provided with every convenience and luxury which art could devise and skill provide, and following roads where the utmost care and precaution were taken to insure ease, safety and comfort of travel, the party proceeded through the southern portion of its route, the President being received in all the large cities and towns with a generous enthusiasm which spoke volumes for the unity of sentiment throughout the country. His appreciative remarks and well-chosen responses to addresses of welcome added greatly to the kindly feeling with which he was everywhere received. Unfortunately the severe illness of Mrs. McKinley, after San Francisco had

17

been reached, put an end to the tour when half completed. The life of the "Lady of the White House" was despaired of, but she recovered sufficiently to be brought back by the shortest route to Washington, attended at every point by her loving husband with the most assiduous and anxious care.

THE SUPREME COURT AND INSULAR COMMERCE

The presence of the President in Washington was needed, for important political questions had arisen which demanded his immediate attention and extended consultation with the members of his Cabinet. These arose in consequence of a decision of the Supreme Court of the United States fixing the status of our insular possessions. In a number of instances duties had been collected on goods imported from Porto Rico and Hawaii to this country, and in one instance fourteen diamonds brought by a soldier from the Philippine Islands had been seized for non-payment of duty. Several lawsuits brought for the recovery of these duties, on the claim that they had been illegally exacted, were decided adversely to the claimants by the lower courts, and appeals were taken to the Supreme Court. A decision was rendered by this court on May 28, 1901, in the suit of De Lima & Co., merchants of New York. which covered all the cases involved except the Philippine one, which was left in doubt. This opinion, announced by Justice Brown, was concurred in by five members of the court, Chief Justice Fuller and Associate Justices Brown, Brewer, Harlan and Peckham, and dissented from by Justices Gray, Shiras, White and McKenna.

The decision was to the effect, that before the Treaty of Paris Porto Rico was a foreign country, and its exports were subject to full duties. After that treaty it became a domestic territory, and, as such, subject to the jurisdiction of Congress while it continued a territorial possession, the decision being that Congress has the right to administer the government of a territory and to lay such duties upon its commerce as it deems suitable. The effect of this decision was that, from the signing of the Treaty of Paris till the passage of the Foraker act, fixing the duties at 15 per cent., no duties could legally be collected on Porto Rican goods. After that act was passed the duties designated by it could be exacted.

This crucial decision fixes the status of all our insular possessions under civil control. But the court adjourned without rendering an opinion on the Philippine case, and as the Philippine Islands differed from Porto Rico in being under military control, the question as to the right of government to collect duties upon Philippine goods remained unsettled. Many held that the President had no authority to exact duties, and that it would be necessary to call an extra session of Congress in order to pass a law governing the Philippine customs; but the President decided that this was not needed, and that existing acts of Congress governed this special case.

The decisions of the Court, so far as they went, made necessary some slight alterations in the plan which President McKinley had formed for proclaiming a full system of civil government in the Philippines on July 4th, but a partial system was put in operation on that date. Late in July, on notice from the Porto Rican Legislature that a system of local taxation had been established in the island which would yield revenue sufficient for the support of its government, the President issued a proclamation declaring the abolition of the import and export duties on the trade of Porto Rico with the United States which had been imposed by the Foraker act, which provided a form of civil government for the island.

AFFAIRS IN CUBA AND CHINA

The above mentioned was one of the questions which confronted President McKinley on his return to Washington from his long journey through the States. Another had to do with Cuban affairs. The Cuban Constitutional Convention had accepted the Act of Congress fixing the relations between the United States and Cuba, and establishing what might be called a mild form of protectorate over the island ; but its acceptance was vitiated by conditions which the President declined to accept, and the question was returned to the convention with the decisive understanding that the Platt amendment, fixing the relations between the United States and Cuba, must be accepted in its entirety, or the military occupation of Cuba would necessarily continue. On June 12, 1901, the Cuban Convention accepted this amendment in its original form, and the sole obstacle to Cuban independence was removed.

Meanwhile the Chinese situation had been modified by the withdrawal of the American troops, except a legation guard ; other nations also ordering the withdrawal of their troops and restoring the government to the Chinese. The indemnity demanded from and accepted by China amounted to $237,000,000, with interest at not over 4 per cent. This large sum was objected to by the United States Government, but was adopted on the demand of the other nations concerned.

OTHER EVENTS OF NATIONAL IMPORTANCE

Among other events of national importance was the settlement of the vexed question of the number of soldiers in the army. The provision to make it 100,000 men was modified on suggestion of General Miles, and the number fixed at 76,000, making one soldier for every 1,000 of the population.

In the spring of 1901, a signal discovery of petroleum was made in the Southwest, a well being opened at Beaumont, Texas, which threw a six-inch stream of oil a hundred feet into the air. Other rich wells were subsequently opened, in that and neighboring States, and great excitement prevailed in the speculative world. The oil differed essentially from that of Pennsylvania, being ill-adapted to refining and principally suitable for fuel.

One of the most striking events of the year was the formation of an industrial combination on an unprecedented scale, a gigantic union of the steel manufacturing interests of the country, with the immense capital of $1,100,000,000. A line of steamships was purchased in the interest of this concern, the railroad magnates of the country added to their holdings, and showed indications of an eventual general combination of transportation facilities, and the public stood aghast at these vast operations, in doubt as to where they would end, or how the interests of the great multitude would be affected. It was with such stupendous financial and industrial operations that the new century began its career, and that the wise and beneficent executive rule of President McKinley neared its end.

CHAPTER XVIII

The President's Last Speech

THE Pan-American Exposition which was formally opened at Buffalo May 1, 1901, had, from the first, President McKinley's earnest support and enthusiastic encouragement. He truly saw that this great exposition would weld together more closely the peoples of North and South America by facilitating trade and commerce and making known to each the resources of the other. It was fitting, therefore, that there should be a President's Day and that he should honor the Exposition with his presence. Therefore he journeyed from his beautiful home at Canton to Buffalo accompanied by his wife, relatives and friends.

President's Day, September 5, 1901, at the Pan-American Exposition, dawned bright and clear, with the temperature sufficiently low to make the day all that could be desired. Business houses and private residences were gayly decorated with flags and bunting, and banners were stretched from windows and across streets, bearing words of welcome to the President and expressive of the sentiment which the great fair was designed to foster, " Peace to Pan-America."

The time announced for the departure of the President from the house of Mr. Milburn, in Delaware Avenue, where he made his home and was most hospitably entertained in Buffalo, was 10 o'clock. Crowds had already begun to assemble in front of the house as early as 9 o'clock. A detail of police kept the crowd back from the sidewalk in front of the house ; but those most eager to catch a glimpse of the President and Mrs. McKinley indiscriminately invaded the beautiful lawns of the adjoining residences, and some even went so far as to climb upon the verandas.

Promptly at 10 o'clock the President emerged from the home of Mr. Milburn, Mrs. McKinley accompanying him, walking by his side without assistance. A great burst of cheers greeted them, which the President acknowledged by bowing and raising his hat. The President and Mrs. McKinley entered the first carriage, and Mr. Milburn, President of the Exposition, and Mrs. William Hamlin, of the Board of Women Managers, the second.

GREETED BY A GREAT THRONG

An escort of twenty mounted police and twenty members of the Signal Corps surrounded the two carriages, and the cavalcade set out at a brisk trot for the Lincoln Parkway entrance to the Exposition grounds. The two carriages were followed by a number of other carriages and tallyhos, their occupants blowing fanfares and adding animation to the scene.

At the entrance to the Exposition grounds the President was met by detachments of the United States Marines and the Sea Coast Artillery, and the 65th and 74th N. G. S. N. Y. Regiments under General S. M. Welch. A President's salute of twenty-one guns was fired. The President was escorted to the stand erected in the esplanade, where probably the greatest crowd ever assembled there greeted him with ringing cheers. The vast assemblage overflowed to the Court of Fountains. In the stands on each side of the President were seated many distinguished men and women, among them representatives of most of the South American Republics.

There was a most absolute quiet when President Milburn arose and introduced the President as follows:

"Ladies and Gentlemen : The President."

THE PRESIDENT'S SPEECH

The great audience then broke out with a mighty cheer, which continued as President McKinley rose, and it was some minutes before he was able to proceed. When quiet was restored the President spoke as follows :

" President Milburn, Director-General Buchanan, commissioners, ladies and gentlemen :

" I am glad to be again in the city of Buffalo and exchange greetings with her people, to whose generous hospitality I am not a stranger and with whose good will I have been repeatedly and signally honored. To-day I have additional satisfaction in meeting and giving welcome to the foreign representatives assembled here, whose presence and participation in this Exposition have contributed in so marked a degree to its interest and success.

" To the Commissioners of the Dominion of Canada and the British Colonies, the French Colonies, the Republics of Mexico and of Central and South America, and the Commissioners of Cuba and Porto Rico, who share with us in this undertaking, we give the hand of fellowship, and felicitate with them upon the triumphs of art, science, education and manufacture which the old has bequeathed to the new century.

TIMEKEEPERS OF PROGRESS

" Expositions are the timekeepers of progress. They record the world's advancement. They stimulate the energy, enterprise and intellect of the people, and quicken human genius. They go into the home. They broaden and brighten the daily life of the people. They open mighty storehouses of information to the student. Every exposition, great or small, has helped to some onward step. Comparison of ideas is always educational, and as such instructs the brain and hand of man. Friendly rivalry follows, which is the spur to industrial improvement, the inspiration to useful invention and to high endeavor in all departments of human activity. It exacts a study of the wants, comforts, and even the whims of the people, and recognizes the efficacy of high quality and new prices to win their favor.

" The quest for trade is an incentive to men of business to devise, invent, improve and economize in the cost of production. Business life, whether among ourselves, or with other people, is ever a sharp struggle for success. It will be none the less so in the future. Without competition we would be clinging to the clumsy and antiquated processes of farming and manufacture and the methods of business of long ago, and the twentieth would be no further advanced than the eighteenth century. But, though commercial competitors we are, commercial enemies we must not be.

THE EXPOSITION'S WORK

" The Pan-American Exposition has done its work thoroughly, presenting in its exhibits evidences of the highest skill and illustrating the progress of the human family in the Western Hemisphere. This portion of the earth has no cause for humiliation for the part it has performed in the march of civilization. It has not accomplished everything; far from it. It has simply done its best, and without vanity or boastfulness, and recognizing the manifold achievements of others, it invites the friendly rivalry of all the powers in the peaceful pursuits of trade and commerce, and will co-operate with all in advancing the highest and best interests of humanity. The wisdom and energy of all the nations are none too great for the world's work. The success of art, science, industry and invention is an international asset and a common glory.

"After all, how near one to the other is every part of the world. Modern inventions have brought into close relation widely separated peoples and made them better acquainted. Geographic and political divisions will continue to exist but distances have been effaced. Swift ships and fast trains are becoming cosmopolitan. They invade fields which a few years ago were impenetrable. The world's products are exchanged as never before, and with increasing transportation facilities come increasing knowledge and larger trade. Prices are fixed with mathematical precision by supply and demand. The world's selling prices are regulated by market and crop reports. We travel greater distances in a shorter space of time, and with more ease, than was ever dreamed of by the fathers.

"Isolation is no longer possible or desirable. The same important news is read, though in different languages, the same day in all Christendom. The telegraph keeps us advised of what is occurring everywhere and the press fore-shadows, with more or less accuracy, the plans and purposes of the nations. Market prices of products and of securities are hourly known in every commercial mart, and the investments of the people extend beyond their own national boundaries into the remotest parts of the earth. Vast transactions are conducted and international exchanges are made by the tick of the cable. Every event of interest is immediately bulletined.

"The quick gathering and transmission of news, like rapid transit, are of recent origin, and are only made possible by the genius of the inventor and the courage of the investor. It took a special messenger of the Government, with every facility known at the time for rapid travel, nineteen days to go from the city of Washington to New Orleans with a message to General Jackson that the war with England had ceased and a treaty of peace had been signed. How different now!

THE TELEGRAPH IN WAR

"We reached General Miles in Porto Rico by cable, and he was able through the military telegraph to stop his army on the firing line with the message that the United States and Spain had signed a protocol suspending hostilities. We knew almost instantly of the first shots fired at Santiago, and the subsequent surrender of the Spanish forces was known at Washington within less than an hour of its consummation.

"The first ship of Cervera's fleet had hardly emerged from that historic harbor when the fact was flashed to our capital, and the swift destruction that followed was announced immediately through the wonderful medium of telegraphy.

"So accustomed are we to safe and easy communication with distant lands that its temporary interruption, even in ordinary times, results in loss and inconvenience. We shall never forget the days of anxious waiting and awful suspense when no information was permitted to be sent from Peking, and the diplomatic representatives of the nations in China, cut off from all communication, inside and outside of the walled capital, were surrounded by an angry and misguided mob that threatened their lives, nor the joy that thrilled the world when a single message from the Government of the United States brought through our Minister the first news of the safety of the besieged diplomats.

A WORD FOR ARBITRATION

"At the beginning of the nineteenth century there was not a mile of steam railroad on the globe. Now there are enough miles to make its circuit many times. Then there was not a line of electric telegraph ; now we have a vast mileage traversing all lands and all seas. God and man have linked the nations together. No nation can longer be indifferent to any other. And, as we are brought more and more in touch with each other, the less occasion is there for misunderstanding and the stronger the disposition when we have differences to adjust them in the court of arbitration, the noblest form for the settlement of international disputes.

"My fellow-citizens, trade statistics indicate that this country is in a state of unexampled prosperity. The figures are almost appalling. They show that we are utilizing our fields and forests and mines, and that we are furnishing profitable employment to the millions of workingmen throughout the United States, bringing comfort and happiness to their homes and making it possible to lay by savings for old age and disability.

"That all the people are participating in this great prosperity is seen in every American community, and shown by the enormous and unprecedented deposits in our savings banks. Our duty is the care and security of these deposits, and their safe investment demands the highest integrity and the best business capacity of those in charge of these depositories of the people's earnings.

" We have a vast and intricate business, built up through years of toil and struggle, in which every part of the country has its stake, which will not permit of either neglect or undue selfishness. No narrow, sordid policy will subserve it. The greatest skill and wisdom on the part of manufacturers and producers will be required to hold and increase it. Our industrial enterprises, which have grown to such great proportions, affect the homes and occupations of the people and the welfare of the country.

" Our capacity to produce has developed so enormously, and our products have so multiplied, that the problem of more markets requires our urgent and immediate attention. Only a broad and enlightened policy will keep what we have. No other policy will get more. In these times of marvelous business energy and gain we ought to be looking to the future, strengthening the weak places in our industrial and commercial systems, that we may be ready for any storm or strain.

RECIPROCITY FAVORED

" By sensible trade arrangements which will not interrupt our home production we shall extend the outlet for our increasing surplus. A system which provides a mutual exchange of commodities is manifestly essential to the continued and healthful growth of our export trade. We must not repose in fancied security that we can forever sell everything and buy little or nothing. If such a thing were possible it would not be best for us, or for those with whom we deal. We should take from our customers such of their products as we can use without harm to our industries and labor.

" Reciprocity is the natural outgrowth of our wonderful industrial development under the domestic policy now firmly established. What we produce beyond our domestic consumption must have a vent abroad. The excess must be relieved through a foreign outlet, and we should sell everywhere we can and buy wherever the buying will enlarge our sales and productions, and thereby make a greater demand for home labor.

"The period of exclusiveness is past. The expansion of our trade and commerce is the pressing problem. Commercial wars are unprofitable. A policy of good will and friendly trade relations will prevent reprisals. Reciprocity treaties are in harmony with the spirit of the times ; measures of retaliation are not.

MORE STEAMERS NEEDED

"If, perchance, some of our tariffs are no longer needed for revenue or to encourage and protect our industries at home, why should they not be employed to extend and promote our markets abroad ? Then, too, we have inadequate steamship service. New lines of steamers have already been put in commission between the Pacific Coast ports of the United States and those on the western coasts of Mexico and Central and South America. These should be followed up with direct steamship lines between the eastern coast of the United States and South American ports.

"One of the needs of the times is direct commercial lines from our vast fields of production to the fields of consumption that we have but barely touched. Next in advantage to having the thing to sell is to have the convenience to carry it to the buyer. We must encourage our merchant marine. We must have more ships. They must be under the American flag, built and manned and owned by Americans. These will not only be profitable in a commercial sense; they will be messengers of peace and amity wherever they go.

"We must build the Isthmian Canal, which will unite the two oceans and give a straight line of water communication with the western coasts of Central and South America and Mexico. The construction of a Pacific cable cannot be longer postponed.

TRIBUTE TO BLAINE

"In the furtherance of these objects of national interest and concern, you are performing an important part. This Exposition would have touched the heart of that American statesman whose mind was ever alert and thought ever constant for a larger commerce and a truer fraternity of the republics of the New World.

"His broad American spirit is felt and manifested here. He needs no identification to an assemblage of Americans anywhere, for the name of Blaine is inseparably associated with the Pan-American movement which finds this practical and substantial expression, and which we all hope will be firmly advanced by the Pan-American Congress that assembles this Autumn in the capital of Mexico. The good work will go on. It cannot be stopped. These buildings will disappear ; this creation of art and beauty and industry will perish from sight, but their influence will remain to

> " ' Make it live beyond its too short living,
> " With praises and thanksgiving.

RESULTS OF THE EXPOSITION

"Who can tell the new thoughts that have been awakened, the ambitions fired and the high achievements that will be wrought through this Exposition ? Gentlemen, let us ever remember that our interest is in accord, not conflict, and that our real eminence rests in the victories of peace, not those of war. We hope that all who are represented here may be moved to higher and nobler effort for their own and the world's good, and that out of this city may come, not only greater commerce and trade for us all, but, more essential than these, relations of mutual respect, confidence and friendship which will deepen and endure.

"Our earnest prayer is that God will graciously vouchsafe prosperity, happiness and peace to all our neighbors, and like blessings to all the peoples and powers of earth."

HOW THE SPEECH WAS RECEIVED

President McKinley's speech was frequently interrupted with applause, his words referring to the establishment of reciprocal treaties with other countries, the necessity of the American people building an isthmian canal and a Pacific cable, and his reference to the work of Blaine in developing the Pan-American idea bringing forth especially enthusiastic cheers. Upon the conclusion of his address a large number of persons broke through the lines around the stand and the President held an impromptu reception for fifteen minutes, shaking hands with thousands.

Throughout the country papers of all parties editorially commented most favorably upon the speech, many predicting that it would become to the present generation what Washington's Farewell Address was to his. It is fitting to record here a few of the many expressions which appeared immediately after the speech—as showing the tenor of all of them.

The Philadelphia *Ledger* (Rep.) says:

"Among the many able addresses the President has delivered in recent years, none will take higher rank than the one spoken yesterday at the Pan-American Exposition. The theme was inspiring and the President in a happy mood to make use of the lessons taught.

"As 'timekeepers of progress' the President bore high and deserving tribute to the value of such expositions. Past experience leaves no room for doubt on that point. The friendly rivalry they bring about and the unexampled prosperity of the nation, with the increasing necessity for wider markets, led the President into some expressions of opinion that will unquestionably be the keynote of the policy of the nation for the immediate future. Above all things, he wants peace and good will—competition, but not enmity. The struggle for success will, in his opinion, be no less sharp in the future than in the past, and he hopes to see it conducted on friendly lines.

"Our great problem is that of securing more markets for our increasing surplus of products. One way to accomplish that is by reciprocity treaties, 'sensible trade arrangements which will not interrupt our home production.' Reciprocity on the President's lines should meet with no opposition in the Republican party or from any friend of the protective tariff. It would be highly advantageous to the nation, and the sooner it can be carried into effect the better.

"In connection with reciprocity treaties, proper encouragement to the merchant marine in the foreign trade and a broad policy of peace and amity toward all nations, the President outlines a policy under which the United States will be certain to go forward with the same unexampled prosperity and contentment that have been the distinguishing characteristics of the McKinley Administration from the beginning."

New York *World* (Dem.) :

"These are the words of a statesman and a wise party leader. They are economically sound as applied to a palpable trade condition. They are politically sagacious in responding to and leading a popular demand which is certain to extend and grow more insistent with the passing of time. They are logically and effectively supplemented by the President's argument for more ships, for an Isthmian canal and for a Pacific cable. Mr. McKinley, always felicitous in his public addresses, has never appeared to better advantage either as an orator or a leader than he does in this admirable speech at the Pan-American Exposition."

MCKINLEY'S LAST MESSAGE

Philadelphia *Times* (Dem.) :

"There will be some dispute as to what were the exact words last spoken by the President who yesterday morning answered to the final roll-call and was summoned from the midst of a sorrowing nation. But it may be taken to be a small matter so long as we remember the hopeful, prophetic message which he delivered to the American people only the day before he was stricken down by the assassin's bullet. This speech has become a dying message. It should linger with us to guide our future policy.

"Mr. McKinley earlier did not hold the liberal economic views of which he had come to be a representative just before his death. The industrial potentiality of the country has increased rapidly within a few years. From his conning-tower at the head of the government he gained a broader outlook. With experience and greater opportunities he surveyed a wider field and was honest and manly enough to change his opinions when he was convinced that those which he had formerly held were no longer for his country's highest good. We honor him for the truth of his character, no less than for the clearness of his sight in regard to questions upon whose correct solution depends the future prosperity of the United States.

" Mr. McKinley has left his message to those who shall come after him. It is to cultivate friendship with all the peoples of the earth, to recognize the changes which modern invention have introduced into modern international relationships, to cast aside ancient sentiments of selfishness and sordidness, and pass out into the sunshine where the nations may buy and sell to each other much more freely. Mr. McKinley was a true friend and advocate of commercial expansion. Some sententious maxims in this farewell address must be remembered :

" 'Our capacity to produce has developed so enormously and our products have so multiplied that the problem of more markets requires our urgent and immediate attention. Only a broad and enlightened policy will keep what we have. No other policy will get more.'

" 'We must not repose in fancied security that we can forever sell everything and buy little or nothing.'

" 'What we produce beyond our domestic consumption must have a vent abroad.'

" 'The period of exclusiveness is past.'

" 'Commercial wars are unprofitable.'

" 'If, perchance, some of our tariffs are no longer needed for revenue or to encourage and protect our industries at home, why should they not be employed to extend and promote our markets abroad?' "

18

It is useful to recall these words in connection with President Roosevelt's promise "to continue absolutely unbroken the policy of President McKinley for the peace and prosperity and honor of our beloved country." We can now but echo the late President's own words in his last speech, when he did not yet foresee the interruption of his earthly term: "The good work will go on. It cannot be stopped." It is for us now to remember his influence as we remember his words and—

> " Make it live beyond its too short living,
> With praises and thanksgiving."

CHAPTER XIX
The Assassin's Fatal Shot

IT was just after the daily organ recitals in the Temple of Music on Friday, September 6th, a day long to be remembered and deplored, that the attempt was made upon President McKinley's life which led to his death. Planned with all the ingenuity and finesse of which anarchy or nihilism are capable, the murderous assassin carried out the work without a hitch. The President, though well guarded by United States secret service detectives, was fully exposed to the attack. He stood at the edge of the raised dais, upon which stands the great pipe organ, at the east side of the structure. Throngs of people crowded in at the various entrances to see the chief executive, and, if possible, clasp his hand. The good-natured mob every minute swelled and multiplied at the points of ingress and egress to the building. The President was in a cheerful mood, and was enjoying to the full the evidences of good-will which everywhere met his gaze. At his right stood John G. Milburn of Buffalo, President of the Pan-American Exposition, who was introducing to him persons of note who approached. Upon the President's left stood his secretary, Mr. Cortelyou.

It was soon after 4 o'clock when one of the throng which surrounded the Presidential party, a medium-sized man of ordinary appearance and plainly dressed in black, approached as if to greet the President. Both Secretary Cortelyou and President Milburn noticed that the man's right hand was swathed in a bandage or handkerchief. He worked his way to the edge of the dais until he was within two feet of the President. President McKinley smiled, bowed and extended his hand in that spirit of geniality the American people so well know, when suddenly the sharp crack of a revolver rang out loud and clear above the hum of voices, the shuffling of feet and vibrating waves of applause that ever and anon swept here and there over the assemblage.

There was an instant of almost complete silence, like the hush that follows a clap of thunder, or the momentary lull that comes after the discharge of a bombshell. The President stood stock still, a look of hesitance, almost of bewilderment, on his face. Then he retreated a step, while a pallor began to steal over his features. The multitude, only partly aware that something serious had happened, paused in the silence of surprise, while necks were craned and all eyes turned as one toward the rostrum where a great tragedy was being enacted.

A GREAT COMMOTION

Then came a commotion. Several men instantly threw themselves forward as with one impulse and sprang toward the assassin. Two of them were United States secret service men, who were on the lookout and whose duty it was to guard against just such a calamity. A negro named Parker, who was near in the line, was said to have instantly struck the assailant and grasped his pistol-hand, but the evidence at the assassin's trial discredited this story. In truth, there was a struggle which rendered the exact facts difficult to obtain. The assailant was hurled to the floor, the pistol struck from his hand, and blows rained upon him by the infuriated detectives and soldiers.

Only now did the multitude that thronged the auditorium begin to come to a realizing sense of the dreadful tragedy which had just been enacted before them. A moment before they had stood mute and motionless, not comprehending the terrible event; but now, as by a single impulse, they surged towards the stage of the horrid drama, while a cry went up from a thousand throats and a thousand men charged forward to lay hands upon the murderous wretch, then helpless in the hands of his captors. For an interval the confusion was terrible. Men shouted, women screamed.

PRESIDENT AND MRS. McKINLEY LEAVING MILBURN HOUSE, BUFFALO

This was on the morning of the assassination.

THE MCKINLEY FUNERAL—THE BODY IN THE EAST ROOM, THE WHITE HOUSE

and children cried. Some of those nearest the doors fled from the edifice in fear of a stampede, while hundreds of others outside struggled blindly forward in the effort to penetrate the crowded building and solve the mystery of excitement and panic which every moment grew and swelled within the congested interior of the edifice.

Inside on the slightly raised dais was enacted within those few feverish moments a tragedy so dramatic in character, so thrilling in its intensity, that few who looked on will ever be able to give a good account of what really did transpire. Even the actors who were playing the principal *roles* came out of it with blanched faces, trembling limbs and beating hearts, while their brains throbbed with a tumult of conflicting emotions, which left behind only a chaotic jumble of impressions which could not be clarified into a lucid narrative of the events as they really transpired.

THE EXALTED VICTIM

Meanwhile, the President, was assisted to a chair. His face was deathly white. He made no outcry, but sank back, with one hand holding his abdomen, the other fumbling at his breast. His eyes were open, and he was clearly conscious of all that happened. He looked up into President Milburn's face and gasped the name of his secretary, Cortelyou.

Mr. Cortelyou bent over the President, who gasped brokenly: "Be careful about my wife. Do not tell her."

Then moved by a paroxysm of pain, he writhed to the left, and his eyes fell upon the prostrate form of his murderer lying on the floor, blood-stained and helpless beneath the blows of the guard. The President raised his right hand, stained with his own blood, and placed it on the shoulder of his secretary.

"Let no one hurt him," he gasped, and sank back as his secretary ordered the guard to bear the murderer out of the President's sight. The outer garments of the President were hastily loosened, and when a trickling stream of blood was seen to wind its way down his breast, spreading its tell-tale stain over the white surface of the linen, their worst fears were confirmed.

A force of Exposition guards were on the scene by this time, and an effort was made to clear the building. The crush was terrific. Spectators crowded down the stairways from the galleries, the crowd on the floor surged forward toward the rostrum, while, despite the strenuous efforts of police and guards, the throng without struggled madly to obtain admission. The President's assailant in the meantime had been hustled to the rear of the building by Exposition Guards McCauley and James, where he was held while the building was cleared and later turned over to Superintendent Bull, of the Buffalo police department, who took the prisoner to the police station, and later to police headquarters. As soon as the crowd in the Temple of Music had been dispersed sufficiently, the President was removed in the automobile ambulance and taken to the exposition hospital, where an examination was made. The best medical skill was summoned, and within a brief period several of Buffalo's best known practitioners were at the patient's side.

THE PRESIDENT'S WOUNDS

The President retained the full use of his faculties while the physicians were consulting about what course to pursue. An examination had revealed the fact that one bullet had grazed the left breast, causing only an unimportant wound. The second bullet had penetrated the abdomen, striking five and a half inches below the left nipple. The abnormally high pulse of the patient indicated that he was dangerously wounded, and the doctors felt that an immediate operation was imperative. One of them told the President this decision. "Gentlemen," he replied, in a low, quiet tone, "I want you to do whatever in your judgment you think is necessary."

Dr. Mann then took charge, and the President was put under the influence of anæsthetics. An incision was made in the abdomen, through the aperture made by the bullet, and the stomach drawn through it. On examination it was found that the bullet had passed straight through this organ.

The bullet could not be found. The holes in the stomach were ugly ones, the posterior hole being much more jagged and torn than the one in front, through which the bullet passed first. The missile had spent some of its force by the time it had traversed the stomach, and thus tore rather than pierced its way through.

After repeated bathing of the wounded parts with antiseptic lotions the apertures in the stomach were sewed up with silk sutures, and the abdominal cut was sewed together with silk-worm gut sutures.

The external wound was then carefully dressed with an antiseptic bath, and a wide abdominal binding was applied. This done, the body was wrapped in sheets, around which blankets were folded, and the President was placed in the ambulance which conveyed him to the residence of Mr. Milburn. Hardly two hours had passed since the firing of the deadly shot.

When it was decided to remove the President from the exposition hospital to the Milburn residence, the news was broken to Mrs. McKinley as gently as might be. She bore the shock remarkably well, and displayed the utmost fortitude. As early as possible in the evening a representative of the press was admitted to the Milburn mansion, where Secretary Cortelyou gave him the official bulletin prepared by the physicians. Secretary Cortelyou arranged for a telegraph office to be established at once in the Milburn residence, and that bulletins, giving the public the fullest information possible, be issued at short intervals. Telegrams poured in by the hundreds, and Secretary Cortelyou was kept busy replying to them. Two stenographers with their typewriters were placed in the parlor, which was quickly transformed into a bustling room.

While the wounded President was being borne from the exposition to the Milburn residence between rows of onlookers with bared heads, a far different spectacle was being witnessed along the route of his assailant's journey from the scene of his crime to police headquarters. The trip was made so quickly that the prisoner was safely landed within the wide portals of the police station and the doors closed before anyone was aware of his presence.

The news of the attempted assassination had in the meanwhile been spread broadcast by the newspapers. Like wildfire, it spread from mouth to mouth. Then bulletins began to appear on the boards, and when the announcement was made that the prisoner had been taken to police headquarters, the crowds surged down toward the terrace, eager for a glimpse of the prisoner. At police headquarters they were met by a strong cordon of police, which denied admittance to all but officials authorized to take part in the examination of the prisoner. In a few minutes the crowd had grown from tens to hundreds, and those in turn quickly swelled into thousands, until the street was completely blocked with a surging crowd of eager humanity. It was at this juncture that some one raised the cry of " Lynch him ! "

Like a flash the cry was taken up. Closer the crowd surged forward. Denser the throng became as new arrivals swelled each moment the swarming multitude. The situation was becoming critical, when suddenly the big doors were flung open and a squad of reserves advanced with solid front, drove the crowd back from the curb, then across the street, and gradually succeeded in dispersing them from about the entrance to the station.

CHAPTER XX
The Last Sad Hours

A S the morning of Friday, September 13th, dawned, and as the eager resident of city and hamlet glanced at the morning bulletins to see the latest reports, hitherto favorable, from the sick room of the President, a great surprise and shock was in store for him. The news was ominous and the history of Thursday and Friday, September 12th and 13th, 1901, is interesting.

On Wednesday the President had a restful night, and the beef juice which the doctors had given him had been relished so keenly that he was given solid food for the first time. He was bathed and then he enjoyed a breakfast of chicken broth, toast and coffee. He felt so good after this somewhat substantial meal that he asked for a mild cigar, which the doctors could not allow him to have. Dr. McBurney, the dean of the corps of attending physicians and surgeons, was thoroughly satisfied with the patient's condition, and went to New York. His intention was to return in a few days. Meantime he and all the physicians kept within call by telephone or telegraph, and were prepared to come back at a moment's notice. Secretary Root also left on the same train, showing his confidence in the recovery of the President.

A SLIGHT REACTION

A slight reaction, however, followed the buoyancy of the morning. The President complained of being tired. The attending physicians at the afternoon consultation, true to their promise to take the public into their confidence, chronicled this fact with scrupulous care, but they displayed no alarm. The doctors said the President's restlessness was only natural and what might be expected.

The slight alarm which was felt when the afternoon bulletin appeared was greatly increased when the physicians hurridly assembled for their evening consultation about an hour earlier than usual. The cheeriness of the morning was succeeded by apprehension, and a dreary rain which began to fall added to the gloomy feeling which prevailed. The bulletin was personally delivered to the members of the press by Secretary Cortelyou, and the frankness with which the physicians announced that the President's condition was not so good, disquieting as it was, was a relief. It was felt to be a proof that nothing was being concealed.

It was explained that the trouble that existed was due to the fact that the solid food taken in the morning had not agreed with the President. It had not been disposed of, and the rise in his pulse was attributed to that fact. It was stated quite positively that the consulting physicians did not believe that the failure to digest the food was due to the condition of the wounds in the sides of the stomach, which were believed to be practically healed, and so pronounced by Dr. McBurney and his associates. The fact that the food would not agree with the patient could not have been anticipated, so it was stated, but as soon as it was found that it had not, the administration of food by the mouth was discontinued. Evidently the surgeons and doctors in attendance were much puzzled by the conditions, which were constantly changing. They were doing their very best for their patient. This was made clear later when, after the lamented President's death, an autopsy was held, and it was found that their's was a hopeless fight. Meanwhile they summoned other doctors.

Dr. Charles D. Stockton, who has a fine reputation as a general practitioner in Western New York, was called in at the evening conference. The problem now was one for the physicians rather than the surgeons, and the advice and counsel of Dr. Stockton were considered advisable.

Secretaries Wilson and Hitchcock reached the Milburn House at 9.35 P.M. They seemed anxious for personal assurances as to the condition of the President, and, when they left their carriage, hurried into the house.

The spirits of the little coterie which Secretaries Hitchcock and Wilson joined in the drawing room of the Milburn House were visibly depressed, although the assurances of Dr. Mann that the President's condition would be better in the morning did something toward offsetting the apprehension they could not conceal.

During the evening the President's pulse increased to 128. This was too high for his temperature. One of the consulting physicians said that, judged by medical records, his pulse should be 96. The acceleration of the pulse was attributed partly to the revulsion of the stomach against the food, and Dr. Mann privately assured Secretaries Hitchcock and Wilson, the President's brother, Abner McKinley, and others assembled below stairs in the Milburn House that the undigested food would probably pass away during the night, and that the President would be better in the morning.

For hours the President failed to respond to the treatment to which he was subjected to relieve him of the difficulty occasioned by the failure of the organs of digestion and assimilation. Nonsuccess of the treatment added to the depression that existed, but just at midnight the relief so much desired came. This gave great encouragement and changed the character of the bulletin, which the physicians were even then preparing. In it they announced that all the unfavorable symptoms had improved since the last bulletin. The decreased rapidity of the pulse, from 128 to 120, which followed the bowel movement, was also exceedingly gratifying.

The physicians were really alarmed about the President's heart. Still the pulse remained much higher than it should be with the temperature at 100.2. The normal pulse for that temperature is about 96.

About midnight the cheering news came from the sick-room that the medical treatment had been effective, and that the unfavorable symptoms of the early evening were all improved.

Abner McKinley, Colonel Brown, his business partner, and Lieutenant James McKinley, the President's nephew, remained at the house during the anxious hours of the evening. After the gratifying intelligence in the midnight bulletin was conveyed to them, they immediately left the house for the night and went to their hotels. Secretary Cortelyou announced, after the bulletin had been issued, that he did not look for any further public statement from the physicians during the night, nor until the regular 6 o'clock bulletin in the morning.

AN IMPRESSIVE SCENE

The scene on the corner across from the Milburn House when Secretary Cortelyou brought out the midnight bulletin was impressive. A hundred newspaper men keyed up to a high tension, and twice that number of anxious watchers who had been alarmed by the 8.30 bulletin, posted everywhere throughout the city, were gathered under the gas light in front of the white tents erected for the accommodation of the newspaper men. Above the suppressed tones of the watchers the only sound was the click of the telegraph instruments. From the gloom into the circle of light the President's Secretary came, accompanied by Mr. Milburn.

"The President has responded to medical treatment, and is better," he said. "The doctors administered calomel and oil, and they proved effective. He is resting nicely now, and the feeling is better."

The cheering news broke the tension of a half night's anxious vigil. After distributing the bulletin, Secretary Cortelyou and Mr. Milburn walked away to get a breath of air and relief from the intense strain of the evening

THE STORY FOR FRIDAY, SEPTEMBER 13TH

Hope and fear alternated all day among the watchers in and around the Milburn house. Every fragment of information was eagerly sought in the hope that it might be construed to mean

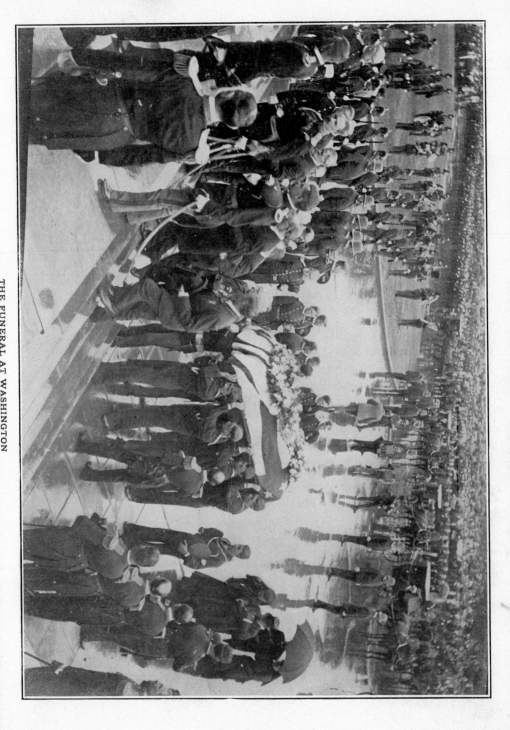

THE FUNERAL AT WASHINGTON

Soldiers and sailors bearing the body up the steps of Capitol, followed by Abner McKinley, the late President's brother and Mrs. Barber, Mrs. McKinley's sister

CARRYING THE CASKET FROM MILBURN HOUSE TO HEARSE

that the danger had passed, and that reasonable hope of the President's recovery might be entertained. Members of the President's family, the physicians, the officials of the Federal Government and all who passed in and out of the house during the day were questioned as to the President's condition, but little of an encouraging nature could be learned. The truth was too evident to be passed over or concealed. The President's life was hanging in the balance. The watchers felt that any moment might come the announcement of a change which would foreshadow the end.

THE LAST RESOURCES EMPLOYED

When the slight improvement noted in the early bulletins was maintained during the afternoon of Thursday, the 12th, and it was learned that the President was taking small quantities of nourishment, hope rose that he would pass the crisis in safety. Everybody knew, and no attempt was made to conceal it, that the coming night would in all human probability decide whether the President was to live or die. It was known that he was being kept alive by heart stimulants, and that the physicians had obtained a supply of oxygen, to be administered if the worst came.

During the day President McKinley was conscious when he was not sleeping. Early in the morning when he woke he looked out of the window and saw that the sky was overcast with heavy clouds. "It is not so bright as it was yesterday," said he. His eyes then caught the waving leaves of the trees glistening with rain Their bright green evidently made an agreeable impression upon him.

"It is pleasant to see them," said he feebly.

The bulletins sent broadcast over the country had brought fearful forebodings to the hearts of relatives and friends. All were praying for the sufferer that, if it be God's will, he might be spared even now when so near death's door.

As fast as steam could bring them the members of the President's Cabinet, his relatives and the physicians, who had left Buffalo, convinced that the President would recover, were whirled back to the city. They went at once to the house in which he was lying, and the information which they obtained there was of a nature to heighten, rather than to relieve, their fears. All night the doctors had worked in the sick-room to keep the President alive.

Day broke with a gloomy sky and a pouring rain, broken by frequent bursts of gusty downpours. It seemed as though nature was sympathizing with the gloom which surrounded the ivy-clad house, about which the sentries were steadily marching. Secretary Cortelyou and Mr. Milburn had announced at half-past 4 o'clock that the efforts of the doctors had produced a rally. Mrs. McKinley was then sleeping, and great care was taken to prevent her from being awakened.

President McKinley fell asleep at half-past 5 o'clock, and slept for an hour. Dr. Wasdin said that this was the most natural sleep that he had had during the night.

Secretary Hitchcock and Mr. Milburn appeared soon after the President awoke at half-past 6 o'clock. They said that both Dr. Rixey and Dr. Stockton believed the President still had a fighting chance.

CROWDS GATHER NEAR THE HOUSE

Almost as soon as it became light men and women began to gather at the ropes which had been stretched across the streets a block away in each direction from the Milburn house. As the day bore on the crowds increased, and were even greater than they were on the day after the President was shot.

It was during the early hours of the morning that the President's sinking spell was at its worst, and but little encouragement was drawn from the bulletin issued at 9 o'clock. It was noted that whilst the President's temperature had fallen his pulse had risen five beats in the minute, from 123 to 128, which showed that his heart was beating like the ticking of a watch. The conclusion was drawn that the apparent improvement in his condition was due solely to the action of the digitalis, strychnine and other medicines that had been given to sustain the heart action.

Senator Hanna, who had gone to Cleveland only two days before, jubilant in the certainty that the President was going to get well, and that he might safely attend the meeting of the G. A. R. in his home city, reached the Milburn house at two minutes before 10 o'clock. In his anxiety to reach the President's bedside he had come from Cleveland, a distance of 183 miles, at the rate of sixty-eight miles an hour.

With Senator Hanna came Mrs. Hanna; Judge Day, of Canton; Colonel Myron P. Herrick, of Cleveland; Senator Fairbanks, of Indiana; Mrs. Duncan and Miss McKinley, sisters of the President; Miss Duncan and Mrs. Herrick. Senator Hanna reached the house first. The members of his party arrived soon afterward. They joined Secretaries Wilson and Hitchcock, Mr. and Mrs. Herman Baer, Abner McKinley, Mrs. Lafayette McWilliams, Mr. Milburn, Wilson S. Bissell, with many others of the relatives and friends, who were in the house. The new arrivals were immediately informed of the critical condition of the President, and their faces, which had been grave, became still graver as they listened.

ANXIETY INTENSE IN BUFFALO

At this time anxiety in regard to the President's condition had become intense throughout Buffalo. Hundreds of men, women and children were massed at the ropes, their faces turned in the direction of the house, though many of them were unable to see it, and, of course, all were too far away to be able to hear anything. So many persons had gathered in the Milburn House that it was crowded. Groups formed on the lawn in front of the house to discuss the situation, and to exchange the latest news from the doctors. The reporters, too, were ever alert for information.

Across the street from the house there were scores of newspaper men waiting for news of the President's condition, and dozens of telegraph instruments were ticking noisily under the tents which had been erected to shelter them.

Secretary Cortelyou was asked whether it was true that the physicians had been compelled to begin feeding the President through the stomach before it was safe to do so because the means first taken to give nourishment had caused irritation, resulting in the rejection of the food which had been injected before it had imparted any nourishment to the patient. This was the explanation commonly accepted of the surprisingly short time that had been permitted to elapse before the President was allowed to receive liquid and even solid food into his stomach.

Mr. Cortelyou said that he had not been informed upon this point. He said that the stoppage of the functions of the bowels had created a poison in the President's system, but that, during the day, this had been practically eliminated.

THE HEART NEEDED BLOOD FOOD

Dr. Roswell Park said: "The President was not given solid food before he could stand it. He was perfectly able to assimilate the food given him, had it not been that the impoverished blood affected the heart. The heart refused to act properly without strong blood food, and that was why the toast, soaked in hot beef juice, was given him. He was not given coffee. He relished the food, and asked for a cigar, but this was denied. Everything known to medical science was done for him, and there was no mistake made." Dr. Hermann Mynter said: "At the time solid food was given him he was able to take it. There can be no mistake about that. I do not believe that the food in his stomach had much effect on the heart."

The President was asleep at half-past 1 o'clock. Only injections of saline solution and digitalis in light doses had been used up to that hour. One of the physicians sat constantly at the bedside, with his fingers on the President's pulse, ready at any alarming change in the action of the heart to apply the remedies which were in readiness to be used as a last resort. Tanks of oxygen were ready at hand to be drawn upon, and all the appliances that medical skill and science could provide were within reach. The beating of the pulse was sufficiently strong to enable the physicians to permit the President to have his sleep out.

Dr. McBurney arrived at the Milburn House a little before 8 o'clock. Shortly after his arrival, oxygen was administered to the President, and under its influence the patient aroused. The Rev. C. V. Wilson of North Tonawanda, pastor of Mr. McKinley's old church in Canton, was with the President and prayed with him. Mr. Wilson left the Milburn house shortly before 9 o'clock. Tears were streaming from his eyes and he was almost completely overcome by grief.

CONSCIOUS THAT THE END WAS NEAR

The President was fully conscious, and whispered to Dr. Rixey that he knew that the end was at hand. He asked to see his wife, and she was sent for. She entered his room, and it was apparent to those present that of the two principal figures in this intense drama President McKinley, about to solve the great mystery, the more fully realized the significance of the awful moment. There was no show of fear in the attitude of the nation's Executive.

Mrs. McKinley sank to her knees at the side of the bed, her husband's hands clasped in hers, and her head bowed and buried in the bed covering. Sobs shook her for a moment, and then she looked at Dr. Rixey, and with almost a smile on her face, said : " I know that you will save him. I cannot let him go ; the country cannot spare him."

THE PRESIDENT'S LAST WORDS

The President, it is said, roused himself sufficiently to recognize her, and whispered : " Good-bye all, good-bye. It is God's way. His will be done." He made a feeble movement, as if he wished to clasp her hand, and lapsed into unconsciousness, and the physicians assisted Mrs. McKinley to her feet and led her from the room.

19

A little later Mr. Milburn explained to Mrs. McKinley that the President was dying, and that he could live till morning only in the event of the direct interposition of Providence. She then came to a full realization of the loss that was upon her, and she showed symptoms of a collapse. Herbert P. Bissell rushed to the assistance of the sorrowing wife, who was being literally supported by Mr. Milburn. Word was sent to Dr. Wasdin, who came from the President's chamber and administered a restorative. Little by little she came back to her normal condition. Several women friends were with her, and in their sympathy she found surcease. To one she whispered : " I will be strong for his sake."

An attempt was made to persuade Mrs. McKinley to retire and get some rest. She refused. She said that her duty was there, and there she would remain within call of those who were with her husband. She said that she hoped that the President would arouse, and she might then have the comfort of a last word with him.

LAST DESPERATE MEANS EMPLOYED

As soon as it was known that oxygen was being administered, all knew that the beginning of the end had come. Then a bulletin was posted as follows :

"The President's physicians report that his condition is grave at this hour. He is suffering from extreme prostration. Oxygen is being used. He responds to stimulation but poorly."

With a sublime display of Christian fortitude, the President soon after lapsed into unconsciousness. The members of the Cabinet, grief-stricken, were gathered in the large drawing-room of the Milburn house. The time had come when they, too, were to look upon the President for the last time in life. They ascended the stairway one after the other, noiselessly approaching the threshold of the chamber where the dying man lay, and gazed within. Those who came first turned back appalled and overwhelmed, and did not pass within the chamber.

Secretary Long, who arrived on a late train, went at once to the chamber and passed directly to the bedside of the President, grasping the hand that was already clammy with approaching death.

Meantime the President had lapsed into a state of complete unconsciousness, and it was only a question of hours, perhaps minutes, when the end would come.

By 10 o'clock there was no perceptible pulse. The extremities had grown cold and the rigidity of death was fast falling upon the sufferer. The physicians who remained at his side detected only the faintest heart-beats. Some of them, knowing that all was over, departed, while others remained, not because there was any further need of their ministrations, but because of respect for the expiring President. Dr. Janeway, the eminent heart specialist, who had been summoned from New York, arrived shortly before midnight and proceeded at once to the bedside of the President. An instant's glance told him the time had passed for the slightest hope ; he turned away, telling the assembled relatives and officials that the end was very near.

Midnight came, and still the tremendous vitality of the President was battling against dissolution. Another hour passed so, and still another. At 2 o'clock Dr. Rixey was the only physician in the death chamber. The others were in an adjoining room, while the relatives, Cabinet officers and nearest friends were gathered in silent groups in the apartments below. As he watched and waited, Dr. Rixey observed a slight convulsive tremor. The President had entered the valley of the shadow of death. Word was at once taken to the immediate relatives who were not present to hasten for the last look upon the President in life.

They came in groups, the women weeping and the men bowed and sobbing in their intense grief.

Grouped about the bedside at this moment were the only brother of the President, Abner McKinley, and his wife ; Miss Helen McKinley and Mrs. Sarah Duncan, sisters of the President ; Miss Mary Barber, niece ; Miss Sara Duncan, niece ; Lieutenant

James F. McKinley, William M. Duncan and John Barber, nephews; F. M. Osborne, a cousin; Secretary George B. Cortelyou, Charles G. Dawes, Comptroller of the Currency; Colonel Webb C. Hayes and Colonel William C. Brown.   With these directly and indirectly connected with the family were those others who had kept ceaseless vigil, the white-garbed nurses and the uniformed marine hospital attendants.   In the adjoining room were Drs. Charles McBurney, Eugene Wasdin, Roswell Park, Charles G. Stockton and Herman Mynter.

The minutes were now flying, and it was 2.15 o'clock.   Silent and motionless, the circle of loving friends stood about the bedside. Dr. Rixey leaned forward and placed his ear close to the breast of the expiring President.   Then he straightened up and made an effort to speak.

" The President is dead," he said.

The President had passed away peacefully, without the convulsive struggle of death.   It was as though he had fallen asleep. As they gazed on the face of the martyr President only the sobs of the mourners broke the silence of the chamber of death. Mr. Cortelyou had been one of the first to rouse himself, after the stunning effect of the announcement of death.   He passed from the room and down the stairway.   There, in the large drawing-room, were still assembled the members of the Cabinet and officials high in the administration and in the confidence of the President.   As he appeared at the threshold of the room, they seemed to realize that the message of death had come.

Mr. Cortelyou halted at the door, and summoning up all of his efforts said: "Gentlemen, the President has passed away." Realizing, too, the momentous nature of the event to the people of the country, Mr. Cortelyou stepped through the outer doorway of the Milburn house and, advancing down the walk to the newspaper men at the front gate, calmly announced: "The President died at 2.15 o'clock."   Thus closed the final chapter in the life of William McKinley.

CHAPTER XXI

Obsequies of the Martyred President

DURING the day that followed the sad death of the martyred McKinley preparations were made for the last sad rites. These, as in the similar instances of Lincoln and Garfield, and of the more recently deceased Victoria, were to consist of public ceremonies and private obsequies. The people demanded the right to gaze upon the lifeless features of their beloved leader, and the request, dictated by respect and affection, could not be ignored. From Philadelphia came an earnest solicitation that the body of the dead President should lie in state for an interval in the Hall of Independence, the hallowed scene of the nation's birth, where the body of Abraham Lincoln had reposed thirty-six years before. But the request came too late, the plans for the funeral ceremonies had been made, and it was deemed best not to change them even for this added honor to the nation's martyr.

Before beginning the preparations for the funeral, it was deemed right and proper that an autopsy should be made to satisfy the family and friends as well as the public that all had been done which could be done to save the President's life. The following is the report of the doctors who made the autopsy:

WHAT THE AUTOPSY TOLD

"The bullet which struck over the breast bone did not pass through the skin and did little harm.

"The other bullet passed through both walls of the stomach near its lower border. Both holes were found to be perfectly closed by the stitches, but the tissue around each hole had become gangrenous. After passing through the stomach the bullet passed

337

into the back walls of the abdomen, hitting and tearing the upper end of the kidney. This portion of the bullet track was also gangrenous, the gangrene involving the pancreas. The bullet has not yet been found.

"There was no sign of peritonitis or disease of other organs. The heart walls were very thin. There was no evidence of any attempt at repair on the part of nature, and death resulted from the gangrene which affected the stomach around the bullet wounds as well as the tissues around the further course of the bullet. Death was unavoidable by any surgical or medical treatment and was the direct result of the bullet wound."

This report of the autopsy upon President McKinley was made not only by the physicians and surgeons who attended him, but by a number of other medical experts. It shows he was beyond medical or surgical aid from the moment he was struck by the assassin's bullet. The surgeons did everything that could be done to help him when they operated upon him promptly and sewed up the two wounds in his stomach. In the ordinary course of events nature would have begun at once to repair the damage, but the autopsy disclosed that nature did nothing. Mr. McKinley was not in as good condition as he was supposed to be. Although not sick, he was "run down" by hard work and sedentary habits. The walls of his heart were unusually thin, and that organ, though sufficient to sustain his ordinarily quiet life, was not strong enough to bear the shock sustained by the assassin's attack. These things could not be known to the physicians and surgeons until the autopsy. They were working more or less blindly, and knew by the pulse that the heart was greatly affected, but there was relatively little fever; it seemed to be abating and the patient gave no sign until the fatal collapse that the parts surrounding the path of the bullet had become gangrenous.

It has been suggested that the bullet of the assassin was poisoned ; but it is not necessary to assume this in order to explain the gangrenous condition, which is a not infrequent result of gunshot wounds. In a healthy young person the gangrene would probably have been accompanied by very high fever; but in the President's case there was relatively little fever, and for this reason the attending physicians were misled into the belief that he was on the high road to recovery. Sad as was his death, it is a relief to know that it was due entirely to the assassin's bullet; that his physicians and surgeons did all that was possible to save him, and that they could not have prolonged his life after the collapse even though they had known exactly what had caused his heart failure.

PLANS FOR THE FUNERAL

The plans for the funeral provided for a private ceremony at the Milburn house on Sunday, September 15th, at 11 A.M., consisting of reading the Scripture, prayer and the singing of a hymn. Immediately after this service the remains of the late President were to be taken to the Buffalo City Hall, under escort of one company of regular troops, one company of marines, one company each of the Buffalo regiments of the National Guard.

At the City Hall the body to lie in state, affording the citizens of Buffalo an opportunity to pay their respects to their dead ruler. The body was then to remain under a guard of soldiers and sailors until Monday at 7.30 A.M., when it would be taken under the same escort to the funeral train at the Buffalo Union Station.

This train, as arranged by the authorities of the Pennsylvania Railroad, to consist of one private car for Mrs. McKinley, one combination car, one dining car, one compartment car, one double drawing room and sleeping car and one observation car, in which the body of the President would be placed.

The train to leave Buffalo at 8.30 Monday morning, and arrive in Washington the same evening, traveling by way of Williamsport, Harrisburg and Baltimore.

At Washington the body to be taken from the train to the Executive Mansion under escort of a squadron of cavalry; and at

9 o'clock on Tuesday morning to be removed to the rotunda of the Capitol, under the same escort of cavalry, when the funeral services were to take place immediately, and afterward the body was to lie in state until evening of Tuesday, when the body would be taken, under military escort, followed by the funeral procession, in accordance with the precedent in the case of President Garfield, to the Baltimore & Potomac Station, and placed upon the funeral train, which would leave for Canton.

The train to reach Canton at 11 o'clock Wednesday morning, where the final funeral services were to be committed to the charge of the citizens of Canton, under the direction of a committee to be selected by the Mayor of that city.

Simple and sincere in life, so was the funeral of William McKinley at the Milburn house in Buffalo on Sunday morning, September 15th. There was no pomp, no harsh stiffness of painful ceremony. It was a sincere tribute of respect to a great and a good man who had died with the words "God's will be done" upon his lips.

THE COFFIN AND ITS DRAPINGS

The coffin rested in the drawing-room on the first floor. It was richly draped in black, with the upper part open, and bearing the simple inscription on a silver plate:

WILLIAM McKINLEY,

BORN JANUARY 29, 1843.

DIED SEPTEMBER 14, 1901.

Across the foot of the coffin was a new silk American flag, which fell in graceful folds to the floor. All about were an abundance of flowers sent from all parts of the country, with a large wreath of roses resting on the mantel near the head of the bier. At every door into the drawing-room soldiers were stationed, and no one was permitted to enter.

Rev. Dr. Locke, of the Methodist Church, and a friend of the family, and the choir from the First Presbyterian Church, of Buffalo, took part in the funeral ceremonies at the house.

At a signal there rose from the hall the words of "Lead, Kindly Light," sung by the quartet. It was President McKinley's favorite hymn. Every one within sound of the music knew it, and, as the voices swelled through the house, half of those in the room put their faces in their hands to hide their tears.

When the singing ended Dr. Locke read from 1 Corinthians, xv. All had risen as he began and remained standing throughout the services. "O Death, where is thy sting? O Grave, where is thy victory?" repeated the minister. Again the voices rose with the words, "Nearer, My God, to Thee." Dr. Locke, who was dressed in the simple garb of a clergyman of the Methodist Church, then advanced to the head of the coffin. Bowing his head and folding his hands as he looked down into the face of the dead President, he invoked the divine help and comfort in the hour of affliction. The services closed with a simple benediction. Four sailors of the navy, two infantry sergeants and two artillery sergeants bore the coffin out of the house. The President, the Cabinet members and the others followed it. Mrs. McKinley and the members of the family remained.

A SOLEMN MOMENT

The trained nurses and the personal attendants of the President gathered on the side porch to see the body taken away. Through their tears from behind the screen of vines they saw it borne from the house, and as long as the hearse in which it was deposited remained in view they strained their dimmed eyes to see it. Those noble women who minister to the sick and who are inured to sorrow were prostrated with grief.

Three long rolls of a muffled drum told those outside the house that the funeral party was about to appear. All the morning a veil of mist had been hanging over the city, but just as the coffin was carried out of the house the sun came out and the warm light illumined the bright colors of the flags on it. All the way from the Milburn house to the City Hall, a distance of nearly four miles, the streets were black with people, but there was no need for police lines, for the people stood in silence with heads uncovered waiting for the procession to pass.

As the coffin was brought out of the house the Sixty-fifth Regiment band, stationed on the opposite side of the street, stepped forward a few paces and began playing in a minor key " Nearer, My God, to Thee." Slowly the coffin was carried on the shoulders of the soldiers across the lawn and placed in the hearse, drawn by four black horses.

As the funeral procession moved south through Delaware Avenue toward the City Hall it passed through a vast concourse of people, filling the walks and cross streets and crowding housetops, windows and every available space along the line of march. It was plain to see from this popular outpouring that the hearts of the people had been deeply touched, and, as the flower-covered coffin passed along, women wept and men gave expression to the universal feeling of grief.

LYING IN STATE IN THE CITY HALL, BUFFALO

As the escort of soldiers swung slowly into Franklin Street a few drops of rain fell. In two minutes it was raining hard. The long line of troops took their positions at attention, facing the City Hall. The coffin was lifted from the hearse to the shoulders of the sailors and marines, and borne into the City Hall. Outside there was not a man who did not stand with hat removed in respect to the dead President. Inside, with slow and measured steps, the bearers made their way to the catafalque. A moment later, and the body of President McKinley was lying in state.

A mighty host of between 75,000 and 100,000 men, women and children swept through the City Hall, where President McKinley lay, during the afternoon between 1.30 and 10.30 o'clock.

The main corridor of the City Hall is oblong. The front opens upon Franklin Street, the rear opening on Delaware Avenue. The front and rear face the east and west. In the centre of the corridor under the dome was the catafalque, about eighteen inches in height. Thirty feet distant from it on either side were two round altar-shaped stands, used for ornamental purposes. These were crape-covered. The sides of the corridor were lined with giant ferns and palms. The chandeliers at the base of the four stairways leading to the second floor were draped with the national colors, overlaid with black and white crape. In the centre of the arch of the south intersecting corridor hung a life-sized portrait of the dead Executive draped with bunting and crape, and with white doves with outstretched wings surrounding it. The coffin was borne into the corridor on the shoulders of eight men.

On the coffin were the national colors, on top of which were placed a wreath of American Beauty roses, and one of white roses. When the lid was removed it was noticed that the President's left hand, which had rested on his waist, had dropped to his side. The top of the coffin was removed and the hand was tenderly replaced. The face of the President bore a look of perfect peacefulness. It was not greatly emaciated. The most noticeable difference was that his usual pallor had been succeeded by sallowness.

President Roosevelt led the Cabinet into the corridor and took a position on the south side, so that he stood on the right and near the foot of the coffin. Scattered about were some of the more prominent citizens of Buffalo, and police and National Guard officials. At the head of the coffin, at attention, stood a sergeant of the coast artillery, and at the foot the Chief Master-at-Arms. President Roosevelt gazed only an instant into the face of the dead, and then, with bowed head, quickly passed toward the Delaware Avenue exit.

First in the throng, a little girl of about seven came along, her brown eyes glistening with excitement. She and her mother had been drenched by the rain. The mother's eyes filled with tears as she looked at the President. The little girl was too short, and, placing her hand on the edge of the glass top, she raised herself on tiptoe and looked in. Her mouth opened with a half-suppressed exclamation as she looked up at her mother. Then a policeman's gloved hand gently pushed her along.

A grizzled war veteran, wearing a Grand Army and a corps badge, limped in. His collar was wilted and his hair was wet. Not a muscle of his grim face moved as he bent slightly over and looked at Mr. McKinley's face. He walked on like one in a dream, perhaps listening in memory to the rattle of musketry at Cedar Creek. Three awe-stricken boys of twelve, somewhat ragged and as wet as rats, came along with linked hands. The policeman tried to get them to separate, but there must have been a boyish Masonry that steeled them against the orders of a bluecoat. Unlink they would not. Each freckled face bent reverently over the convex glass, a look of something like terror came into their eyes, and then they were swept on, still linked together, a sort of faith, hope and charity in ragged knickerbockers and shoes that oozed water at the toes. Out into the rain they went, down the outer steps, with their heads together, holding in their chalice of memory a picture that will be retold to children and grandchildren in the days to come. The corridor became wet from the tramping feet, and still the hero-worshippers surged through the portals. As long as the doors were open, late into the night, did the people, in an orderly and continuous line, pass the bier and view the pallid features. Then the casket was closed and the gates locked. A guard of honor stood sentinel through the night.

THE BODY TAKEN TO WASHINGTON

At early dawn of Monday morning, escorted by military, the body was taken to the funeral train, and started for the Capital City, acccompanied by relatives, high officials and many friends. Through a long living lane of bareheaded people, stretching from Buffalo up over the Alleghenies, down into the broad valley of the

Susquehanna, and on to the marble city on the banks of the shining Potomac, the nation's martyred President made his last journey to the seat of government, over which he presided for four and one-half years. The whole country seemed to have drained its population to the sides of the track over which the funeral train passed. The thin lines through the mountains and the sparsely-settled districts thickened at the little hamlets, covered acres in towns suddenly grown to the proportions of respectable cities and were congested into vast multitudes in the larger cities. Work was suspended in field and mine and city. The schools were dismissed, and everywhere appeared the trappings and tokens of woe. A million flags at half mast dotted hillside and valley, and formed a thicket of color over the cities, and from almost every banner streamed a bit of crape. The stations were heavy with the black symbols of mourning. At all the larger towns and cities, after the train got into Pennsylvania, militiamen, drawn up at present arms, kept back the enormous crowds.

A REMARKABLE DEMONSTRATION

The silence with which the countless thousands viewed the remains of their hero and martyr was oppressive and profound. Only the rumbling of the train wheels, the sobs from men and women with tear-stained faces and the doleful tolling of the church bells broke on the ear. At several places, Williamsport, Harrisburg and Baltimore, the chimes played Cardinal Newman's grand hymn. Taken altogether, the journey home was the most remarkable demonstration of universal personal sorrow since Lincoln was borne to his grave. Every one of those who came to pay their last tribute to the dead had an opportunity to catch a glimpse of the flag-covered bier, elevated to view in the observation car at the rear of the train.

There was no other bit of color to catch the eye on this train of death. The locomotive was shrouded in black, the curtains of the cars, in which sat the lonely, stricken widow, the relatives of the

President, Cabinet and others were drawn. The whole black train was like a shuttered house, save only for that hindmost car where the body lay guarded by a soldier of the army and a sailor of the navy.

Mrs. McKinley stood the trip bravely. In the morning, soon after leaving Buffalo, she pleaded so earnestly to be allowed to go into the car where her dear one lay, that reluctant assent was given, and she spent half an hour beside the coffin.

PILOT ENGINE PRECEDED THE TRAIN

All the way the train was preceded about fifteen minutes by a pilot engine sent ahead to test the bridges and switches and prevent the possibility of an accident to the precious burden it carried.

The train had the right of way over everything. Not a wheel moved on that section of the railroad system thirty minutes before the pilot engine was due, or for the same length of time after the train had passed. The General Superintendent had sent out explicit instructions covering every detail. The order concluded :

" Every precaution must be taken by all employees to make this movement absolutely safe."

In the twelve hours between Buffalo and Washington, it is estimated over half a million people saw the coffin which held all that was mortal of President McKinley.

It was with simple ceremony and a silence that fitted perfectly the sadness of the occasion that the body of the late President was borne up Pennsylvania Avenue to the White House and laid upon the bier in the great East Room where he had stood so often in the pride of his manhood to receive the greetings of the common people he loved better than himself.

It was fitting that such ceremony as there was should be severely military in its character, in recognition of the fact that the President was the Commander-in-chief of the United States army and navy. Nowhere was there a show of civilian participation. The streets about the station were filled with mounted troops, and the station itself was occupied by stalwart soldiers and sailors in uniform. The blue-coated policemen and the railroad employes were nearly all that stood for civil life.

It was not so on the broad stretch of avenue that led to the White House. There the people strained and crowded in a vast multitude against the stiff wire ropes which restrained them from the space marked out for the line of procession. The silence that marked the progress of the funeral party through the national capital was profound. The people as a whole did not talk even in whispers, and the only sign of agitation in the great crowd was the silent pressing and striving against the ropes to see the mournful cortege which swept slowly along. The afternoon was cloudy, and with the close of day began the dull, depressing boom of a great gun at intervals of five minutes. It was the signal which gave notice of the approach of the funeral train.

At the Pennsylvania Railroad Station men in bright uniforms gathered, a mixture of soldiers and sailors, and, with lowered voices, talked in groups while waiting to take up their parts in the ceremony. From the brigadier-general and naval captain down to the humblest lieutenant and ensign, every officer on duty in the Capitol was there, save a few of high rank who composed the guard of honor, and waited at the White House.

The casket was moved from the observation car, and tenderly received upon the bent shoulders of the body-bearers. Four artillerymen, from Fort McHenry, Maryland, were on the right and four sailors on the left. Straightening themselves under their burden, they walked slowly towards the hearse. As the casket emerged a bugle note rose clearly, and " taps " rang out. That was the only sound that broke the dead silence.

Just beyond the entrance to the station President Roosevelt, with the members of the Cabinet, had paused and had taken station so as to leave a broad space for the funeral cortege. They ranged themselves on the sidewalk in double rows opposite each other and stood with bared heads as the corpse was carried to the hearse, drawn up at the side gate.   The hearse was an exquisitely carved affair, and was drawn by six coal-black horses, each of which was led by a colored groom in black livery.

When the sad cortege arrived at the White House the hearse stopped under the *porte-cochere*.   The body-bearers took the coffin upon their broad shoulders, and, passing up three or four steps, waited until President Roosevelt and the members of the Cabinet had alighted from their carriages, and then followed them through the wide-open doors into the East Room.   Just in the centre of the room, under the great crystal chandelier, they deposited their precious burden upon a black-draped base, and stood at salute while the Chief Executive and Cabinet members, with bowed heads, passed by.

Following them came the chief officers of the army and navy now in the city, the guard of honor consisting of officers of the Loyal Legion, members of the Union Veterans' organization and the Grand Army of the Republic.

The casket was placed lengthwise of the East Room, the head to the north.   Piled about it were a half hundred floral emblems of exceptional beauty, and as many more were placed in the inside corridor to wait the morrow.   Two marines, a soldier and a sailor, stood guard, one at each corner of the casket, while seated on either side were two members of the Grand Army, and two members of the Loyal Legion.   These were relieved at intervals of two hours during the night.

Before midnight the household had retired to rest, and the only lights to be seen were those in the room where his comrades kept watch over their dead chief.

There in the East Room of the White House, where for more than four years he had made his home as the Chief Magistrate of the great American Republic, he rested undisturbed.   Upstairs his widow mourned for her dead in the family apartments that brought back but the saddest of memories.

CHAPTER XXII

The Impressive State Funeral Ceremonies

THE last sad services at the Nation's Capital began on Wednesday, the 17th of September, when the body-bearers silently and reverently raised to their stalwart shoulders the casket, containing all that was mortal of the illustrious dead. As they appeared at the main door of the White House the Marine Band, stationed on the avenue opposite the mansion, struck up the hymn the President loved so well, " Nearer, My God, to Thee," and, as the last sad strain of the music died away, the throng in the building lifted their heads, but their eyes were wet.

Slowly along the White House driveway, through a fine drizzling rain, the solemn cortege wound its way down to the gate leading to the avenue and halted. Then, with a grand, solemn swing, the artillery band began the " Dead March from Saul," a blast from a bugle sounded " march" and the head of the procession was moving on its way to the Capitol. The casket, in a black carved hearse and drawn by six coal-black horses, caparisoned in black net with trailing tassels and a stalwart groom at the head of each, moved down through the gateway toward the distant Capitol. In the great funeral procession were bodies of troops representing the army and navy, high dignitaries of State, including the Judiciary, members of both houses of Congress and representatives of foreign governments; also many civic organizations from all sections of the country.

At 10.12 o'clock the head of the procession arrived at the north end of the Capitol plaza. The troops swept around to the south end of the plaza and then marched to position fronting the main entrance to the Capitol. As soon as they had been formed at rest, the artillery band on the left and the Marine Band on the right of the entrance, the funeral cortege with its guard of honor entered the plaza from the north.

The guard of honor ascended the steps, the naval officers on the right and the army officers on the left, forming a cordon on each side, just within the ranks of the artillerymen, seamen and marines. As the eight sturdy body-bearers, four from the army and four from the navy, tenderly drew the flag-draped casket from the hearse the band sweetly wailed the pleading notes of " Nearer, My God, to Thee." Every head in the vast attendant throng was bared. Tear-bedimmed eyes were raised to heaven and silent prayers went up from the thousands of hearts.

With careful and solemn tread the body-bearers began the ascent of the staircase with their precious burden and tenderly bore it to the catafalque in the rotunda.

Here, under the great dome of the Capitol, on whose vast canopy the artist has painted the apotheosis of Washington, there rested the body of William McKinley, whose apotheosis is in the hearts of his countrymen. In the centre of the rotunda that has resounded to the tread of statesmen for almost a century stood the bier of the dead President, while on either side passed 60,000 men, women and children who sought a last glimpse of the face of the man they all loved so well.

The obsequies, from the moment the remains of the President were carried from the White House to the Capitol until they were placed upon the train which bore them to the old home in Canton, were simple and democratic. There was no display of pomp and splendor. The ceremonies were majestic in their simplicity. The occasion was historic, though sorrowful, and the greatest in the land paid humble tribute to the dead President. The new President of the United States, the only living ex-President, the Supreme Court, the highest officers of the army and navy, the Senate and House of Representatives, the representatives of the foreign powers, delegations of the great patriotic orders of the country, representatives of States and municipalities, all met with bowed heads about the bier of William McKinley. Through its representatives a nation paid the last honors to its martyred President.

A DAY OF GLOOM

It was a genuine day of mourning, and Nature added to the gloom. Gray clouds overcast the sky early in the day and at intervals rain deluged the city. Despite the frequent downpours, the tens of thousands of Washington's citizens who besieged the Capitol to look upon the dead form of the President held their places in line, drenched to the skin, but determined to show their affection for him who had been so ruthlessly taken from them.

In the services in the rotunda of the Capitol all interest centred, as they expressed the sympathy of the nation and the acquiescence in God's will according to the President's last prayer of resignation. The place was well chosen and already hallowed by the religious services over the bodies of the other two martyred Presidents. President McKinley's remains rested directly in the centre of the Capitol beneath which it had been the purpose of the designers of the building to have placed the body of the Father of his Country, George Washington. On the walls surrounding the rotunda hang immense paintings depicting the great events in the early history of the country. Its discovery by Columbus, the embarkation by the Pilgrim Fathers, the surrender at Yorktown, and other great events marking the birth of the nation, are shown ; while from pedestals on the east and west side of the circle the marble statues of Lincoln and Grant looked down upon the bier of the martyred President.

This was a spot which always attracted Mr. McKinley when a member of Congress. Hundreds of times had he stood gazing on these pictures, pointing them out to friends and visitors, and thousands of times, in the pursuit of his duties as Congressman, had he traversed this rotunda, a familiar figure to the guides and employees of the Capitol. To-day the guides, grown gray in the service, who used to point out Major McKinley to the curious visitors as the leader of the House and a great man, acted as ushers and seated the audience of 800 or more that gathered about Major McKinley's coffin to pay their last respects.

A NOTABLE OCCASION

It seemed peculiarly fitting that the body of this distinguished man should lie amid the scenes of his great achievements as a statesman and legislator. How strong he was in the affections of Congressmen was shown by the large attendance of Senators and Representatives. His old colleagues in the House and members of the Senate, with whom he labored and accomplished great work of legislation, were inexpressibly affected as they gathered about his remains.

Few of the older Congressmen could hide their feelings. There was Payne, of New York; Hopkins, of Illinois; Bingham and Dalzell, of Pennsylvania, who served many years in the House when William McKinley was one of its foremost Republican members, and Allison, of Iowa; Hawley and Platt, of Connecticut; Burrows, of Michigan; Spooner, of Wisconsin; Cullom, of Illinois; Cockrell, of Missouri; Daniel, of Virginia, and others of the Senate who had the most pleasant recollections of their associations with Mr. McKinley when he was a member of Congress. The faces of these distinguished statesmen reflected their heartfelt sorrow. Senator Hawley, an intense admirer of President McKinley before and after the latter entered the White House, tottered into the rotunda almost in a state of collapse. He had come from Buffalo with the funeral party, and, though broken in health and shaken by age, he was determined to pay his respects to the beloved dead.

It was a most distinguished and august body that gathered about the casket. There was President Roosevelt, sitting at the head of his Cabinet, conscious of the great responsibilities suddenly thrust upon him, but with sorrow depicted in every line of

THE PRESIDENT POSES FOR THE CHILDREN'S CAMERAS AT EL PASO, TEXAS

FUNERAL PROCESSION TO THE CAPITOL
Senators and Representatives in line

his face. In full command of his feelings, it was only the firm set of his jaw that revealed the effort to preserve a calm exterior.

Across a narrow aisle from him sat the only living ex-President of the United States, Grover Cleveland, who now visited Washington for the first time since he resigned the reins of Government into the hands of William McKinley on March 4, 1897. Mr. Cleveland seemed affected by the services and the surroundings, reverently bowed his head in prayer and joined with the audience in repeating the Lord's Prayer at the close of the minister's invocation.

SERVED UNDER THREE MARTYRED PRESIDENTS

With President Roosevelt there sat all the members of Mr. McKinley's Cabinet. Secretary Hay sat on his left, a heartbroken, sorrow-stricken man. For the third time in his life he attended services held over the bodies of murdered Presidents. It has been his fate to have been intimately associated with the three Presidents of the United States who have fallen at the hands of assassins. He was private secretary to the first martyred President, Abraham Lincoln, and was Assistant Secretary of State under President Garfield. This third cruel blow was much more than he deserved. Besides Secretary Hay, there were the other members of the late President's two Cabinets.

SERVICES IN THE CAPITOL

Mrs. McKinley was unable to attend the services at the Capitol, but the other members of the dead President's family gathered near the casket and listened to the simple prayers, hymns and address that composed the service. The two hymns, which were special favorites of Mr. McKinley, were sung by a double quartet. Everybody was affected by the sweet music and touching words. "Lead, Kindly Light" and "Nearer, My God, to Thee" seemed to have deeper significance as the strains of the well-known tunes rang through that vast rotunda and were re-echoed from the lofty dome.

There was a profusion of floral gifts in all forms of magnificent and costly flowers, sent from all parts of the country and expressing the love, affection and esteem of representatives of all governments, organizations and bodies of men. The railing about the rotunda was lined with exquisite floral pieces, while the flag-draped casket was banked with some of the finest wreaths and designs.

The funeral services were simple and beautiful. They were of the form prescribed in the Methodist Church. Two hymns, a prayer, an address and a benediction comprised all of it, yet the impression left at the end was of perfection.

When the noise occasioned by seating the late-comers had ceased a hush fell upon the people and then the choir softly sang " Lead, Kindly Light," Bishop Newman's divine anthem, while every one stood in reverence. At the conclusion of the hymn Rev. Dr. Henry R. Naylor, presiding elder of the Washington District M. E. Church, delivered the invocation, while the distinguished company listened with bowed heads.

As the pastor ceased the voices of the choir swelled forth, and the rich, pure soprano notes of a soloist led the hymn "Some Time We'll Understand." The music was remarkably effective and touching as the notes came back in soft echoes from the fulness of the dome overhead. As soon as the hymn ceased Bishop Edward G. Andrews, of the Methodist Episcopal Church, who had come from Ohio to say the last words over the remains of his lifelong friend and parishioner, arose. He stood at the head of the casket and spoke in sympathetic voice and with many evidences of deep emotion.

As the bishop concluded every one in the vast rotunda rose and, the choir intoning the air, hundreds of voices joined in the grand old hymn " Nearer, My God, to Thee."

The last notes died away softly, and with uplifted hands the benediction was pronounced by Rev. Dr. W. H. Chapman, acting pastor of the Metropolitan Church. This ended the religious service.

EULOGY BY BISHOP ANDREWS

' Blessed be the God and Father of our Lord, who of His abundant mercy hath begotten us again into a lively hope by the resurrection of Christ from the dead, to an inheritance uncorruptible, undefiled, and that fadeth not away, reserved in Heaven for you who are kept by the power of God through faith unto salvation, ready to be revealed in the last time.'

" The services for the dead are fitly and almost of necessity services of religion and of immortal hope. In the presence of the shroud, and the coffin, and the narrow home, questions concerning intellectual quality, concerning public station, concerning great achievements, sink into comparative insignificance, and questions concerning character and man's relation to the Lord and giver of life, even the life eternal, emerge to our view and impress themselves upon us.

VALUE OF CHARACTER

" Character abides. We bring nothing into this world; we can carry nothing out. We ourselves depart with all the accumulations of tendency, and habit, and quality which the years have given to us. We ask, therefore, even at the grave of the illustrious, not altogether what great achievement they had performed, and how they had commended themselves to the memory and affection or respect of the world, but chiefly of what sort they were; what the interior nature of the man was; what were his affinities. Were they with the good, the true, the noble? What his relation to the Lord of the universe and to the compassionate Saviour of mankind; what his fitness for that great hereafter to which he had passed.

" And such great questions come to us with moment, even in the hour when we gather around the bier of those whom we profoundly respect and eulogize and whom we tenderly love. In the years to come, the days and the months that lie immediately before us will give full utterance as to the high statesmanship and great achievements of the illustrious man whom we mourn to-day. We shall not touch them to-day. The nation already has broken out in its tears, and is still pouring them, over the loss of a beloved man. It is well.

HIS CHILDHOOD TRAINING

" But we ask this morning of what sort this man is, so that we may, perhaps, knowing the moral and spiritual life that is past, be able to shape the far-withdrawing future. I think we must all concede that nature and training and—reverently be it said—the inspiration of the Almighty conspired to conform a man admirable in his moral temper and aims.

"We none of us can doubt, I think, that even by nature he was eminently gifted. The kindly, calm, and equitable temperament, the kindly and generous heart, the love of justice and right, and the tendency toward faith and loyalty to unseen powers and authorities—these things must have been with him from his childhood, from his infancy; but upon them supervened the training for which he was always tenderly thankful and of which even this great nation from sea to sea continually has taken note.

"It was a humble home in which he was born. Narrow conditions were around him; but faith in God had lifted that lowly roof, according to the statement of some great writer, up to the very heavens and permitted its inmates to behold the things eternal, immortal and divine; and he came under that training.

"It is a beautiful thing that to the end of his life he bent reverently before that mother whose example, and teaching, and prayer had so fashioned his mind and all his aims. The school came to him but briefly, and then came to him the Church with a ministration of power. He accepted the truth which it taught.

"He believed in God and in Jesus Christ, through whom God was revealed. He accepted the divine law of the Scripture; he based his hope on Jesus Christ, the appointed and only Redeemer of men; and the Church, beginning its operation upon his character at an early period of his life, continued even to its close to mould him. He waited attentively upon its ministrations.

"He gladly partook with his brethren of the symbols of mysterious passion and redeeming love of the Lord Jesus Christ. He was helpful in all of those beneficences and activities; and from the Church, to the close of his life, he received inspiration that lifted him above much of the trouble and weakness incident to our human nature, and, blessings be to God, may we say, in the last and final hour they enabled him confidently, tenderly, to say, 'It is His will, not ours, that will be done.'

HIS PERFECT HONESTY AND FAITH IN MAN

"Such influences gave to us William McKinley. And what was he? A man of incorruptible, personal and political integrity. I suppose no one ever attempted to approach him in the way of a bribe; and we remember, with great felicitation at this time, for such an example to ourselves, that when great financial difficulties and perils encompassed him he determined to deliver all he possessed to his creditors, that there should be no challenge of his perfect honesty in the matter. A man of immaculate purity, shall we say? No stain was upon his escutcheon; no syllable of suspicion that I ever heard was whispered against his character. He walked in perfect and noble self-control.

"Beyond that, this man had somehow wrought in him—I suppose upon the foundations of a very happily constructed nature—a great and generous love for his fellow-men. He believed in men. He had himself been brought up among the common people. He knew their labors, struggles, necessities. He loved them; but I think beyond that it was to the Church and its teachings concerning the fatherhood of God and universal brotherhood of man that he was indebted for that habit of kindness, for that generosity of spirit, that was wrought into his very substance and became him so that, though he was of all men most courteous, no one ever supposed but that courtesy was from the heart. It was spontaneous, unaffected, kindly, attractive, in a most eminent degree.

"What he was in the narrower circle of those to whom he was personally attached I think he was also in the greatness of his comprehensive love toward the race of which he was part. If any man had been lifted up to take into his purview and desire to help all classes and conditions of men, all nationalities beside his own, it was this man.

HIS DOMESTIC LOVE

"Shall I speak a word next of that which I will hardly advert to—the tenderness of that domestic love which has so often been commented upon? I pass it with only that word. I take it that no words can set forth fully the unfaltering kindness and carefulness and upbearing love which belonged to this great man.

"And he was a man who believed in right, who had a profound conviction that the courses of this world must be ordered in accordance with everlasting righteousness, or this world's highest point of good will never be reached; that no nation can expect success in life except as it conforms to the eternal will of the Infinite Lord and pass itself in individual and collective activity according to that Divine Will. It was deeply ingrained in him that righteousness was the perfection of any man and of any people. Simplicity belonged to him. I need not dwell upon it, and I close the statement of these qualities by saying that underlying all and over-reaching all and penetrating all there was a profound loyalty to God, the great King of the universe, the Author of all good, the Eternal hope of all that trust in Him.

HIS MORAL QUALITIES

"And now, may I say further that it seems to me that to whatever we may attribute all the illustriousness of this man, all the greatness of his achievements—whatever of that we may attribute to his intellectual character and quality, whatever of it we may attribute to the patient and thorough study which he gave to the various questions thrust upon him for attention, for all his successes as a politician, as a stateman, as a man of this great country, those successes were largely due to the moral qualities of which I have spoken.

"They drew to him the hearts of men everywhere, and particularly of those who best knew him. They called to his side helpers in every exigency of his career, so that when his future was at one time likely to have been imperiled and utterly ruined by his financial conditions, they who had resources, for the sake of helping a man who had in him such qualities, came to his side and put him on the high road of additional and larger successes.

HONORED BY OPPONENTS

"His high qualities drew to him the good-will of his associates in political life in an eminent degree. They believed in him, felt his kindness, confided in his honesty and in his honor. His qualities even associated with him in kindly relations those who were his political opponents. They made it possible for him to enter that land with which he, as one of the soldiers of the Union, had been in some sort at war and to draw closer the tie that was to bind all the parts in one firmer and indissoluble union.

"They commanded the confidence of the great body of Congress, so that they listened to his plans and accepted kindly and hopefully and trustfully all his declarations. His qualities gave him reputation, not in this land alone but throughout the world, and made it possible for him to minister in the style in which he has within the last two or three years ministered to the welfare and peace of human kind.

"It was out of the profound depths of his moral and religious character that came the possibilities of that usefulness which we are all glad to attribute to him. And will such a man die? Is it possible that He who created, redeemed, transformed, uplifted, illumined such a man will permit him to fall into oblivion? The instincts of immortality are in all good men. The Divine Word of the Scripture leaves us no room for doubt. 'I,' said One whom he trusted, 'am the resurrection and the life. He that believeth in Me, though he were dead, yet shall he live, and whosoever liveth and believeth in Me shall never die.'

HIS NAME ILLUSTRIOUS

"Lost to us, but not to his God. Lost from earth, but entered Heaven. Lost from these labors and toils and perils, but entered into the everlasting peace and ever-advancing progress. Blessed be God who gives us this hope in this hour of calamity and enables us to triumph through Him who hath redeemed us.

"If there is a personal immortality before him, let us also rejoice that there is an immortality and memory in the hearts of a large and ever-growing people who, through the ages to come, the generations that are yet to be, will look back upon this life, upon its nobility and purity and service to humanity and thank God for it.

"The years draw on when his name shall be counted among the illustrious of the earth. William of Orange is not dead. Cromwell is not dead. Washington lives in the hearts and lives of his countrymen. Lincoln, with his infinite sorrow, lives to teach us and lead us on. And McKinley shall summon all statesmen and all his countrymen to purer living, nobler aims, sweeter faith and immortal blessedness."

CHAPTER XXIII

The Last Home-Coming to Canton

THE last chapter of the sad ceremonial, the removal of the remains of the late President to the grave at his old home at Canton, Ohio, began on Tuesday evening, September 17th, when the funeral train left Washington over the Pennsylvania Railroad.

The great bronze doors of the Capitol in which the body had lain in state had closed while there were still thousands of people waiting to get a last glance at the casket.

The guards at the Capitol, who had patiently throughout the long day held the crowd in leash, were permitted a hurried look at the face of the deceased. The cover of the casket was screwed down by the undertakers, it was lifted once more upon the shoulders of the body-bearers, and by them borne to the hearse at the foot of the east steps of the Capitol.

The escort from the Capitol to the train consisted of a committee from the army and navy and two squadrons of the Eleventh Cavalry. The route was down Pennsylvania Avenue, which was lined on either side by troops of the District of Columbia.

It was a quiet, noiseless journey, without music. Not a drum was heard, nor a funeral note. Nor was there a sound from the crowd which lined the broad street. Notwithstanding the hour was late, the air chill and a light mist was falling, hats were uniformly removed as the cortege passed.

At the railroad station there was a dense throng, and the remains were received by large delegations of army and naval officers. There the soldiers and seamen carried the casket from the hearse to the observation car placed in the second section of the funeral train.

The casket was placed on standards draped with the national colors, and was covered with floral emblems. No less than twenty cars were required for the transportation of the funeral party to Canton.

Remarkable demonstrations of a stricken people's grief marked the last home-coming of the martyred President, William McKinley. All along the path of the sombre funeral train, from Washington, on the Potomac, to Canton, in Ohio, mourning thousands stood to bid their dead chief a last, sad farewell. Although the journey was made in the dead of night, not a city, town or hamlet but contributed its quota. Silent they stood in the black darkness as the cars bearing the beloved dead flashed by in the gloom, unlit, except that bearing the remains of the President. Illuminated by lights within the car, the casket stood out in bold relief, visible to the watchers in the night.

THE SILENT PEOPLE LINE THE TRACK

Daylight was dawning as the train arrived at the foot of the eastern slope of the Alleghenies. But through the semi-darkness the forms of many people could be seen strung along the track.

Extra engines were coupled on, and the train was pulled laboriously up the mountains. The morning was raw, foggy and cheerless. Mountaineers, with axes on their shoulders, came down from the steep slopes to pay their homage with uncovered heads.

Men, women and children all were there. Miners, with lamps in their caps, had rushed forth from the tunnels at the train's approach, and the steel mills along the Conemaugh River were emptied. These were men who felt that their prosperity was due to the system for which the dead statesman stood, and their loss seemed of a personal character. Four women, with uplifted hands, were noticed on their knees and handkerchiefs were at the lips of others; and from the smoke-covered city came the sound of the church bells clanging out the universal sorrow.

A little further on the train passed a string of coke ovens, the tenders standing at the mouths of the glowing furnaces with their hats in their hands. The train slowed down that the people might better see the impressive spectacle at the rear of the train within the observation car, the elevated flag-covered casket with its burden of flowers and the two grim, armed sentries on guard at the head and foot and outside, on the platform, a soldier with his bayoneted gun and a sailor with drawn cutlass, both at salute. So rigid they stood they might have been carved out of stone.

As the train passed through Harrisburg, Altoona, Pittsburgh, Allegheny, and other Pennsylvania towns and cities in the route of the sad cortege, people were seen in thousands, standing in silence and with bared heads as the train passed.

The climax of the great sorrow was observed when the train reached the Ohio line and entered the President's own State. The signs of grief and mourning were evident on every hand. The people were grieving the death as of their well beloved son.

Church bells tolled most mournfully, and the train slackened speed. The humblest cottage was draped in mourning, and thus was McKinley's return heralded with silent and deeply-felt sorrow.

Canton received the remains of the late President McKinley shortly before noon on Wednesday, the 18th. Two weeks previous, upon the same day, and almost at the same hour, in the full vigor of life and the buoyancy of health, surrounded by loving friends and admiring neighbors, who cheered his departure for Buffalo, he started upon the journey that terminated in assassination. The same friends and neighbors, augmented by a vast multitude that included nearly the entire population of Canton, patiently, silently, with hearts overshadowed with grief and heads bowed in humiliation, awaited the coming of the train that brought to them the lifeless form of the President. There was no lack in the preparation for this sad duty. No detail was omitted, and the entire service was performed with a thoroughness which so strongly marked the bringing of the body to Washington. There was a degree of simplicity and tenderness that gave it additional impressiveness and left no doubt as to the depth of the affection of the people, and the sincerity of their grief.

Canton's little railroad station and the streets in its vicinity were crowded with people. Infantrymen of the State National Guard performed patrol duty in the inside, and Troop A, of Cleveland, which had twice escorted President-elect McKinley from the White House to the Capitol at Washington, sat erect and motionless on their horses on the outside. A reception committee of citizens, including men of all parties and sects, at the head of which was Judge Day, an intimate friend, close associate and near neighbor of the late President, was at the station, not only to tenderly receive the remains of the dead President, but to care for the comfort and look after the safety of his successor and the Cabinet Ministers, who were among the chief mourners.

There was no apparent need for the services of soldiers and police. There was no crowding or pushing among the people, no fretting or fussing on the part of those charged with the conduct of affairs. All were seemingly impressed with the solemnity of the occasion and actuated by the common purpose to assist in successfully carrying out the object for which they were assembled.

LYING IN STATE IN CANTON

The casket was borne from the funeral car to the hearse by the soldiers and sailors who had performed this service since the departure from Buffalo. The funeral procession moved between lines of sorrowing people to the Court House, in which the remains reposed in state until evening, when they were escorted to his late residence. During the hours the remains were exposed the people passed continuously in two lines on each side of the casket.

The casket rested in the main corridor of the Court House, with the head toward the south entrance, by which the people were admitted to view the remains. The walls and ceiling were completely covered with a black fabric, which gave it the appearance of an immense vault, dimly lighted by incandescent electric lamps. Entering this long chamber from the clear sunlight of the outside the effect was awe-inspiring upon the visitor. This was heightened by the presence of the dead President, resting upon a plain black catafalque, surrounded by the military and naval guards, standing rigidly at the head and foot and on either side. The people passed into the building, upon entering which the men divided to the right and left and walked past the remains on either side, moving to the exit on the north of the building. The entire proceeding was conducted with the utmost good order and without any crowding.

When the lying in state was terminated, the line of people awaiting admission to the hall extended several blocks. At the request of Mrs. McKinley, the casket remained at the residence from Wednesday evening until Thursday afternoon, when, after the services in the church, it was removed to West Lawn Cemetery and deposited in a vault.

FUNERAL SERVICES AT CANTON

Thursday opened with lowering clouds that threatened to envelop the closing scene with a pall and deluge the vast multitude of sorrowing spectators. Fortunately, as the sun rose in the sky, the clouds were dissipated ; the atmosphere, which had been damp and penetrating, became bright and cheering, bringing assurances of better weather than that which had been experienced at Buffalo and Washington. All through the night and early morning, trains loaded with pilgrims to Canton rumbled into the stations. Before the morning was far advanced, the streets were packed with people of both sexes, all sizes and conditions, who moved in solid mass about the Court House and passed in orderly procession through the vault-like chamber, with its mournful drapery and its oppressive funeral light, where the remains had reposed in state and had been exposed to view for the last time.

As the noon hour came and passed, preparations were completed for the funeral procession, which soon formed and took up

21

its mournful journey, passing under the sweep of giant arches robed
in black, between two living tides of humanity massed along the
streets, covering house-tops and filling windows.   The church bells
still were tolling, mingling their dismal tones with the cadence of
the funeral dirge.

The Methodist Church in which the services were held was
filled to its utmost capacity, and was surrounded on the outside by a
vast multitude, which was held back by the military escort, formed in
line to await the closing of the religious exercises and to make the
last march to the cemetery with the pomp and ceremony befitt-
ing the occasion.   Mrs. McKinley did not go to the church.   She
was desirous of being with her beloved to the end, but was finally
prevailed upon, by her relatives and her physician, to remain at
home.   President Roosevelt and the members of the family were
in position directly in front of the hearse as the representatives of
a stricken nation and mourning people.   The funeral procession
reached the church about 2 o'clock.   The relatives and officials of
State and Nation were shown to seats reserved for them.   The
McKinley pew, four seats from the communion rail on the right
central aisle, was vacant and covered with black.   Abner McKinley
and his family and the other relatives sat immediately in front and
to the rear of it.   President Roosevelt and his Cabinet were to the
left of the central aisle, just across from the relatives.   Admirals
and generals were in the front row.   Members of the Senate and
House of Representatives were present in large numbers.

The services conducted after the manner of the Methodist Church
were wholly appropriate, their simplicity adding to their impressiveness.   The music was by a quartet, two male and two female voices.
There was no organ accompaniment to conceal the sweetness and
tenderness of the voices, which filled the edifice, floating harmon-
iously across the groined ceiling and through the auditorium.   The
delivery of the eulogy by Rev. Dr. Manchester, the pastor, friend
and neighbor of the late President, was a most touching and beautiful tribute to the public services and personal worth of the

deceased. The services closed with singing " Nearer, My God, to Thee," by the quartet. When the benediction was pronounced by Father Voltman, of Chicago, the organ began in murmuring tones Chopin's funeral march, which swelled into a volume of melody as the congregation slowly moved from the church after the removal of the casket.

Upon emerging from the church the remains were again received by the troops with the prescribed honors, the column of march was resumed and, passing between two lines of solid humanity that stretched from the church to West Lawn Cemetery, every constituent unit of which stood reverently and mournfully as the cortege passed, they were borne to the tomb.

No greater reverence has ever been shown to any man, living or dead, than was exhibited toward the dead President. As the funeral car passed men and women sobbed convulsively. When the casket had been born to the catafalque at the door of the vault, all realized that the last and saddest moments were upon them.

BRIEF BURIAL SERVICE

There was a moment's pause, then Bishop Joyce, of Minneapolis, read the burial service of the Methodist Church slowly, but in a voice that could be heard distinctly by all who were grouped around the vault. As his words ended there was a brief silence, and then eight bugles sounded out the notes of the soldier's last call—"taps." The notes of the buglers died away so softly that all who heard them remained listening for a few seconds to hear if the dying strain was really ended. When the final note had died away, Secretary Wilson and Secretary Root were weeping, and President Roosevelt was gazing mournfully at the walk. It was the last moment for the men who had been so long and closely associated with the deceased President, and the thought seemed greater than most of them could bear.

Nature has been kind in selecting the last resting place for President McKinley. West Lawn Cemetery is on a high knoll overlooking the peaceful valley, with the busy little city of Canton laid out below. If it were not for an intervening church spire, one might get from this elevation a glimpse of the McKinley home. On this elevation, looking out on his native city and his native State, the body of William McKinley was laid to rest. The beauty of the grounds has attracted the attention of the country's best landscape gardeners, who have journeyed here to study its attractions. On this funeral day it was doubly beautiful, with the rustling trees shedding the first yellowed leaves of Fall and adding a golden touch to the green-clad slopes. Just inside the stately entrance stands the gray stone vault where for a time the coffin will repose. Its dreary exterior was relieved by great masses of flowers, banked all about until the gray walls were shut out from view. But in due time the body will be taken from the vault and committed to the little plot of ground further on. This is the McKinley lot, and here lie his father, whose name he bore, the mother he guarded so tenderly in life, his brother James, his sister Anna, and his two children. When that time comes a stately shaft of granite will rise above the grave, telling of the civic virtues, the pure life and the martyr death of William McKinley.

DR. MANCHESTER'S EULOGY

"Our President is dead.

"'The silver cord is loosed, the golden bowl is broken, the pitcher is broken at the fountain, the wheel broken at the cistern. The mourners go about the streets.' One voice is heard—a wail of sorrow from all the land; for 'the beauty of Israel is slain upon Thy high places. How are the mighty fallen. I am distressed for Thee, my brother. Very pleasant hast Thou been unto me.'

"Our President is dead. We can hardly believe it. We had hoped and prayed, and it seemed that our hopes were to be realized and our prayers answered, when the emotion of joy was changed to one of grave apprehension. Still we waited, for we said, 'It may be that God will be gracious and merciful unto us.' It seemed to us that it must be His will to spare the life of one so well beloved and so much needed. Thus, alternating between hope and fear, the weary hours passed on. Then came the tidings of defeated science and of the failure of love and prayer to hold its object to the earth. We seemed to hear the faintly muttered words: 'Good-by all, good-by. It is God's way. His will be done,' and then 'Nearer, My God, to Thee.' So, nestling nearer to his God, he passed out into unconsciousness, skirted the dark shores of the sea of death for a time, and then passed on to be at rest. His great heart had ceased to beat. Our hearts are heavy with sorrow.

MOURNING FOR THE MAN

"The cause of this universal mourning is to be found in the man himself. The inspired penman's picture of Jonathan, likening him unto the 'beauty of Israel,' could not be more appropriately employed than in chanting the lament over our fallen chieftain. It does no violence to human speech, nor is it fulsome eulogy to speak thus of him, for who has seen his stately bearing, his grace and manliness of demeanor, his kindliness of aspect, but gives assent to this description of him? It was characteristic of our beloved President that men met him only to love him. They might, indeed, differ with him, but in the presence of such dignity of character and grace of manner none could fail to love the man. The people confided in him, believed in him. It was said of Lincoln that probably no man since the days of Washington was ever so deeply imbedded and enshrined in the hearts of the people, but it is true of McKinley in a larger sense. Industrial and social conditions are such that he was, even more than his predecessors, the friend of the whole people.

"A touching scene was enacted in this church last Sunday night. The services had closed. The worshippers were gone to their homes. Only a few lingered to discuss the sad event that brings us together to-day. Three men in working garb of a foreign race and unfamiliar tongue entered the room. They approached the altar, kneeling before it and before his picture. Their lips moved as if in prayer, while tears furrowed their cheeks. They may have been thinking of their own King Humbert and of his untimely death. Their emotion was eloquent, eloquent beyond speech, and it bore testimony to their appreciation of manly friendship and of honest worth.

"It is a glorious thing to be able to say in this presence, with our illustrious dead before us, that he never betrayed the confidence of his countrymen. Not for personal gain or pre-eminence would he mar the beauty of his soul. He kept it clean and white before God and man, and his hands were unsullied by bribes. 'His eyes looked right on, and his eyelids looked straight before him.' He was sincere, plain and honest, just, benevolent and kind. He never disappointed those who believed in him, but measured up to every duty, and met every responsibility in life grandly and unflinchingly.

"Not only was our President brave, heroic and honest; he was as gallant a knight as ever rode the lists for his lady love in the days when knighthood was in flower. It is but a few weeks since the nation looked on with tear-dimmed eyes as it saw with what tender conjugal devotion he sat at the bedside of his beloved wife, when all feared that a fatal illness was upon her. No public clamor that he might show himself to the populace, no demand of social function was sufficient to draw the lover from the bedside of his wife. He watched and waited while we all prayed—and she lived. This sweet and tender story all the world knows, and the world knows that his whole life had run in this one groove of love. It was a strong arm that she leaned upon, and it never failed her. Her smile was more to him than the plaudits of the multitude, and for her greeting his acknowledgments of them must wait. After receiving the fatal wound, his first thought was that the terrible news might be broken gently to her. May God in this deep hour of sorrow comfort her! May His grace be greater than her anguish! May the widow's God be her God!

"Another beauty in the character of our President, that was a chaplet of grace about his neck, was that he was a Christian. In the broadest, noblest sense of the word that was true. His confidence in God was strong and unwavering. It held him steady in many a storm where others were driven before the wind and tossed. He believed in the fatherhood of God and in His sovereignty. His faith in the Gospel of Christ was deep and abiding. He had no patience with any other theme of pulpit discourse. 'Christ and Him crucified' was to his mind the only panacea for the world's disorders. He believed it to be the supreme duty of the Christian minister to preach the word. He said : 'We do not look for great business men in the pulpit, but for great preachers.'

MCKINLEY'S CHRISTIAN CHARACTER

"It is well known that his godly mother had hoped for him that he would become a minister of the Gospel, and that she believed it to be the highest vocation in life. It was not, however, his mother's faith that made him a Christian. He had gained in early life a personal knowledge of Jesus which guided him in the performance of greater duties and vaster responsibilities than have been the lot of any other American President. He said at one time, while bearing heavy burdens, that he could not discharge the daily duties of his life but for the fact that he had faith in God.

"William McKinley believed in prayer, in the beauty of it, in the potency of it. Its language was not unfamiliar to him, and his public addresses not infrequently evince the fact. It was perfectly consistent with his lifelong convictions and his personal experiences that he should say, as the first critical moment after the assassination approached, 'Thy kingdom come ; Thy will be done' ; and that he should declare at the last, 'It is God's way. His will be done.' He lived grandly ; it was fitting that he should die grandly. And now that the majesty of death has touched and calmed him, we find that in his supreme moment he was still a conqueror,

"My friends and countrymen, with what language shall I attempt to give expression to the deep horror of our souls as I speak of the cause of his death? When we consider the magnitude of the crime that has plunged the country and the world into unutterable grief, we are not surprised that one nationality after another has hastened to repudiate the dreadful act. This gentle spirit, who hated no one, to whom every man was a brother, was suddenly smitten by the cruel hand of an assassin, and that, too, while in the very act of extending a kind and generous greeting to one who approached him under the sacred guise of friendship.

"Could the assailant have realized how awful the act he was about to perform, how utterly heartless the deed, methinks he would have stayed his hand at the very threshold of it. In all the coming years men will seek in vain to fathom the enormity of that crime.

CONSOLATION IN SORROW

"Had this man who fell been a despot, a tyrant, an oppressor, an insane frenzy to rid the world of him might have sought excuse. It was the people's friend who fell when William McKinley received the fatal wound. Himself a son of toil, his sympathies were with the toiler. No one who has seen the matchless grace and perfect ease with which he greeted such can ever doubt that his heart was in his open hand. Every heart throb was for his countrymen. That his life should be sacrificed at such a time, just when there was an abundant peace, when all the Americans were rejoicing together, is one of the inscrutable mysteries of Providence. Like many others it must be left for future revelations to explain.

"In the midst of our sorrow we have much to console us. He lived to see his nation greater than ever before. All sectional lines are blotted out. There is no South, no North, no East, no West. Washington saw the beginning of our national life. Lincoln passed through the night of our history and saw the dawn. McKinley beheld his country in the splendor of its noon. Truly he died in the fulness of his fame. With Paul he could say, and with equal truthfulness, 'I am ready to be offered.' The nation was at peace. We had fairly entered upon an era of unparalleled prosperity. Our revenues were generous. Our standing among the nations was secure. Our President was safely enshrined in the affections of a united people. It was not at him that the fatal shot was fired, but at the very life of the Government. His offering was vicarious. It was blood poured upon the altar of human liberty. In view of these things we are not surprised to hear from one who was present when this great soul passed away, that he never before saw a death so peaceful or a dying man so crowned with grandeur.

LESSONS FROM THE TRAGEDY

"But our last words must be spoken. Little more than four years ago we bade him good-by as he went to assume the great responsibilities to which the nation had called him. His last words as he left us were : 'Nothing could give me greater pleasure than this farewell greeting—this evidence of your friendship and sympathy, your goodwill and, I am sure, the prayers of all the people with whom I have lived so long, and whose confidence and esteem are dearer to me than any other earthly honors. To all of us the future is as a sealed book, but if I can, by official act or administration or utterance, in any degree add to the prosperity and unity of our beloved country and the advancement and well-being of our splendid citizenship, I will devote the best and most unselfish efforts of my life to that end. With this thought uppermost in my mind, I reluctantly take leave of my friends and neighbors, cherishing in my heart the sweetest memories and thoughts of my old home—my home now, and, I trust, my home hereafter, so long as I live.'

"We hoped with him, that when his work was done, freed from the burdens of his great office, crowned with the affections of a happy people, he might be permitted to close his earthly life in the home he loved.

" He has, indeed, returned to us, but how? Borne to the strains of ' Nearer, My God, to Thee,' and placed where he first began life's struggle, that the people might look and weep over so sad a home-coming.

"But it was a triumphal march. How vast the procession ! The Nation rose and stood with uncovered head. The people of the land are chief mourners. The nations of the earth weep with them. But, oh what a victory ! I do not ask you in the heat of public address, but in the calm moments of mature reflection, what other man ever had such high honors bestowed upon him and by so many people ? What pageant has equaled this that we look upon to-day? We gave him to the nation but a little more than four years ago. He went out with the light of the morning upon his brow, but with his task set, and the purpose to complete it. We take him back a mighty conqueror.

> " The churchyard where his children rest,
> The quiet spot that suits him best,
> There shall his grave be made,
> And there his bones be laid.
> And there his countrymen shall come,
> With memory proud, with pity dumb,
> And strangers far and near,
> For many and many a year,
> For many a year, and many an age,
> While History on her ample page,
> The virtues shall enroll
> Of that paternal soul.''

CHAPTER XXIV

The World in Mourning

IT was one great funeral day throughout the United States and its distant possessions. Wherever the stars and stripes waved they were placed at half mast, and the people over whom they waved were found, during the funeral hour at Canton, bowed down in their places of worship or hushed in silence at their places of business. Signs of mourning were seen on every hand, both public and private houses being heavily draped in black and decked with flags at half mast with sable streamers. This was not a show of pomp, nor meant as an effusive and sudden display of sorrow. It was from the people's hearts and indicated their grief.

The President's proclamation, setting apart Thursday, September 19th, as a day of mourning, met the universal approval and was everywhere observed. In every city, town and hamlet the churches were opened, and the dead President was mourned as a personal friend.

No phase of the nation's sorrow over the death of President McKinley embodies a higher tribute to the man than the spontaneous sincerity shown in the memorial sermons preached in a thousand pulpits of all denominations throughout the United States, and even in Europe. From the humblest chapel and from the largest cathedral came the same note of personal loss. The emotion shown by congregations in every part of the United States, notably while singing the two favorite hymns of the dead President, was at once a vindication of the sentiment and power of these hymns and an involuntary testimonial to the genuineness of affection inspired by the man. The same sincerity rang through the sermons preached at these services.

In London, in Berlin, in St. Petersburg, in Rome ; in churches throughout Europe, in Asia and in the Philippines ; the services were devoted to memorials of the assassinated President of the United States.   Such a tribute from the religious bodies of the world is an honor more to be desired than a monument.   No less significant is the passionate voice of the churches against anarchy and on behalf of law and order.   Never has the pulpit of this country voiced the emotions and convictions of the whole nation more completely or more worthily than it did regarding the assassination of the President and the vital questions connected therewith. The whole episode is a reassuring answer to any who may have entertained doubts as to whether the United States was at heart a religious nation.

We need but refer to what took place in a few of our larger cities to understand the feeling throughout the country.

In Washington, D. C., twenty years after the death of Garfield, the nation's capital was again in mourning.   The wheels of government were locked, and the voices of the people were uplifted in prayer for the soul of William McKinley while his body was being committed to the tomb in his Ohio home.

There was no need of a proclamation to insure a proper observation of the sad event there.   Everywhere were to be seen badges of mourning, and on every flag staff the national ensign was at half-mast.   Private and public business was absolutely suspended, and every face showed signs of sadness.   The city gave evidence in most impressive manner that its heart was at Canton in the solemn hour of President McKinley's funeral.   At exactly 3.30 o'clock (2.30 o'clock in Canton) the city ceased from labor, practically from locomotion, for five minutes.

There was no official proclamation requiring such observance of the funeral hour, and there had not been any general agreement for such observance, but when the hour arrived, as if by common instinct men, women, and children, white and black, came to a sudden halt in the tasks in which they were engaged, and sat or stood still as statues wheresoever they chanced to be. Men on foot and on bicycles, the drivers of carriages and draught wagons, chauffeurs and trainmen stood in mute supplication for the dead. Streetcars throughout the city were at a standstill, and generally the car operatives and their passengers united in a silent service, which caused spectators to look on as if it were "the hush of being newly born." Telegraph instruments, typewriting machines, elevators, indeed, all the appurtenances of business throughout the capital, were for the time motionless, and the great city was as quiet as a prairie at midnight.

It was a beautiful contribution to the nation's prayer, and it is safe to say that Washington never before in its history beheld so unique and striking, so spontaneous and unconventional, a token of respect and love for any man.

To the people of Washington the late President McKinley was more than an official, he was their kindly guardian, and they rendered their tributes of respect with their whole hearts. The people, in accordance with President Roosevelt's proclamation, repaired to their churches to attend the memorial services, and rarely have the places of worship been so crowded. All denominations—Protestant, Catholic and Jew—united in these. The Metropolitan Methodist Episcopal Church, where Mr. McKinley worshipped, was the centre of interest, and here the services were more impressive than elsewhere. The President's pew was draped in black and left vacant. It was originally set apart for President Grant, and has ever since borne the inscription, "Our President." The crowd could not be accommodated in the main body of the church, and a second service was held simultaneously in the lecture hall. Bishop Warren and Dr. Crawford spoke in each place.

NEW YORK CITY

New York never saw a day such as the one on which the President was laid to rest. It had witnessed solemn funeral processions, like that of General Grant; it had taken part in splendid parades of triumph, like that in honor of Admiral Dewey; it had been aroused to patriotic enthusiasm, as on the day the Seventh Regiment marched to the front at the outbreak of the Civil War; it had experienced days of terror, as in the time of the draft riots; but this day was different from any of these, yet as deep in feeling and as significant in meaning. It was Thursday in a great commercial metropolis, with a population representing every race and language on the globe; yet a solemn hush, deeper than that of any Sunday, fell on the entire city. All work ceased. All play was stopped. The theatres were closed. The games were postponed. Even many of the saloons shut their doors. Only for the crowds in the streets, one might have thought some awful calamity, like a plague or famine, had visited the city. Never before was there so complete a suspension of all the usual activities of a busy people. And for what? No hero had arrived, who was to be welcomed. No funeral procession was to pass. No army was to parade. But many miles away the nation's martyred President was being borne to his last resting place, and this city of 3,500,000 gave up one whole day to tearful meditation on the life and death of the nation's honored dead. Immense crowds thronged the principal squares and avenues and viewed the draperies of mourning. The churches —the only buildings wide open—were filled with worshippers during the memorial services held in response to President Roosevelt's proclamation. As the time approached when it was known that the procession would start in Canton, the silence of the city grew more intense, and a solemnity of feeling pervaded all, as if the people were in the very presence of death itself. And when the hands on the clocks pointed to half-past 3, an extraordinary scene was enacted. Every street car stopped suddenly, as if by magic, and the people stood with tense faces, indicative of the sorrow they felt. The only sound to be heard was the tolling of the bells, and as these clanged out their dirgeful melody men reverently uncovered their heads. Six thousand people stood in front of the Herald Building, with heads uncovered, while the great bells on the roof were tolled. Those who witnessed the spectacle will never forget it. This was a day memorable in the history of New York.

IN PHILADELPHIA

Philadelphia paid full measure to the world-wide tribute of sympathy, grief and respect that centered at Canton, Ohio. The community, without distinction of race or creed, united in memorial services that filled churches of every denomination. Nearly all branches of business were absolutely suspended during the whole day, and there were very few establishments, large or small, that did not close for the afternoon, or, at least, during the time announced for the funeral of the late President.

A memorably impressive incident of the day was the stopping of the trolley cars all over the city for ten minutes in the afternoon, suggesting the almost complete pause that was occurring in the ordinary affairs of the country, and concentrating public attention upon the sad final scene at the home of the late President. It was a reminder of the railroad trains that, at the same time, had been halted in their rushing; of the motionless machinery in establishments where usually myriads of hands were busy, and of the innumerable avenues of ordinary trade and business that had been closed in one great expression of sympathy and sorrow. It was at half-past 3 o'clock that the trolley cars were brought to a standstill on every line; on some of them motormen and conductors briefly uncovered their heads, in mute token of their realization of the solemn meaning of it all—an example that was followed by many passengers and observers. Here, as in the case of the Postal Telegraph Co., below mentioned, the power was cut off at the dynamos and the stop was everywhere simultaneous.

GATHERED ABOUT INDEPENDENCE HALL

In the vicinity of the old State House, where so many memorable scenes have transpired, and where the remains of the martyred Lincoln had lain in state, there was assembled a crowd of about 2,000 people at this time, and here numbers of men remained, with heads bared and bowed, as a knell sounded over the solemn scene. It was a minute or two after the half hour when a silence that seemed strange in this ordinarily busy centre was broken by the plaintive tones of the muffled bell in Independence Hall tower, and which continued to toll at half minute intervals until 4 P. M. At the first stroke hundreds of men removed their hats, and remained uncovered for several minutes, and many a head was bowed in reverent sympathy, uniting in spirit with those who, in distant Canton, were paying the last earthly honors to the remains of the nation's dead. With half-masted flags gently fluttering overhead, emblems of mourning wherever the eye rested, and traffic of every kind in suspense, the decorous multitude at once evidenced and realized that sympathy which extended not only over all the country, but embraced countries beyond in its gracious bond.

CHICAGO, THE WESTERN METROPOLIS

The noises of the great city of Chicago were hushed and its commerce suspended for a few moments on this the day of grief, while mourning thousands paid their last tribute to the memory of William McKinley. The silence was broken only by muffled bells, tolling off the fifty-eight years of the dead President's life.

In the forenoon services were held in nearly all churches and the virtues of William McKinley as a President were sung. A big memorial meeting was held at the Auditorium in the evening.

Between twenty and twenty-five thousand men marched in the funeral procession which followed a draped carriage. Its empty seats were more eloquent than words of the nation's loss. In this carriage two years ago the President rode through long aisles of applauding people. Unfurled near the carriage was a flag which had flown over the President on occasions of rejoicing in Chicago, in Canton and in Washington. In common with other cities, all business, not already suspended, stopped at 2.30 P.M. for five minutes. For almost the first time in history the pulsing heart of Chicago's commerce ceased entirely, while sorrowing citizens stood with doffed hats in respectful silence. Business generally was suspended during the day and the streets were draped in mourning.

CALIFORNIA SHOWS GRIEF

California offered reverence to the dead Chief Magistrate. Every city, town and village in the State observed the occasion by some public demonstration. In the larger cities impressive memorial services had been arranged, and business of all kinds was suspended.

At Sacramento, Los Angeles, San Diego, and other large cities, in addition to the general observance of the day by the different religious denominations, public memorial services were held. In San Francisco the public services were held at Mechanics' Pavilion, and 20,000 people crowded within the structure. The program consisted of music, prayers and addresses. Gen. W. H. L. Barnes delivered the eulogy. It was General Barnes who had made the address of welcome at the reception given in the President's honor by the Knights Templar.

TELEGRAPH WIRES HUSHED

One feature absolutely unique in history characterized the McKinley funeral. It was the silencing of the telegraph, not only in Chicago, but throughout the country. Never before since electricity was first put to use as a means of communication from city to city, and from country to country, has there taken place, it is said, anything paralleling, even in a small way, what was done the afternoon of the funeral at Canton on a scale that was gigantic.

Upon orders from the officials of the different telegraph companies, or upon the common impulse of the operators where direct instructions were not received, the entire telegraph system of the United States was hushed for five minutes, at 2.30 P.M., Canton time, the hour set for lowering the President's body into the burial vault. At that moment on all the huge network of wires, from the Atlantic to the Pacific, not a "sounder" in the land gave a single tick, and the great ocean cables were pulseless as the corpse of the Chief Magistrate himself.

More than once before to-day thousands of miles of railways and vast armies of men, industrial or military, have paused as a tribute to the dead, but the cessation of the telegraph for such a cause, or, indeed, for any reason, is without precedent in the world's record. It is estimated that fully 100,000 telegraphers thus simultaneously paid homage to McKinley.

The total number of miles of wire affected was upward of 1,000,000. In the Western Union Chicago office, the hundreds of operators all arose at their desks when the moment came, and, joining their voices, sang with deep feeling the President's hymn, "Nearer, My God, to Thee." The wires of the Associated Press, the Postal Telegraph Company, the North American Company, the Chicago and Milwaukee Company and all similar organizations were included in the general stoppage.

Probably the most remarkable method of producing complete silence on the wires, free from any possible interruption, was employed by the Postal Telegraph Company. At a given signal the dynamos were disconnected at the ends, literally draining the circuits of electricity, so that everywhere all the wires were technically and literally "dead."

ONE TOUCH OF NATURE

Never before the day on which William McKinley was laid to rest was there so powerful a demonstration of the truth of the words which Shakespeare put into the mouth of Ulysses, " One touch of nature makes the whole world kin." The touch of nature was a woeful one. But in that woe the whole world seemed involved. Tributes to America's dead were paid by distant lands the world around. The French Republic tempered its welcome to the Russian Czar, who was then her guest, with signs of mourning for our loss.   The German Emperor sent his personal representative to a memorial service and put the flags at half-mast on the vessels of his navy.   And so the tale went around the world, to the antipodes and back again.   Differences of race and of form of government seemed for the time forgotten.   There was something in America's bereavement which transcended all such artificial lines. There was a sharp, deep touch of elemental nature, and it made the whole world kin in bonds of sympathy.

We can not but remark upon the manifestations of sympathy made in the British Empire, both in Europe and in America.   It was a unique thing for the King to order his court into mourning for an American President, and so it was for such notable services as those which were held at St. Paul's and Westminster.   It was a notable thing for the great commercial exchanges throughout the kingdom to be closed, for the flags to be half-masted in the navy, and for memorial services to be held in cathedrals and churches everywhere.   A memorial service at the British Embassy at Constantinople, a salute from the guns of Gibraltar, and the closing of all banks, exchanges and places of business in Bombay, are only a few items from an innumerable host telling of the unfeigned sympathy of our "kin beyond the sea."

In the Dominion of Canada the demonstration was perhaps of all most marked.   The heir apparent to the throne had just landed, and all the country had prepared to welcome him with fulness of rejoicing.   But for the time of our mourning Canada, too, mourned scarcely less generally than we.   The sad occasion was made one of cessation from business and from pleasure, and a day of mourning and prayer, north of the border as well as south of it.   In that respect the traveler would scarce have been conscious of having crossed the line from the one country into the other.   For the day the dream of continental union was in sentiment realized.   Canada and the United States were one in some of the tenderest and not least strong bonds that can bind humankind together.   The generous and sympathetic messages and actions of England's King in this sad drama will henceforth cause Americans to regard him with added friendliness. So the fact of his participation in the mourning of the Dominion for our lost President will cause the Duke of Cornwall to be esteemed with love and gratitude by this nation, which would have been glad under happier auspices to welcome him to its soil.

Our day of mourning was thus gently illumined with the light of sympathy and gratitude. The American people are a grateful people and look upon these tokens of neighborly sympathy with gratitude and appreciation, and surely will not forget in the years to come that the nations of the world were one with them in their grief.

THE ASSASSINATION OF PRESIDENT McKINLEY

While holding a reception in the Temple of Music at the Pan-American Exposition, Buffalo, September 6, 1901

OATH OF OFFICE BEING ADMINISTERED TO THE PRESIDENT
BY CHIEF JUSTICE FULLER

CHAPTER XXV

The World's Sympathy with the Nation's Grief

THE murder of President McKinley by the fell hand of Anarchy not alone threw the American nation into a stupor of grief, but also gave a shock which was felt round the world; the nations of Europe could not have shown greater horror or manifested more fervent sympathy had the assassin's bullet reached the heart of one of their own most honored rulers. From princes and people alike came warm expressions of sympathy with their stricken sister nation, as deeply inspired with feeling as though our murdered ruler had been President of the world instead of the United States. It is our purpose in the present chapter to present some of the more important and significant of these contributions.

From England, with which, a few months before, the United States had so warmly sympathized in the death of her beloved Queen, the fatal act of September 6th called forth the following earnest expression of grief and regret. King Edward VII. hastened to send the following message to the Foreign Office:

"Kiel, Sept. 7.—Please send at once to the American Embassy to offer my deepest sympathy at the dastardly attempt on the President's life. I have telegraphed direct. Please keep me informed of his condition."

Lord Roberts was as prompt to speak for the military establishment of Great Britain, sending the following message to the American Embassador Choate:

"Please convey to President and Mrs. McKinley, on behalf of myself and the British army, our profound regret at what has occurred and our earnest hope that the President's valuable life may be spared.   "ROBERTS."

Mr. Chamberlain, the Colonial Secretary, wired from Birmingham :

" I have heard with sorrow and detestation of the atrocious, cowardly act of which the President of the United States is a victim. Every Englishman deeply sympathizes with the people of America and with the family of the President, whose high character is well appreciated on this side."

Germany was equally earnest in her expressions of sympathy, the Emperor and Empress at once writing the following message to Mrs. McKinley :

" Koenigsberg, September 7, 1901.

" The Emperor and I are horrified at the attempt planned against your husband. Express our deepfelt sympathy, hoping that God may restore to health Mr. McKinley.

" WILLIAM I. R.
" VICTORIA I. R."

The President of France cabled directly to his fellow President :

" Rambouillet, September 7, 1901.

" With keen affliction I learn the news of the heinous attempt of which your Excellency has just been a victim. I take it to heart to join with the people of the United States in wishing the early recovery of your Excellency and I earnestly desire in this sorrowful juncture to renew to you the assurance of my sentiment of constant and cordial friendship.

" EMILE LOUBET."

Of the American Republics, Guatemala was the first to express its sorrow, President Estrada telegraphing to Mrs. McKinley :

" Guatemala, Sept. 6, 1901.

" My Government and I most heartfully lament the unhappy event. Be pleased to receive our profound sorrow.

" M. ESTRADA C."

Many more expressions of sympathy were received immediately after the shot was fired. In the days following, constant inquiries were made as to the condition of the distinguished patient. When, on September 14th, President McKinley passed away, the nation was officially notified of it by President Roosevelt's proclamation, given elsewhere, as his first official act. Official notice was given to foreign governments by a circular note addressed by the Secretary of State to their representatives accredited to the Government of the United States.

"DEPARTMENT OF STATE,
WASHINGTON, September 14, 1901.

"Sir: It is my painful duty to announce to you the death of William McKinley, President of the United States, in the city of Buffalo, at fifteen minutes past two in the morning of to-day, September 14th.

"Laid low by the act of an assassin, the week-long struggle to save his life has been watched with keen solicitude, not only by the people of this country, who raised him from their own ranks to the high office he filled, but by the people of all friendly-nations, whose messages of sympathy and hope, while hope was possible, have been most consolatory in this time of sore trial.

"Now that the end has come, I request you to be the medium of communicating the sad tidings to the government of the honored nation you so worthily represent, and to announce that, in obedience to the prescriptions of the Constitution, the office of President has devolved upon Theodore Roosevelt, Vice-President of the United States.

"Accept, sir, the renewed assurance of my highest consideration.
"JOHN HAY."

From England

The replies were instantaneous. King Edward of England sent the following telegram from Fredensborg, Denmark, to Mr. Choate, the American Ambassador in London:

"Most truly do I sympathize with you and the whole American nation at the loss of your distinguished and ever-to-be-regretted President. "Edward, Rex."

The Archbishop of Canterbury, the Most Rev. Frederick Temple, sent the following despatch to Mr. Choate:

"I desire to express in behalf of the Church of England the deep grief with which we have heard of the death of the President. The loss of so great a ruler is a calamity to the whole world. The triumph of wickedness fills us with sorrow. Our prayer and good-will will be an earnest for the American people."

Following is the text of the message of the Lord Mayor of London to the American Embassy:

"The citizens of London are profoundly moved and deeply affected at the sad intelligence of President McKinley's death. They had hoped that under Providence so valuable a life might be spared for the welfare of his country. In their name I beg to tender your Excellency their heartfelt sympathy. I shall be grateful if you will convey this to Mrs. McKinley and the people of the United States. The eminent career and public services of President McKinley were widely appreciated here and will long be remembered by the English people, who, having themselves sustained the loss of a beloved sovereign this year, are able to sympathize keenly with the United States in the sudden removal of their distinguished President."

On Sunday there was an immense congregation at St. Paul's Cathedral. Among those present were Ambassador Choate and the staff of the Embassy. The Rev. Henry Scott Holland, Precentor of the Cathedral, said:

"A great hope that once filled humanity lies slain. We once dreamed that the New World had awaked from the nightmare of evil memories and set out to live its free life unburdened and uncursed, but the new has like bitterness to work through as the old. We must face it calmly and patiently. Not that we may be driven into a fierce reaction by the sting of this insane crime does the poor man lie dead. With renewed humility and with severer resolution we must work together for a new order of social intercourse, in which it will become impossible for passions which issue in such an outrage to exist."

Sir Henry Irving wired to Mr. Choate :

" May I add personally my deep grief to that of the people of this nation and of the nations of the earth for the loss of a great and good life, so ruthlessly snatched away in the fullness of love and honor."

With brief but well-chosen words the London *Times* thus ended its editorial :

" He died as he lived, with simple, manly courage and unaffected piety, which mark the best men of his race."

The *Daily Telegraph* said :

" There was the same anxious look in the faces of Londoners yesterday as they wore when our late beloved Queen was fighting her battle with death. It was then that America stretched out her hand to us. To-day, in her hour of bitter trial, we return the grasp."

The *Daily Chronicle*, discussing the world-wide sympathy displayed, said :

" This sympathy is intensified by a full realization of the calamity, until we are almost inclined to say that there is no precedent for such a display of emotion and fellow-feeling on these particular lines. It is not impossible that the assassination of Mr. McKinley will advance that international comity of governments to which some political students look as the keynote of future peace and harmony."

The *Westminster Gazette* said :

" To us in this country the loss of President McKinley is a family bereavement. We have had our differences with the

American people. We know full well how more true it becomes every day that they are our keenest and most dangerous trade competitors, but above and beyond the conflict of competition is the outstanding fact that they are our next of kin. We are linked by common ties that exist nowhere except with the United States. Just as Queen Victoria was sincerely mourned on the other side of the Atlantic, so now we claim a special right to share the sorrow and indignation which the American continent feels at the death of its President."

From Germany

Nothing was more appreciated in this country than the quick action of the German Emperor William. His despatch to Mr. Hay was as follows :

" I am deeply affected by the news of the untimely death of President McKinley. I hasten to express the deepest and most heartfelt sympathy of the German people to the great American nation. Germany mourns with America for her noble son, who lost his life while he was fulfilling his duty to his country and people. " WILLIAM I. R."

The Emperor also sent the following despatch to Mrs. McKinley :

" Her Majesty the Empress and myself beg you to accept the expression of our most sincere sorrow in the loss which you have suffered by the death of your beloved husband, felled by the ruthless hand of a murderer. May the Lord, who granted you so many years of happiness at the side of the deceased, grant you strength to bear the heavy blow with which he has visited you.

" WILLIAM I. R."

On hearing of the death of President McKinley, the Emperor, with characteristic and generous thought, ordered the German fleet assembled off Danzig to half-mast their flags and to hoist the Stars and Stripes at their maintops, and also ordered flags to be half-masted on all German public buildings. German opinion is reflected by the *Berliner Neueste Nachrichten*, which said :

"The German nation expresses to the American people sincere sympathy in the loss of a leader who was an out-and-out American, and who firmly undertook the realization of aims he deemed worth obtaining, and corresponding with the wishes of a majority of the people."

From Austria

In Austria the hearty feeling was well voiced by the Vienna *Neues Weiner Tageblatt*, which said:

"The ocean is not wide enough to hold all the sympathy that is streaming from the Old World to the New."

From Russia

In Russia, perhaps the most important editorial utterance was that of the St. Petersburg *Boerse Gazette*, which said :

"Mr. McKinley was one of the most popular figures in American history and one of the best representatives of American ideals. On account of the extraordinary purity of Mr. McKinley's character, the American people will find sympathy wherever civilized men dwell. Opinion in Europe regarding Pan-Americanism may possibly be divided, but it is comprehensible from the American point of view. Mr. McKinley died firmly believing that the work he had begun in domestic and foreign policy would find suitable instruments for its continuation."

From France

President Loubet, of France, telegraphed as follows to Mrs. McKinley :

" I learn with deep pain that his Excellency Mr. McKinley has succumbed to the deplorable attempt on his life. I sympathize with you with all my heart in the calamity which thus strikes at your dearest affections and which bereaves the great American nation of a President so justly respected and loved."

The Paris *Gaulois* said :

" The death of President McKinley will have a greater reverberation throughout Europe than had the disappearance of Garfield, Lincoln, or Carnot. He played a bigger part on the world's stage than any of his predecessors."

From Italy

In Italy the sympathy was specially strong by reason of the late King's assassination a year ago. The Dowager Queen Margherita said on Thursday to a friend, when talking of Mrs. McKinley : " Both of us know what it is to be kept from the bedsides of our dear ones, I by Humbert's instantaneous death, she by weak health. I cannot get her out of my mind. She is constantly in my thoughts and prayers."

From Mexico

The most significant and welcome message from the head of any government in this hemisphere was from President Diaz, of Mexico :

" I have been deeply shocked by this crime. President McKinley was not a ruler of exclusive or aristocratic tendencies. He was a good friend of the people, a genuine democrat in the best sense of the word. With regard to Mexico, President McKinley had ever evidenced such friendly sentiments that his death will be mourned in this country hardly less keenly than in the United States."

CHAPTER XXVII
Memorial Tributes

THAT William McKinley was a great man, his acts will show when history has recorded his deeds. It is to his honor to say that political opponents have rated his abilities more highly than his political supporters, and that European observers have rated them more highly than have Americans. Posterity will ratify the higher judgment, and history will rank President McKinley more highly than his contemporaries have done, not only as an astute politician, but also as a popular leader and a broad-minded and cautiously progressive statesman. His death was felt as a personal loss by thousands who knew him only through his public life, and by the entire Nation as a great public calamity. The world itself turned into mourning and joined in expressions of sorrow and grief. With these expressions are many noble tributes of distinguished men and women in all walks of life, and also of the newspaper press of the country where editors speak from the vantage ground of closest knowledge of events. We give only a few of the many memorial tributes which have been uttered.

His Characteristic Virtues

By Cardinal Gibbons

"In the annals of crime it is difficult to find an instance of murder so atrocious, so wanton and meaningless, as the assassination of Mr. McKinley. Some reason or pretext has been usually assigned for the sudden taking away of earthly rulers. Balthasar, the impious king of Chaldæa, spent his last night in reveling and drunkenness. He was suddenly struck dead by the hand of the Lord. How different was the life of our Chief Magistrate! No court in Europe or in the civilized world was more conspicuous for moral rectitude and purity, or more free from the breath of scandal, than the official home of President McKinley. He would have adorned any court in Christendom by his civic virtues.

"The Redeemer of mankind was betrayed by the universal symbol of love. If I may reverently make the comparison, the President was betrayed by the universal emblem of friendship. Christ said to Judas, Fiend, betrayest thou the Son of Man with a kiss? The President could have said to his slayer. Betrayest thou the head of the nation with the grasp of the hand? He was struck down surrounded by a host of his fellow-citizens, every one of whom would have gladly risked his life in defense of his beloved chieftain.

"The domestic virtues of Mr. McKinley were worthy of all praise. He was a model husband. Amid the pressing and engrossing duties of his official life he would from time to time snatch a few moments to devote to the invalid and loving partner of his joys and sorrows. Oh, what a change has come over that afflicted woman! Yesterday she was the first lady of the land. To-day she is a disconsolate and broken-hearted widow. Let us beseech Him who comforted the widow of Nain that He console this lady in her hour of desolation.

"The strongest shield of our Chief Magistrate is the love and devotion of his fellow-citizens. The most effective way to stop such crimes is to inspire the rising generation with greater reverence for the constituted authorities, and a greater horror for any insult or injury to their person. All seditious language should be suppressed. Incendiary speech is too often an incentive to criminal acts on the part of many to whom the transition from words to deeds is easy. Let it be understood, once for all, that the authorities are determined to crush the serpent of Anarchy whenever it lifts its venomous head.

"What a beautiful spectacle to behold prayers ascending from tens of thousands of temples throughout the land to the throne of mercy! Is not this universal uplifting of minds and hearts to God a sublime profession of our faith and trust in Him?"

His Memory Will Live

ARCHBISHOP IRELAND

"The nation mourns. Well may she mourn. She has lost her Chief Magistrate whom she loved so dearly, in whom she so willingly reposed her pride. William McKinley is now dead; his memory will live down the ages, as that of one of the most worthy to have been the President of the Republic of the United States.

"I knew him closely; I esteemed him; I loved him.

"He was the true man, honest, pure of morals, generous-minded, conscientious, religious. He was the noble citizen, proud of being a son of the people, brave on the battlefield in his country's peril, zealous of its glory, unswervingly loyal to its honor and its interests.

"He was the typical President of the Republic, large-minded in his vision of the questions bearing upon the country's fortune; resolute in using his authority for what seemed to him its best weal; ready as the leader of a self-governing people to hearken to the popular voice, and, so far as principle and conscience permitted, obey its behests, even to the sacrifice of his personal view. Political opponents differed from him in matters of public policy; they did not, they could not, mistrust his sincerity, or his spirit of justice and patriotism.

"William McKinley is now dead—stricken down by the hand of a vile assassin. This makes the nation's sorrow doubly deep, for to sorrow is added shame—shame before her own eyes, before those of the world, that in this land of civil liberty there should have been found a man so overwhelmingly bad as to murder her President, to murder him who served so well his fellow-man, to murder him who cherished so tenderly the free institutions of America—shame that within her own borders the majesty of the Republic should have been outraged and its name disgraced, the honor of humanity assailed and its most sacred rights imperilled.

"In our hour of sorrow we turn to the God of nations and commend to Him our country. In His mysterious designs He judges best to take from us our friend, our President, despite our earnest prayers that we be allowed to retain him among the living. We murmur not against His holy will, which we know to be wisdom and goodness, but in compensation for our great loss we pray that peace be given to the nation, that blessings descend upon our people."

History has no Precedent

Senator Joseph B. Foraker

Senator Foraker said in part: "In the vigor of robust manhood; at the very height of his powers; in the possession of all his faculties; in the midst of a great work of world-wide import-ance; in the enjoyment of the admiration, love, and affection of all classes of our people to a degree never before permitted to any man; at a time of profound peace, when nothing was occurring to excite the passions of men; when we were engaged in a celebration of the triumphs of art, science, literature, commerce, civilization, and all that goes to make up the greatest prosperity, advancement, and happiness the world has ever known; surrounded by thousands of his countrymen, who were vying with each other in demonstrations of friendship and goodwill, the President of the United States, without a moment's warning, was stricken down by an assassin, who, while greeting him with one hand, shot him to death with the other.

" History has no precedent for such treachery and wickedness since Joab, stroking his beard as though to kiss him, inquiring, 'Art thou in health, my brother?' smote unsuspecting Amasa in the fifth rib and 'shed out his bowels to the ground.'

SORROW YET TOO FRESH

" We can scarce realize that such a crime was possible, much less that it has been actually committed, and our sorrow is yet too fresh, our grief too poignant, and our indignation too acute for us to contemplate it dispassionately or discuss it considerately.

"But, while we cannot speak becomingly of the murderer and his awful crime, we can fittingly employ this hour to commemorate the virtues of his victim, and to recount in part at least his great services to his country.

" The allotted age of man is three score years and ten, but William McKinley was not yet fifty-nine when his career ended. In these short years he did a wondrous work. In its accomplishment he was unaided by fortuitous circumstances. He was of humble origin, and without influential friends, except as he made them.

" No language can adequately tell of his devoted love and tender affection for the invalid partner of all his joys and sorrows. Amidst his many honors and trying duties she ever reigned supreme in his affections.

" The story of this love has gone to the ends of the earth, and is written in the hearts of all mankind. It is full of tenderness, full of pathos, and full of honor. It will be repeated and cherished as long as the name of William McKinley shall live.

" It was these great qualities of the heart that gave him the place he holds in the affections of other peoples. They claim him for humanity's sake, because they find in him an expression of their highest aspiration. By common consent he honored the whole human race, and all the race will honor him.

" But he was more than gentle. He was thoroughly religious;

23

too religious to be guilty of any bigotry. His broad, comprehensive views of men and his duty in his relations to God, enabled him to have charity and respect for all who differed from his belief.

"His faith solaced him in life, and did not fail him when the supreme test came. When he realized the work of the assassin, his first utterance was a prayer that God would forgive the crime. As he surrendered himself to unconsciousness, from which he might never awake, that surgery could do its work, he gently breathed the Lord's prayer : 'Thy kingdom come, thy will be done.'

"And when the dread hour of dissolution overtook him, and the last touching farewell had been spoken, he sank to rest murmuring 'Nearer, my God, to Thee.'

"This was his last triumph, and his greatest. His whole life was given to humanity, but in his death we find his most priceless legacy. The touching story of that death-bed scene will rest on generations yet unborn like a soothing benediction. Such Christian fortitude and resignation give us a clearer conception of what was in the apostle's mind when he exclaimed : 'O Death, where is thy sting ? O Grave, where is thy victory?'"

A Truly Great Man

DR. FRANK GUNSAULUS, OF CHICAGO

"Still, still we linger at his grave. Once and again we make brave effort to leave it with the silence and the securities of God and the immeasurable time. We say we will forget, if possible, in order that we may go forth to our tasks and accomplish them. But we have waited so long that we now see that we shall be saved to all loftiness of life and generous confidence, not by forgetting, but by remembering. Not in any mist-covered pool of oblivion in which we may put out of sight the agony and the loss but in the absolving fountains of memory and love must we seek baptism and consecration toward the attainment of ends worthy of the American's past and the American's future.

" The three great graves which have received the dust of our martyred Presidents have three points toward which in each instance God has led his Moses, and on the mountain top lit by a moment of divine success Moses has been seen looking into the promised land. How little have we thought that our Moses was to die there and enter his grave before his nation reached its Canaan.

MCKINLEY A TRULY GREAT MAN

" William McKinley's career has been the career of a truly great man. His greatness has not a solitary element of the theatrical or romantic in its composition or influence. His was the genius which is so full-orbed and harmonious that it is most likely to require years for its completeness and serviceableness to be rightly estimated.

" Washington was no brilliant genius, and he beneficently inaugurated the movement of American Republicanism. A Napoleon at the beginning of our governmental experiment would have napoleonized our youth. Equally unfortunate would we have been had our experiment been fathered by a political philosopher of extraordinary visions.

" Lincoln's greatness was Republican greatness. His arm was strong when public sentiment lifted it, and he was able to incarnate the intellect and conscience of the republic.

" McKinley's greatness is of this type. He did listen with an ear close to the ground for the tread of the millions, and after a moment, which assured him of the righteousness and wisdom of public sentiment, he was erect and leading them Zionward. His imperialism was that of absolute loyalty to the people's will, after the people's will had been educated by a knowledge of the facts in the case. The quality of the man's nature, his great public services, his practical faith in the institutions and processes of Republican government, make his grave a rallying point for all those elements of order and progress which will at last achieve for earth in many spirited reality the city of God."

A Great President

Chauncey M. Depew

" President McKinley held a position among the rulers of the world which no other of our Presidents filled. He not only had the confidence of Americans to an unusual degree, but, now that we are a world power, he was regarded in all European cabinets as the wisest and safest custodian of the conditions attendant upon this new and critical position of the United States among the nations of the world. The position which he took in China led to modifications of terms and protests against partition of territory which made possible a settlement without war. The comments of the European press upon his speech at the Pan-American Exposition show that in European opinion he was the greatest factor for the peace of the world. His death is a national and international calamity. Roosevelt will make an excellent President—strong, masterful and able. But no man living could, for the next three years of adjustment and settlement, possess the confidence as a ruler which attached to President McKinley. His opinions on domestic and foreign affairs were the judgment of the country because of the wisdom of his administration and utterances. The new President will have to go through the trial before he can hold such a place and have so much resting upon his individuality. In other words, the country in its industrial and commercial conditions, in its relations with capital and labor, in the processes of its development, in its entrance and expansion into foreign markets, and in its diplomatic relations with other countries, felt, with the tried and trusted McKinley, as a voyager on the Atlantic does in a ship commanded by an experienced and famous captain, who, with the storms, hurricanes and cyclones of the sea, has never had an accident and has always brought his ship safe and on time to port."

Imitate His Great Virtues

GROVER CLEVELAND *

" To-day the grave closes over the dead body of the man but lately chosen by the people of the United States from among their number to represent their nationality, preserve, protect, and defend their Constitution, to faithfully execute the laws ordained for their welfare, and to safely hold and keep the honor and integrity of the republic. His time of service is ended, not by the lapse of time, but by the tragedy of assassination. He has passed from the public sight, not joyously bearing the garlands and wreaths of his countrymen's approving acclaim, but amid the sobs and tears of a mourning nation. He has gone to his home, not the habitation of earthly peace and quiet night, with domestic comfort and joy, but to the dark and narrow home appointed for all the sons of men and then to rest until the morning light of the resurrection shall gleam in the east.

" All our people loved their dead President. His kindly nature and lovable traits of character, and his amiable consideration for all about him will long live in the minds and hearts of his countrymen. He loved them in return with such patriotism and unselfishness that in this hour of their grief and humiliation he would say to them : ' It is God's will ; I am content. If there is a lesson in my life or death, let it be taught to those who still live, and leave the destiny of their country in their keeping.' Let us, then, as our dead is buried out of our sight, seek for the lessons and the admonitions that may be suggested by the life and death which constitutes our theme.

* From an address to the students at Princeton University.

"First in my thoughts are the lessons to be learned from the career of William McKinley by the young men who make up the student body of our university. These lessons are not obscure or difficult. They teach the value of study and mental training, but they teach more impressively that the road to usefulness and to the only success worth having will be missed or lost, except it is sought and kept by the light of those qualities of the heart which it is sometimes supposed may safely be neglected or subordinated in university surroundings. This is a great mistake. Study and study hard, but never let the thought enter your mind that study alone, or the greatest possible accumulation of learning alone, will lead you to the heights of usefulness and success. The man who is universally mourned to-day achieved the highest distinction which his great country can confer on any man, and he lived a useful life. He was not deficient in education, but with all you will hear of his grand career and his services to his country and to his fellow-citizens, you will not hear that the high plane he reached or what he accomplished was due entirely to his education. You will instead constantly hear as accounting for his great success that he was obedient and affectionate as a son, patriotic and faithful as a soldier, honest and upright as a citizen, tender and devoted as a husband, and truthful, generous, unselfish, moral and clean in every relation of life. He never thought any of those things too weak for his manliness. Make no mistake. Here was a most distinguished man, a great man, a useful man—who became distinguished, great and useful because he had, and retained unimpaired, qualities of heart which I fear university students sometimes feel like keeping in the background or abandoning.

LESSONS TO LEARN

"There is a most serious lesson for all of us in the tragedy of our late President's death. The shock of it is so great that it is hard at this time to read this lesson calmly. We can hardly fail to see, however, behind the bloody deed of the assassin, horrible figures and faces from which it will not do to turn away. If we are to escape further attack upon our peace and security, we must boldly and resolutely grapple with the monster of Anarchy. It is not a thing that we can safely leave to be dealt with by party or partisanship. Nothing can guarantee us against its menace except the teaching and the practice of the best citizenship, the exposure of the ends and aims of the gospel of discontent and hatred of social order, and the brave enactment and execution of repressive laws.

" The universities and colleges cannot refuse to join in the battle against the tendencies of Anarchy. Their help in discovering and warring against the relationship between the vicious councils and deeds of blood, and their steadying influence upon the elements of unrest, cannot fail to be of inestimable value.

" By the memory of our murdered President, let us resolve to cultivate and preserve the qualities that made him great and useful, and let us determine to meet any call of patriotic duty in any time of our country's danger and need."

Bright with Good Deeds Done

Secretary John D. Long

" President McKinley, of blessed life, is now and, more and more as time goes on, will be of blessed memory. The asperities which afflict a public servant during his official career will quickly be forgotten, and the calm, just verdict of history will pronounce him a man of ideally pure, true character, a patriot of single and disinterested devotion to his country and a statesman unexcelled for tact, prudence and practical competency. His domestic life is one of the precious sanctities of American sentiment.

" As an Executive, his administration has been a series of remarkable achievements. It has been attended by great military successes, by an abounding prosperity.

"It has put out the last embers of sectional bitterness. It has been marked by appointments of high character and especial fitness to places of great trust. The tone of the public official, the efficiency of the civil service, the integrity and fidelity of all departments and branches of the executive government were never so high as to-day.

"President McKinley leaves an unblemished record in public and private life.

"And a record not merely free from blemish, but bright with good deeds done, with great service rendered."

His Simple Greatness

John W. Griggs, ex-Attorney-General

"Hear the concordance of praise that comes from every mind under the heavens!

"The East cries, 'We loved him, for he was of our stock. He thought with us. He brought us prosperity. We knew him; therefore we loved him.'

"The West says, 'He was of us; he was our perfect product. We knew him; therefore we loved him.'

"The North cries, 'He fought for us; he wrought for us. We understood him; he was loyal and true; therefore we loved him.'

"The South cries, 'We loved him, for he was magnanimous and just to the South; in war an honorable foeman, in peace a friend and a brother.'

"Gallant soldier, successful politician, wise legislator, powerful debater, matchless orator, courtly gentleman; courtly in manner because courteous in feeling.

"If I were to seek a phrase to describe his public demeanor, I should say it was, 'Simple greatness.'

"And he was no mere theoretical academic statesman, filled with great zeal and small sense. His mind and methods were of the practical kind. No man ever appreciated more truly than he the real nature and quality of public sentiment, and none ever understood better how to mould and use it for the public good. He had faith in the common sense of the average citizens, and it was to their reason, not their passion or their prejudice, that he always made his appeals—and rarely in vain.

" He was no trimmer, watching the shifting impulses of the populace that he might trim his sails to the momentary gusts, but a great pilot scanning always the waters ahead to shun the rocks and whirlpools and discover where the deep, safe channel of national progress lay. His pilot stars were truth and loyalty.

" He was the sanest man and the one most free from hasty impulse and unreasoning prejudice that ever graced so high a station."

A Great Figure

Senator Henry Cabot Lodge

"President McKinley was the leader and chief in a momentous period of his country's history, and he rose fully to the great situation. His policies have become the policies of the United States.

" When the history of his time is written he will stand forth as the great figure in the years which have been so crowded with events. He gained the entire confidence of the nation by his patriotism, wisdom and ability, just as he won its love by his kindness and goodness to all men. This is not the time, especially for those whose personal sorrow mingles with that of the public at his loss, to say more. We all bow our heads with grief and are grateful for the sympathy other nations offer us so strongly.

" Deeply conscious of our loss, and with our hearts full of sadness and sorrow for her to whom President McKinley gave such beautiful and unselfish devotion, the sympathy of all Americans goes out to the Vice-President, called so suddenly and so painfully to take the place of one who was his friend as well as his associate, and with whose well-considered policies and patriotic purposes he is in such complete accord. Words at such a moment are vain. It is a tragic end of a great career. Murder cut short a brilliant and beneficent life. It is a national loss and a profound sorrow. It is all inexpressibly sad."

Of Blameless Life

Adlai E. Stevenson, former Vice-President

" Blameless in private life, of personal integrity unquestioned, firm in his convictions of duty, true to his friendships, patriotic in all his impulses, of lofty aims and purposes, gentle and loving to those to whom his toils and cares were given—he will be to the young men of our country at once an example and an inspiration.

"It is well that upon this day all business be suspended, the ordinary cares for a while laid aside, the symbols of mourning displayed, and that the people of all shades of belief and of all sections of our country should assemble to do honor to the memory of our Chief Magistrate. The candidate of a party, he was the President of an entire people. Such occasions as this touch the responsive chords of the great American heart. The Government will live. The feeling of devotion to country, of determination to maintain our free institutions in their purity and their vigor, was never stronger than at this moment. Let those now upon the threshold, and who may yet witness the passing of the noon of the century, realize something of the dignity and the grandeur of American citizenship.

"In this hour of national sorrow it is a gratifying reflection that during the more than 100 years of our history as a government no man has been elected to the Presidency who was unworthy of the great office. The eminent statesman whose memory we how honor has with ability and fidelity met the requirements of his exalted station. His work is done. His hands are folded. His name is henceforth upon the list of the illustrious dead. Peace to his ashes! May God comfort the one most of all bereaved!

"In establishing our government, our fathers wisely provided by constitutional methods for contingencies such as that we now deplore. In less favored countries revolutions are often the immediate result of the death of rulers. By peaceable succession the officer designated by law is now the incumbent of the great office. Coming in such a manner and in the hour of the nation's gloom it brings to its incumbent responsibilities of no ordinary character. It is the earnest prayer of all that his discharge of the solemn duties that await him may redound to the continued welfare of our common country."

The People Bowed as One Man

William Jennings Bryan

"As monuments reared by grateful hands to the memory of heroes testify to the virtues of the living, as well as to the services of the dead, so the sorrow that has overwhelmed our nation, obliterating the distinctions of party, race, and religion, is as complimentary to the patriotism of our people as to our departed Chief Magistrate. But it is not strange that the people bow as one man over the bier of their illustrious fellow-citizen—not strange that the solemn stillness is broken only by the music of the sacred hymns which he was wont to sing—not strange that all hearts turn in sympathy to the husbandless home at Canton.

"The President's position made him a part of the life of all his countrymen, and the circumstances which attended his taking off added indignation to grief—indignation that even one murderous heart could be found in all the land, and grief that the wicked purpose of that heart should have been consummated against one so gentle in spirit and so kind in word and deed.

"This.is neither the time nor the place for a discussion of remedies for anarchy. It can have no defenders in the United States. Government is a necessity, and the delusion that society can exist without it is harmful, even when no violence is advocated, for it is the duty of every citizen of a republic to strive to make his government perfect in every detail, and this purpose is not only weakened but entirely destroyed by the doctrine that all governments are bad and should be overthrown."

A Leader of All

A. G. Schurman, President of Cornell University

"We have come together with bowed heads and heavy hearts to join in a solemn service in memory of the late President of the United States. What manner of man he was we can now only vaguely discern, for our eyes are blinded with tears and analysis is overwhelmed by emotion. Yet, that a great and good man walked with us, and shall walk with us no more, we are somehow vividly aware.

"Strong he was, and firm even to the point of obstinacy. Yet he was so deferential to the judgment of others, so willing to listen to everybody, so truly democratic in his search for truth and wisdom, that his very lack of dogmatic self-conceit and even the deliberateness of his method were at first construed as signs of weakness, and in the early days of his Presidency it was a not uncommon criticism that he had no mind of his own. Never was there a greater mistake, as the men who came closest to him and had most to do with him will universally testify. His Cabinet was made up of strong men, but the President dominated the Cabinet. He saw everybody, heard everybody, but followed nobody. Yet, somehow, he was leader of all, and all fell into line and marched

behind or beside him. He acquainted himself with all the facts of
a given case, listened to all manner of advice from those who
might be supposed to know all about it, even suffering fools gladly,
and then reached a decision or adopted a policy of his own, which,
being well considered, was sure to command general assent. It
was his own view, yet it was the quintessence of the public mind.
He was the greatest inductive philosopher who ever experimented
with American politics. And it did not take the American people
long to discover his method or to show their appreciation of it.
Even before his re-election, the talk that he lacked independence
of judgment had entirely ceased.

" I have dwelt upon this point, because it is here that William
McKinley has suffered most injustice at the hands of his critics."

A Man Who Knew His Own Mind

W. R. Harper, President of Chicago University

" President McKinley, I believe, showed the highest ability as a
statesman. He carried the country through one of its most critical periods, and his administration will be known hereafter from the
fact that under him the United States took its place in the world
at large. As a man, he was simple, strong and lovable, simple-
minded and yet firm. He was a man who knew his own mind and
could carry with him his party and the people. He was a man of
high culture and high ideals, a man whose interest in all that was
great was manifest. He was a friend of education in every form,
from the lowest to the highest."

" The Well Beloved," McKinley's Title

Dr. Angell, President of the Michigan University

" The title that is most likely to come to our martyred President is that of ' The well beloved.' Washington had a dignified

severity that left a space between himself and the people. Lincoln was loved by only half the nation when he died. Old animosities between the North and the South had not expired when Garfield passed away. But since McKinley came into office the Blue and the Gray have been united. He won the hearts of the Southern people and cemented a nation.

" His was the average American life in a glorified form. He was pure, simple, genial and kind. So long as he dominated our affairs, he could be dealt with by foreign powers with sincerity, and this is the secret of the great influence of this nation in the administration of foreign affairs."

Living for Others

A. T. Hadley, President of Yale University

" As we lay President McKinley's body to rest to-day, we do not think of him as one apart from ourselves, but rather as one who, in life and death, identified himself with the American people. His was not a career of self-centred isolation. In his ambition and in his work he was a man among men—living for others as he understood their needs, and reaching his best results through that co-operation from others which he so well knew how to secure.

" It is a noteworthy fact in American history that the men who have attained the chief office in the land have not been those with whom brilliancy was the chief characteristic. The prize did not fall to the lot of men like Calhoun, or Clay, or Webster, or Seward, or Blaine. It came rather to those men of plainer purpose whom the people felt to be more truly representative of themselves. It detracts not one whit from the glory of McKinley's administration that men like Hay and Root and Long and others with whom he knew how to surround himself contributed so large a part to its success. For the work of a single individual, be he as brilliant as Napoleon, is apt to stand apart from the life of the people and the world, as compared with that of him who knows how to pursue aims in which his country has its full share, and to enlist the help of that country in carrying them to a completion."

An Awful Mystery

John Wanamaker

"The passing on of William McKinley is an awful mystery. There are millions of hearts that are overwhelmed with agony. As against the miserable creature, called a man, who destroyed this noble life, there are thousands and thousands of men in the United States, noble and true, who would unhesitatingly and gladly have given their lives if his could have been spared, so full was it of gifts and graces, of growth and of genuine goodness.

"Almost like a flash in the sky, he passed on without spot or decay or the withering of powers to the eternal and enduring. He lived and died nobly. 'Good-by,' he said, 'good-by, to all. It is God's way.' Always a sage and a soldier, and now a saint."

"To-day, O Mother Earth, take back thy clay !
   The spirit that employ'd it, by its flight
Beyond the stars into th' eternal day
   Bequeaths it thee — it is thy lender's right.
We only plead that thou wilt safe enfold
   This dust made sacred by a people's grief.
'Twas honor's tent — a patriot's pure stronghold —
   The watch-room of the nation's loyal chief !

"He loved his native land and used his life
   To serve her larger growth in strength and fame.
Insuring arts of peace, deploring strife,
   Resisting all that threaten'd wrong or shame.
Though senseless anarchy made him its mark,
   His mortal death was but immortal birth !
Each freeman's heart shall be his memory's ark,
   While Liberty extols his peerless worth !''

          —Sam'l W. Small, in *The Constitution*, Atlanta, Ga.

Mrs. Florence Earle Coates, in the "Memorial Ode" written by her on the request of the city of Philadelphia for the Peace Celebration, and read at Independence Hall on October 8, 1898, coupled Lincoln and McKinley in two stanzas to which our latest national tragedy has given a yet deeper significance. She wrote of them as the chieftains of the nation, each of whom had piloted the United States through war to peace. Their deaths by assassination have now linked their names inseparably and forever. We append the stanzas, the first being a tribute to Abraham Lincoln and the second a tribute to William McKinley:

Lincoln-McKinley

"And one there is, one image, full of rest,
A memory of manhood singly blest,
The saviour of our Nation, and her Chief;
Matchless in judgment, love, compassion, power—
The Man meet for the hour.
    Assailed by ignorance and half-belief—
Each searching, from too near a view,
To read the soul of all our souls most true—
He went his way, unselfish, minist'ring;
But in the bud and promise-time of Spring,
He died—and then we knew.

"So in the years to come, when we shall sleep,
    Tired pilgrims, at life's everlasting goal,
And the hid hand that faithful minutes keep
    Shall all the record of our times unroll,
    Our sons shall read, emblazoned on the scroll,
        His name, revered and great,
    Who sways our continent with mild control;
Pilot whom war tempestuous could not whelm,
Who stood, through every peril, at the helm,
    Guiding to peaceful port our Ship of State.
He neither needs our praise nor vindication,
    Who, in the coming years, shall take his place
    With the wise rulers of the English race,
A leader of the strength that fits a free-born nation."

Roswell P. Flower   S. G. Payne   J. McKenna   T. M. Bayne

C. P. Breckenridge   R. M. La Follette   Nelson Dingley, Jr.   Wm. McKinley, Jr., Chairman

J. G. Carlisle   J. H. Gear   J. C. Burrows   B. McMillin

Roger Q. Mills

A MEETING OF THE WAYS AND MEANS COMMITTEE OF THE HOUSE DRAFTING THE McKINLEY TARIFF BILL

CHAPTER XXVII

Characteristics and Incidents

QUITE as impressive as anything else in the developments of the last four days of his life on earth was the clear light in which they showed how President McKinley's personal charms and qualities as a man had won the affection of the country. Particularly was this noticeable in Washington, where, from his long service in Congress, and his more than four years in the Presidential chair, he became known personally as to no other part of the country, except, perhaps, to his neighbors in Canton. Dr. David J. Hill, Assistant Secretary of State, once remarked to a friend when Mr. McKinley's personality was under discussion, that if "the Lord had ever breathed the breath of life into a more gracious and amiable man than Mr. McKinley," Dr. Hill had yet to find it out. This is a thoroughly characteristic estimate, and one that is by no means confined in its expression to occasions of grief and strain like the present.

ALWAYS DID THE AMIABLE THING

Mr. McKinley, according to the best estimates of those who knew him well, always did the amiable and courteous thing. He was thoughtful and considerate. If he ever had any feeling of injured dignity or ill-temper, he never let it be discovered even by those nearest to him. Everybody who went to the White House came away pleasantly impressed, whether Republican, Democrat, Populist, anti-Imperialist, or Socialist; a negro, a Chinese, or a Caucasian. It had not been uncommon with other Presidents for men of more or less prominence to come away from the White House saying rather unpleasant things about the treatment they had received. With McKinley it was different, and in

422

that personal equation doubtless lay a large share of his success as a public man and party leader, in securing acceptance of the policies for which he stood. When before, it is frequently asked, has a President carried the House of Representatives in three Congresses in succession? When before has a President sustained such friendly relations with the Senators that they have rejected none of his nominations for office, or that he, in turn, has had to veto none of their bills? For this is substantially the situation. The very few vetoes and rejected nominations—and their number has been trifling—have rarely been unwelcome to the other side, but were rather in the nature of the correction of errors due to newly discovered evidence.

COURTESY TO CRITICS

When the Secretary of the Anti-Imperialist League first visited Washington, the President came out of a Cabinet meeting to receive him—a most unusual courtesy. Many a President who had been flattered as McKinley has been, would have taken affront at some of the utterances of the league, and, standing on his dignity, have refused altogether to see its representative. One of McKinley's predecessors steadily refused to see during his term of office an eminent doctor of divinity who several times called on public business, because he had as a preacher alluded to his alleged Sabbath-breaking propensities. President Arthur, with all that graciousness of manner which has associated itself with his name, proved a hard master for the clerical force in his immediate employ. If he desired a letter or a paper from the files for any purpose, he could brook no delay, and was seemingly unwilling to grant that time might be necessary even for those who served a President.

In fact, those who know the White House best, in its various aspects toward the public, are able to relate a great many incidents showing considerable human nature on the part of the various Presidents who have occupied it, but of McKinley they have nothing to relate but pleasant things, kindly acts, and genial ways. He seemed never offended at those who have most severely criticised him. We read in the newspapers one day that Senator Tillman declared that McKinley was gradually becoming a dictator to the subversion of the old Republic; the next day we read that Mr. Tillman went to the White House to ask for a small consulship for one of his constituents, and strange to relate that, although an opposition Democrat, he readily obtained it.   In fact, Tillman has said in a public way that, in his opinion, no finer gentleman from George Washington's time to the present had ever occupied the Presidential chair. He never went to the White House in the latter part of Mr. Cleveland's administration, just as there were many Republicans of prominence that were not very neighborly with Mr. Harrison, and others who did not like Mr. Arthur.

It has long become notable to outside observers, who have talked with public men after they came away from a conference with the Chief Executive, how generally he made their wishes his own.   In the organization of the first Philippine Commission, one of the men, provisionally selected, hastened to Washington to tell Mr. McKinley that he was not much of a believer in his expansion policy, and that, probably knowing this, Mr. McKinley would want somebody else to serve.   "Quite the contrary," was the President's answer.   "We need just the element of opinion on the Commission which you represent.   I am glad that you feel as you do about it."   Another man whom Mr. McKinley was about to appoint to a high office expressed, in the same way, his skepticism on the subject of protection, as indentified with Mr. McKinley's name.   In the same spirit, Mr. McKinley assured him that the view of the case which he held was the very one which the President was eager to have represented.

SAW BOTH SIDES OF A QUESTION

McKinley was always so able to see both sides of questions, to recognize personal and local limitations, that his relations with the world and with the American public were always very pleasant. It will be recalled how enthusiastic the Democratic South became when, on his visit to that section he allowed a Confederate badge,

WILLIAM McKINLEY

The 25th President

Born January 29th 1843.   Assassinated September 6, 1901.   Died September 14, 1901

PRESIDENT ROOSEVELT AT THE BIER, BUFFALO

pinned playfully on the lapel of his coat, to remain there all day, and how it is said that he recommended that the Federal Government join with the Southern States in the care of the cemeteries in which were buried the Confederate dead. Wherever he traveled on earth, east, west, or south, he always fell in so acceptably with the prevailing views and aspirations of the people as to win their most marked favor. By his diplomatic way, he led a great many persons to his manner of thinking, when they did not realize that they were being led.

MR. MCKINLEY'S CONSIDERATION

A touching tribute has been paid by a former stenographer of an Ohio State Senator to Mr. McKinley's kindheartedness. Before going on the stage, Louise Dresser was the private secretary of Senator Earnshaw, of Franklin County, Ohio, and, while acting in that capacity, was told one day that she was wanted in the room of Mr. McKinley, who was then Governor of Ohio. On entering the room she approached Mr. McKinley's secretary, thinking that he wanted to dictate a letter to her. On being told that the Governor wanted to dictate to her, she approached him nervously, and when she tried to work could scarcely hold the pencil. Seeing her plight, the kindhearted Governor said with a smile : " Don't be nervous. You'll get it all right. Think you are writing for Earnshaw." Miss Dresser speaks most feelingly of his consideration, and among the millions of mourners she feels the loss as keenly as though she had lost a personal friend.

LOYAL TO OLD FRIENDS

Loyalty to old friends, absolutely without regard to their worldly station, was a conspicuous trait of Mr. McKinley's character. At the second inauguration, among the White House guests were Jack Adams, who runs the President's farm near Canton, and a friend, Mr. Alexander, a tinsmith, from Minerva, Columbiana County, Ohio. Mr. Adams came to Washington at the President's invitation, but had no idea of doing more than " eating one meal in the White House," as he expressed it.   Here is Mr. Adams' own story of how he happened to be stopping at the White House during the inauguration week :

"Just before the inauguration of 1897, Mr. McKinley asked me if I did not want to come to Washington. Well, I was pretty busy on the farm just then, so I said no, I would come to the next one. The President laughed, and said to remind him and he would send me a pass. I got it. When my friend Alexander and I went up to the White House the President held out his hand and said : ' I'm glad to see you,' and asked me about my health and my family and how everybody was doing. I told him I had just come to town and got a room. He said : ' Not a bit of it. You are to stay right here in the White House, you and your friend.' I said that I did not like to impose upon him, but he replied that it was no imposition, and that I must bring my grip and stay the week out as his guest, and he would see that I had a good time and do everything for me that he could do. He made out a ticket that passed us to the grand stand to see the parade, and also gave us seats at the Capitol and admission to the inauguration ball."

POLITICAL REMINISCENCES

The following anecdotes of the late President were written for the Detroit *Free Press*, by David M. Carey, of the editorial staff of that paper :

"Columbiana County was the Republican stronghold in the old Eighteenth Congressional District of Ohio, made famous through the public career of the lamented McKinley, as was the adjoining district through the achievements of Garfield. After the late President had served as prosecuting attorney of Stark County, he decided to stand for Congress, and early in his initial campaign set about to securing to himself the overwhelming party majority in Columbiana. At the head of the men fitted for counsel was Judge J. A. Ambler, an ex-member of Congress, while among the young men for war were Hon. R. W. Tayler, now the representative of that district, then editor of the *Buckeye State* ; Ed. Moore, owner of that veteran party organ ; Major Monaghan, who recently died in the Philippines while filling an appointment given to him by the President; Frank McCord, collector of customs at Cleveland, and several others who have since attained greater or less distinction.

" One morning McKinley entered my office, and after telling who he was, though I knew him on sight, said : 'Squire, they tell me that you know everybody in Columbiana County, and particularly in the vicinity of Salem. I wish that you could give me a few days in canvassing this section.' The title given me was due to the fact that I was burning out my political ambitions by serving as justice of the peace under the fee system in a community then notorious for its reverence of law. I acknowledged my extended acquaintance in the community, for I had been reared there, presided over a preparatory academy that attracted scores of pupils from as many families, and had a weakness for driving over the hills of one of the prettiest spots on the map instead of groaning over a fifty to one shot while waiting for business as 'squire.'

" McKinley was 'Major' to the misses and 'Billy' to the political rustlers. While he did not adopt the traditional methods of the popular campaigner, he was one of the most effective in this line of activity that I ever encountered. He did not toss the babies in the air and kiss them on the rebound. He did not tell stories to the voters or run the risk of 'jollying' them beyond their actual worth. But there was an insinuating personality that it is difficult to describe. He could find a seat on the top of a stake-and-rider fence as though he had always been accustomed to it. A blade of grass or straw always found its way to his mouth, and the act made the farmer feel the presence of a congenial spirit. The major's smile, breaking over a beautiful set of teeth, was worth an election in a close district, and there was always a suggestion of reserve force that was more impressive than any amount of talk could have been.

"When the old soldiers saw the broad-brimmed slouch hat turned back from an expansive forehead and a magnetic pair of eyes that beamed the strongest ties of comradeship, they were up in arms for McKinley and no second choice. They dropped everything else to help fight his battle. And it must not be inferred that his lack of effusiveness was attended by a lack of effectiveness. To the farmer he talked about the tariff on wool, to the laboring man about the protection with which he would be surrounded, and to the manufacturer about the advantages that could be secured to them only through Republican control of national affairs. Right or wrong, his words carried conviction, and how well he made them good when he fathered the bill bearing his name is a matter of history.

"No cleaner man, in every sense of the word, ever came to the public view. Even in the heat of a political fight he never uttered a sentiment nor a sentence unfit for publication or for use in a model home. His self-containment was phenomenal and his voice never betrayed passion or menace. It ever had a pleasing conversational tone, except when emphasis was required from the stump. He was never bitter or unfair even in the secrecy of political conference, clearly denoting that what many have designated as diplomacy was a part of the man's nature. He would address a dozen farmers in a district schoolhouse with the same care and detail as he did his audiences of thousands, and nothing could have been more conscientious than the manner in which he made every engagement, even though its bearing upon his prospects could be but slight.

MCKINLEY LOSES HIS HAT

"While he was speaking in a school-house in one of the few Democratic districts of the county, some one hid his hat, and it required fifteen minutes after the meeting to find it in the wood box under some beech chunks. During the Minneapolis convention, which I reported for the *Free Press*, McKinley presided at one stage of the proceedings, during which an attempt was made by

Foraker and Ambler, of the Ohio delegation, to start a movement for his nomination to the Presidency. His protest was prompt and earnest, but would not have availed had his own State been able to swing the convention. In the excitement of the event he forgot at adjournment where he had left his hat, and as I approached him from the reporters' table he quickly remarked: 'Remember when I lost my hat down in Wayne Township, squire,' and then laughed, as staid men will over their earlier recollections.

"The best impressions now given of McKinley's character are those that I formed when his national career was yet to be made, and when I was with him as an incident of local politics. There was an attraction in his dignity and reserve, for they were accompanied by a democracy of speech and action such as would mark a paradox in a man less consistent and tactful. He was always approachable, and had a faculty of making friends who remained friends. He grew constantly in the stature of statesmanship and broadened his distinguishing views as the development of the country demanded, but to the end he maintained the same calm courage, the same personal attractions, the same virtues of private life that marked him when he first aspired to Congress."

HOW THE PRESIDENT TRANSACTED STATE BUSINESS

In a recent number of the *Independent*, Albert Halstead contributes an interesting article, entitled "The President at Work," which gives a good insight into Mr. McKinley's business habits :

"The President is methodical, completing each day's task as it comes to him. He does not postpone business from day to day until, with a dash of determination and despair, he rushes through it hastily and carelessly. He has the important executive faculty of making others work for him. He knows how to direct, to place responsibility on other shoulders; not that he avoids it, but that while making decisions and outlining policies himself, he leaves the drudgery to others. This relieves him of much routine that would weary and prevent him from paying the faithful attention to affairs which a successful administration requires.

"President McKinley is not naturally combative. He prefers to employ peaceful rather than aggressive methods in the accomplishment of an object. He never fights unless circumstances force it; yet he dominates always, and when a policy is determined upon, it is carried out. He has often been pictured as yielding, but that is unjust. When he has a purpose in view it matters not to him whether he wins what might be termed a personal victory, so long as the purpose is accomplished. He uses tact, is courteous and considerate at all times and avoids enmities. This is both natural and a matter of policy, a course far more successful in the long run than aggression.

HIS FREQUENT CONSULTATIONS

"The President consults unreservedly with his Cabinet on all important questions, with Congressional leaders of both parties and with prominent men throughout the country, giving due weight to all judgments and opinions. He keeps in close touch with public sentiment in this way and by reading the newspapers thoroughly. He is, certainly, not self-opinionated, and yet he is self-confident, and has an exact measure of his own abilities. He invariably listens to arguments, hears all sides of a question, then makes up his mind and acts accordingly. Perhaps he might be called a harmonizer. This quality is seen in the unity and solidity of his party. He is its acknowledged and undisputed leader, and it has never been more effective or harmonious. In his Cabinet are men selected for their intellectual force and especial capacities, men of strong individualities and vigorous opinions. They are his counselors, but he is the dominant force. He advises with them fully, but when a decision is reached it is his; and it is he, the President, who acts. The Cabinet is always in harmony with the determination that has been reached. This absence of Cabinet dissension shows the persuasive yet determined President, whose arguments have brought conviction.

Each Cabinet officer is supreme in his department, but is held to strict account for its work. And the policies of those departments are, to a surprising degree, inspired by the President, who is fully informed of their needs and the duties of each official.

HIS PERSONAL DIGNITY

"One of Mr. McKinley's striking characteristics is his personal dignity. No one ever slaps him on the back or becomes familiar; nor does any one tell a doubtful story in his presence. He is courteous and affable, friendly and at times jovial, yet ever by his bearing requiring the fullest respect and consideration for the great office he occupies. He never forgets that it is due to the people who elected him to preserve and even increase the dignity of his office. Despite his unexpressed demand that respect be shown him as President, he is most approachable, simple in his tastes, absolutely unaffected, detesting pomp and ostentation. He always realizes his responsibility to the people and their claims on him. He is clear-minded, conscientious and earnest, a model husband and typical Christian American. His ambition is to perform his duty faithfully, to protect and advance the nation's best interests, to support its highest traditions, and to promote the general welfare.

AIDED BY CORTELYOU

"While the Presidency is, of necessity, a laborious office, its cares may be much lessened if the secretary to the President is capable and diplomatic, able to relieve his chief of many burdens, a good counselor, who is broad and big enough mentally to make an efficient Cabinet officer. President McKinley has such a man in George B. Cortelyou, who is not only his secretary, but his trusted friend. Though a staunch Republican, Mr. Cortelyou was not selected through political influence, but because he had proven himself efficient and trustworthy. In this difficult position he makes friends rather than enemies for the President. He is the most popular secretary who has served a President in a quarter of a century. When it is remembered how many people he must disappoint each day; that he must tell the newspaper correspondents what they should know without seeming to suppress information; that he must remember every public man he has ever met; that he must be quick to grasp what each caller wants and be fully informed on every subject, and that he must be the buffer between the President and the public, it becomes apparent that unusual talents are required of him. Mr. Cortelyou has earned the President's confidence, and he does more executive work than any previous secretary. He has been so successful in systematizing the work of his office that it is better and more promptly done than ever before.

VOLUMINOUS CORRESPONDENCE

"The extent of President McKinley's correspondence can be appreciated from the fact that 400,000 communications were received and disposed of at the executive offices in his first term. Mr. Cortelyou, with a force composed almost exclusively of stenographers, who read each other's notes with facility, has dispensed with an immense amount of unnecessary work. When a letter or document is received, a memorandum, to show what is to be done with it, is written in shorthand in its upper left-hand corner. This is kept on the paper until it comes back to the secretary for approval. A letter is then written by a clerk in conformity with the memorandum. Thus in most of the correspondence there is no dictation. A 'precedent index' prepared by Secretary Cortelyou, covering practically every case that is likely to arise, serves as a guide to the clerks in answering correspondence and lessens the work materially. When a letter is of sufficient importance to be filed in the executive offices, the shorthand notes are preserved with it, so the exact action taken can be learned at a glance. Every important paper is briefed in typewriting, and when necessary the brief is filed with the papers, giving an accurate record.

5

THE FUNERAL AT CANTON

THE FUNERAL AT CANTON

Casket leaving the church

"Appreciating the importance of expediting business, Mr. Cortelyou prepared and had printed a number of endorsement pasters, which are attached to papers referred to other departments. Consequently when a communication comes to the White House that should go to the Department of State a paster referring it there is attached and, thus endorsed, it is forwarded. A rule of the executive offices requires that the work of each desk be finished on the day of its receipt. This prevents an accumulation of work and keeps it up to date.

"When the President makes a journey, his secretary and several members of the White House clerical force accompany him. All speeches made on the trip are reported stenographically. Copies are furnished the newspaper men with the party, and a special copy is preserved for the office records. Telegraphers from the office force are also with the President, and he is kept in constant touch with Washington. The 'war room,' where several telegraphers are always on duty, puts the President in communication with every part of the world. Here cipher dispatches are received and he is kept advised of every important event. With such a system, so much work and such a force, there is no idling in the executive offices."

CHAPTER XXVIII

The Assassin and the Anarchists

IT is unfortunate that the name of an assassin must be linked with that of his victim, and in that way perpetuated; yet we are sure that whenever mentioned it will be only with reprobation for his conduct and to hold up his name to execration. Such were the names of the assassins of Lincoln and Garfield, and the story of this awful tragedy by which William McKinley was so suddenly taken off brings into prominence another name which will likewise be execrated.

Czolgosz, the name of the man who shot President McKinley, offers a lingual problem to nine-tenths of those who attempt to pronounce it. It is one of those names which the English alphabet cannot spell phonetically, and which the average English-speaking person stumbles over in trying to express after hearing it spoken by a Russian. Written according to its sound, the name of Czolgosz, or its nearest equivalent, is "Tchollgosch," or, more broadly speaking, "Schollgosch."

The former pronunciation is given by one who is familiar with the varied dialects in Polish Russia, from whence the parents of Leon Czolgosz came to this country.

"Cz" is represented in the Russian alphabet by a character which is pronounced much the same as though one were suppressing a sneeze—"tch." The next two letters—"ol"—are pronounced in combination as though written "oll," and the remaining letters of the name—"gosz"—may be given the sound of "gosch."

Leon Czolgosz, the self-avowed disciple of Emma Goldman and the other radical anarchist leaders, who shot President McKinley, insisted from the very first moment he was taken into custody, that he alone was responsible for his crime. He stated that he had talked the matter over in advance in a general way with his friends, but that he was not advised by them, and that there was no plot or conspiracy to take the life of the President in which any one else took a part. He declined to furnish the names of the men with whom he discussed the crime.

Czolgosz was subjected to six hours of examination and questioning at the hands of the police officials. This lengthy examination proved to be fruitless, save in so far as his own individual fate was concerned, for while he told nothing that would implicate any one else in his crime, he went over the scene at the Temple of Music, when he shot the President, again and again, completing a confession as ample as the law ever exacted. He even went to the extent of illustrating to the officers the manner in which he shot the President, and told with manifest pride how he had deceived the President and his detective protectors with the bandaged hand that held the revolver.

CZOLGOSZ MAKES A STATEMENT

The following is a statement that the assassin is reported as having made upon his examination before the police of Buffalo :

"I was born in Detroit nearly twenty-nine years ago. My parents were Russian Poles. They came here forty-two years ago. I got my education in the public schools of Detroit, and then went to Cleveland, where I got work. In Cleveland I read books on socialism and met a great many socialists. I was pretty well known as a socialist in the West. After being in Cleveland several years, I went to Chicago, where I remained several months, after which I went to Newburg, on the outskirts of Cleveland, and went to work in the Newburg wire mills.

"During the last five years I have had as friends anarchists in Chicago, Cleveland, Detroit and other Western cities, and I suppose I became more or less bitter. Yes, I know I was bitter. I never had much luck at anything, and this preyed upon me. It made me morose and envious, but what started the craze to kill was a lecture I heard some little time ago by Emma Goldman. She was in Cleveland, and I and other anarchists went to hear her.   She set me on fire.

"Her doctrine that all rulers should be exterminated was what set me to thinking, so that my head nearly split with the pain. Miss Goldman's words went right through me, and when I left the lecture, I had made up my mind that I would have to do something heroic for the cause I loved.

"Eight days ago, while I was in Chicago, I read in a Chicago newspaper of President McKinley's visit to the Pan-American Exposition at Buffalo.   That day I bought a ticket for Buffalo, and got there with a determination to do something, but I did not know just what.   I thought of shooting the President, but I had not formed a plan.

"I went to live at No. 1078 Broadway, which is a saloon and hotel.   John Nowak, a Pole, a sort of politican, who has led his people here for years, owns it.   I told Nowak that I came to see the fair.   He knew nothing about what was setting me crazy.   I went to the Exposition grounds a couple of times a day.

"Not until Tuesday morning did the resolution to shoot the President take a hold of me.   It was in my heart; there was no escape for me.   I could not have conquered it had my life been at stake.   There were thousands of people in town on Tuesday.   I heard it was President's Day.   All those people seemed bowing to the great ruler.   I made up my mind to kill that ruler.   I bought a 32-calibre revolver and loaded it.

"On Tuesday night I went to the fair grounds, and was near the railroad gate when the Presidential party arrived.   I tried to get near him, but the police forced me back.   I was close to the President when he got into the grounds, but was afraid to attempt the assassination, because there were so many men in the body-guard that watched him.   I was not afraid of them, or that I would get hurt, but afraid I might be seized and that my chance would be gone forever.

"Well, he went away that time, and I went home. On Wednesday I went to the grounds and stood right near the President, right under him, near the stand from which he spoke.

"I thought half a dozen times of shooting while he was speaking, but I could not get close enough. I was afraid I might miss; and, then, the great crowd was always jostling, and I was afraid lest my aim fail. I waited until Thursday, and the President got into his carriage again, and a lot of men were about him and formed a cordon that I could not get through. I was tossed about by the crowd, and my spirits were getting pretty low. I was almost hopeless that night as I went home.

"Yesterday morning I went again to the Exposition grounds. Emma Goldman's speech was still burning me up. I waited near the central entrance for the President, who was to board his special train from that gate, but the police allowed nobody but the President's party to pass out while the train waited. So I stayed at the grounds all day waiting.

"During yesterday I first thought of hiding my pistol under my handkerchief. I was afraid if I had to draw it from my pocket I would be seized by the guards. I got to the Temple of Music the first one, and waited at the spot where the reception was to be held.

"Then he came—the President—the ruler—and I got in line and trembled and trembled, until I got right up to him, and then I shot him twice through my white handkerchief. I would have fired more, but I was stunned by a blow in the face—a frightful blow that knocked me down—and then everybody jumped on me. I thought I would be killed, and was surprised at the way they treated me."

Immediately upon the arrest of the assassin of President McKinley and the news that it was an attempt of anarchists, active and strenuous measures were taken to ferret out the conspiracy, if there were any, and to arrest the conspirators. Immediately, in Chicago, Ill., Paterson, N. J., and other large cities, the police

25

located suspicious characters and those affiliated with anarchistic organizations. In Chicago nine men were arrested and lodged in jail upon very strong suspicion that they had criminal knowledge at least of the crime. Emma Goldman, whom the assassin had named as the author of writings and speeches by which he was inflamed, was also arrested and held to answer to the charge of inciting to murder, but was later discharged for lack of evidence.))

ANARCHY AND ANARCHISTS IN CHICAGO

The circumstances surrounding the arrest in Chicago of Emma Goldman, the high priestess of Anarchy, and nine of her followers recall the anarchistic affairs in which Chicago has had part in the past. In the circumstances, the following review of the course of the Chicago group, so far as known to the police and to the public, will not be uninteresting at this time:

The conspiracy which culminated in the blaze of dynamite and the murder of policemen on the night of May 4, 1886, had its origin far away from Chicago, and under a social system very different from ours. Anarchy in Chicago is the direct result of social revolt in Europe, which, under more lax laws and a greater freedom of press and speech, has been able to develop to a degree impossible in the Old World.

Chicago has well been named "the hotbed of Anarchy," for, after the enactment of the stringent laws in Germany against social democracy and the determined opposition of Prince Bismarck, as well as laws passed and precautions taken in other European countries, the exodus to the United States began, and Chicago, unfortunately, seemed to be chosen as the favored abiding-place of Anarchy, notwithstanding its public sentiment, which was strongly against such a state of affairs.

Even the sudden awakening that occurred in 1873 was little more than political froth, but it had its lasting effect, however small. It was about this time that the movement for an eight-hour day began. The communists in the East began the agitation.

This was taken up with added zest in Chicago, and culminated in the "bread riots" and other disgraceful proceedings.

The first point of attack was the Relief and Aid Society, which was helping the destitute. The communists asserted that they had $600,000 which was being misappropriated. In December a procession formed and a committee called on the officers of the Aid Society, but did not receive an interview. This incensed them so that violence was resorted to, and a full-fledged anarchist society was the result, with a number of well known "Reds" as officers and leaders.

CLAMORING FOR BLOOD

The next step was to gain control of a German daily paper. This at first failed, but by the end of four or five years one was started, which became so rabid later as to be the real instigator of the Haymarket riot. The organization was fast drifting away from its methods of peace for bringing about reforms, and had already begun to clamor for blood.

A secret meeting was held, where a declaration of principles was adopted. This was followed by others, and on July 25, 1877, a fight between the communists took place near the Halsted Street viaduct; coming closely after the accession to power of Parsons and Schilling as leaders of the "Reds."

The communists lay dormant for some time after this, and the next notable step was the purchase of the *Arbeiter Zeitung*, which became the official organ of anarchy. Shortly after June 16, 1878, another paper was started, known as *The Alarm*, with Albert Parsons as editor.

After the second election of Carter H. Harrison, Sr., as Mayor the communists let politics entirely alone, and began to depend solely on force to gain their point. Military companies began to be formed, and rifle practice was the order of the day. Processions filled the streets, and women standard-bearers, carrying red and black banners, invariably headed the columns. One of the most notable of these took place on Tuesday night, April 28, 1885, on the occasion of the opening of the new Board of Trade building. Fielden and Parsons held an open-air meeting, and gathered together 2,000 of their followers, and, headed by a brass band, marched through the principal thoroughfares Winding up in front of the Board of Trade, they indulged in a fight with the police and then withdrew.

For inspiration the Chicago anarchists were wont to look to Rensdorf, who attempted the life of the Emperor of Germany, and his accomplices, Hœdel and Nobling, who were executed with him, were reverenced as martyrs.   Herr Most now began to figure as a bright star in the firmament.   February 16, 1886, was the day on which the movement which culminated in the murder of eight policemen and the maiming of a large number more at Haymarket Square may be said to have been born. On this day occurred the lockout at the McCormick Harvester Works.

WITH RIFLES AND BOMBS

On February 27th, and March 3d, meetings were held at Grief's Hall, and 140 men set out from this hall armed with rifles, revolvers and bombs, with a determination to prevent the "scabs," who were then operating the McCormick plant, from going to work. The waylaying of men on their way to work now began, and a little later a lively battle took place between the guards at the gate, the police and workmen, combined against the " Reds," who were determined to wreak vengeance on all who were on the opposite side of the fence. The anarchists were defeated, but a large number on both sides went away with broken heads and some with bullet holes in their bodies.

Soon after the riots at McCormick's the notorious "Revenge Circular" was distributed. On May 4, 1886, appeared the announcement of the mass meeting at Haymarket Square. It was printed in German and English, and announced that good speakers would denounce the atrocious acts of the police, and urged all workmen to be present.   That night a meeting was held in a cave in West

Lake Street. Here Parsons, Spies, Ling and others gave out dynamite bombs and perfected the scheme for the overthrow of the city government. The signal for action was the lighting of a huge bonfire in Wicker Park. Ling was the manufacturer of the bombs, and he carried them about with him in a satchel.

The plan adopted for action was to cut the telegraph wires between police stations, to make communication impossible; proceed to one station after another and destroy it with bombs; to fire buildings on the way, so as to call out the fire department, to prevent its being called on to suppress the riot, and to kill every policeman they came in contact with. The meeting was to be held in Haymarket Square—a widening in Randolph Street, between Halsted and Desplaines Streets, half a block from the Desplaines Street police station. Spies, Schwab, Fielden, Parsons, Fischer, Engel, Ling and Neebe were to speak and direct the movement of the rabble. Spies, Parsons and Fielden were late, but the mob stood patiently in the falling rain waiting for them. Finally they arrived, and each in turn made an inflammatory speech. Part of the plot had come to the ears of the police, and because of the complaints from residents and the general uneasiness of the police officials every man was on reserve.

THE HAYMARKET MURDERS

As the rabble increased and became more demonstrative and uneasy, it was deemed best that a detachment of policemen be sent to disperse it. Lieutenant Bonfield deserves the credit of the *coup* which prevented the carrying out of the anarchists' plan. On his own responsibility he formulated a plan, kept every man on reserve, and when the right time came, Captain William Ward set out with his men to disperse the mob.

At the head of a column of "bluecoats," he marched up to the barrel on which Fielden stood and commanded him to desist. Turning about, he commanded the crowd to disperse. Suddenly a terrific explosion occurred. A dynamite bomb had been flung into the group of policemen. Eight of them were killed and sixty-nine injured. Immediately following the explosion the discharge of small arms began, Lieutenant Bonfield rallied his men, and the anarchists were scattered in every direction. Fielden, on the appearance of the police, drew a revolver, fired from under cover and fled. Parsons was waiting in a saloon for the explosion. He also fled.

Fischer and Spies, the anarchists, got away from the scene of action as soon as they could. Ling, Engle and Neebe were also not to be found. How many in the mob were killed or wounded or afterward died of their injuries it is impossible to tell. That a large number paid dearly for their attendance at that treasonable gathering is certain, but the wounds of many were hidden and the deaths of others covered up.

The discovery of quantities of bombs, dynamite and arms under sidewalks, in lumber yards, and other places plainly showed that concerted action had been determined on. The sensational capture of Ling by Captain Scheuttler, and his subsequent suicide; the flight and return of Parsons, the long trial, the speeches, the sentence, the appeal, the new sentence, the appeal to the Supreme Court to interfere, the sentences commuted, the alarm and excitement preceding November 11, 1887, the suicide of Ling by blowing off his head with a bomb, and the execution of Parsons and Spies and Schwab on the above date, need only to be mentioned.

RECENT PLOTTINGS IN CHICAGO

From the closing of the Haymarket case until the present day anarchists in Chicago remained in a dormant state, although at times they asserted themselves. Up to the time of the assassination of King Humbert of Italy the anarchists all over the world had been working for the building up of their organization. They had expended their efforts in making converts, in educating leaders, and had given not a little attention to training up children in the disbelief in law, order and religion. Chicago was the great meeting-place of the anarchists, and supplied the literature that went out to the world.

The assassination of King Humbert, July, 1900, was the most fiendish act of the anarchists up to that time after the Haymarket riot. Bresci, who committed the deed, was from Paterson, N. J., yet he was not unknown to the anarchists in Chicago, and it is suspected that funds were raised there to send him to Italy to murder the ruler of that country.

The plot said to have been discovered for the killing of the heads of five governments seems to have originated in Chicago. Czolgosz, the assassin of President McKinley, was believed to have been in Chicago only a short time before he committed the deed. In jail in Chicago there were lodged nine anarchists accused of being conspirators with him; and it was there that Emma Goldman lectured and was afterward captured. Chicago is the city where *The Fire Brand*, the official organ of the anarchists, is published. From Chicago have emanated teachings that have fairly set the world afire. It has been the scene of the greatest anarchistic demonstration and wholesale murder in history. And when the police of the whole country and the United States Secret Service were working to place the guilt for the murder of President McKinley, Chicago again proved to be a hotbed of anarchistic sentiment.

CHAPTER XXIX

Czolgosz Pays the Penalty

WE propose to make this chapter brief, for the trial of the assassin was brief, yet, dignified and solemn. Justice was rendered surely and swiftly. All the forms of law were complied with, as would have been done for the slayer of the humblest citizen.

First was the indictment before the grand jury. Czolgosz was arraigned in court on September 16th, immediately following the death of his victim.

Bereft of the power of speech, white-faced, haggard and disheveled, Leon Czolgosz stood before the officers of the law to answer for the crime which had robbed the nation of a noble and generous ruler. Standing at the bar of justice, arraigned on the charge of murder, this blue-eyed, mild-faced youth moved his lips as if to speak, but no sound issued forth. There was the shadow of hopeless despair in his eyes, and on his brow the pallor of awful terror, for what he knew he could not escape. Death must be his portion, as surely as the sea of faces that hemmed him in showed not one countenance with a sign of mercy or pity.

When brought before Justice Edward K. Emory, in the County Court of Buffalo, Erie County, New York, the prisoner stubbornly refused to answer questions repeatedly asked of him by District Attorney Penney as to whether he had counsel or wanted counsel. The District Attorney then suggested that inasmuch as the defendant refused to answer counsel should be assigned. Judge Emory assigned Lorin N. Lewis and Robert C. Titus, former Supreme Court Justices of Buffalo, whose names had been suggested by the Erie County Bar Association.

448

Aside from the surgeons and physicians in the case, no witnesses were sworn other than those who were in the Temple of Music and witnessed the shooting.

Late in the afternoon, just exactly ten days after the shooting, the Grand Jury voted unanimously to indict Czolgosz for murder in the first degree, and the indictment was presented to Judge Emory in the County Court.

CZOLGOSZ IN COURT

After indictment was reported the prisoner was driven from the penitentiary, a mile from the City Hall, to the jail across the street from the hall. Czolgosz was then taken under strong guard from the jail through the tunnel under Delaware Avenue to the basement of the City Hall and up the stairs to the court-room on the second floor.

The prisoner was shackled to a detective and another detective held his other arm. Assistant Superintendent Cusack marched in front and a number of patrolmen behind. When the prisoner was taken before the bench the crowd in the court-room surged about him on all sides. They were compelled to resume their seats.

Czolgosz was of medium height, of fairly good build, and had light curly hair, but a ten days' growth of beard on his face gave him an unkempt appearance. Apparently he feigned insanity, not stupidity, and his glance roamed about, but his eyes were always downcast. Not once did he look the county prosecutor or the judge in the face.

Judge Emory asked the prisoner if he had counsel, but there was no answer, despite the fact that the peace officers told him the judge was speaking and that he must answer. Czolgosz trembled like a leaf. His eyes dilated and his face twitched all over. Then his eyes wandered to the steel band glistening on his right wrist.

The court then said :

"Czolgosz, you having appeared for arraignment in the court, without counsel, the law makes it the duty of the court to assign counsel. The Bar Association of your county has considered the matter and suggested the names of certain gentlemen of high character for such assignment. The court has seriously considered the question, and after much consideration has concluded to follow the suggestion made by the Association. The Court therefore assigns Lorin L. Lewis and Robert C. Titus as your counsel."

These gentlemen, both distinguished members of the bar and able lawyers, felt it their duty to accept the commands of the Court and defend the prisoner. This insured dignity and decorum for the trial.

THE TRIAL

On Monday, September 23d, the assassin, Leon F. Czolgosz, was placed upon trial in Buffalo charged with the murder of President William McKinley. He entered a plea of "guilty," which was subsequently changed to "not guilty" by direction of the Court.

The Court convened at 10 o'clock, and within two hours eight jurors had been secured. Technicalities were not raised by the examining counsel, but it was significant that every man who had said he had not formed an opinion on the case was excused by the District Attorney. Those who acknowledged they had formed an opinion, but admitted that their opinion could be changed by evidence, were accepted by each side.

Justice Truman C. White, one of the oldest and most experienced of the Supreme Court Judges, was on the bench. Immediately after the opening of the Court, and after the prisoner had pleaded, Justice Lorin L. Lewis, senior counsel for the defendant, announced that he, with his colleagues, ex-Justice Robert C. Titus and Carlton E. Ladd, was ready to act in behalf of the prisoner.

The work of completing the jury was then undertaken with a celerity that was amazing. Before the day was over the entire panel had been sworn, the jurors had listened to a description of the Temple of Music, where the crime occurred, had seen photographs of the interior of that structure, and had been told by three surgeons what caused the death of the President, and the effect of the assassin's shot upon the various organs of the body. They had also learned why the fatal bullet had not been located.

The presentation of the Government's case followed, shortly before three o'clock, when Assistant District Attorney Haller began, with much deliberation, to address the Court. After stating what the prosecution expected to prove, he summoned witnesses to testify to the facts in the case.

All the testimony for the prosecution had been received soon after noon of Tuesday, the 24th. The counsel for the defence had but few questions to ask, as their client had stubbornly refused to assist them. The eminent alienists summoned by the Erie County Bar Association and by the District Attorney to examine Czolgosz and to determine his exact mental condition had declared him to be perfectly sane, and thus destroyed the only system of defence that Judges Lewis and Titus could have put together.

Judge Lewis arose slowly, and, addressing the Court, said that the sudden close of the case against Czolgosz was a surprise to him and his colleagues. They had no witness to call for the defence. He asked the Court that he be allowed to address the jury at once. The Court consented, and the venerable jurist began an address that will long be remembered by those who heard it.

THE JURY'S VERDICT

In it he gave a clear and concise statement of the legal right to trial and defence of every person accused of crime. He also dwelt upon the importance of deciding whether the prisoner were in his right mind. When he had closed, Justice White charged the jury upon all the points of law involved, and dismissed the jurors to their room for deliberation.

Czolgosz had been seated in his chair all the afternoon, his hands clasped on the arms of the chair, and his head bent forward and a little to the left. The room was not warm, but he frequently took his handkerchief from his pocket, and mopped the perspiration from his forehead and cheeks. At no time during the absence of the jury did he raise his eyes or lift his head, or seem to know that he was the object of interest to several hundred men and women.

After an absence of the jury of less than half an hour, the crier rapped for order, and the jury filed into the room. The clerk read their names, each juror responding "present" as his name was called.

No time was wasted. The jurors did not sit down. Addressing them, Justice White said : " Gentlemen, have you agreed upon a verdict ? "

" We have," responded foreman Wendt.

" What is your verdict ? "

" That the defendant is guilty of murder in the first degree."

There was a moment of silence, and then a murmur arose from the lips of the crowd. It ended there. There were no hand clappings ; no cheers. Justice White's voice could be clearly heard in every part of the room when he thanked the jurors for their work, and allowed them to go.

Czolgosz was immediately handcuffed to his guards, and hurried from the court room downstairs, to the basement, and through the tunnel under Delaware Avenue to the jail. He appeared to be in no way affected by the result of the trial.

Thus had the wheels of justice moved swiftly. The trial of the assassin consumed eight hours and twenty-six minutes, and covered a period of only two days. Practically all this time was occupied by the prosecution in presenting a case so clear, so conclusive that, even had the prisoner entered the plea of insanity, it is doubtful if the jury would have returned a verdict different from the one given.

SENTENCED TO DEATH

On Thursday afternoon, September 26th, Leon F. Czolgosz received his sentence. He was duly asked if he had any legal reason why sentence should not be passed. He gave no reason, but declared in a feeble voice, through his counsel, that no one else knew anything of the crime but himself. The Judge then uttered these solemn words, while Czolgosz stood erect, looking straight at the Judge. He did not tremble ; not a muscle quivered.

"In taking the life of our beloved President, you committed a crime which shocked and outraged the moral sense of the civilized world. You have confessed that guilt, and, after learning all that at this time can be learned from the facts and circumstances of the case, twelve good jurors have pronounced you guilty, and have found you guilty of murder in the first degree.

"You have said, according to the testimony of creditable witnesses and yourself, that no other person aided or abetted you in the commission of this terrible act. God grant it may be so ! The penalty for the crime for which you stand convicted is fixed by this statute, and it now becomes my duty to pronounce this judgment against you.

"The sentence of the Court is that in the week, beginning October 28, 1901, at the place, in the manner and means prescribed by law, you suffer the punishment of death.

"Remove the prisoner."

As soon as the death sentence was finished Czolgosz took his seat in the same indifferent manner that had characterized him throughout the trial. He was brought to his feet quickly by the officers, who shackled him and led him away to the jail to await his removal to Auburn prison, there to pay the penalty of his crime, but in no sense to lessen the sorrow and grief of the people whose chief and friend he had slain.

We need not dwell upon the scene enacted in the death chamber, where the slayer of the good man took his seat in the death chair. Only a few witnesses—those allowed by law—were present to see the majesty of the law vindicated, and with this chapter closed the fearful tragedy which startled the world on September 6, 1901.

CHAPTER XXX

Anarchy's Awful Crimes for the Past Century

LITTLE did the American people dream that this land of the free and the home of the brave would be red in the blood set free by an Anarchist's hand. How freely our gates have been swung open to all comers, whatever the color, nationality, or creed, none know better than the American people. They have had faith in man, and believed in the protection which comes with American freedom. What the results of this sad awakening will be we cannot foresee. In this place it may be well to note the progress of the *Anarchistic* teachings during the past century.

The attempt against the life of President McKinley at Buffalo follows by a little more than a year the assassination of King Humbert of Italy. A few months before the death of Humbert an effort was made in Belgium to kill the Prince of Wales, now King Edward of England. In the Autumn of 1898 Empress Elizabeth of Austria-Hungary was assassinated in Switzerland. In the Summer of 1897 the Prime Minister of Spain, Canovas del Castillo, was slain. In June, 1894, President Carnot of France was murdered. Eighteen hundred and ninety-four marks an epoch—the anarchistic epoch—as may be seen from a study of the assassinations of the past 100 years.

The nineteenth century ran red with the blood of rulers, beginning in 1801 with the killing of the Czar Paul of Russia by some of his nobles. There were over fifty assassinations or attempts at assassinations of ruling statesmen and crowned heads, beginning with the Czar Paul and ending with President McKinley. But a clear distinction can be drawn between those which occurred prior to 1894

454

and those which have crowded the few years since Carnot fell. Bellingham, the assassin of Spencer Perceval, Prime Minister of England, was actuated by personal grievances. The dozen attempts on the life of Louis Philippe were due to the unsettled political conditions in France and also to the restlessness of the republican revolutionists throughout Europe who were in the foreground of the revolutionary movement of the middle of the century. During that period there was scarcely a European monarch whose life was not attacked by some republican fanatic. Orsini, the Italian patriot, who tried to kill Napoleon III in 1858, was clearly inspired by Mazzini's views as to the way to overthrow monarchical governments and establish republics in their place. The late Signor Crispi, the Italian statesman, was in those days a fervent disciple of Mazzini, but he used to say : "To obtain the unity and independence of Italy it does not seem to me necessary to beg from kings, or to humiliate ourselves before them as Manin proposes, or to murder them as Mazzini believes." The slaying of Marshal Prim, in 1870, when he was at the head of the Spanish provisional government after the deposition of Queen Isabella, was an act inspired by local political conditions, and so was the assassination of Czar Alexander of Russia in 1881.

These numerous assaults on established government, prior to 1894, through attacks on the person of official representatives of government were for the most part the acts of political conspirators, or republican revolutionists, or crazy people. Even Queen Victoria's life was in peril four times from the murderous tendencies of persons insane. The celebrated *mot* of King Victor Emanuel, after the attempt upon his life in 1878, illustrates the general conditions that have always prevailed since the work of rulers began. It was his opinion that being shot at was part of the business of kings. Yet in different periods the motive for assassination, sheer insanity aside, has varied. The Orsini school of assassins worked for the political object of changing the form of government. They aimed their daggers and bullets at political despotism, as did the slayers

of the Czar Alexander II.   Now between the assassination of the
Russian Emperor in 1881, and the tragedy of Carnot in 1894, there
was a period of thirteen years, during which not even an attempt at
the murder of rulers was made, excepting the assassination of
President Garfield in America, which followed Alexander's death
within three months.   No such length of time, unmarked by an
attack on a ruler's life, had passed before during the nineteenth
century.   Those thirteen years were stainless.

THE FIRST CRIME OF MODERN ANARCHY

The assassination of President Carnot, in 1894, was the first
avowed work of the modern revolutionary anarchists, whose propaganda of murder is aimed against all government of whatever
character and however liberal and free.   Every assassination and
attempt at assassination since then has been their work.   They
have been exceedingly busy, and their bloody harvest has been
uncommonly fruitful.   Within seven years they slew the Presidents
of the two greatest republics in the world, besides killing the Monarch of a great power, the Empress of another great power, the
Prime Minister of still another European kingdom, and attempting
the life of the heir of Britain's throne.   Their success in their murderous attack upon the President of the United States, completed
a record of five persons of high estate slain within seven years, for
no other reason than that those persons stood for government in
whatsoever form.

It is quite clear that the anarchistic epoch in assassination is
upon us, and that the United States is not free from the atrocities
and terrors which it carries in its train.   Revolutionary anarchy
evidently regards the liberal institutions of America with as much
hatred as it does the harshest despotism in Europe.   It is a wild
insensate thing, and it has struck a cruel blow at the cause of personal liberty and human freedom in the very land where that cause
was most deeply rooted in the affections of the people.

Before we give further details of their accursed work, let us here give an able editorial upon the

SUPPRESSION OF ANARCHISTS

"The assassination of the President of the United States at the hands of a man who professes himself an anarchist challenges the careful consideration, by the people and their representative bodies, of the question whether it is not full time to enter upon a certain and stern repressive treatment of fanatics of his class. The United States has been easy with them, has given them license of speech, liberty of organization, privilege of parade; it has thus afforded free field for the propaganda of murder. It has kept open its ports to this society of European destructives, under the old custom of asylum to political offenders,—for assassins of monarchs and plotters of assassination have been held to be such in Great Britain and America, sometimes also in Switzerland and in a few other countries. Perhaps the time has come when this tolerance should no longer be extended. It does not work well.

"There is no sort of doubt that there is a real society of enemies of all government, made up for the most part of men bred under European conditions, whose aim is the overturn of government of any sort by means of terror; and thus they strike at law and order by the murder of those who represent them, Presidents of republics as well as Kings, constitutional sovereigns as well as autocratic monarchs; and, as was shown in Chicago some years ago, also the legally appointed instruments of the law's enforcement, the police, chosen from the people for the protection of the people from crime and violence. The lesson of Chicago should not be lost upon us. No more effective blow has been delivered at this blind assault on order than the hanging of the men who, either in person or by their speech and printed words, brought on and carried out the massacre of policemen in Haymarket Square. Yet, in this year, in New Jersey, societies have been allowed to celebrate the assassin of the King of Italy as a martyr, making him the hero

26

of a play in which were reproduced the circumstances of the murder. This tolerance transcends the bounds of reasonable freedom, and the plea of free speech, the pretext of political opinion, must no longer avail to protect what is simply a criminal organization.

"Its members should be dealt with as criminals, and should be put under the surveillance that attends criminals. Every man of them should be marked and followed by the oversight of the law, and be subject to arrest wherever found. There should be permitted no more publications of their evil teachings; there should be no more meetings allowed, no more street parades with "Death to Tyrants" and other angry legends on their banners; they should be driven to holes and corners. We have tried the plan of keeping everything in the open, and it has failed; now it is time to treat these conspirators to rigorous law. It might be well to consider whether the members of an anarchistic society should not be punished, on the proof of that fact, with imprisonment for life?"

AN ANARCHIST SLAYS PRESIDENT CARNOT OF FRANCE

There are several points of striking resemblance between the assassination of President Sadi Carnot and the assassination of President McKinley. President Carnot was killed with a poignard in Lyons, by an anarchist named Cesario Santo, on June 24, 1894. Santo was executed for his crime.

Like President McKinley, President Carnot was a visitor at an exposition. He had gone to Lyons with Premier Dupuy and other officials of the government to attend the Exhibition of Arts, Sciences and Industries. Also alike is the manner in which the assailants approached. Santo carried a newspaper to conceal his poignard, and was allowed to approach, because it appeared like a petition he desired to present.

The President had left the banquet of the Chamber of Commerce on the Exposition grounds at half-past nine o'clock in the evening to drive to the Grand Theatre, where a gala performance had been arranged in honor of his visit to the city. His carriage stood in the Place de la Bourse, and he had just seated himself in it when Santo appeared. Running quickly forward, Santo sprang upon the steps of the carriage. President Carnot had no warning until the narrow knife was plunged into his body. The carriage was driven at once to the Prefecture, where the dying man was cared for. He lived until a few minutes past midnight, and was semi-conscious to the last.

Santo was seized at once by the police, who had hard work to protect him from the frantic crowd. Balked in their desire to tear him to pieces, the mob stormed the Italian Consulate and demanded that the flag and coat-of-arms be removed. Beaten back again, they rushed upon an Italian restaurant, stripped it of its furnishings, and set it on fire. It was found that Santo was an Italian anarchist, who had been employed in Cette as a baker. He bought the poignard on Friday and on Saturday left, after a quarrel with his employer. He arrived in Lyons Sunday morning, and in the evening killed the President. In his pocket was found a map, showing the route of the President's progress for the day, and upon this he had marked several advantageous points for his crime.

Physicians found that the knife had penetrated through the lung and severed the aortic artery. There was no hope from the first, although an operation was performed in an attempt to stop the flow of blood. The President suffered great pain until the end. Mme. Carnot and her children were in Paris and left for Lyons on a special train at one o'clock in the morning. They did not know that they were too late until they arrived at six o'clock. Premier Dupuy returned to Paris at once to make sure of the stability of the government.

Santo was tried and executed by the guillotine on August 16th.

King Humbert of Italy was assassinated at Monza, Italy, on July 29, 1900, by Gaetano Bresci, an Italian anarchist, who lived in West Hoboken, N. J.   Bresci was sentenced to solitary confinement for life.   He afterwards committed suicide in his cell.

While living at his summer villa near by, King Humbert had gone to the grounds of the Gymnastic Society, at Monza, to distribute the prizes to the victorious athletes.   He rode in his carriage, attended only by his aide-de-camp, and with neither escort nor guards.   When the work of distributing the prizes had been finished the King re-entered his carriage.   He was smiling, happy and perfectly at ease.   The crowd was cheering.   In the midst of the crowd was Bresci pushing about to obtain an advantageous position.   Just as the horses were about to start he drew a revolver and discharged it three times.   One bullet went through King Humbert's heart and he fell back into the arms of his aide.   As the attendant bent over him he opened his eyes.

HOW KING HUMBERT OF ITALY WAS SLAIN

"It is nothing," he said, and became unconscious.

Bresci had been seized by many hands.   Police, athletes and spectators pounced upon him, and before the police in sufficient force could act, his clothes had been torn to shreds, his face and body battered and his hands and arms torn.   The horses were lashed into a gallop and a dash was made for the villa, where medical attendance could be obtained.   The drive was made in three minutes, but before the gates were reached the king was dead.

When Queen Margherita arrived at the villa after a drive, a few minutes later, the news was broken to her.

"It is the greatest crime of the century," she cried.   "Humbert was good and faithful.   No king could have loved his people more.   He was one who bore ill will to no one."

Bresci confessed his crime, and boasted of it.   He said first that he came from Prato, in Tuscany, where his parents live, but later he said:

"Tell them I came from America, where I was a silk weaver, on purpose to kill Humbert."

JOHN HAY.
SEC. OF STATE UNDER PRES. McKINLEY.

JOHN D. LONG.
SEC. OF THE NAVY UNDER PRES. McKINLEY.

SECRETARY OF THE TREASURY UNDER PRESIDENT McKINLEY.

LYMAN J. GAGE.

It was soon discovered that he had worked in a silk mill at Paterson, N. J., and lived in West Hoboken, where his wife and family still are. He was well known in the colony of anarchists there, and for a time it was believed he had been chosen by lot to perform the deed as the representative of some fanatical circle. Later it appeared he acted of his own volition, and had sailed for Italy with the purpose of killing the King. He was known in Paterson as a moody, quiet man, who never talked about his ideas to anyone save a few cronies. His wife knew nothing of the plan he had formed and was anxiously awaiting his return from a visit to his home.

There is no capital punishment in Italy, but after a speedy trial Bresci was sentenced to a punishment worse than death. For nearly a year he was confined in a stone cell, barely large enough for his body, and just before his suicide was confined in one a trifle larger. There was but little light, no reading matter, no writing utensils, no work, and no one to whom he could speak.

Owing to the absence from Italy of the Prince of Naples, it was thought at first that a temporary regency would be necessary. The Prince arrived in time, however, and, as King Victor Emmanuel III., succeeded his father. King Humbert was careless of his personal safety, although he had been repeatedly warned.

ATTEMPTED ASSASSINATIONS OF RULERS

Prior to 1800 the attempts to assassinate rulers were rare compared with the record of the nineteenth century. The French Revolution, which maddened an entire nation, seems to have left throughout the world the seeds of a disposition to destroy those in authority. The assassins have been as active in their assaults upon Presidents of republics as upon Kings or despots.

On May 15, 1800, James Hatfield made an unsuccessful attempt upon the life of George III. of England, and in the same year an attempt was made to kill Napoleon I. by an infernal machine.

Spencer Percival, Premier of England, was killed by Bellingham, May 11, 1812.

An attempt upon the life of George IV. of England when regent, was made in January, 1817, and Andrew Jackson, President of the United States, was attacked by an assassin in January, 1835. Many attempts were made upon the life of Louis Philippe of France between 1835 and 1846. Frederick William IV. of Prussia was murderously attacked in 1850, and Francis Joseph of Austria in 1853. Ferdinand Charles III., Duke of Parma, was killed by assassins March 27, 1854. Three unsuccessful attempts were made upon the life of Queen Isabella of Spain, in 1847, 1852 and 1856.

Several attempts were made to assassinate Napoleon III. between 1855 and 1858, in one of which bombs thrown by Orsini killed or wounded 150 persons. All of his assailants were Italians. Daniel, Prince of Montenegro, was killed August 13, 1860. Then followed the greatest tragedy of the kind the world had known, the assassination of President Lincoln by John Wilkes Booth, April 15, 1865.

Michael, Prince of Servia, was killed June 10, 1868, and Prim, Marshal of Spain, in December, 1870. Georges Darboy, Archbishop of Paris, was assassinated by anarchists May 24, 1871, and Richard, Earl of Mayo, Governor-General of India, was killed by a native convict in February, 1872. An attempt was made to kill Amadeus, Duke of Aosta, when King of Spain, in May of the same year. Two attempts were made on the life of Bismarck in 1866 and 1874. Abdul Aziz, Sultan of Turkey, was assassinated in June, 1876, and in the same year, Hussein Avai and other Turkish Ministers were killed by Hassan, a Circassian officer. Three attempts were made on the life of William I. of Prussia and Germany between 1861 and 1878, and Humbert I. of Italy was attacked by John Passananti in the latter year, when the Nihilists were especially active. They made unsuccessful attempts upon Lytton, Lord Viceroy of India, and Alfonso XII., King of Spain. An attempt was made upon the life of Loris Melikoff, Russian General, in 1879, and Alexander II. of Russia was pursued relentlessly. After three attempts by individual assassins had been made, a railway train, on which he was supposed to be traveling, was undermined in December, 1879; this was followed by an explosion in the Winter Palace, in February. 1880. The Emperor was finally killed by an assassin, who lost his own life, in March, 1881.

The second President of the United States to die at the hands of an assassin was James A. Garfield, who was shot by Charles Jules Guiteau, July 2, 1881, and died of his wounds September 19, 1881. Guiteau was hanged June 30, 1882. Marie François Sadi Carnot, President of France, was mortally stabbed by Cesare Santo, an anarchist, on June 24, 1894.

In March, 1895 an unsuccessful attempt was made upon the life of King Humbert of Italy, and in 1897 he was again attacked. President Borda, of Uruguay, was assassinated in 1897, and in the same year attacks were made upon President Diaz, of Mexico, and President Morales, of Brazil, the latter assault resulting in the death of the Minister of War. Elizabeth, Empress of Austria, was assassinated in September, 1898. President Heureux, of San Domingo, was assassinated July 26, 1899. In the same year an anarchist youth shot at the Prince of Wales, in Holland. The third attempt, on July 29, 1900, upon the life of King Humbert, of Italy, was successful. On August 2d an anarchist, named Saison, attempted to kill the Shah of Persia, during his visit to Paris. In August, 1901, a suspected anarchist was found secreted in the shrubbery of the Vatican gardens while the Pope was visiting the grounds.

CHAPTER XXXI

Theodore Roosevelt, the 26th President

BY the death of William McKinley on Saturday morning, September 14, 1901, Theodore Roosevelt succeeded to the high office of President of these United States.

HIS ANCESTRY

Theodore Roosevelt was born October 27, 1858, and is therefore not quite forty-three years old. He was born in New York City, at 28 East Twentieth Street. His people originally lived on the Battery, but as the town changed gradually moved away from the business centre. His grandfather once owned a fine residence at one of the corners of what is now Fourteenth Street and Broadway. In blood Mr. Roosevelt is a quarter Hollandish and three-quarters Scotch, Irish and French Huguenot. His mother was a Bonhill and had relatives of the name of Lukin and Craig. The Lamontaigne family is in his ancestry, and the Devoes, of Georgia and South Carolina. His uncle, James D. Bullock, built the noted privateer *Alabama*, and another of the Bullocks fired the last gun aboard her. But after all this is said of the ancestry, chronicles agree that Mr. Roosevelt owes a great deal to his father. The elder Theodore Roosevelt was one of the leading men of his day in the metropolis—the days of the Civil War. He was a merchant, philanthropist and a lover of out-door life. He, more than anyone else, founded the present newsboys' lodging-house system. He devised and carried out the plan of the war time allotment commission. He could drive a four-in-hand team better than any other New Yorker in his day. He died in 1878, idolized by the son who was to take up the lines of the ambitious part of his life and carry them on.

"What strong direction did your home influence take in your boyhood?" was asked Mr. Roosevelt.

FOND OF ATHLETICS

"Why," he replied, "I was brought up with the constant injunction to be active and industrious. My father, all my people, held that no one had a right to merely cumber the earth ; that the most contemptible of created beings is the man who does nothing. I imbibed the idea that I must work hard, whether at making money or whatever. The whole family training taught me that I must be doing, must be working—and at decent work. I made my health what it is. I determined to be strong and well, and did everything to make myself so. By the time I entered Harvard College I was able to take my part in whatever sports I liked. I wrestled and sparred and ran a great deal while in college, and, though I never came in first, I got more good out of the exercise than those who did, because I immensely enjoyed it and never injured myself. I was fond of wrestling and boxing; I think I was a good deal of a wrestler, and though I never won a championship, yet more than once I won my trial heats and got into the final round. I was captain of my polo team at one time, but since I left college I have taken most of my exercise in the 'cow country' or mountains, hunting."

HIS ENTRY INTO POLITICS

He was graduated at Harvard University in 1880, being then twenty-two years old, and took a European trip for a rest before entering on his life career. His first view of the Alps inspired him with a desire to surmount them, and he climbed the Jungfrau and the Matterhorn before that desire was satisfied.

Returning to New York, his native city—for he was born as we have said, at No. 28 East Twentieth Street—he began the study of law, but soon became engrossed in politics. He has described his entry into the political field thus : "I have always believed that every man should join a political organization and should attend the primaries ; that he should not be content to be merely governed, but should do his part of that work. So after leaving college I went to the local political headquarters, attended all the meetings and took my part in whatever came up. There arose a revolt against the member of Assembly from that district, and I was nominated to succeed him, and was elected."

ELECTED ASSEMBLYMAN

It was in the Fall of 1881 that he was elected to the Assembly from the XXIst District, and he was twice re-elected, serving in the legislatures of 1882, 1883 and 1884. At Albany he found an ample field for that aggressiveness of his nature which wrong always arouses. Some of the veterans were at first only amused at his straightforward and ingenuous speeches, but they soon realized that "this ridiculously candid youngster," as one of them called him, was a fighter who could not be cowed, either by open or by secret methods.

Few men looked more unfitted for public life. His eyeglasses led the Tammany Hall members to think him effeminate, until they learned that he was a fine boxer, and two or three encounters, which did not, however, lead to any blows, convinced them that he was a courageous man, but the fact being disclosed that he had written a book, the opinion gained ground that he was merely a writer, and therefore would take no prominent part in legislation.

The member from the XXIst Assembly District, however, soon began expressing his sentiments, and the serious-minded members of the Assembly became convinced that his judgment on New York City matters was sound. He spoke rapidly, spoke attractively, hit hard, was good-humored, but savagely sarcastic in dealing with well-known rascals, and public opinion outside the Capitol was soon in his favor.

For several years attempts had been made to pass a reform charter for New York City. All failed, because the threatened departments united and were too strong for the reformers.

Assemblyman Roosevelt made his attacks on certain departments of New York City separately, and bowled them over one by one. His rise in rank in the Assembly was startlingly rapid. The second year of his membership he was the Republican candidate for Speaker. It was a Democratic House, but the honor was nevertheless a great one for a young man. In his third year as an Assemblyman he was put at the head of the Committee on Cities, having proved his thorough knowledge of the affairs of New York and other cities.

He served his constituency particularly well by aiding in the passage of bills abolishing fees in the offices of the Register and the County Clerk, and while chairman of the Committee on Cities he introduced reform legislation which proved immensely beneficial. One of his measures was the act taking from the Board of Aldermen power to confirm or reject the appointments of the Mayor. He was chairman of the noted legislative investigating committee which bore his name, and which revealed many of the abuses existing in the city government in the early '80s.

Assemblyman Roosevelt was highly popular with his associates, irrespective of party. It is seldom a man receives more genuine expressions of sympathy than he did from his fellow Assemblymen when his mother and his wife both died in one week. The Roosevelt of that period was already a national figure. Attending the Republican State Convention of 1884, he was elected one of New York's four delegates-at-large to the Republican National Convention, as a delegate desirous of nominating George F. Edmunds for the Presidency.

CIVIL SERVICE COMMISSIONER

In 1886 Mr. Roosevelt was the Republican candidate for Mayor against Abram S. Hewitt, United Democracy, and Henry George, United Labor. Mr. Hewitt was elected by about 22,000 plurality.

Mr. Roosevelt was appointed a member of the United States Civil Service Commission by President Harrison in 1889. His ability and rugged honesty in the administration of the affairs of that office greatly helped to strengthen his hold on popular regard. There were 14,000 places under the merit and capacity rules of the Commission when he went in. There were 40,000 when he went out, a record he may well point to with pride.

Mr. Roosevelt continued in that office until May 1, 1895, when he resigned to accept the office of Police Commissioner from Mayor Strong. He found the administration of police affairs in a demoralized condition, but the same energetic methods that had characterized all his work—the same uncompromising honesty that is the most prominent note in his character—when applied to police affairs soon brought the administration of the department to a high degree of efficiency.

BECOMES POLICE COMMISSIONER IN NEW YORK CITY

In the period between Mr. Roosevelt's election to the legislature and his appointment as Civil Service Commissioner he had spent most of his Summers in the West on a ranch, and had written several books on the life of the Western plains and mountains. Some surprise was expressed, therefore, by a friend, when Mr. Roosevelt became Police Commissioner, that a literary man should volunteer for police work, and Mr. Roosevelt gave this reason: " I thought the storm centre was in New York, and so I came here. It is a great piece of practical work. I like to take hold of work that has been done by a Tammany leader and do it as well, only by approaching it from the opposite direction. A thing that attracted me to it was that it was to be done in the hurly-burly, for I don't like cloister life."

His enforcement of the excise law produced an abundance of hurly-burly. Many said it was the most potent factor in the overthrow of the Strong reform administration at the next election and the return of Tammany to power; but Roosevelt answered all criticism by asserting that he had sworn to enforce all the laws and would not stultify himself. Moreover, he maintained that the best

MRS. THEODORE ROOSEVELT
The Lady of the White House

THEODORE ROOSEVELT

way to obtain the repeal of an obnoxious law was by enforcing it rigidly, and not by ignoring it.

His unheralded personal tours of inspection about the city by night caught many a policeman napping, and resulted in many humorous situations, until the force had thoroughly assimilated the idea that their president was not a man to be trifled with.

Jacob A. Riis, author of "How the Other Half Lives," saw a great deal of Police Commissioner Roosevelt. Touching on the man's single-minded fearlessness in that office, Mr. Riis afterward wrote:

"I read a story when I was a boy about a man who, pursued by a relentless enemy, dwelt in security because of his belief that his plotting could not hurt an honest man. Mr. Roosevelt constantly made me think of him. He spoke of it only once, but I saw him act out that belief a hundred times. Mulberry Street could never have been made to take any stock in it. When it failed to awe Roosevelt, it tried to catch him. Jobs innumerable were put up to discredit the president of the board and inveigle him into awkward positions. Probably he never knew of one-tenth of them. Mr. Roosevelt walked through them with perfect unconcern, kicking aside the snares that were set so elaborately to catch him. The politicians who saw him walk apparently blindly into a trap and beheld him emerge with damage to the trap only, could not understand it. They concluded it was his luck. It was not. It was his sense. He told me once after such a time that it was a matter of conviction with him, that no frank and honest man could be in the long run entangled by the snares of plotters, whatever appearances might for the moment indicate. So he walked unharmed in it all."

Of Mr. Roosevelt's attitude toward strikers Mr. Riis has written:

HIS ATTITUDE TOWARD STRIKERS

"I had watched police administration in Mulberry Street for nearly twenty years, and I had seen many sparring matches between workingmen and the Police Board. Generally there was bad

faith on one side ; not infrequently on both.   It was human that
some of the labor men should misinterpret Mr. Roosevelt's motives
when, as president of the board, he sent word that he wanted to
meet them and talk strike troubles over with them.   They got it
into their heads, I suppose, that he had come to crawl ; but they
were speedily undeceived.   I can see his face now as he checked
the first one who hinted at trouble.   I fancy that man can see it,
too—in his dreams.

" 'Gentlemen,' said Mr. Roosevelt, 'I have come to get your
point of view, and see if we can't agree to help each other out.   But
we want to make it clear to ourselves at the start that the greatest
damage any workingman can do to his cause is to counsel violence.
Order must be maintained, and, make no mistake, I will maintain it.'

"I tingled with pride when they cheered him to the echo.   They
had come to meet a politician.   They met a man, and they knew
him at sight."

IN THE NAVY DEPARTMENT

From the presidency of the New York police force he was
called by President McKinley to be Assistant Secretary of the
Navy in April, 1897.   There again his energy and quick mastery
of detail contributed much to the successful administration of the
department and the preparation of the navy for the most brilliant
feats in naval warfare in the history of the world.

From the very first he foresaw, it is said, the possibility of a
conflict with Spain, and he set about preparing his department for
it.   He pushed repairs on the ships, worked earnestly for the Navy
Personnel Bill, and visited the various naval reserves throughout
the country.   He left nothing undone that would in his opinion
secure the highest efficiency in the service when the time for action
came.   It is said that he it was who first realized the tremendous
opportunity that the war would open in the East, and who had
Dewey, in whom he recognized the right man for the place,
appointed to command the Eastern Squadron. Many naval experts
agree that the remarkable skill in marksmanship displayed by the

American gunners was due to his foresight. He saw the necessity of practice, and he thought it the best kind of economy to burn up ammunition in acquiring skill.

A CHARACTERISTIC STORY OF HIS INSISTENCE

A characteristic story is told regarding Roosevelt's insistence on practice in the navy. Shortly after his appointment he asked for an appropriation of $800,000 for ammunition. The appropriation was made, and a few months later he asked for another appropriation of $500,000 for the same purpose. When asked what had become of the first appropriation, he replied : " Every cent of it was spent for powder and shot, and every bit of powder and shot has been fired." When he was asked what he was going to do with the $500,000, he replied : "Use every dollar of that, too, within the next thirty days in practice shooting." When the *Maine* was blown up Roosevelt had no doubt, it is said, that war would follow, and his energies were bent with redoubled force to getting the navy ready. When war did finally break out Roosevelt is credited with a plan for taking Havana at once, and dictating terms from there.

"ROOSEVELT'S ROUGH RIDERS"

Of course he could not sit still behind a desk after war had been actually declared. He submitted his resignation to the President on April 16th, and tried to get an appointment on General Lee's staff. Then came the Rough Rider idea, hardly thought of before realized. "Roosevelt's Rough Riders "—the name struck the popular fancy, and the regiment became famous before it was organized. During Roosevelt's Summer months upon his ranch in Dakota he learned to know cowboys, not simply as the picturesque objects who appear in Wild West shows, but as courageous men, strong to bear the hardships of warfare. From such men the famous Rough Riders were chiefly recruited. Four years' membership in the Eighth Regiment of the New York State National Guard, to which Roosevelt belonged from 1884 to 1888, and in which he was for a time a captain, furnished at least a basis for his brilliant military career. But more than all else that induced him to go to the front were his devotion to the cause for which the war was fought and his love for an active life. These same reasons drew to him scores of young men of prominent families from all parts of the country, who joined the Western cavalrymen to go and fight the Spaniards. The regiment thus formed was known as Roosevelt's Rough Riders, although it was commanded by Colonel Wood, of the regular army, Colonel Roosevelt being second in command, with the rank, until promoted, of lieutenant-colonel.

SAN JUAN HILL AND LAS GUASIMAS

His conduct at the jungle fight of Las Guasimas and in the bloody charge up San Juan Hill made him a popular hero, and gave rise to a large number of most interesting stories concerning his personal bravery and his influence over the men he led. At the very start he drilled this band of independent, high-spirited ranchers, cowpunchers and athletes into regimental shape with no uncertain hand. In one of his first speeches to them he said : " You've got to perform without flinching whatever duty is assigned you, regardless of the difficulty or danger attending it. No matter what comes, you must not squeal." These words of Roosevelt became almost a religion with his men. " To do anything without flinching and not to squeal" was their aim, and to hear the colonel say "Good" was reward enough. One of his troopers, who was invalided home, thus answered a reporter who had asked concerning the colonel, " He is a fighter, isn't he ?'

"A fighter ! You'd give a lifetime to see that man leading a charge or to hear him yell. Talk about courage and grit and all that—he's got it ! Why, I used to keep my eye on him whenever I could, and I've seen him dash into a hail of bullets, cheering and yelling all the time, as if possessed. He doesn't know what fear is, and seems to bear a charmed life. All the Rough Riders adore him."

Another told of how Colonel Roosevelt acted when slightly hurt by a fragment of a Spanish shell on San Juan Hill.   He said :

"Teddy was with four or five other officers just below the brow of a hill upon which one of our batteries was placed, when a Spanish shell, well aimed, flew over the crest and exploded just above the heads of the group.   Two of the officers were painfully wounded, but Teddy, with his usual good luck, escaped with a graze of the back of his right hand.   It was trivial, but the scratch bled.   I shall not forget the delight on Teddy's face as he saw his own blood leak out.   Whipping out his handkerchief after a moment, he bound it around his hand.   A little later, when he was near our line he held up his bandaged hand and exclaimed gayly, 'See here, boys ; I've got it, too !'   I never saw anybody so anxious to be in the thick of trouble as Teddy.   The first day the Rough Riders were held in reserve. Teddy chafed terribly.   He kept saying, 'I wish they'd let us start.'   We all idolize Teddy.   He wears a flannel shirt most of the time, and refuses to fare any better than his men.   Why, he wouldn't have a shelter tent when they were distributed.   There isn't one of our fellows who wouldn't follow our Teddy to Hades if he ordered us to."

Writing afterward of the battle of Las Guasimas, Colonel Roosevelt himself told of another narrow escape he had, as follows :

"At every halt we took advantage of the cover, sinking down behind any mound, bush or tree-trunk in the neighborhood.   The trees, of course, furnished no protection from the Mauser bullets. Once I was standing behind a large palm, with my head out to one side, very fortunately, for a bullet passed through the palm, filling my left eye and ear with the dust and splinters."

GENERAL WHEELER'S ESTIMATE OF THE ROUGH RIDER

General Wheeler said of the colonel on his return from Cuba : "Roosevelt is a born fighter, and his men were absolutely devoted to him.   While we were together on board the transport I had an opportunity of observing Roosevelt more closely than was possible in the hustle and excitement of the camp. What impressed me most about him is his absolute integrity. I am told that he is likely to be chosen as a candidate for the Governorship of New York, and certainly no better selection could be made. Some day his splendid qualities may earn for him the highest position it is in the power of the United States to give."

Private Will T. Palmers, of the Rough Riders, wrote home to Kansas, as follows :

"When we came to make the final charge that took this position, some of the officers wanted to fall back and leave it in possession of the Spaniards, but Colonel Roosevelt pulled his pistol and said : 'You can fall back if you want to, but my men will hold it till the last man dies.' We held it, and did not die, either. I tell you, Wood and Roosevelt are proud of their regiment. Our boys are proud of their colonel. We fought ninety hours without sleep or rest."

The colonel never ordered his men to do what he would not do himself under like circumstances. Here is what Sergeant Jacob Judson, of Co. E. First Illinois Volunteers, wrote to his brother, John Judson, of Passaic, under date of Santiago, July 30th :

"The Rough Riders and our regiment have for a week camped together. They are a fine body of men, and Colonel Roosevelt is a fine fellow. I have talked to him personally three times. He is one of the boys. In the campaign against Santiago he was digging trenches with a pick, like his men. He sleeps in a miserable tent and chews hardtack like the rest. When we first came our food consisted of one piece of hardtack for each meal and some water. This lasted two days, and along came Colonel Roosevelt on his horse. I was on my way to cut some grass to sleep on. He stopped me, and said : 'I know you boys are starved for food, but I am going to do all I can for you. So far I have managed to get some coffee and a number of cases of hardtack, which will start you. We are going to fight together, and I want to see you all in good trim.'

If it wasn't for him I am sure we would have been without supplies for some time."

A grateful father, William Tudor, of Boston, wrote as follows to a newspaper under date of August 9, 1898 :

"At the time of the long journey of the Rough Riders from San Antonio, Texas, to Tampa, made unbearable from the excessive heat and deficient food, my son, now slowly recovering from typhoid fever, taken in Texas, was prostrated by a sudden and violent attack of vomiting, brought on by the hot weather. Colonel Roosevelt, hearing of this, gave up to him his berth in the sleeper, taking the boy's place with the other men during the remainder of the journey."

AN INCIDENT OF DISCIPLINE

When it came to discipline, Colonel Roosevelt never let his kindness of heart degenerate into anything like laxity. It is related of him that one day in camp, before Santiago, one of his troopers objected to the performance of some menial work which was unpleasant, but necessary. Colonel Roosevelt, who had striven to impress every man while the command was being recruited at San Antonio that no picnic was ahead of them, and that there would be many unpleasant and distasteful duties to perform, was vexed that the lesson had been so imperfectly learned, or, if learned, so quickly forgotten, and he became angry when the man got obstinate. He gave him a lecture that made his ears ring.

When he had finished the trooper said : "All right, Colonel ; I'll do it." Then he paused for a minute. "Colonel," he went on, "haven't you got a few beans to spare? I'm kinder holler." The commander of the Rough Riders had been scowling savagely, but the appeal for beans made the scowl die away. "I'll see," he said, "come over here." The trooper followed to where Colonel Roosevelt's belongings were lying. The colonel found a small can three-quarters full. "Here," he said, emptying out half of them, "take 'em and fill up your ' holler,' but you bury that dead horse at once, or there'll be trouble in this camp, and you'll be in it."

The regiment distinguished itself in the campaign, and Colonel Roosevelt became famous for his bravery in leading the charge up San Juan Hill on July 1st. This is the way it was described in press dispatches from the field :

"Roosevelt was in the lead waving his sword. Out into the open and up the hill where death seemed certain, in the face of the continuous crackle of the Mausers, came the Rough Riders, with the Tenth Cavalry alongside. Not a man flinched, all continuing to fire as they ran. Roosevelt was a hundred feet ahead of his troops, yelling like a Sioux, while his own men and the colored cavalry cheered him as they charged up the hill. There was no stopping as men's neighbors fell, but on they went, faster and faster. Suddenly Roosevelt's horse stopped, pawed the air for a moment, and fell in a heap. Before the horse was down Roosevelt disengaged himself from the saddle and, landing on his feet, again yelled to his men, and, sword in hand, charged on afoot."

HIS FAMOUS LETTER TO GENERAL SHAFTER

Roosevelt's care for his men was shown by the circulation of the famous "round robin" which he wrote, protesting against keeping the army longer in Cuba. Here he showed how little he is bound by mere conventionalities. People shook their heads when they heard what he had done, and talked of precedents. Colonel Roosevelt makes precedents. He made one that time when he sent the famous letter to his superior officer, General Shafter, which Shafter made public as an explanation of the situation, and which contained such a powerful presentation of the facts that it resulted in the recall of the perishing army from Cuba after it had won the fight. The letter bore date of August, 1898, and ran as follows:

"*Major-General Shafter :*

"SIR :—In a meeting of the medical and general officers called by you at the palace, this morning, we were all, as you know, unanimous in view of what should be done with the army. To keep us here, in the opinion of every officer commanding a division or a brigade, will simply involve the destruction of thousands. There is no possible reason for not shipping practically the entire command north at once. Yellow fever cases are very few in the cavalry division, where I command one of the two brigades, and not one true case of yellow fever has occurred in this division, except among the men sent to the hospital at Siboney, where they have, I believe, contracted it. But in this division there have been 1,500 cases of malarial fever. Not a man has died from it; but the whole command is so weakened and shattered as to be ripe for dying like sheep when a real yellow fever epidemic, instead of a fake epidemic like the present, strikes us, as it is bound to if we stay here at the height of the sickly season, August and the beginning of September. Quarantine against malarial fever is much like quarantine against the toothache. All of us are certain, as soon as the authorities at Washington fully appreciate the conditions of the army, to be sent home. If we are kept here it will, in all human probability, mean an appalling disaster, for the surgeons here estimate that over half the army, if kept here during the sickly season, will die. This is not only terrible from the standpoint of the individual lives lost, but it means ruin from the standpoint of the military efficiency of the flower of the American army, for the great bulk of the regulars are here with you. The sick list, large though it is, exceeding 4,000, affords but a faint index of the debilitation of the army. Not 10 per cent. are fit for active work. Six weeks on the North Maine coast, for instance, or elsewhere where the yellow fever germ cannot possibly propagate, would make us all as fit as fighting cocks, able as we are and eager to take a leading part in the great campaign against Havana in the Fall, even if we are not allowed to try Porto Rico. We can be moved north, if moved at once, with absolute safety to the country, although, of course, it would have been infinitely better if we had been moved north or to Porto Rico two weeks ago. If there were any object in keeping us here, we would face yellow fever with as much indifference as we face bullets. But there is no object in it. The four immune regiments ordered here are sufficient to garrison the city and sur-rounding towns, and there is absolutely nothing for us to do here, and there has not been since the city surrendered. It is impossible to move into the interior. Every shifting of camp doubles the sick rate in our present weakened condition, and anyhow the interior is rather worse than the coast, as I have found by actual reconnoisance. Our present camps are as healthy as any camps at this end of the island can be. I write only because I cannot see our men, who have fought so bravely and who have endured extreme hardship and danger so uncomplainingly, go to destruction without striving, so far as lies in me, to avert a doom as fearful as it is unnecessary and undeserved.

"Yours, respectfully,

"THEODORE ROOSEVELT,

"*Colonel, Commanding First Brigade.*"

GOVERNOR OF NEW YORK

Colonel Roosevelt returned to the United States to find that he was already talked of as the next Governor of New York. But his regiment, which he had "breathed with and eaten with for three months," was still on his hands, and he had no time for anything but it. Not until he became a plain citizen on September 15th would he talk of politics. And then he found the tide of events bearing him along inevitably and irresistibly.

Previous to the State Convention he was nominated by the Citizens Union, but he declined, replying that he was a Republican. The Democrats tried to frustrate his nomination by attempting to prove that he had lost his legal residence in that State. That plan failed, and he was nominated in the convention by a vote of 753 to 218 for Governor Black. The campaign throughout the State was spirited. Colonel Roosevelt took the stump and delivered many speeches. His plurality was 18,079.

When Colonel Roosevelt arrived in Albany as Governor it was felt that the State would have as an executive a man of such high integrity that every officeholder in Albany would understand that his accounts must be absolutely correct, that there would be no stealing and that there would be no jobbery attempted in the Legislature. It was also felt that the standard of official efficiency would be raised; that inefficient public servants would be retired and replaced with men of undoubted capacity. Governor Roosevelt apparently saw that he must act conservatively and cautiously. The newspaper correspondents could testify to the great care he took in appointing heads to both the Insurance Department and the Department of Public Works. Under the care of Francis Hendricks the Insurance Department became an honor to the State, and Governor Odell was applauded when he reappointed Colonel John N. Partridge as Superintendent of Public Works, who had been selected for the position by Theodore Roosevelt.

HIS IMPETUOUS SPIRIT TO GOOD EFFECT

It had been predicted by Democratic orators that Governor Roosevelt would be "too impetuous" at times. Governor Roosevelt acknowledged that he was impetuous by temperament, but said he thought he had subdued this trait of his nature. However, a day came when his impetuous spirit blazed forth, but no one of eminence has ever criticised him for that day's action. It was the final day of the session of the Legislature of 1899 when he frankly expressed his opinion that the Franchise Tax Act ought to be passed and it was passed. The members of the Legislature felt that public opinion was supporting the Governor, and they did not venture to defeat the measure. It is therefore a law to-day.

Another "impetuous" act of the Governor was the removal from office of the District Attorney of New York County, Asa Bird Gardiner, on the charge that he gave aid and comfort to Chief of Police Devery after that officer had been indicted for issuing a seditious order to the police force regarding violence at the polls. The record made by Eugene Philbin, an independent Democrat, whom the Governor appointed to succeed Gardiner, soon disarmed the criticisms of all those who desired an honest administration of that important office, and proved Governor Roosevelt's ability to estimate men aright.

Measures which he pressed with his personal as well as official influence provided for the prevention of the adulteration of food products and fertilizers, the betterment of the wage workers in tenement houses, improvements in the labor law and the system of factory inspection, the protection of game, and especially the honest and efficient administration of the State canals and the extension of Civil Service regulations. The notorious Ramapo job found in him an insurmountable obstacle, and by the "Confessions of Judgment" Bill the strong hand of the Governor saved New York City's treasury from much heavy legalized looting.

VICE-PRESIDENT AT WASHINGTON

Governor Roosevelt's disinclination to become the nominee for Vice-President of the United States is well remembered. At his party's imperative call, however, he laid aside the desire he had to be re-elected Governor of New York and accepted the position on the national Republican ticket alongside William McKinley. The enormous amount of work Mr. Roosevelt performed in the campaign which resulted in the re-election of Mr. McKinley, called forth admiration for his endurance, vitality and perseverance even from his bitterest enemies.

AUTHOR OF SEVERAL BOOKS

That President Roosevelt is in reality a man of many sides is shown by the fact that in the midst of his intensely active life he has found time to do considerable literary work. The year after he was graduated from college he published his "Naval War of 1812"; in 1886 there came from his pen a "Life of Thomas H. Benton," published in the "American Statesmen Series"; the following year he published a "Life of Gouverneur Morris," which was followed, in 1888, by his popular "Ranch Life and Hunting Trail." In 1889, were published the first two volumes of what he considers his greatest work, " The Winning of the West." In 1890 he added to the series of " Historic Towns," a " History of New York City." " Essays on Practical Politics," published in 1892, was followed the next year, by " The Wilderness Hunter," while in 1894 he added a third volume to his " Winning of the West." In 1898 he collected a volume of essays, entitled " American Political Ideas." Since the Spanish war he has written a book on " The Rough Riders " and a series of articles on Oliver Cromwell. Most of these books have either been written while on his vacations on his Western ranch, or in the intervals of the labors of his public offices. They are marked by facility, vigor and clearness of expression, rich descriptive power, and his historical writings by accuracy, breadth and fairness.

In expressing his political views and experiences President Roosevelt's pen is a trenchant one. Here are two extracts from his political essays which demonstrate the truth of that statement, are fair samples of his style and also show the trend of the man's mind pretty clearly :

HIS IDEA OF PRACTICAL POLITICS

" Practical politics must not be construed to mean dirty politics. In the long run the politics of fraud and treachery and foulness are unpractical politics, and the most practical of all politicians is the politician who is clean and decent and upright. But a man who goes into the actual battles of the political world must prepare himself much as he would for the struggle in any other branch of our life. He must be prepared to meet men of far lower ideals than his own, and to face things, not as he would wish them, but as they are. He must not lose his own high ideal, and yet he must face the fact that the majority of the men with whom he must work have lower ideals. He must stand firmly for what he believes, and yet he must realize that political action, to be effective, must be the joint action of many men, and that he must sacrifice somewhat of his own opinions to those of his associates if he ever hopes to see his desires take practical shape.

"The prime thing that every man who takes an interest in politics should remember is that he must act and not merely criticise the actions of others. It is not the man who sits by his fireside reading his evening paper and saying how bad our politics and our politicians are who will ever do anything to save us; it is the man who goes out into the rough hurly-burly of the caucus, the primary and political meeting, and there faces his fellows on equal terms.

"Of all the forces that tend for evil in a great city like New York, probably none are so potent as the sensational papers. Until one has had experience with them it is difficult to realize the reckless indifference to truth or decency displayed by papers such as the two that have the largest circulation in New York City. Scandal forms the breath of the nostrils of such papers and they are quite as ready to create as to describe it. To sustain law and order is humdrum, and does not really lend itself to vaunting woodcuts; but if the editor will stoop, and make his subordinates stoop, to raking the gutters of human depravity, to upholding the wrong-doer and furiously assailing what is upright and honest, he can make money, just as other types of pander make it. The man who is to do honorable work in any form of civic politics must make up his mind (and if he is a man of properly robust character he will make it up without difficulty) to treat the assaults of papers like these with absolute indifference and to go his way unheeding. Indeed, he will have to make up his mind to be criticised, sometimes justly and more often unjustly, even by decent people, and he must not be so thin skinned as to mind such criticism overmuch."

Not only a maker of books, Colonel Roosevelt is an ardent lover of books. They accompany him in all his travels. No day is complete to him unless he has read something of decided interest, either in a famous old book or in a popular new one. One day is a specimen of many. Roosevelt had spoken in his Vice-Presidential campaign at Little Valley, in Cattaraugus County. N. Y., and at a big meeting in Buffalo, and then at midnight had started from Buffalo in his sleeping car for Watertown. Most men would have felt the need of rest after a day of such exhausting travel and work. Not so Colonel Roosevelt. He remained up till 2 o'clock in the morning reading an article on trusts by President Hadley, of Yale.

HIS LIFE ON THE RANCH

Colonel Roosevelt's popularity with the cowboys of the West was won by his personal ability to hold his own with them in the roughest of their sports and in the severest of their hardships. He was one of the first of the Eastern men of culture to enter upon the cattle business with the serious purpose of making money, and for years he spent so much of his Summers as could be spared from business to live among the rough riders of the plains, eating with them, sleeping with them, hunting with them and competing with them in trials of strength and skill. To them he is always "Teddy." Investing some money in cattle, he pastured the herd on the public ranges of Dakota. He told his hired cowboys that he intended to be one of them. As he was a college graduate and wore glasses, they set him down for a typical "tenderfoot" at first, but were soon undeceived. This story has been published of the way he won their respect:

AN INCIDENT OF COWBOY LIFE

At the first big roundup of which Roosevelt took part the "bad man" who is always present on such occasions was known as "Long Ike." He had the reputation of being quick on the trigger. One of his favorite tricks was to line up alongside a drinking bar, select the filled glass of one man he thought he could cow and drain it. A glass half filled with whiskey had been poured out by a cowboy and placed in front of Roosevelt. Long Ike reached out and took it, and so certain was he that the stranger would submit that he did not take the precaution to make his customary bluff with his revolver.

Before he could swallow the liquor Roosevelt was on him like a catamount. He is an expert wrestler, and threw Long Ike heavily. Then he turned him over and stood him up and ran him outdoors, taking the bully's revolver away from him in the run. Outside Ike was thrown again, harder than before, and couldn't get up for five minutes. When he did he was dazed and amazed. The style of attack was so unusual, and withal so vigorous, that he was afraid to resent it. He sneaked out of camp. The young man with eyeglasses and gleaming teeth enjoyed the respect of the cowboys from that day forward.

AS A HUNTER OF BIG GAME

As a hunter of big game Colonel Roosevelt has earned a reputation second probably to none in America. Not a few moose, elk, mountain lions and grizzlies have fallen to his gun. His habitual coolness when in tight places has stood him in good stead over and over again. A Western correspondent wrote to an Eastern paper:

"It was in 1890 that I spent the night in a cabin on the eastern shore of Kootenai Lake. Another man had sought refuge there who said that he was a trapper, and that he had just come down from a point in the Selkirks, where he had accompanied Colonel Roosevelt on a bear hunt. The Colonel had heard that there existed in the Selkirks a kind of grizzly bear which he had not as yet shot, and he had determined to secure a specimen. The guide said that they came across this bear rather unexpectedly, and that the animal charged them. He added: 'You know Colonel Roosevelt is very nearsighted, and he carries more kinds of glasses than an Englishman; one pair to read with, one to shoot with, and another to walk with. When the bear charged us he had on his walking glasses, and when I told him that the beast was upon him he coolly took off these glasses, folded them up, put them away in his pocket, took out and wiped his shooting glasses, and put them on as quietly and deliberately as if there was not a bear in the whole country. By the time he had got his glasses adjusted the bear was near, but he pulled up his gun and killed him in his tracks, and did not seem in the least bit excited.'"

ROOSEVELT'S SWIFT RIDE FROM THE ADIRONDACKS

Now we come to the moment when he was summoned to the deathbed of his friend and chief. Immediately upon the first news of the assassination of President McKinley, he had hastened to Buffalo. After three days it seemed that the President would recover, and Mr. Roosevelt left for the mountains to be with his family.

When Mr. Roosevelt and his guides left the Tahawus Club, in the Adirondacks, where his family was staying, early Friday morning September 13th, for a tramp in the mountains, the then Vice-President fully believed that President McKinley was entirely out of danger and on the rapid road to recovery. That this was so was made manifest by his private secretary, William Loeb, while the special train which bore him to Buffalo was on its record-breaking rush to the scene of the nation's tragedy. During the brief stop of the train at Rochester Secretary Loeb said :

"The President wishes it understood that when he left the Tahawus Club house yesterday morning to go on his tramping into the mountains he had just received a dispatch from Buffalo stating that President McKinley was in splendid condition and was not in the slightest danger."

The Roosevelt tramping party moved in the direction of Mount Marcy, the highest peak in the Adirondack region. They had not been gone over three hours when a mounted courier rode rapidly into Tahawus Club with messages to the Vice-President stating that President McKinley was in a critical condition. The messages had been telegraphed to North Creek, and from there telephoned to a point ten miles south of Tahawus Club. Extra guides and runners were at once deployed from the club in the direction of Mount Marcy with instructions to sound a general alarm in order to find the Vice-President as soon as possible.

The far-reaching megaphone code and the rifle-cracking signals of the mountain-climbing guides, as hour after hour passed away, marked the progress of the searching mountaineers as they climbed the slope of Mount Marcy. Just as the afternoon began to merge with the shades of early evening and as the searchers were nearing the summit of the lofty mountain, the responsive echoes of distant signals were heard and answered, and gradually the scouts and the Roosevelt party came within hailing distance of each other.

THRILLING RIDE THROUGH STORM

When Colonel Roosevelt was reached and informed of the critical condition of the President, he could scarcely believe the burden of the messages personally delivered to him. Startled at the serious nature of the news, the Vice-President, at 5.45 o'clock, immediately started back for the Tahawus Club. In the meantime the Adirondack Stage Line placed at his disposal relays of horses covering the thirty-five miles to North Creek. A deluging thunderstorm had rendered the roads unusually heavy.

All through the long, dreary night the stage coach with the distinguished passenger boomed along through the woods, the thick foliage of the trees furnishing a sombre canopy which somewhat protected the party from the downpour of rain. Hours passed with the Vice-President torn by conflicting emotions, in which grief at the unexpected tidings was uppermost. The gray of the morning had not yet begun to light the heavens when Alden's Lane was reached at 3.15, and, although he was then within the reach of telephone communication, he was not apprised of the death of President McKinley. The stop at Alden's Lane was only of sufficient duration to allow a change of horses, and again the stage coach dashed forward. From the latter place to North Point, where the special lay waiting with all steam on, the road was through heavy forest timber and the journey was attended with actual peril. The driveways are very narrow in many places, with deep ravines on either side. A slight deviation would have meant a broken carriage or more serious trouble. But the expert guides piloted the Vice-President safely to his objective point, and Colonel Roosevelt, looking careworn but expressing no fatigue, alighted and dashed up to the special train at North Creek.

That was 5.22 o'clock that morning, and for the first time the traveler of the night learned that President McKinley had passed away at Buffalo at 2.15 o'clock. Mr. Loeb, his secretary, was the first to break the news to him. The new President was visibly affected by the intelligence, and expressed a desire to reach Buffalo as soon as possible.

The trip was a record-breaker in point of speed, in many places exceeding a mile a minute. There was a brief stop at Ballston to permit the Vice-President to send some telegrams. It was 7 o'clock, and a crowd at the little station received the new President in sympathetic silence.

A three-minute stop was made at Rochester, the train leaving that city for Buffalo at 12.18 P.M., and at 1.40 the special came rushing into that city, the President going at once to the home of Ansley Wilcox, where he arrived five minutes later.

CHAPTER XXXII

Theodore Roosevelt—President and Man

BY the laws of the land the death of William McKinley at 2.15 A. M. on Saturday the 14th of September, elevated to the Presidency the Vice-President. This contingency had occurred previously four times in our history. Two of our Presidents had died a natural death during their term of office, William Henry Harrison, succeeded by John Tyler, and Zachary Taylor, succeeded by Millard Filmore.

Then, two were assassinated, Abraham Lincoln, succeeded by Andrew Johnson, and James A. Garfield, succeeded by Chester A. Arthur.

William McKinley was the fifth President to die in office and to be succeeded by his associate.

ROOSEVELT TAKES THE OATH OF OFFICE

After Mr. Roosevelt's arrival in Buffalo he visited the Milburn house to see the face of his former friend and chief and to comfort the widow. In the afternoon he was sworn in as President at the house of his friend, Ansley Wilcox.

To this impressive ceremony came a few prominent officials and near friends. Among the first were Secretary Root, Attorney-General Knox and United States District Judge John R. Hazel, of Buffalo. The party proceeded immediately to the library of the house, where Mr. Roosevelt awaited them. They were closely followed by Secretaries Long, Hitchcock and Wilson, and the deceased President's Secretary, Mr. Cortelyou, President Milburn, of the Exposition Company, Senator Depew, Justice Albert Haight, of the Court of Appeals, and others. Other friends of the Vice-

President entered the house within a few minutes, and at 3.35 o'clock Mr. Wilcox came out on the lawn and said to the press representatives that it was the desire of the Vice-President that they be admitted to the house to witness the solemn ceremony. A score, or more, of newspaper men walked noiselessly into the dusky library of the old house, where, with bowed heads, stood the members of the Cabinet and those who had been asked to be present. The room was as silent as the house of death itself. No word was spoken above a whisper. Several women were in the little room, and all stood with bowed heads, as if the presence of death were there.

A SOLEMN CEREMONY

The Vice-President stood on the south side of the room, with his back to a small window, and the members of the Cabinet and the men present stood in a circle facing him. For some time Mr. Roosevelt talked earnestly with Secretary Root, whose friendship and counsel he so highly valued. Then Secretary Root stepped back a few paces, and the Vice-President stood motionless by the side of Judge Hazel. There was a dead silence of several seconds, and then Secretary Root said :

" Mr. Vice-President,"—another long pause,—" I have been requested by all of the members of the Cabinet of the late President McKinley who are present in the city of Buffalo, being all except two, to request that for reasons of weight affecting the administration of the government you shall proceed without delay to take the constitutional oath of office as President of the United States."

He spoke with great deliberation, and so still was the room that, had his words been uttered in whispers, they might easily have been heard by every one present.

Mr. Roosevelt's face was stern and rigid. Lifting his eyes, he looked steadfastly into the face of the Secretary for a moment, and in a voice with marked firmness and all of his characteristic distinctness, replied :

28

"Mr. Secretary, I shall take the oath at once, at the request of the members of the Cabinet, and in this hour of deep and terrible national bereavement I wish to state I shall continue absolutely unbroken the policy of President McKinley for the peace, prosperity and honor of our beloved country."

ADMINISTERING THE OATH

Judge Hazel then administered the constitutional oath, Mr. Roosevelt repeating the sentences as spoken by the magistrate :

"I do solemnly swear that I will faithfully execute the office of President of the United States, and will, to the best of my ability preserve, protect and defend the Constitution of the United States."

When the last words were said, President Roosevelt signed the document in the usual form. All was silent, and scarcely a movement of hand or foot was made during the solemn procedure. As soon as the oath was taken the President turned to the circle of Cabinet officers about him and said :

"I will ask the gentlemen of the Cabinet to stay that I may have a talk with them alone."

The President then stepped out into the hall and shook hands with those who passed out. In a few seconds the library was cleared of all those except the members of the Cabinet, and there President Roosevelt sat down with them for his first Cabinet meeting.

ROOSEVELT'S PROCLAMATION

President Roosevelt, on September 14th, issued the following proclamation as his first official act :

"By the President of the United States of America a proclamation :

"A terrible bereavement has befallen our people. The President of the United States has been struck down ; a crime committed not only against the chief magistrate but against every law-abiding and liberty loving citizen.

"President McKinley crowned a life of largest love for his fellowmen, of most earnest endeavor for their welfare, by a death of Christian fortitude; and both the way in which he lived his life and the way in which, in the supreme hour of trial, he met his death will remain forever a precious heritage of our people.

"It is meet that we, as a nation, express our abiding love and reverence for his life, our deep sorrow for his untimely death.

"Now, therefore, I, Theodore Roosevelt, President of the United States of America, do appoint Thursday next, September 19th, the day in which the body of the dead President will be laid in its last earthly resting place, as a day of mourning and prayer throughout the United States. I earnestly recommend all the people to assemble on that day in their respective places of divine worship, there to bow down in submission to the will of Almighty God, and to pay out of full hearts their homage of love and reverence to the great and good President whose death has smitten the nation with bitter grief.

"In witness whereof I have hereunto set my hand and caused the seal of the United States to be affixed.

"Done at the city of Washington, the 14th day of September, A. D., one thousand nine hundred and one, and of the independence of the United States the one hundred and twenty-sixth.

(Seal)   THEODORE ROOSEVELT.

 By the President,

   JOHN HAY, Secretary of State."

ROOSEVELT'S SPEECH AT MINNEAPOLIS

The last carefully prepared public utterance made by President Roosevelt, before succeeding to his high office, on questions of national import was his speech at the Forty-second Annual State Fair at Minneapolis on Monday, September 2d, three days before President McKinley made his ever-to-be-remembered address at Buffalo. In view of the fact that Mr. Roosevelt became President of the United States, his speech on that occasion is of special interest, and the most important parts of it are here reprinted.

"Our country has been populated by pioneers, and therefore it has in it more energy, more enterprise, more expansive power than any other in the wide world. You whom I am now addressing stand for the most part but one generation removed from these pioneers. You are typical Americans, for you have done the great, the characteristic, the typical work of our American life. In making homes and carving out careers for yourselves and your children, you have built up this State; throughout our history the success of the home-maker has been but another name for the upbuilding of the nation.

ATTITUDE OF THE STATE TOWARD PROPERTY

"The vast individual and corporate fortunes, the vast combinations of capital which have marked the development of our industrial system, create new conditions, and necessitate a change from the old attitude of the State and the nation toward property. It is probably true that the large majority of the fortunes that now exist in this country have been amassed not by injuring our people, but as an incident to the conferring of great benefits upon the community; and this, no matter what may have been the conscious purpose of those amassing them. There is but the scantiest justification for most of the outcry against the men of wealth as such; and it ought to be unnecessary to state that any appeal which directly or indirectly leads to suspicion and hatred among ourselves, which tends to limit opportunity, and therefore to shut the door of success against poor men of talent, and, finally, which entails the possibility of lawlessness and violence, is an attack upon the fundamental properties of American citizenship.

"Our interests are at bottom common; in the long run we go up or go down together. Yet more and more it is evident that the State and, if necessary, the nation has got to possess the right of supervision and control as regards the great corporations which are its creatures; particularly as regards the great business combinations which derive a portion of their importance from the existence of some monopolistic tendency. The right should be exercised with caution and self-restraint ; but it should exist, so that it may be invoked if the need arises.

" But our country, as it strides forward with ever-increasing rapidity to a foremost place among the world-powers, must necessarily find, more and more, that it has world duties also. There are excellent people who believe that we can shirk these duties and yet retain our self-respect ; but these good people are in error.

" Right here let me make as vigorous a plea as I know how in favor of saying nothing that we do not mean and of acting without hesitation up to whatever we say. In private life there are few beings more obnoxious than the man who is always loudly boasting, and if the boaster is not prepared to back up his words his position becomes absolutely contemptible. So it is with the nation. It is both foolish and undignified to indulge in undue self-glorification, and, above all, in loose-tongued denunciation of other peoples. Whenever, on any point, we come in contact with a foreign power, I hope that we shall always strive to speak courteously and respectfully to that foreign power. Let us make it evident that we intend to do justice. Then let us make it equally evident that we will not tolerate injustice being done to us in return. Let us further make it evident that we use no words which we are not prepared to back up with deeds, and that while our speech is always moderate, we are ready and willing to make it good. Such an attitude will be the surest possible guarantee of that self-respecting peace, the attainment of which is and must ever be the prime aim of self-governing people.

ATTITUDE AS REGARDS MONROE DOCTRINE

" This is the attitude we should take as regards the Monroe Doctrine. There is not the least need of blustering about it. Still less should it be used as a pretext for our own aggrandizement at the expense of any other American State. But, most emphatically,

we must make it evident that we intend on this point ever to maintain the old American position. Indeed, it is hard to understand
how any man can take any other position, now that we are looking
forward to the building of the Isthmian Canal. The Monroe Doctrine is not international law, but there is no necessity that it
should be. All that is needful is that it should continue to be a
cardinal feature of American policy on this continent; and the
Spanish-American States should, in their own interests, champion it
as strongly as we do. Commercially, so far as this doctrine is concerned, all we wish is a fair field and no favor; but if we are wise
we shall strenuously insist that under no pretext whatever shall
there be any territorial aggrandizement on American soil by any
European power, and this no matter what form the territorial
aggrandizement may take.

"No nation capable of self-government and of developing by
its own efforts a sane and orderly civilization, no matter how small
it may be, has anything to fear from us.

OUR RELATIONS TO CUBA

"Our dealings with Cuba illustrate this, and should forever be
a subject of just national pride. We speak in no spirit of arro-
gance, when we state as a simple historic fact that never in recent
times has any great nation acted with such disinterestedness as we
have shown in Cuba. We freed the island from the Spanish yoke.
We then earnestly did our best to help the Cubans in the establishment of free education, of law and order, of material prosperity,
of the cleanliness necessary to sanitary well-being in their great
cities. We did all this at a great expense of treasure, at some
expense of life; and now we are establishing them in a free and
independent commonwealth, and have asked in return nothing
whatever, save at no time shall their independence be prostituted
to the advantage of some foreign rival of ours, or so as to menace
our well-being. To have failed to ask this would have amounted
to national stultification on our part.

"In the Philippines we have brought peace, and we are at this moment giving them such freedom and self-government as they could never under any conceivable conditions have obtained had we turned them loose to sink into a welter of blood and confusion, or to become the prey of some strong tyranny without or within. The bare recital of the facts is sufficient to show that we did our duty.

"If you study our past history as a nation you will see we have made many blunders and have been guilty of many shortcomings, and yet that we have always in the end come out victorious because we have refused to be daunted by blunders and defeats—have recognized them, but have persevered in spite of them. So it must be in the future. We gird up our loins as a nation with the stern purpose to play our part manfully in winning the ultimate triumph, and therefore we turn scornfully aside and, with unfaltering steps, tread the rough road of endeavor, smiting down the wrong from the paths of mere ease an l idleness and battling for the right, as Greatheart smote and battled in Bunyan's immortal story."

ROOSEVELT THE YOUNGEST PRESIDENT.

Theodore Roosevelt is the youngest man ever inducted into the office of President of the United States. He had not yet completed his forty-third year, having been born on October 27, 1858. Up to the time of President Roosevelt's accession the youngest man to assume the functions of Chief Executive of the republic was General Grant, who was forty-seven when he was first inaugurated, and Grover Cleveland was the third, being aged forty-eight years at the beginning of his first term.

Franklin Pierce and General James A. Garfield were each forty-nine, while James K. Polk and Millard Fillmore had each rounded their half century. The latter was the second of the Vice-Presidents to succeed to the higher office.

John Tyler, who became President on the death of William Henry Harrison, being the first of the Vice-Presidents to so attain the highest place in the nation, was fifty-one. "Old Tippecanoe," the popular appellation of his predecessor, was the oldest man ever chosen to the Presidency, being sixty-eight at the time of his inauguration. General Chester A. Arthur, a fortuitous incumbent of the high office through the assassination of his predecessor, General Garfield, was fifty-one. Abraham Lincoln was fifty-two, William McKinley fifty-three, General Rutherford B. Hayes fifty-four, Martin Van Buren and Benjamin Harrison, fifty-five each.

George Washington, the first President, was fifty-seven when first inaugurated, and that was the age of Andrew Johnson, who became President on the assassination of Mr. Lincoln. Thomas Jefferson and his immediate successor, James Madison, were each fifty-eight when first installed, and that was the age of John Quincy Adams, while James Monroe was a year older when he began his first term. John Adams was sixty-two, as was Andrew Jackson, "Old Hickory." James Buchanan was sixty-six, being, next to the first Harrison, the senior in the list of our Chief Magistrates.

The longest lived of the Presidents was the first Adams, who succumbed to general debility at the ripe age of ninety years. The youngest to die was General Garfield, who died by the assassin's bullet when he was forty-nine. The next youngest was his predecessor, James K. Polk, who came to a natural death when aged fifty-three. President McKinley was fifty-eight when laid low by his anarchist murderer.

The only living ex-President at time of Mr. Roosevelt's accession was Grover Cleveland, who was in robust health at the age of sixty-four.

The Vice-Presidents who attained the Presidency besides those who reached the office through the death of their predecessors were John Adams, Thomas Jefferson and Martin Van Buren, all of whom were elected after having filled entire terms in the second place.

All of the Presidents who succeeded through the death of their predecessors, namely, Tyler. Fillmore, Johnson and Arthur, were candidates for renomination, but all failed in their ambition. Fillmore at a subsequent period was nominated by the American party in the quadrangular campaign which resulted in the first election of Lincoln. The Presidents who have striven for re-election after having served full terms and been rejected by the arbitrament of the ballot were: John Adams, his son, John Quincy Adams, Martin Van Buren, General Benjamin Harrison and Grover Cleveland. The last named was defeated in his second campaign, but was victorious in the third. The only avowed candidate for a third term in the Presidency was General Grant, who was defeated in the Republican Convention of 1880, after a memorable conflict. President Franklin Pierce was defeated for renomination by the Democratic Convention of 1856. George Washington, the first President, publicly refused a third term, and his example, followed twelve years later by Thomas Jefferson, became a precedent that has not since been violated in almost a century.

PRESIDENT ROOSEVELT'S LONG ISLAND HOME

Trophies of the chase form a large part of the decorations of Colonel Roosevelt's home at Oyster Bay, Long Island. The house is on Cove Neck, three miles by carriage from the village of Oyster Bay. It is approached by a steep, winding roadway, which takes the visitor through a dense wood before revealing to him the house itself. Once on the crest of the little hill which the colonel selected for his home, the visitor has a beautiful view in every direction, especially to the north and east, where the waters of the Sound and Cold Spring Harbor are seen. Around the house on all sides is a closely cropped lawn, studded with shade trees, big and little, and of many kinds. The main entrance to the house, on the south, is under a beautiful *porte-cochére* laden with heavy vines and bearing a pair of spreading antlers. The walls of the dwelling are of red brick to the second story, and above that of wood, painted in many colors. A broad porch runs around three sides of the structure, covered, except in front, by a shingled roof, and shaded here and there by a luxurious Virginia creeper. Within, the house is beautifully furnished from cellar to attic. In nearly every room are trophies of the colonel's life on the Western plains, and not a few relics from his Cuban campaign. Just at the right of the front door is Remington's bronze of the " bronco buster," which was presented to the colonel by the Rough Riders at Camp Wikoff. In the library, on the ground floor, are many long shelves, well filled with books, and a collection of bronzes and hunting trophies. A fireplace of old-fashioned proportions is at one side of the room, and near the windows is the desk at which the colonel does most of his literary work and correspondence. On the walls of the study are portraits of Washington, Grant and Lincoln, and photographs of Henry Cabot Lodge and of the colonel himself, holding in his arms the rightful heir to his name and fame, Theodore Roosevelt, Jr.

HIS WIFE AND CHILDREN

The President is never so happy as when he is sitting quietly in his home with his wife and children. Home is to him the most sacred place on earth, and he has never allowed his family circle to be disturbed by the many cares which fell upon him as a civil or military servant of his country. The present Mrs. Roosevelt is the second wife of the colonel. She was Miss Edith Kermit Carow, and he married her in 1886. President Roosevelt has six children, ranging in age according to the order in which they are here named : Alice, Theodore, Kermit, Ethel, Archibald and Quentin.

Mrs. Roosevelt, who will be known as the lady of the White House, is rather petite, has brown hair and brown eyes, a clear skin, with some color when she is excited, but her chief beauty is her mouth, which is marvelously expressive. She dresses neatly and simply with a quiet elegance. Her wealth of tresses is pushed back from the forehead, except a few curly ringlets that play about her temples. She is not an athlete, but she is a finished horsewoman and is fond of outdoor exercise.

Mrs. Roosevelt has long been identified with a score of charities. She possesses the great talent which made Mrs. Cleveland so popular, of remembering the faces of people she meets once or twice and also being able to remember all about them. She is the boon companion, as well as the very wise and tender mother, of her stepdaughter and her own children, who are much younger than Miss Alice Roosevelt. She is a frail-looking woman, but has much more strength than she apparently possesses. She is deeply religious.

MR. ROOSEVELT'S SISTERS

Mr. Roosevelt's two sisters are women noted for their rare charm, intelligence and their most gracious manners. Mrs. Cowles, formerly Miss Anna Roosevelt, has been married only a few years, although she is older than her brother Theodore. When her cousin, J. Roosevelt, was in charge of the American Embassy in London, she went over as his guest and stayed with him for a time, taking charge of his household. Her success as a hostess was marvelous in London—in fact, in England, where she made countless warm friends, and where she met Commander Cowles, whom she married the following year. She is now living in Washington, where she is a very marked personality, and comes nearer to having a *salon* than any other American woman.

Mrs. Douglas Robinson, the youngest sister, is the wife of a well-known real estate man in New York, and is considered one of the cleverest women in the city. Like her sister, Mrs. Cowles, she holds weekly receptions for not only the smart set but for people from all over the country who have talent, charm or any gift that makes them in any way prominent. Mrs. Robinson resembles strongly Mrs. Theodore Roosevelt—in fact, they are often taken one for the other.

LEAD, KINDLY LIGHT.

DYKES.

NEWMANN, 1833.

1 Lead, kind-ly Light, a-mid th' en-circling gloom. Lead Thou me on;
2 I was not ev - er thus, nor pray'd that Thou Shouldst lead me on;
3 So long Thy pow'r has blest me, sure it still Will lead me on

The night is dark, and I am far from home, Lead Thou me on.
lov'd to choose and see my path; but now Lead Thou me on.
O'er moor and fen, o'er crag and tor-rent, till The night is gone,

Keep Thou my feet; I do not ask to see
I lov'd th gar - ish day; and, spite of fears,
And with th morn those an-gel fa - ces smile,

The dis - tant scene one step e - nough for me.
Pride rul'd my will: re - mem - ber not past years.
Which I have lov'd long since, and lost a - while.

This beautiful hymn composed by Cardinal Newman was the especial favorite of William McKinley and was sung at Memorial Services.